Social Anthropology in Perspective

I. M Lewis

Social Anthropology in Perspective

The Relevance of Social Anthropology

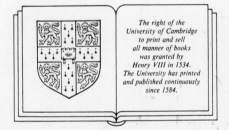

The right of the
University of Cambridge
to print and sell
all manner of books
was granted by
Henry VIII in 1534.
The University has printed
and published continuously
since 1584.

Cambridge University Press

Cambridge
London   New York   New Rochelle
Melbourne   Sydney

Published by the Press Syndicate of the University of Cambridge
The Pitt Building, Trumpington Street, Cambridge CB2 1RP
32 East 57th Street, New York, NY 10022, USA
10 Stamford Road, Oakleigh, Melbourne 3166, Australia

Originally published in a paperback edition by Penguin Books, Ltd,
1976
© I. M. Lewis, 1976

Paperback edition reissued (with amendments), and hardcover
edition first published, by Cambridge University Press, 1985
© Cambridge University Press, 1985

Printed in Great Britain at
the University Press, Cambridge

British Library cataloguing in publication data
Lewis, I. M.
Social anthropology in perspective:
the relevance of social anthropology.
1. Ethnology
I. Title
306   GN316

Library of Congress catalogue card number: 85-12776

ISBN 0 521 30854 2 hard covers
ISBN 0 521 31351 1 paperback

sⱼ

Contents

Preface

Public reputations do not always do full justice to their subjects. So the old image of the anthropologist as a bearded professor, stalking skulls with his callipers at the ready, is gradually yielding ground to that of the professional explorer and chronicler of exotic tribal customs. The latter is indeed the traditional role of the social anthropologist (in contrast to the physical anthropologist) and provides our subject with most of its romantic appeal and much of its intellectual force and academic rigour. Social anthropology, however, is more than this. Social anthropologists are indeed dedicated to the study of distant civilizations, both in their traditional and changing, contemporary forms, but we have also a larger aspiration: the comparative study of *all* human societies in the light of those challengingly unfamiliar beliefs and customs which expose our own ethnocentric limitations and put us in our place within the wider gamut of the world's civilizations. It is in this spirit that this introduction to social anthropology is offered, and this is why I make so many deliberate comparisons between esoteric alien customs and more familiar native practices and beliefs. My theme throughout is the social setting and cultural expression of identity.

As the comparative study of human societies and with its special concern for the alien and remote, social anthropology is an ambitious enterprise and notoriously difficult to expound. The basic problem is where to begin. Particularly in the small-scale societies traditionally frequented by anthropologists, social relationships are usually so densely interwoven that as soon as one begins to unravel one strand in the tangled skein, other knots appear that have to be untangled before any further progress can be made. If, in the Marxist tradition, we start with environmental resources and their utilization in production and consumption, we immediately encounter complex patterns of kinship, political organization and religion. In modern European communities this may not entail serious difficulties since our forms of kinship, politics and religion are familiar enough. In such circumstances much can be taken for granted, and institutions and relationships are in any case more impersonal and less socially involuted. But when our immediate (though never final) concern is with exotic communities where social relationships are of labyrinthine complexity and sustained by beliefs as bizarre as they are unfamiliar, all these have to be understood in depth before we can make much sense of the economic infrastructure. If, for instance, property and religion are so much a part of kinship that it makes as much sense to see the former as expressions of the latter as *vice versa*, we will clearly not get far until we grasp the basic principles of kinship organization. Thus, whatever one begins talking about, one ends up discussing many other things. Our many-sided subject matter stubbornly refuses to be broken down into tidy watertight compartments. Some repetition is therefore inevitable as we are forced to examine the same phenomena from many different points of view. This, of course, is as much a tribute to the richness of our material as a commentary on the inadequacies of our methods.

Where we decide to breach this charmed circle is, consequently, an arbitrary matter. My preference, which will not commend itself to everyone, is to start with religion, so in effect beginning at the top and working down. An introductory first chapter outlines my conception of social anthropology, then chapter 2 discusses its main historical trends. In chapter 3 we launch into a wide-ranging examination of the forms and functions of religion; we begin with the problem of suffering and affliction and we end in chapter 5 with the trinity of myth, rite and eschatology. Having established our spiritual superstructure, we proceed in chapter 6 to probe its environmental and economic foundations. Thence, we move on (in chapter 7) to explore systems of exchange (of goods, services and prestige), emphasizing throughout the vital social content of these transactions. This leads us naturally in chapter 8 to the traditional heartland of social anthropology (and of most tribal societies): marriage and kinship, where women constitute the most valuable and productive currency of all. Since kin and marital ties are heavily impregnated with political significance in such small-scale communities (as well as in specialized areas of industrial societies), this brings us to the more explicit analysis of politics and power in our concluding chapters. The first of these, chapter 9, deals with the more familiar world of centralized political organization, with states and chiefdoms. The second, chapter 10, concentrates on less centralized communities close to anarchic spontaneity. There we also explore the dynamic interplay between this political form and its antithesis, the state; in closely scrutinizing in their contemporary setting those frequently opposed phenomena 'tribalism' and 'nationalism', we return to our central theme, the quest for identity.

In pursuing this theme in this fashion, I have tried to present most of the fundamental theory of social anthropology in a coherent form for reading rather than reference. I have made extensive use of ethnographic illustrations, but have attempted to embed these firmly in the structure of the text so that they participate in and advance the argument rather than merely embellishing or, worse still, interrupting it. If I have not always succeeded, it is not the fault of my eloquent sources!

In this context it is appropriate to note that social anthropologists are prone to rely excessively on the 'ethnographic present', offering static descriptions and analyses of particular societies at the time they happen to have been studied without consideration of any subsequent developments. I share the orthodox view that exotic social phenomena are of intrinsic interest, whatever their time-depth, and thus possess a timeless validity *sub specie aeternitatis*. But believing that they are as methodologically important as they are topical, I also sympathize with criticisms of this lack of historical sense. For if the picture painted by the anthropologist of what he sees at a particular time is true, it must possess some predictive force. Within limits, it should be possible to extrapolate into the future. Certainly we have grounds for serious disquiet if future developments make no sense in the light of an earlier anthropological report. Thus the time dimension – both in retrospect and prospect – offers us a fuller and more rounded picture of the institutions and beliefs we study, enabling us to distinguish between the ephemeral and enduring, and so helps us to reach a more definitive assessment of the significance of the phenomena confronting us. Hence, I have tried to follow my main ethnographic excursions through to the present, giving as up-to-date an account as I can. I hope this will confirm how contemporary developments in Africa and Asia both illuminate, and are illuminated by, earlier anthropological research.

It only remains to be added that this book has grown out of an introductory course of lectures which I have given for a number of years at the London School of Economics. Like this book the course is directed towards a mixed audience and designed to appeal at different levels and in different ways to different people. In the ensuing give and take, I learned many things which I have tried to incorporate here. Thanks are also due to my long-suffering colleagues at L.S.E. and elsewhere in London University, who have been extraordinarily generous with advice and help. Here Dr Maurice Bloch's advice on economic issues has been helpful and Dr Peter Loizos's criticism of the economic and political chapters has enabled me to improve the presentation of my argument. The comments of Katie Platt, who prepared the bibliography and index, have been equally helpful. And, as is usual in this Pelican series, more than ritual tribute is due to its editor, Professor Isaac Schapera, for his astringent but always stimulating criticism. I owe a special debt to the secretaries in our Anthropology Department for their ready assistance and forbearance, and particularly to Mrs Isabel Ogilvie who so expertly typed so much of the manuscript. I am also grateful to the L.S.E. for granting me a term's sabbatical leave without which I would not have been able to complete this book.

Finally, as those who are familiar with the process will know, writing an introduction to a subject forces one to attempt a wide-ranging stock-taking, and consequently involves a return to one's intellectual roots. Anthropologists have two sorts of teachers: those under whom they study as students at universities, and those whom they study in the course of their field-work. My debt to the latter is mainly to the Somali, and if individuals are to be named, above all to Musa Galaal; to the former it is to Noel Stevenson, Franz Steiner, Godfrey Lienhardt, E. E. Evans-Pritchard, Clyde Mitchell and Daryll Forde.

London, October 1974   I.M.L.

Preface to the 1985 Edition

Not long ago, Sheikh Yamani, the Saudi Arabian Oil Minister, was being interviewed for American television news by a friend and former student. At the end of the interview, Sheikh Yamani politely asked his interviewer what subject she had studied at University. When she replied 'social anthropology', the Oil Minister expressed keen interest and approval, adding that, in his opinion, all leading politicians should include some training in this subject in their studies. Such preparation, Sheikh Yamani declared, would help politicians to appreciate and understand other people's cultures and, at least as important, sensitise them to their own cultural ethnocentricities. In the same vein, if in a more specific practical context, Jomo Kenyatta's successor, President Arap Moi of Kenya, proclaims that social anthropology is indispensible for the effective, culturally informed administration of an ethnically plural African state.

These authoritative endorsements by leading figures in the Third World (where social anthropology has not always been regarded positively), emphasise the role of the subject, as a bridge to inter-cultural understanding, proposed in this book. In preparing this new edition, I have made a number of corrections and amendments to the text of the first edition (1976) which some reviewers considered ended rather abruptly.

I have thus also added a new concluding chapter which reviews, reflectively, current (1980s) trends in what some anthropologists call the 'post-structuralist' era. This brief survey makes no claims to exhaustive coverage, but seeks rather to signpost what I take to be significant directions in the contemporary practice of social anthropology which, it is suggested, is often much closer to cultural anthropology than we British anthropologists generally suppose. The areas we touch on include: Marxist anthropology; gender studies; ethnographic interpretation; semantic and medical anthropology; urbanism and ethnicity; applied anthropology; and, finally, what our subject means today at home as well as in distant 'other cultures'. My necessarily compressed treatment of such a wide range of topics is inevitably selective and, compared with earlier chapters, programmatic; but it is buttressed by quite extensive bibliographic references to enable the reader to follow-up areas of special interest. In preparing this review, I have noted with keen interest, how many contemporary anthropologists, breaking free of the shackles of epistemological puritanism, see the present state of our subject as having transcended the vogue movements and 'isms' (functionalism, structuralism, Marxism, etc.) of earlier periods. This eclectic position is very close to that adopted and advocated in this book. This consideration of recent developments has benefited greatly from the friendly comments of David Brokensha, Murray Last and James Lewton-Brain, which I gratefully acknowledge without, of course, implying any common doctrinal concensus.

As I note later, we should in any case be cautious in identifying and evaluating theoretical trends since the historiography of social anthropology is still in its infancy. Important developments are however, in train. Already, one hundred years after his birth in 1884, the cultural anthropologist who founded social anthropology, Malinowski (together with all his works) has acquired a status comparable to an exotic society[1] – a fitting subject for study by anthropologists, historians and literary men, whose ranks will in due course no doubt include (most appropriately), Trobriand Island scholars.

London, March 1985   I.M.L.

---

1. See below, p. 55. In the 1984 centenary year, conferences bringing together anthropologists, historians and philosophers to evaluate Malinowski's significance were held in his native Cracow, in London (at the London School of Economics), at Bologna and Florence and no doubt elsewhere: see e.g., J. Overing (ed.), *Rationality and Rationales*, London, Tavistock Press, 1986.

To my mother

'New things are made familiar, and familiar
things are made new.'   SAMUEL JOHNSON

Chapter One
Aims and Methods

Ethnocentricity is the natural condition of mankind. Most peoples of the world do not, in their conservative heart of hearts, like foreigners and display feelings of hostility (often tinged with fear) towards them. This indeed is one of the most widespread ways in which people declare and affirm their identity – by saying who they are not. Today, however, especially among the younger generation, we see a very different set of attitudes in western countries. Under this new dispensation things foreign and far removed from our own polluted urban world acquire an exotic piquancy, an exciting glamour, which causes them to be approached with a mixture of reverence and hope. For all its faults, it can at least be said for the modern world that it has produced a substantial body of articulate opinion that blends passion with compassion in its concern for the impoverished and starving peoples of the world. This expanding (though by no means unambiguous) sense of common humanity is encouraged by the rapidity and intensity of modern communications and by a growing awareness that mankind as a whole may face extinction unless some more harmonious and rational adjustment can be achieved between the world's rapidly growing population and its dwindling natural resources. Ironically, the sudden realization by the oil states of the Third World that they possess a powerful weapon capable of commanding world attention and respect adds a new element of self-interest to this wider sense of common human identity.

 This extension of the boundaries of acknowledged humanity, however fitful or partial, is especially favourable to social anthropology, which is by tradition a Third World subject. In fact it is *the* Third World subject, the authentic founder of Black Studies, the original academic discipline devoted to the study and understanding of alternative cultures, institutions and beliefs. Here comparison is of the essence, and concentration of social anthropology on the differences and similarities between tribal and industrial cultures and institutions the world over gives it its unique character. Writing in 1783, long before social anthropology had assumed any coherent shape or even possessed a name, the eighteenth-century French social philosopher, J. J. Rousseau proclaimed our guiding assumption: 'One needs to look near at hand if one wants to study men: but to study man one must learn to look from afar: one must first observe differences in order to discover attributes.' It is this comprehensive perspective on the human condition that social anthropology seeks to achieve.

Clearly there are many ways of studying man, and the phrase 'I am interested in people' that is often used to express and justify an interest in social anthropology is encouraging – but not very enlightening. We need to be much more precise about the aspects of man that engage our attention and the methods of study we propose to adopt. This book seeks to present social anthropology as a humanistic discipline which, by its very nature, claims to be less ethnocentric and insular than history or sociology but which has strong and significant links with both these subjects as well as with social psychology and psychiatry. (I use 'psychiatry' here in the broad sense to refer to psychiatric theory as much as therapy and to include depth psychology, i.e. various forms of psychoanalytic theory.) That it has also close ties with comparative religion scarcely needs to be said.

We study *peoples* rather than *people*. Our primary units of reference are 'societies', that is, distinct and relatively autonomous communities whose members' mutual social relations are embedded in, and expressed through, the medium of a common culture. Culture is a key term here. Not only does the possession of culture conventionally mark the great divide separating humans from other animals, but different human societies tend to possess distinctive cultures. Culture is thus the protective shell of a community and cultural distinctions become, to some extent, an index of social identity. We assume this, of course, when we associate variations in speech or accents and life style, that is cultural differences, with variations in social class or place of origin. Our everyday awareness of these value-laden distinctions makes it all the more necessary to stress that in social anthropology (and sociology) 'culture' is a neutral term. It is not something that I have and you do not, or *vice versa*; nor is it a commodity with which some people have the good fortune to be more generously endowed than others. It is thus *not* employed in the sense in which people speak of being more 'cultured' (or 'cultivated') than others. For our purposes, culture is simply a convenient term to describe the sum of *learned* knowledge and skills – including religion and language – that distinguishes one community from another and which, subject to the vagaries of innovation and change, passes on in a recognizable form from generation to generation. Culture thus transcends the lives of its living exponents in any one generation: if it did not it could not survive. Its component elements are absorbed in the first few years of life largely unconsciously, and later more deliberately by informal and formal learning processes. Socialization inevitably takes place within and through the medium of a particular cultural tradition. When people do not know how to bring up or what to teach their children their cultural heritage is indeed in jeopardy.

CULTURE AND RACE

This is the place to emphasize that culture is a very different thing from 'race' – if, that is, we are to understand race in its scientific sense of a genetically distinctive breed. In popular speech, when people expatiate upon the virtues or vices of the British, Scottish, Welsh, Irish, Jewish or any other so-called 'race', they are really talking about particular *cultural* attitudes and characteristics. By appropriating the term 'race' they seek to invest these cultural stereotypes with a unique finality and metaphysical value, implying that culturally patterned behaviour is genetically determined. But there is no general evidence that distinctive cultural traits are associated with particular genes. No geneticist has yet isolated a Jewish gene or a British gene transmitting specific cultural attributes. If culture were transmitted genetically it would scarcely be necessary to expend such time and energy training children: it would be so much easier! It is precisely because there is no direct correlation of such a kind between genetic make-up and culture that we can afford to ignore race as a significant variable in our discussion of different social and cultural arrangements. Genetics and biology have little to tell us that is relevant, except in so far as these sciences throw light on human nature in general.

Racism, and racial antagonism and conflict are therefore, paradoxically, essentially social and cultural rather than biological phenomena : it is not biology but culture that makes 'race' socially significant. Social racism, which is a form of chauvinistic nationalism or tribalism, exists quite independently of the geneticists and biologists for whom alone the term race has some residual scientific validity. Social circumstances in which one dominant ethnic group or 'race' confronts others may engender a climate favourable to research aimed at exploring possible relationships between genetic and cultural phenomena. The recent revival of interest in the relationship, if any, between race and intelligence (notoriously difficult to assess in absolute terms that are cross-culturally valid) is itself a social phenomenon, reflecting our ethnically mixed contemporary environment.

On a wider front, men everywhere seek to view their way of life and culture as part of the natural order of things, as indeed a fact of nature. So, as the song has it, we do what comes naturally, and we 'naturalize' those whom we adopt fully into our own community – those who are born into it need only be 'socialized'. In the same idiom which would transform facts of culture into facts cf nature we speak of 'natural rights' and 'natural justice'.

Our more significant and currently fashionable meeting-point with biology is not at the level of race, but at that of species. As the immense success of works by Desmond Morris and other popularizers of ethological research on primates demonstrates, *Homo sapiens* never tires of contemplating the behaviour of his nearest animal kin. Some presumably find this reassuring. Certainly the popularity of ethology is a testimony to the deep-seated character of western civilization's abiding concern with the nature–nurture problem. In fact, as Lévi-Strauss has helped us to recognize in his distinction between 'nature' and 'culture', it is in all likelihood a universal human obsession. Having invented and evolved culture, man, it seems, never ceases to marvel at his own creation. In the process he endlessly ponders the point at which his culture stops and his nature begins, where – as Shakespeare poses the issue in *The Tempest* – Prospero ends and Caliban begins.

CULTURE AND COMMUNITY

But we must now leave these tangential matters and return to the task of establishing what social anthropology is and does. We study different cultures and the communities that produce them, placing our primary emphasis on *social relations* and treating culture as a vehicle or medium for social interaction rather than an end in itself. Here British social anthropologists part company with many of their American colleagues, who give priority to culture and to cultural patterns, underestimating (as it seems to us) the social dimension. Naturally those anthropologists who grant culture such imperative force tend to see social relations as the product of cultural patterning and conditioning, and thus tend to concentrate on child-rearing practices, enculturation, and socialization. Continuity and discontinuity are similarly measured and interpreted as essentially cultural phenomena and so discussed in terms of 'acculturation'. For us, on the other hand, the dialectic between culture and society is weighted in the opposite direction. Social relations rather than their cultural vestments have priority.

Social life obviously encompasses a vast range of activities and beliefs and is of bewildering complexity. Our first aim, therefore, is to isolate significant typical events and units of social life and activity, and then to probe for the underlying blueprint, often implicit rather than explicit, that will show how they fit together into a meaningful pattern. Our interest is not simply in any one department of social life but rather in all these in a community, and especially in their mutual interdependence as parts of a whole. If communities can be thought of as houses, we are as concerned to discover what goes on in the bedroom, bathroom and kitchen as in the dining-room and sitting-room. We see action in one area not as self-contained or hermetically sealed, but as spilling over to affect and be affected by what goes on elsewhere under the same roof.

This holistic, comprehensive, catholic approach (whose history we shall briefly review in the next chapter) is usually called 'functionalism' or 'structural functionalism'. Its abiding concern is with the interconnectedness of things, with all the links in the social chains that bind individuals together as members of a community. Words and actions are full of subtle meanings which, to be fully explored and understood, have to be set in a much wider social context than that of their immediate occurrence. What people do, and say, and say they think, has a logical coherence and consistency that relates to the overall social structure of the community. Community life cannot continue successfully unless there is some such orderly structure of mutually reinforcing expectations and 'roles', some organization of interlocking parts which click together to form a harmonious whole. This stress on the interdependence of social phenomena, though it may be circular and is not exhaustive, takes us a long way in understanding the basic dynamics of community life.

Social life can thus be viewed as a kind of theatre, an image which, of course, has always appealed to dramatists and poets. From this perspective, we set out to discover the plot of the social drama which the members of a particular community are in effect engaged in presenting, the parts or 'roles' that its members assume, and their mutual interaction as the play proceeds. What is the play really about? Are there significant sub-plots which cast some of the characters in the drama in a very different light from that in which they are officially cast? What room for manoeuvre is there in different productions of the same play? How far can the actors depart from their parts with improvization and ad-libbing and yet remain within the accepted, culturally defined, conventions? How do we evaluate their performance?

In real life the situation is more complex than in our simple analogy. For a start, the actors all play many different roles, shedding old and assuming new parts with bewildering speed and ease: sometimes indeed they play several different roles at the same time, representing different things in different relationships. Nor do they necessarily all share the same interpretation of the events in which they participate; rival themes are thrust forward, and the same lines are used to justify contradictory claims and interests. How these are to be assessed poses delicate problems for the social anthropologist as he attempts to evaluate local ideology and its relationship to economic and political commitments. What binds all these discordant currents into something that can be called a community? What weight is to be attached to environmental and other external pressures in understanding how its members live together? If these pressures increase or decrease dramatically how will this affect the stability of the society? What will it take to shake the actors out of their accustomed parts, forcing them to assume completely novel roles? What, finally, is the vital, dynamic core of the community that gives it its uniquely distinctive character? What *really* makes it tick?

ALLIED APPROACHES

Particularly if we adopt a 'transactional' perspective, emphasizing inter-personal exchanges and transactions, study of the forces animating community life inevitably brings us very close to psychiatry and social psychology where the roles people play are also of critical importance. There are many problems which cut right across the artificial frontiers separating these subjects, particularly when attempts are made to interpret thought and feeling. It is very unfortunate therefore that, in Britain especially, social anthropologists have, on the whole, displayed towards colleagues in adjacent disciplines so little of the ecumenical tolerance with which they habitually approach exotic tribesmen. There are many reasons for this. The most significant is probably the persistence of past misunderstandings. In the name of their founding ancestors, some British social anthropologists still feel obliged to take up defensive positions against imaginary enemies who died long ago. They seem blissfully unaware that their opponents have long since abandoned the positions at issue and now share important common ground with them.

Disciplinary frontiers should be channels of communication, not iron curtains of mutual unintelligibility and mistrust; this regrettably narrow-minded approach misconstrues the complementary aims and interests of these cognate subjects. As social anthropologists our major concern is with those ideas and ways of behaving which a given community takes for granted as the 'natural' order of things. These deeply ingrained socially appropriate patterns of thought and behaviour we call 'norms', since they are endowed with normative force and moral value by their adherents. Of course, in our actual observation and collection of data we move from particular individuals and instances to the general, abstracting from the particular what we see to be shared and are told is socially expected and approved. We look at the individual to discern the imprint of society: it is what he shares with his associates, not what distinguishes him from them, that directly interests us. For us the individual is a microcosm of the social macrocosm. His private emotions and idiosyncracies, and difficulties he experiences in internalizing the social norms of his community are his business. They are not on our agenda, at least not until they become such a common feature, shared by so many others, that they qualify as 'social phenomena'. Here, of course, as at so many other points in the blurred frontier zone between social anthropology, psychiatry and social psychology, the key question becomes: What is the threshold incidence which transforms individual into social phenomena? The more individualistic the inner life of individuals the more clear-cut the demarcation line between our subjects.

If the Anthropologist studies alien communities the psychiatrist or analyst (once known as 'alienist') thus treats alien symptoms in individual patients. He examines why certain individuals cannot easily accept the ways of thinking and behaving that their social milieu thrusts upon them. The psychiatrist explores the roots of personal deviance, 'inadequacy' and 'alienation' – not the grounds of conformity and compliance. But the treatment usually consists in trying to help the alienated patient to come to terms with his situation, which means accepting his position in society and the norms of conduct he finds so disturbing. Despite the impact of liberalizing currents which encourage more give and take, this modifying or normalizing function contiues to play a major role in psychiatry. The patient, if the treatment is successful, learns 'to live with his problem'.

Nevertheless, despite his vital if sometimes reluctantly assumed role in maintaining the norms of society, the psychiatrist is often in danger of under-valuing the weight of the social pressures bearing on his patient and of assuming ethnocentrically that his own and his society's moral standards enjoy universal validity. Psychiatrists are more easily shocked than is generally supposed. The practitioner in psychological medicine may over-emphasize the physiological dimensions of his patient's illness, or, if psycho-analytically inclined, exaggerate the significance of childhood and prenatal experience. The social anthropologist, for his part, while stressing the importance of social interaction (and thus joining forces with much that is practised in the name of 'psycho-dynamics') is often over-simplistic in the unacknowledged psychological assumptions he makes about people's inner feelings and mental states. He is prone to speak and write at one moment as though motives were transparently obvious, and at the next as though they were inscrutable mysteries far beyond the range of his competence.

In reality both the social anthropological and the psychiatric (or psychological) approaches are mutually helpful and necessary if we are to achieve a balanced perspective on man as a sentient being. In order to define mental alienation and abnormality, the psychiatrist must first know what is normal, accepted and socially approved; since these vary in different cultures and sub-cultures he will be completely at sea outside his own milieu unless he takes account of the cultural factor. In this process in which the psychiatrist (or psychoanalyst) looks *outwards* from the individual psyche into his patient's social network, he inevitably moves into territory which the social anthropologist (and in Europe the sociologist) regards as his – hence, of course, the boundary disputes alluded to above.

Equally, when the social anthropologist attempts to assess the impact of socially enjoined behaviour or beliefs on the inner feelings of the people he studies, he likewise trespasses upon the psychiatrist's (and psychologist's) territory. This is especially obvious, for instance, when we examine culturally stereotyped responses to danger and stress, and attempt to evaluate their impact on the feelings of our informants. Social tension, as we shall see, is an assessment of social relations that springs readily to the lips of anthropologists but is rarely examined with much psychological sophistication, or even an awareness that it is a psychological phenomenon as well as a social one.

Then there is the problem of deviance. Stereotyped deviant behaviour is inevitably a social phenomenon, and concerns us almost as much as it does social psychologists or psychiatrists. We cannot afford to ignore the fact that mental illness is culturally patterned, and even goes in fashions. Again, different 'normal' individuals play their social roles with more or less commitment and conviction, and the individual's actual repertoire of roles usually does not exhaust his range. Actors are often bigger than their parts. The unfulfilled potential for new roles cannot be completely and unreservedly surrendered to the psychiatrist. We are interested in the social implications of personal ambition, greed, anger and hatred. No one who aims to study real life can possibly ignore these factors. Social life is very far from being governed by shrewd logic and sweet reason.

If our frontiers with psychiatry and psychology (including social psychology) are problematic and ill-defined, the situation is even more confused with sociology (and in some respects history). Some authorities hold that social anthropology is really a sub-division of sociology, a broadly-based comparative 'trans-cultural' or cross-cultural sociology. Others assert that anthropology is the tree and sociology the branch. Fortunately, since both cases can be argued persuasively, we can ignore these contentious reflections of academic imperialism and simply note the more striking differences in emphasis in the work of those who study man under these rival, though sometimes combined, banners. Distinctions exist both in the kinds of problems that are selected for study and in the manner in which they are tackled.

THE PARTICIPATING OBSERVER

Let us take methods first. The modern social anthropologist relies heavily on the research procedure known as 'participant observation'. This requires him to immerse himself as thoroughly as he can in the life of the community he is trying to understand. He must know the local language sufficiently well to follow what is going on round him and to record it with accuracy and subtlety. Within the limitations imposed by his hosts and his own inhibitions and scruples, the anthropologist has to mix in with local society and become the life and soul of the party. Total immersion is impossible or extremely rare and few anthropologists go completely native: most guardedly keep their distance yet observe and participate sufficiently to allow them to study things in their context.

Empathizing as far as possible with his hosts, the anthropological research worker seeks to seize the essence of life around him and to incarnate its animating spirit. He dashes about from place to place and function to function endeavouring to record all aspects of the local scene, trivial as well as tragic. His range of interests is as large as life: births, marriages, deaths, quarrels, reconciliations, rhetoric, religion, cultivation, animal husbandry, home-crafts, politics – all claim his attention and are (or should be) faithfully reported – warts and all. The minimum required of the social anthropologist is that he should write the biography of the people he studies. If he has no contribution to make to anthropological theory, he can at least do that.

As he rushes hither and thither, his note-books become crammed with an amazing collection of miscellaneous information which is so diverse and uneven that it gives colour to and so in a way explains Robert Lowie's famous definition of culture as a 'thing of shreds and patches'. All this material he gets, whenever possible, at first hand, or at any rate from those to whom he is prone to refer in unguarded moments as 'reliable informants'. In some cases the problem is to get taciturn people to talk. In others the difficulty is to stop loquacious informants from pouring out an endless stream of words which they positively insist on having recorded. Whichever way round it is, the task, complicated by the anthropologist's limited mastery of the vernacular, is apt to be taxing and to require tact and patience of a high order.

As he pores over all this raw data the field-worker discovers certain interesting patterns and principles in terms of which his information makes sense. These have to be tested and followed up in new lines of inquiry. The anthropologist's appetite for information and his curiosity are boundless, and he is naturally particularly attracted by those avenues of inquiry where the answers come hard, suggesting that he has touched on a sensitive and hence significant vein. The field anthropologist is thus in some respects a kind of cross-cultural private eye, relentlessly pursuing clues to lay bare the soul of his foreign hosts.

The social anthropologist is equally, of course, an entrepreneur whose special expertise lies in mediating between exotic cultures and his own, and he has the same vested interests as other go-betweens. So it is not surprising that each field-worker tries to select an unstudied people, or if that fails, a community whose present circumstances render them acutely interesting for 'theoretical reasons'. For each piece of field research aims at achieving a 'scoop' which will redound to the anthropologist's credit, and the more interesting and exciting the raw data the better. There is always the lurking fear that some hostile critic will ask the returned voyager the old, but still highly relevant question: was his journey really necessary? Did he really need to go so far to learn so little? It is at this point that the anthropologist, when pressed, retreats into impenetrable jungles of ethnographic fact. And it is by the quality of these records that he brings back that he will ultimately be judged. The 'ethnographic facts' are indeed our golden fleece.

If you identify strongly with those you study you may not appreciate the extent to which you have been brain-washed. In the culture in which he specializes the anthropologist is admirably sociological; but as soon as he steps outside it to engage in comparative studies and generalization he becomes paradoxically culture-bound, unwittingly taking unique cultural forms as universal facts. Hence, to an extent which is often hard to gauge accurately, high-sounding 'theoretical' debates between leading members of the profession are partly arguments between the cultures they were privileged to study. In this ethnographic imperialism if in no other way, the cultures anthropologists study and plagiarize gain their revenge.

As Malinowski's own posthumously published field diaries record,[1] this cross-cultural experience, involving a massive ex-

1. B. Malinowski, *A Diary in the Strict Sense of the Term*, Routledge & Kegan Paul, 1967. This work, apparently not intended for publication and perhaps bowdlerized in translation from the Polish original, gives nevertheless a revealing picture of the conditions under which Malinowski carried out his epoch-making research in the Trobriand Islands between 1914 and 1918.

For a contrasting account of field-work experience in Africa by an American researcher (Dr Laura Bohannan), see E. S. Bowen, *Return to Laughter*, Gollancz, 1954.

posure to what we nowadays call 'culture-shock', is likely to be as gruelling psychologically as it is physically. Foreign communities, whether tribal or otherwise, are no more anxious than you or I to be subjected to intensive and embarrassingly close scrutiny by a tiresome stranger whose aims and intentions may be, to say the least, puzzling. Although surprisingly few of our colleagues have died 'in the field', it is nonetheless fitting that field-work should have assumed the character of a tribal ordeal or initiation rite the performance of which, under appropriate conditions, is virtually indispensable if one is to gain professional status. C. G. Seligman did not exaggerate when, many years ago, he declared: 'Field research in Anthropology is what the blood of the martyrs is to the Church.' It is our counterpart to the psychoanalyst's 'training analysis' (or simulated illness and cure), a traumatic endurance test in which the tyro anthropologist discovers almost as much about himself as about the people he has come to study.[2]

In this type of work the researcher's personality inevitably bulks large and has to be taken into account in the evaluation of his reports (a critical task which colleagues assume with unbecoming zeal). Not all traditional or other communities singled out for study get the anthropologists they deserve, or *vice versa* – although a surprisingly high proportion seem to. Nevertheless there are few social anthropologists whose field experiences are so hair-raising and disastrous that they fail to develop strong loyalties towards their exotic patrons. Here Colin Turnbull's much publicized indignation at the depraved behaviour of the famine-stricken Ik is exceptional.[3] Every anthropologist, after all, lives off those he studies, and he should not fail to recognize and respond to this basic fact. While one may sometimes wonder whether some of one's colleagues were quite as warmly welcomed as they make out, most returned field-workers readily assume the role of genial impresarios or spokesmen for their exotic hosts. They may indeed be able to voice interests and demands which their sources are unable to express through any other channel.

2. For a fuller discussion of these issues see I. M. Lewis, *The Anthropologist's Muse: An Inaugural Lecture,* London School of Economics, 1973.
3. Colin Turnbull, *The Mountain People,* Cape, 1973.

This traditional spokesmanship, which can imply serious responsibilities, is naturally becoming less significant today as modern communications and education reach into the furthest quarters of the globe. We catch an echo of it however in that curiously possessive rather than patronizing way in which anthropologists are given to speaking of 'their people' (just as the people sometimes speak of 'their anthropologist'). What this implies and should express is the field-worker's moral commitment to his foreign hosts; this can be the source of much personal anguish and heart-searching. Whatever his private political convictions, and whether he angrily denounces it as 'ethnocide' or not, no anthropologist worth his salt can dispassionately contemplate the destruction of a traditional way of life which he has learnt to appreciate and admire. And yet this may be part of the price which has to be paid if a larger population is to survive. For the wider economic and political interests of a country may be in complete conflict with the wishes and needs of a constituent community which an anthropologist happens to have studied. If, as is sometimes the case, he is actually in a position to influence the course of events, how should he then act? Ethnocide or something approaching it revolts him, but he does not usually wish to champion the preservation of cultures simply as museum pieces. The dilemma is a very real one in the contemporary Third World and does not, unfortunately, admit readily of simple, universally valid answers.

FACTS AND FIGURES

Subjectivity and personal involvement are part of the price the social anthropologist pays for his most cherished and characteristic research strategy which, within the limits we have indicated, we can succinctly describe as 'going native'. On the surface at least, the methods of sociology are very different. The empirical sociologist is nothing if not business-like, 'objective' and above all 'scientific'. He designs careful and often elaborate questionnaires which he or his assistants administer to statistically significant sample groups in the population under investigation. Statistical (and often computer) analysis of the respondents' answers may

with luck reveal statistically significant trends in opinion, attitudes, or behaviour. The research procedure here usually
assumes that people can read and write (which can be a serious
limitation), and it also conveniently throws the burden of veracity
on one's informants. People must fill up their questionnaires conscientiously and honestly. Since, however, those who carry out
surveys of this kind are seldom able to control their sources,
even cleverly-designed trick questions may fail to yield anything
but superficial or ambiguous results. Certainly it is frequently
difficult to know 'what to make of' (a revealing phrase) data collected in this fashion, unless the whole enterprise is very carefully
controlled and supplemented by on-the-spot observations made by
experienced researchers. However sophisticated the machinery of
'data-processing' and costly the enterprise, the outcome is unlikely
to be of value if the information collected is spurious in the first
place. Here the old adage 'ask a silly question and get a silly
answer' still applies. As a contributor to a recent survey on 'com-
parability in social research', published under the auspices of the
British Social Science Research Council, sagely observes: 'a great
deal can go wrong at the recording stage which may make subsequent analysis difficult or even impossible'.

The most amusing commentary on the limitations which are
inherent in this type of research, however, is perhaps that enshrined in the Indonesian concept of a 'statistical Muslim' (or
Islam statistique), a person who, while not actively practising the
faith, so records his identity for census and other purposes. Imagine
what the results would be if someone were to base a study of active
religious adherence on the laconic entries made under the heading 'religion' on hospital admission forms in Great Britain! For
all its faults and notwithstanding the low reputation it has
acquired through its use to collect trivial information, the social
survey technique can undoubtedly produce a wide range of useful
statistical data. In literate urban societies it can provide valuable
quantitative information on such topics as education, health,
housing, social class, racial attitudes, income distribution, family-
structure, the mass media and so on, thus contributing to the
identification and understanding of important social issues.

This of course is not the end of the sociologist's interest or expertise. The sociologist can also examine his data analytically in the light of hypotheses developed by his more theoretically inclined colleagues on such matters as urban alienation, juvenile delinquency, football hooliganism, dangerous driving, the generation gap, secularization, and race relations. What is often lacking, however, in sociological research is a concerted effort to examine social data functionally in order to discover significant, rather than merely self-evident, correlations between different patterns of belief and behaviour. Here the missing link is frequently the directly observed contextual detail which is so crucial in anthropological field work. The proliferation of statistical data is, paradoxically, often ultimately less illuminating than a much more narrowly based, but correspondingly more intensive, case-study.

From this caricature [4] (for that is all there is time for here), it can be seen that in its empirical tradition, sociology (and to a considerable extent social psychology also) deals primarily with western industrial society, which it examines descriptively in a somewhat piecemeal fashion. Thus, except where comparative material from more exotic regions is included (as it may be), sociology tends to take western values and assumptions for granted; like history it is consequently inclined to be more ethnocentric than social anthropology. Hence, there is perhaps a certain poetic justice in the traumatic methodological heart-searching in which so many sociologists are at present engaged as they roundly reject the old 'value-free' claims of their intellectual ancestors and aggressively expose the latent political biases of their colleagues. But as we contemplate these bitter internecine struggles we should not be too unsympathetic or complacent. It is silly to exaggerate differences when the similarities are also significant. When it is fortified by 'in-depth' interviews, and addressed to the intensive observation of what people actually do as well as what they say they do, sociological research merges indistinguishably with the work of social anthropologists.

4. In his *Invitation to Sociology*, Penguin, 1970, Chapter 1, Peter Berger offers a very similar characterization to that outlined here. For a more trenchant and witty, if sometimes a little extreme, self-critique, see S. Andreski, *Social Science as Sorcery*, Penguin, 1974.

This blurring of disciplinary frontiers is further encouraged when those few social anthropologists who can count, or have convenient access to mathematical aids, follow sociologists in succumbing to the lure of statistics and the computer. Methods can easily converge and so can the problems and topics studied as well as their location. So in fields such as economic and social development, and urban studies, social anthropologists no longer exercise a monopoly in Third World research. From the other side, an increasing number of social anthropologists are bringing their subject home to investigate small communities or self-contained sectors of western society, the traditional domain of sociologists. Our colleagues thus are now to be found participating and observing in villages and urban enclaves in Britain and America as well as on the ski-slopes of Europe, and are also making forays into factories, prisons and hospitals to see whether they can produce more interesting and unexpected findings than those already provided by other techniques of research.

It would be narrow-minded and bigoted not to welcome these convergent developments. For the social sciences have more to gain from each other than they have to lose, and the precise origin and pedigree of new findings and theories is of little importance so long as they extend and expand our understanding of the world. Once these ecumenical gestures have been graciously made, however, it needs to be repeated emphatically that the most valuable thing about social anthropology is its uniquely privileged relationship with exotic traditional societies. The beliefs and behaviour of remote cultures challenge most profoundly our own ethnocentric experience and assumptions, and compel us to recognize the amazing variety and versatility of human social arrangements, moral standards, and cosmologies.

TIME AND SPACE

This cross-cultural spatial perspective complements the temporal perspective of the historian, which it enlarges and enriches. In their encounters with the ghostly figures of past eras and periods, historians frequently adopt much the same holistic approach as we do. As one member of the profession has aptly observed: 'It is not too difficult – it does not wrench the mind too painfully – for the historian or the humanist to accept the notion of "living his way" into the totality of a culture. On the contrary his heart may be gladdened by the new and heady sense of actuality that accompanies this type of study.'[5]

It would be a cold anthropological heart that would not respond to these stirring words. But the mind-stretching impact of the historian's research tends to be limited by the fact that (usually at least) he is working within his own cultural tradition. Unlike the anthropologist he can never have the excitement of actually directly confronting his subjects in the flesh; and he is dealing with people who, temporally distant though they may be, are ultimately his own kith and kin. The past that historians study thus normally embraces, and even plays a part in shaping, the world they themselves inhabit. As it unfurls the panoramic vistas of past periods and epochs within the European cultural tradition, history builds a view of ourselves as the inevitable continuation and culmination of everything that has gone before. It traps us and pins us down in time, urging us to agree with Kierkegaard, that if life can only be lived forwards, it can only be understood backwards. History thus cuts man down to size by reminding him of his origins: its characteristic insight is hindsight. Our subject points towards wider horizons, offering a further dimension of perception and perspective, giving us at least the illusion that we transcend the confines of time.

This, however, is one of those voyages in which ultimately, and often without warning, the traveller confronts himself. We discover how exotic peoples meet the universal basic human needs of food, shelter and sex in unexpected ways and with highly original and thought-provoking theories about the meaning of life and the nature of the human condition; in so doing we begin to perceive the relativity and arbitrariness of our own basic postulates. We thus engage in cultural confrontations in which we suddenly perceive how our vision is clouded and distorted by hidden assumptions that we did not know we entertained. This is

5. H. S. Hughes, 'History, the Humanities, and Anthropological Change', *Current Anthropology*, vol. 4, 1963, p. 141.

humbling. But it is also exhilarating, liberating and profoundly humanizing.

THE CROSS-CULTURAL PERSPECTIVE

This new self-awareness, which the contemplation of alien cultures and institutions promotes, throws light on our own past as well as present. We are prone to over-emphasize our rationality and to under-rate the very significant part played in our lives by beliefs and ideas that we normally categorize as irrational and absurd, and readily disavow. We are equally ready to project this highly idealized picture of ourselves onto our own past and do not know what to make of the weird mystical 'fantasies' in which our ancestors seem to have indulged. Perhaps they did not *really* believe in them – or did they? Our study of exotic tribal religions, however, enables us to come to terms with this tantalizing problem at a safe distance; indirectly it makes it easier to realize that it is not the presence of such beliefs that is odd or unusual but their absence.

We also learn that family structure and sentiments which we take for granted are by no means universal, that forms of government that seem inevitable and natural are not necessarily so; we confront the unpalatable finding that a strong sense of brotherhood and identity within a community usually implies equally strong hostilities towards outsiders. More positively, we discover how problems that result from the shrinking of family ties to what we call the 'nuclear family' are alleviated or avoided in the more flexible kinship arrangements of many tribal peoples. But such benefits as we may find here and elsewhere entail countervailing disadvantages. Those who live permanently in them do not always share our nostalgia for big, happy extended families: nor do all those who participate in that often-associated matrimonial arrangement, polygyny, find it equally attractive.

Any careful cost–benefit analysis will show that every social practice and institution has limitations and presents difficulties as well as opportunities. Some societies and cultures may indeed be more pleasant to live in, just as some seem more exciting and others nastier. However, social anthropology can offer no general panacea for our present ills and discontents. Although it certainly has a romantic streak, our subject is a serious academic discipline; it is not an intellectualized transcendental meditation in which exotic beliefs are wrenched crudely from their setting to be appropriated in the selfish pursuit of some second-hand, simulated, and ultimately spurious nirvana. Nor do we seek to pass judgements, or to rate one social system as morally superior to another in any overall sense. I know of no scientifically valid calculus that would enable to to do that, and in any case the project would be stultifying. Our findings have relevance for moral philosophy, but the philosophers can be left to draw their own conclusions – as they will do in any case.

Finally, in this brief introduction, what of the unflattering charge that social anthropology is the 'child of imperialism' (some would say bastard) and so carries an incapacitating stigma?[6] It is not surprising that this denunciation is so regularly and vehemently levelled by Americans, especially bourgeois 'children of capitalism', who have evidently commendably sensitive consciences. Understandably outraged by the revelations that colleagues had been implicated, however unwittingly, in the notorious Project Camelot, linked with CIA activities in Cambodia, American Anthropologists have often tended to assume that those working in 'colonial situations' elsewhere must have been similarly employed as, in effect, government agents. It is not difficult to understand this assumption, even when its projection elsewhere may be unjustified or oversimplistic. At the same time, American anthropologists are acutely aware, to the point of self-caricature, that the North American Indians have for generations provided a conveniently accessible exotic backyard for ethnographic research. So in the United States, perhaps more clearly and explicitly than elsewhere, social and cultural anthropology is frequently perceived as a form of academic activity rarely purged of exploitation. Put simply; our subjects are our copy, their customs the 'trophies' we collect. No wonder the mysterious Amerindian guru, Don

6. Some views on this issue are discussed in I. M. Lewis, *The Anthropologist's Muse: An Inaugural Lecture*, London School of Economics, 1973. See also Talal Asad (ed.), *Anthropology and the Colonial Encounter*, Ithaca Press, 1973; A. Kuper, *Anthropologists and Anthropology: The British School, 1922–1972*, Allen Lane, 1973; Dell Hymes (ed.), *Reinventing Anthropology*, Vintage, New York, 1974.

Juan, with uncharacteristic directness calls his anthropological mouth-piece, Carlos Castaneda, a 'pimp'.[7] The description is embarrassingly accurate. Beyond providing local amusement as a curiosity and practical help during his actual field-work, the crucial issue thus becomes: what more comprehensive return is the anthropologist to make to his former hosts after he has left them?

With this in mind we must consider the derogatory accusation of colonial compliance (if not complicity) in British social anthropology. I think that, as children have a habit of doing, British social anthropologists and many of their French, Belgian and American colleagues rebelled against their colonial 'parents'. Above all else it was the circumstantial and highly sympathetic accounts of complex and sophisticated tribal institutions and beliefs produced in the crucial inter-war period which finally destroyed the archaic stereotype of the rustic tribesman as a congenitally incapacitated simpleton, incapable of rational reasoning or civilized living. Whatever their private political opinions (in many cases left-wing), they collected and published with dedication and enthusiasm exciting new evidence which forced informed European opinion to discard the hackneyed image of the poor, benighted savage. This first-hand testimony, delivered with appropriate scholarly documentation, helped restore to the so-called 'primitive' his full humanity and dignity; it became intellectually inadmissible for tribesmen to be regarded as museum specimens who would remain for ever wayward children of nature and wards of paternalistic colonialism.

7. Carlos Castaneda, *Journey to Ixtlan*, Penguin, 1974.

Chapter Two

The Rise of Modern Social Anthropology

Our Victorian founding fathers did not, of course, hold such enlightened views on the mind and character of the 'savage tribesman'. This is not surprising; and we should not fall into the obvious trap of righteous indignation after the event nor judge them too harshly. The information available over a century ago on the customs and beliefs of exotic tribal peoples was incomparably poorer than it is today. Scientific field-research, treating the cultures of tribal societies with the same respect and scholarship as that lavished upon the great civilizations of antiquity and the East, is scarcely more than fifty years old. A hundred years ago the reports of travellers, colonial officials and missionaries were, with a few striking exceptions, amateur works which, however well-intentioned, often conveyed a misleading and partial picture. Such incomplete and imperfect evidence naturally limited the validity of inferences and generalizations based on it, although this was seldom apparent at the time.

Let us, however, also pay tribute to the high-minded humanitarian concern displayed, however patronizingly, by so many of our Victorian predecessors. No matter how wild their theories (and some were very wild), their hearts were often manifestly in the right place. Tribesmen might indeed be benighted savages, but they could still stir the liberal conscience – especially when their very primitiveness and simplicity made them all the more vulnerable to exploitation by unscrupulous Europeans. It is thus a matter for pride that some of the most eminent of the first anthropologists were really 'philanthropologists', men of the moral calibre of Thomas F. Buxton (1786–1845) and Thomas Hodgkin (1798–1866). These great Quaker figures, both of whom had played leading roles in the anti-slavery movement, founded the Aborigines Protection Society in the early 1830s. And this organization, which sought to protect the rights of the newly colonized, provided much of the original intellectual and moral impetus which led ultimately to the formation of the Royal Anthropological Institute of Great Britain.[1] The Institute was opened in 1871 with the object of promoting the scientific study of man, past and present, from all points of view – biological, social, and cultural. It remains the major national learned society for British anthropologists and is without doubt the most prestigious body of its kind in the English-speaking world.

It was several years, however, before social anthropology was to emerge as a distinct discipline, separate from other branches of anthropology, and to receive that accolade to which all subjects aspire – a secure place on university curricula. In practice, the subject was first introduced under the older and more inclusive names 'anthropology' and 'ethnology'[2] at Oxford in 1884 and at Cambridge in 1900. The first university professorship bearing the title 'social anthropology' was that held on an honorary basis at Liverpool University in 1908 by Sir James George Frazer (1854–1941), author of the mammoth Victorian best-seller *The Golden Bough* (first edition 1890) which, with its strong appeal to a readership brought-up on the classics, did much to establish the new subject's credentials. Courses at the London School of Economics, which became social anthropology's chief centre in Great Britain (and for a time in the world), began with the appointment in 1910 of C. G. Seligman. With Rivers he had participated in the famous Torres Straits expedition and was freshly returned from new research in the Sudan.

Despite, or perhaps because of, this late arrival social anthropologists are much given to tracing their intellectual pedigree to as remote and as illustrious ancestors as they can uncover. Some indeed go back to Plato; others have recourse to Herodotus. Rather than strain the reader's credulity by indulging in equivalent flights of genealogical fantasy, I shall start with our Victorian predecessors, since most of the currents of modern social anthropology (as of sociology) can be traced directly back to them.

1. See G. W. Stocking, 'What's in a Name? The Origins of the Royal Anthropological Institute (1837–71)', *Man* (N.S.), vol. 6, 1971, pp. 369–90.

2. This word is still sometimes used on the continent to describe what in Britain would now be called social anthropology.

Our curtain rises, then, in the nineteenth century, when the study of man was treated as a kind of history and more especially of that generalizing sort usually known as 'universal history' which is so well represented today in the works of Arnold Toynbee. At that time, European scholars were fascinated by the technological and, as they saw them, moral triumphs of their age, and obsessed with the necessity for progress in all fields of human endeavour; they felt a positive obligation to contemplate continually the long, hard road along which man had struggled in his search for perfection. Perhaps it was reassuring to ponder the primeval origins from which man's ascent had commenced long, long ago. It seems also that the regular equation of 'primitive' tribal customs with the earliest forms of European prehistoric culture provided an acknowledgement of common humanity, but one which was appropriately abridged and indirect. Our colonizing ancestors could not deny (although some attempted to) that they were dealing with representatives, however imperfect, of a single human species – *Homo sapiens*; but they could assert that the tenuous affinities they were prepared to recognize lay with their own most remote and primitive forebears. And if some savage peoples had so clearly fallen behind in the race, others, as some authorities maintained, might well represent not simply retarded, or imperfectly evolved, but actually degenerate forms of earlier civilization. Such backsliding was not necessarily incompatible with the general movement of mankind: evolution did not rule out devolution. Such views, of course, helped to justify the treatment of newly colonized tribesmen as savages urgently requiring the European's civilizing attentions. When Darwin appropriated this evolutionary perspective, and the morally convenient notion of the survival of the fittest, all nature seemed to chorus her approval of the unchallengeable truth of these basic facts of human and animal existence. As Bertrand Russell remarks: 'Darwinism was an application to the whole of animal and vegetable life of Malthus's theory of population, which was an integral part of the politics and economics of the Benthamites – a global free competition in which victory went to the animals that most resembled successful capitalists.'[3]

3. B. Russell, *History of Western Philosophy*, Allen & Unwin, 1946, p. 808.

It would be unfair to suggest that our Victorian predecessors deliberately compared tribal customs with those of early man in order to discredit the indigenous peoples they were colonizing. The truth is that they had a narcissistic preoccupation with their own past; any information they could glean about 'savage society' was eagerly seized upon in the hope that it might shed further light on their own origins.[4] As one critic caustically observed, these early armchair anthropologists, who seldom had any direct acquaintance with the tribal customs that so intrigued them, appeared to be only interested in the living in order to better understand the dead. This historical fascination inspired their limitless appetite for novel titbits of information on savage customs which would give substance to the shadowy forms of their own distant ancestors. This method of reclaiming the dead, we may note in passing, survives in modern archaeology. As he racks his brains to discover the purpose of some otherwise unintelligible artefact, the prehistorian turns hopefully to 'ethnographic parallels' from living cultures. In this fashion the stone-age men of today throw light on those who have long disappeared from view. So while we may decry our predecessors' excessive self-absorption, we have again to salute their ingenuity in developing a valuable and indispensable part of the archaeologist's armoury of techniques. But this is a digression.

Victorian scholars were divided in their views of the precise nature and order of the stages of man's evolutionary progress. But most agreed on the basic characteristics of the earliest 'state of nature' from which the great evolutionary adventure had begun. As might be anticipated, this primordial zero-point represented the antithesis of almost everything they most cherished. It was seen as an anarchic slough of disorder and despair. In this primeval chaos man's unbridled egotism reigned supreme with no government to restrain it; property was not respected and no orderly means existed for its transfer from one generation to the next; marriage was unknown and mating was savagely haphazard and competitive. This Hobbesian state was christened, not it seems without a certain relish, 'primitive promiscuity'. This fantasy world of natural lust, ironically, can scarcely ever have been more

4. See J. W. Burrow, *Evolution and Society*, Cambridge University Press, 1966.

closely realized than in the appalling conditions of the urban poor in the sordid back streets and alleys of prosperous Victorian cities; but it could not, of course, be permitted to endure for long in the theoretical world. So, in this science fiction view of human evolution, primitive promiscuity was soon replaced by more orderly patterns of existence. Intriguingly foreshadowing our contemporary women's liberation movement, some of these stalwart Victorians envisaged that the evolutionary struggle then involved domination by the female since, they argued, women first rebelled against these loose promiscuous relations to queen it over men. Others stoutly denied this matriarchal ascendency, insisting that, following its promiscuous episode, early society soon settled down under a patriarchal régime in which the opposite sex knew its place and kept it. Ultimately the final culmination was the same: anarchy eventually gave place to patrician capitalism.

This, for instance, was largely the thesis developed by the great English comparative jurist, Sir Henry Maine (1822–88). Maine considered that laws inevitably bore the stamp of the social conditions within which they were enacted and applied, so the best way to discover the course of social evolution was to examine the changing character of legal codes. He saw himself as an empiricist, attacking such woolly concepts as 'natural equality' and the imaginary 'state of nature' beloved of the political philosophers. His expert knowledge of classical history was sharpened by a deep interest in Indian law based upon his years of service there as a senior legal official. Maine's most influential book, *Ancient Law*, was first published in 1861, ten years after the Great Exhibition. This is a brilliant if, as we can now see, overconjectural study of the development of legal ideas and forms of social organization. The argument runs as follows. The typical organization of early society was based upon the patriarchal family. By natural increase in population and with the adoption of strangers (who were treated as fictitious kinsmen), patriarchal families grew into clans such as those found in ancient Rome. These later evolved into tribes, and these in turn swelled in size and complexity eventually to become fully-fledged states. (A very similar evolutionary typology is still employed today, as we shall see, by one school of contemporary American anthropologists.)

Maine summed up the crucial developments of human history in his famous formula of the 'movement of the progressive societies from Status to Contract'. By this Maine meant that in archaic and primitive society a man's rights and duties were rigidly determined by his position at birth in a given family or clan. However hard he strove, his destiny was fixed at birth by his parents' position, and such limited social mobility as might be achieved was rationalized (and thus concealed) in the language of kinship. As society evolved, however, relations between people became at once more individual and flexible with a greater scope for the exercise of choice and free will. Kinship was no longer the sole idiom for legitimate relations; voluntary contractual connections began to appear and gained ascendancy over those determined from birth by kinship. This interpretation of the universal direction of progress is of course in keeping with the more liberal Victorian assumptions. Maine was writing in the wake of the Chartist movement and a decade after the formation of the Amalgamated Society of Engineers, the first professional union in Britain with a membership exclusively of apprenticed craftsmen. Had he lived to see the present development of union organization, with its emphasis on restrictive employment and job-demarcation, he might have wished to revise some of his views. The British National Union of Students, with its mandatory membership, would have astonished him.

Unlike so many contemporaries whose first-hand experience of savage society rarely extended outside the senior common-rooms of Oxford and Cambridge, Maine had at least lived in India. The importance of such direct, if only fleeting and superficial, contact with exotic cultures is further demonstrated by Maine's contemporary, Lewis Henry Morgan (1818–81), an American lawyer who inaugurated the study of kinship and whose works had an important influence on Marx and Engels. After graduating, Morgan spent some time amongst the Iroquois Indians, who had fascinated him since his college days, and published his famous *League of the Iroquois* in 1851. Amongst other things, it records a kinship system which struck Morgan as distinctly odd. The Iroquois had, he reported, a 'system of classification of kindred, both unique and extraordinary in its character, and wholly unlike any with which we are familiar'. A year later, however, he was intrigued to discover that the Ojibwa Indians, who were of different linguistic stock, had the same system. Further research revealed that what had at first appeared to be a bizarre anomaly was in fact a cultural feature shared by many different Indian peoples. This stimulated Morgan into mounting a much wider-ranging inquiry in the course of which, with the assistance of the American Department of Indian Affairs and other official bodies, he sent out questionnaires to government officials and missionaries in many different parts of the world seeking further information on kinship terminologies.

From an analysis of this large body of data, Morgan concluded that two contrasting principles underlay the terms used by different societies to describe and classify relatives. The American Indian system tended to group together under a single term categories of kinsfolk whom we should recognize as distinct. The word we translate in English as 'brother', for instance, would include those we distinguish as 'cousins'; similarly a term such as 'father' might also include paternal 'uncles'. This economical use of a few key terms to embrace large clusters of kinsfolk Morgan called 'classificatory'. He contrasted this with the other type of terminology found amongst speakers of the 'Celtic' and Semitic languages, where most relatives had separate and unique kinship terms. This type, which we find to some extent in English, clearly emphasized differences rather than shared properties, and Morgan labelled it 'descriptive'.

The classificatory system can be conveniently illustrated by the patrilineal Omaha Indians among whom a man calls his mother's father, mother's brother, mother's brother's son, and mother's brother's son's son by a single term. He uses one term to refer to his mother, to his mother's brother's daughter and to his mother's brother's son's daughter. Thus here we see two terms used to distinguish relatives on my mother's side according to their sex. In effect, all my mother's female paternal kin are called by the same term that I apply to my 'mother'; and all her male paternal kin are designated 'mother's brother' without reference to their generational position. Here the generation-gap is very effectively bridged.

Like so many of his contemporaries, Morgan was an evolutionist. Consequently he assumed that tribes possessing the classificatory kinship system, even if now separate and speaking different languages, must once have shared a common origin. As he saw it, his discovery of the two types of kinship terminology afforded a powerful new research tool to investigate historical connections and to reconstruct links which had otherwise disappeared or been forgotten (as well they might, since they had probably never existed!). Although this interest in pseudo-historical connections was Morgan's primary concern, he was also one of the first anthropologists to understand that the names used to designate relatives are not simply determined by linguistic rules without reference to social factors; kinship terms have an important social dimension, since relatives grouped together and called by the same term exhibit, at least in certain respects, shared patterns of behaviour. If, for example, I call my mother's brother's son by the same term that I apply to my mother's brother, the implication is that I share a common relationship with both. Again, if I call my mother and her sister by the same term ('mother'), then both behave maternally towards me – though not necessarily with the same intensity of feeling. Having thus grasped the important principle that kinship terms reflect social usage, Morgan was able to go further and indeed to anticipate later research in his perceptive assessment of the social advantages of the classificatory system. Such a system, as he saw, minimized the differences which might otherwise be drawn between distant and close kin. It extended the web of relationships under the mantle of a few comprehensive terms of relationship connoting close, primordial loyalties. The brotherhood of man did not end with the immediate family of siblings at which it began.

For these and other achievements Morgan has indeed some claim to be considered 'the founding father of kinship studies', as Meyer Fortes has pointed out.[5] But we must now return to England to consider briefly part of the lively contribution to the developments we are discussing made by Sir Edward Tylor (1832–1917). It was Tylor who first taught anthropology under this name at Oxford in 1884 and he carried forward and extended

5. M. Fortes, *Kinship and the Social Order*, Aldine, Chicago, 1969, p. 15. See also Ward H. Goodenough, *Description and Comparison in Cultural Anthropology*, Aldine, Chicago, 1969.

some of the theoretically more important strands in Morgan's work. When he noticed that linguistic usage could reflect social usage and that classificatory kinship systems encouraged group solidarity, Morgan made what we would now call a 'functional' interpretation of social phenomena. Tylor's work which, especially in the field of religion, is currently enjoying something of a revival, displays further and more explicitly recognized examples of this functionalist way of understanding society. But, like Morgan, his main orientation was historical and he contributed to evolutionary theory by introducing the term 'survival' for those customs or beliefs which, like the human appendix, linger on anachronistically out of context. These, he argued, can often provide the keen evolutionist with important clues to earlier historical connections.

In the present context, Tylor's most interesting contribution was his pioneering application of statistics to the analysis of social phenomena. This 'piece of social arithmetic', as he modestly called it, was published in 1889 and was addressed to the problem of understanding the exaggerated lengths to which many tribesmen were reported to go in avoiding their in-laws. Very sensible, the reader may think. Quite true. But, as Tylor noticed, while some cultures prescribed very strong avoidance behaviour between *sons* and parents-in-law, others were more concerned to keep *daughters* and parents-in-law from each others' throats. Other societies again seemed remarkably latitudinarian, scarcely appearing to notice that a problem existed. Were such variations arbitrary, or could they be explained in any logically consistent fashion? Tylor decided to investigate, guided by the shrewd hunch that there might be statistically valid correlations between avoidance behaviour and choice of residence at marriage. Surveying reports on the relevant customary behaviour in 350 separate 'societies', Tylor was able to demonstrate that, when the newly-weds set up house with the *wife's kin*, avoidance behaviour between the latter and the *husband* occurred more frequently than could be expected on the basis of mere chance. Similarly, when the wife lived with her husband's kin, *she* was then obliged to avoid *them*. To clinch the matter, Tylor discovered that in those cases where the couple lived independently of either group of kin, avoidance behaviour was haphazard.

Tylor's next step was to show that these statistical correlations, or 'adhesions' as he quaintly called them, could also shed light on other puzzles. Thus a particularly bizarre practice, for which with typical resourcefulness Tylor coined the name *teknonymy*, involved calling a married person not by his own name but by that of his children. Here Johnny's father, David, would be referred to as 'Father of Johnny', and Johnny's mother Mary would similarly be called 'Mother of Johnny'. (This procedure is reminiscent of the Christian and especially Catholic usage in which the Virgin Mary is known as the 'Mother of Jesus'.) Again, Tylor was able to prove that these curious forms of reference were not distributed round the globe by arbitrary acts of providence. On the contrary, they went hand-in-hand with the correlations already established between avoidance behaviour and residence at marriage. If, for example, a man was known as 'Father of James' the probability was that he lived with his wife's people and dutifully avoided his mother-in-law in the appointed manner.

Tylor had thus isolated three separate customary practices and elegantly demonstrated that they formed a mutually associated complex, each element varying with the others. Although he was more concerned with the general evolutionary history of mankind than in analysing societies as self-sustaining wholes, here he was busy making functional associations almost in spite of himself! What is more, he was demonstrating the functional inter-relation of social phenomena with greater statistical skill and sophistication than most British social anthropologists could manage today. The work of his modern American successor in this field, George Peter Murdock, covers a wider range of kinship data and is generally more ambitious in scope in its systematic search for the determinants of different systems of kinship terminology.[6]

These achievements do not exhaust Tylor's contribution to the developing trend of functionalist logic which we can detect in these evolutionary writers. Anticipating much later research, Tylor also made the seminal suggestion that the choice of resi-

6. G. P. Murdock, *Social Structure*, Macmillan, New York, 1949.

dence at marriage exerted a crucial effect on the way kinship was reckoned in a society. This link between marriage and kinship, the two abiding pillars of much anthropological theory, was further emphasized in Tylor's pithy comment that, in the history of human development, the choice facing many tribal peoples was the stark one of marrying out or dying out. Threatened groups bring in wives from outside and thus establish important social links promising external support and succour. Such ties of marriage create alliances which, as Tylor shrewdly saw, may help to discourage enmity or to compose differences between otherwise mutually hostile tribes. This 'survival-kit' view of the functions of out-marriage (or 'exogamy' as the Scottish writer J. F. McLennan christened it, in contrast to 'endogamy' or in-marriage) has a thoroughly modern ring about it. As we shall see later, there is therefore some force in the stock examination question: was Tylor the first alliance theorist?

FUNCTIONALISM: DURKHEIM'S CONTRIBUTION

The functionalist tendencies we have detected in Tylor loom much larger in the work of his French contemporary, Émile Durkheim (1858–1917), the last and greatest of the forerunners of modern social anthropology to be discussed here. Durkheim is generally regarded as the founder of modern comparative sociology (a distinction which to some extent Marx and Weber must also be allowed to share). In common with other scholars we have considered, Durkheim was essentially an armchair theorist who seldom stirred outside his study, or beyond his own milieu, except to give lectures or to participate in learned debates. He was a socialist, a democratic reformer rather than a Marxist or revolutionary syndicalist, and believed passionately in the transforming power of secular education. Sociology in the final analysis existed to provide a theoretical basis for socialism and secular education which were its practice. Thus educational policy (over which Durkheim succeeded in exerting a dominant influence in France), rather than revolutionary political change, represented the true key to the utopian transformation which he envisaged.

Born at Épinal in the Vosges, Durkheim was Jewish and brought up to be a rabbi which, however, he did not become, turning instead to the new science of sociology. He taught this subject first at Bordeaux and then from 1902 until his death in 1917, at Paris. His doctoral thesis took the form of an analysis of the effects of various degrees of economic differentiation in different societies, and was not very favourably received by his examiners. Nevertheless, the book which he based upon it and published in 1893 under the title *De la Division du travail social: étude sur l'organisation des societés supérieures*[7] is without question one of the most influential and stimulating in the whole field of the social sciences. Although Durkheim remains less well-known popularly than Marx, his ideas have exerted a greater formative influence in the development of anthropological (and sociological) theory.

In contrast to Maine and others including the English social philosopher Herbert Spencer, Durkheim maintained that increasing economic specialization did not necessarily entail the growth of individualistic competitiveness and social atomization. Nor, *pace* Marx, did industrialization inevitably result in capitalistic alienation (although Durkheim did acknowledge that in 'abnormal' circumstances *anomie* might result). On the contrary, under favourable conditions (which were never clearly specified) the rise of economic specialization led to the development of a new and improved kind of social cohesion and one largely inspired, it would seem, by utopian socialism. The division of labour itself was not, as economists had long held, caused by a desire for greater productivity. Rather, increased productivity followed from increasing economic specialization which, in turn, had been produced by a massive increase in the 'density' of society.

Durkheim developed this ingenious thesis by contrasting the economic and social conditions in primitive and modern societies. As he read the evidence on primitive societies, where of course there was far less economic specialization, social cohesion was of a very rudimentary kind. Its basis lay in the simple attraction of like for like, since the constituent units in such 'segmental' societies were all-of-a-piece. Carve them up however you wished,

7. English translation: *The Division of Labour in Society*, Free Press New York, 1947.

you would always end up with an array of monotonously similar looking bits. In a passage which reads very oddly indeed today and betrays his naïveté, Durkheim even went so far as to claim that such was the depressing degree of homogeneity in primitive society that its members were actually *physically* indistinguishable from each other! The primitive sympathetic magic which kept such simple tribesmen together Durkheim christened 'mechanical solidarity'. In striking contrast, modern industrial societies were characterized by heterogeneity, and were held together by a superior bonding principle which, following the centuries' old analogy between the body-politic and the human organism, Durkheim chose to call 'organic solidarity'. Its basis lay in the attraction of opposites.

In an argument where the central issue was social cohesion it was clearly necessary to find some means of measuring this elusive force. Here Durkheim took a leaf out of Maine's book and decided to adopt law as an objective measure of social solidarity. This led him to compare the legal codes of archaic and modern societies in much the same manner as Maine had done. He concluded that legal processes could be divided into two contrasting types. One species of law, which he called 'restitutive', was concerned essentially with restoring social harmony; the other, its opposite, was repressive penal law, inherently punitive and vengeful. The latter, Durkheim asserted (wrongly, as later anthropological field studies were to show) predominated in primitive conditions and could thus be employed as a measure of the mechanical solidarity present. Punishment, Durkheim maintained, was neither corrective nor deterrent in intention; it was a passionate reaction on the part of society which, in taking what amounted to collective revenge on the criminal, symbolically reaffirmed and restored the moral values and common loyalties which he had desecrated: symbolic lynching in which an outburst of punitive indignation against the criminal healed the injuries which he had inflicted on society. Such punitive gestures fulfilled the important function of maintaining mechanical solidarity at the requisite pitch. And, paradoxically, as Durkheim was to recognize, a certain amount of crime might even be necessary to keep society in a healthy state, on its toes – as it were.

Criminals were thus in some sense public benefactors (this clearly being a case where crime does pay !). Modern industrial society with its superior 'organic' solidarity could dispense with these primitive aids to cohesion and develop the more civilized, less emotional and, above all, rational legal processes which Durkheim took to be characteristic of progress. This in essence is Durkheim's utopian version of Maine's thesis.

As I have implied, many of Durkheim's conclusions are tautological or based upon inaccurate assumptions and evidence. But it is an impressive tribute to the persuasive power of his challenging presentation that despite so many deficiencies his argument remains fresh and stimulating. Why is this so? Mainly, I think, because he finally established the explanatory power of functionalism; he showed more clearly than any of his predecessors how much more profoundly we understand man's social life when we see it in all its functional complexity. Earlier writers had given hints of the rewards that lay in store for those who followed this intellectual path. Durkheim opened the floodgates and offered what amounted to a radically new way of making sense of social institutions and their inter-relations. It is a measure of his success in launching this new functional approach that we now take it so much for granted that we forget, and even find difficulty in appreciating, the novelty which it represented at the time.[8]

That said, we must note that in common with so many other innovators, Durkheim's insights can also be found to some extent in the works of others. Apart from his own native predecessors (principally Condorcet and Comte), and the post-Kantian German philosopher, J. G. Fichte, there are many parallels (as well as differences) in the ideas of the English schoolmaster, inventor, philosopher and Fabian, Herbert Spencer (1820–1903), whose exceptionally voluminous writings make him the father of British sociology. Yet, somehow, even when he gets his facts wrong and becomes trapped in a spiral of tricky tautologies, Durkheim's way

8. For a valuable assessment see J. A. Barnes, 'Durkheim's Division of Labour in Society', *Man* (N.S.), vol. I, 1966, pp. 158–75. A. Giddens, *Capitalism and Modern Social Theory*, Cambridge University Press, 1971, compares Durkheim's contribution with those of Marx and Weber.

of putting things has a brilliant radiance which few other sociological theorists can match, far less surpass. Where Marx's
analysis emphasized the importance of economic resources and
their control, Durkheim maintained the primacy of social institutions, which he saw as functionally linked components of the
composite social organism. From this perspective, Durkheim enabled us to see how different social structures (rather than
systems of production) 'generate', as we would now say, distinctive patterns of belief. Whatever their ultimate truth or falsity,
beliefs and ideologies could thus be subjected to exactly the same
kind of functional analysis as other social phenomena. They had
no specially privileged status. This treatment removed ideology
and conceptual systems from the sequestered domains of philosophy and theology which have never been quite the same since !
Here, as a subtle and admirably thorough critique of his achievement by a philosopher, Steven Lukes, points out, Durkheim
anticipated Wittgenstein by at least half a century in showing
how concepts were (socially generated) collective representations.[9]

This highly illuminating way of regarding beliefs and concepts
not in terms of their ultimate truth or falsity, but as the product
of specific social conditions, is best illustrated in Durkheim's
book *Les Formes élémentaires de la vie religieuse* (1912).[10] In
The Division of Labour primitive and industrial societies were contrasted, since each was held together in a different way and by a
distinctive kind of social glue. Here the argument is rather
different; Durkheim argues that, if it is desired to penetrate and
isolate the quintessential features of religion, then the best way
of proceeding is to examine religion in its most primitive (earliest),
purest, and most elemental form. First, of course, you have to
locate your most primitive tribe. Fortunately for Durkheim this
did not present too many difficulties. There was a relative abundance of recent information on the totemic beliefs of the supremely
'simple' hunting and gathering Australian Aborigines, who were
generally regarded as, in Frazer's phrase, 'humanity in the
chrysalis stage'. Durkheim had little difficulty in employing this
material to demonstrate how beliefs in the mystical powers of

9. S. Lukes, *Émile Durkheim: His Life and Work*, Allen Lane, 1973; Penguin, 1975; p. 437.
10. English translation: *The Elementary Forms of the Religious Li e*, Allen & Unwin, 1915.

animals and other 'totemic' forces reflected the structure of Aboriginal hordes and their component divisions. Totems, he argued, were mystically charged symbols of group cohesion and identity – badges of belonging. They acted as emblems or mascots, symbolizing group loyalties.

Religion, which for Durkheim involved the separation of the sacred and the profane (as in Judaism), was an essentially *social* phenomenon. Likewise Durkheim's thoroughly Jewish God was a commendably sociable figure charged above all else with the maintenance of social order and morality amongst the faithful. Indeed, God was society deified. Or, as he put it slightly differently on another occasion, 'religion' is 'the system of symbols by means of which society becomes conscious of itself; it is the way of thinking characteristic of collective existence'. In the final analysis, religion was thus to be seen as the emotionally charged product of intense social interaction ('collective effervescence') – *esprit de corps* elevated to the metaphysical plane. (With the privilege of hindsight, some may see here an anticipation of the modern emphasis on transactions and interaction as the basic nexus of symbolic life.) And as the handmaid of religiosity, ritual's part was to express and impress those sentiments of group adherence on which the orderly life of the social organism depended for its survival. This arguably 'establishment' and certainly consensual presentation of religion finds surprisingly strong echoes in some of Marx's writing on the same topic. But it contrasts with the latter's general emphasis on religion as an abortive form of protest by the underprivileged: '. . . the sigh of the oppressed creature, the sentiment of a heartless world, and the soul of soulless conditions . . . the opium of the people !' [11]

The general theory of society which is enshrined in these two books is spelt out with great verve, but not without ambiguity, in Durkheim's methodological manifesto *Les Règles de la methode sociologique*.[12] Here we need only underline a few key concepts. Durkheim defines the sociologist's data as consisting of 'social facts'. These are customary ways of thinking and acting

11. T. B. Bottomore and M. Rubel (eds.), *Karl Marx: Selected Writings in Sociology and Social Philosophy*, Penguin, 1970, p. 41.

12. English translation: *The Rules of Sociological Method*, Free Press, New York, 1965.

to which each individual member of society feels compelled to conform. Personal idiosyncracies are not relevant here: what really matter are those sentiments and axiomatic patterns of thought and action which come, as we would say 'naturally', as a result of having been brought up or 'socialized' in a particular society and culture. Since these 'facts' belong to the group as a whole and since the latter is more than the sum of its parts, they have a transcendent reality of their own and cannot simply be *reduced* to the individuals in whose conduct they manifest themselves. By the same token, collective beliefs and behaviour cannot be explained in terms of individual psychology. They require a special new social psychology for, as Durkheim circuitously asserted, only the social can explain the social.

Hence Durkheim insisted that to understand one set of social phenomena we must see them in the round – in their wider, social context. Society is a dynamic organism: the destiny of its component parts and their significance lie in their contribution to the survival of the whole. This holistic approach, a kind of social determinism, is the essence of functionalism, and its discovery frees those who seek to understand social institutions from the dead hand of historical determinism. If history is not quite bunk, at least it is far from everything. Origins are certainly often interesting, but they do not necessarily have much to do with the present functioning and meaning of things. The contemporary meaning and significance of phenomena may have little to do with the shape and form which links them, however remotely, with the past. Like words, social institutions, customs, and beliefs all change drastically over time. To take a rather obvious example, women's liberation today is better understood in the light of its ambient social and economic circumstances than as the inevitable culmination of the nineteenth-century suffragette movement.

MALINOWSKI AND RADCLIFFE-BROWN

Durkheim's work marks the turning point between evolutionism and functionalism and provides the bridge to Malinowski and Radcliffe-Brown, the authentic founders of modern social anthropology. As befits two rival *prima donnas*, each of these formidable figures gave a characteristically distinctive twist to his version of functionalism. Malinowski (1884–1942), an emigré Pole, was trained first as a scientist and this may explain the strongly biological orientation of his functionalist theories. These were developed in England where he had come in search of further anthropological inspiration after reading Frazer's *Golden Bough*. In Malinowski's view man is an animal, even if sometimes a relatively cultured and social one. His physiologically based needs, or appetites, demand satisfaction, which is achieved through society's various culturally defined institutions. Thus marriage regulates sexual drives, economic institutions provide sustenance, and law and politics establish a regularized basis for necessary social cooperation and interaction. This Hobbesian approach finds difficulty in offering a plausible explanation for the existence of religion and art. These less direct consequences of man's animality could, Malinowski argued, be understood in the light of their integrative contribution to man's social existence. Thus magic was a crutch to which men turned when their technical expertise failed them, myth provided a justification or 'charter' for existing social and political activities, and ritual offered comfort in time of distress and despair. All this was consistent with Malinowski's over-riding view of culture as man's distinctive form of biological adaptation.

This down-to-earth, no-nonsense conception of man as an imperfectly socialized animal places much less stress than Durkheim on society as a metaphysical good to the preservation of which all activities are ultimately directed. Malinowski's natives were real people; not over-socialized cardboard figures locked in everlastingly mindless mechanical soldarity. Social life for Malinowski was like capitalism for Keynes: 'a going concern', in which individuals interacted with each other in pursuit of mutually rewarding transactions. Here the guiding motto was: you scratch my back, and I'll scratch yours – a process to which Malinowski usually referred in more dignified language as 'reciprocity' or 'give and take'. Since Malinowski made no secret of his earthy, materialist view of man's motives it is odd that it has taken modern exponents of transactional analysis and game theory so long to recognize his pioneering achievements in this field.

These ideas on culture and society are, as one would expect, a product both of Malinowski's own flamboyant personality and of his experience as a field-worker. Durkheim belonged to that contemplative school of armchair theorists epitomized by Sir James Frazer, who is supposed to have solemnly replied 'God forbid!' to the innocent questioner who asked if he had ever lived amongst 'savages'. Frazer's disciple, Malinowski, was of a very different mettle. Although he was not the very first, he has come to be regarded as the pioneer, bush-whacking anthropologist, the originator of the doctrine that until you have lived cheek by jowl with an exotic tribe and spoken their language fluently you cannot claim full professional status. Ironically enough, his main field experience occurred as a fortuitous consequence of the First World War. He had been a research student at the London School of Economics under the direction of C. G. Seligman since 1910. The outbreak of war found him in Australia where, with his teacher's patronage, he was attending a meeting of the British Association as secretary of the anthropology section. As soon as hostilities started, the question of Malinowski's possible internment arose since, although Polish, he was technically an Austrian subject. The Australian authorities took a commendably enlightened view of the matter, however, and allowed him to carry out research on the Trobriand Islands close to New Guinea. There he flung himself into the local setting with characteristic abandon and commitment, participating in the daily round of village life with an eagerness and zest which he attributed partly to his Polish temperament; there he established standards of meticulous and painstaking observation and inquiry which have been an inspiration to social anthropologists ever since. His graphic accounts of this experience established him as anthropology's Conrad and gave the subject the fiercely empirical tradition which is its hallmark in Britain to this day.

Malinowski was a prolific writer and also a uniquely gifted teacher, training, largely by the socratic method, a whole generation of brilliant disciples; true to their master in their fashion they have created modern social anthropology with cross-fertilization from Radcliffe-Brown. These are remarkable achievements and it would be unreasonable to expect Malinowski also to have made theoretical contributions of comparable significance. The functionalist method which he so strenuously championed amounted, in fact, to little more than acknowledging that every custom or institution, however strange and bizarre, served some contemporary purpose. Life was vivid and alive. It was not cluttered up with redundant 'survivals', to be understood retrospectively by reference to assumed evolutionary historical stages. Such a nostalgic obsession with the past was a natural outcome of the chair-bound anthropologist's myopic glance. Once you abandoned the theorist's armchair and his gloomy study and actually got out there among living tribesmen, then and only then could you really understand what was going on. With this fresh perspective exotic rituals which made no sense in the silence of the scholar's study except as echoes of past glories fell into their natural place as living parts of the throbbing actuality of real flesh-and-blood communal life. Redundant customs had no place in Malinowski's view of the world. There everything was, as the modern phrase has it, 'all go'.[13]

This healthy utilitarianism was, as has been said, ultimately referable to biologically grounded needs and drives. The sociological strain is weak in Malinowski's writing, and this may be connected with his unique absorption in a single exotic culture. In any event, it fell to Professor Radcliffe-Brown (1881–1955), Malinowski's contemporary and rival, to redress the balance in the direction of the sociological theorists. In the process, Radcliffe-Brown, who was a more skilful theorist than fieldworker, supplied British social anthropology with a theoretical framework to temper and guide the empiricism which it derived from Malinowski. Indeed, it is largely through Radcliffe-Brown's writing that Durkheim has made such an impact on social anthropology. Radcliffe-Brown was also a functionalist but of a less programmatic sort; he developed a more sophisticated terminology and theoretical approach, and in many respects improved on Durkheim. Where Malinowski had invoked the aid of reductionist principles borrowed from biology, and concentrated on man's *cultural* adaptation, Radcliffe-Brown re-asserted the

13. See R. Firth (ed.), *Man and Culture: An Evaluation of the Work of Bronislaw Malinowski*, Routledge & Kegan Paul, 1957; H. C. Payne, 'Malinowski's Style', *Proceedings of the American Philosophical Society*, vol. 125, No. 6, December 1981, pp. 416–40; G. W. Stocking, 'The Ethnographer's Magic: fieldwork in British Anthropology from Tylor to Malinowski', in G. W. Stocking (ed.), *Observers Observed*, University of Wisconsin Press, Madison, 1983, pp. 70–120.

social basis of all customs and institutions. Society for him, as for Durkheim, was an organism of which each constituent part existed to contribute to the well-being of the whole. He introduced the term *structure* to emphasize that social life must be founded upon an orderly, organized basis, a determinate framework of positions, roles and expectations which remains constant over considerable periods of time. It is only within and in relation to this 'structure' that institutions have functions to fulfil. Their primary purpose is the conservative one of helping to sustain and maintain the existing order of things. Thus for the structural functionalist we may say that the ends (social solidarity) always justify the means (social institutions).

That institutions work in this way, contributing to the general *status quo*, becomes taken for granted by Radcliffe-Brown. Once this is accepted we can seek out the logical consistencies in contextual use which constitute 'structural principles' and which make sense of otherwise apparently baffling practices and beliefs. At the same time and again harking back to Durkheim, at least in the case of tribal societies we usually know very little of their past through lack of documentary sources, so we can ignore this 'conjectural history'. If the past is inscrutable, it is better to concentrate on the more accessible present, which is sufficiently complicated to require our fullest concentration. This is Radcliffe-Brown's prescription.

One of the most impressive demonstrations of the virtues of this contextual, or holistic, approach is that offered by Radcliffe-Brown himself in a paper entitled 'The Mother's Brother in South Africa' and first published in 1925.[14] The factual data concern a South African people called the BaThonga, who had been meticulously studied by the Swiss missionary Junod and described in impressive detail in his classic monograph, published in 1913, *The Life of a South African Tribe*. Junod was particularly struck by the behaviour expected of people in their capacity as 'sister's son' or 'mother's brother'. The salient characteristics of this relationship were:

14. Reprinted in A. R. Radcliffe-Brown, *Structure and Function in Primitive Society*, Cohen & West, 1952. See also A. Kuper (ed.), *The Social Anthropology of Radcliffe-Brown*, Routledge and Kegan Paul, London, 1977.

1. Throughout his life the uncle is expected to display particular care and attention towards his sister's son.
2. Thus, if his sister's son fell sick, the maternal uncle would readily sacrifice on his behalf.
3. Despite the kindness on the uncle's part, however, the nephew was permitted many liberties at his expense. Such indeed was the uncle's indulgent good humour that the nephew could even steal his dinner without incurring his wrath.
4. In the same spirit, the nephew could with impunity even steal the sacrifice prepared in honour of the spirits by his uncle. Surprisingly this otherwise sacrilegious act was readily condoned.
5. Finally, on his uncle's death, the nephew inherited some of his property and might even claim his widow !

What is to be made of this extraordinary permissiveness on the part of the maternal uncle? First of course we need more information. The BaThonga are a patrilineal people, that is, kinship in blood is traced principally through the male line on the father's side. A son belongs to his father's clan and inherits property and position in his father's patriline. This makes the special position of the maternal uncle seem even more anomalous, and led Junod to suppose that we could only understand this peculiar relationship if we assumed that it represented an anachronistic throwback or 'survival' of an earlier matriarchal stage. This evolutionary explanation was, Junod proposed, the 'only one possible'.

Radcliffe-Brown, however, elegantly shows us how we can make sense of all this without invoking the tenuous spectre of an earlier 'matriarchal' stage which he points out would actually have quite the opposite influence. He notes first that the 'permissive maternal uncle' is by no means a phenomenon unique to the BaThonga. On the contrary it is quite common – though by no means universal – in other patrilineal societies. It must, logically, be explicable in terms of other shared social circumstances. When we approach the problem in this open-ended, context-sensitive way, probing deeper into linked relationships, we notice that the permissive relationship is paralleled by another which is its opposite in some respects. This is the coldly correct relationship which prevails in these patrilineal societies between the nephew and his *paternal* aunt. If my maternal brother is all sweetness and light, my father's sister is a real dragon – a cold, formally distant aunt with whom no liberties are possible at all. If then, we have two significant relationships here rather than one, and each is the counterpart of the other, what common factors make sense of both?

The solution, Radcliffe-Brown argues, lies in the underlying 'logic' of classificatory kinship systems, and especially in the principle he calls the *equivalence of siblings*. What this means is: if I have a particular type of relationship with someone, I will enjoy the same relationship (more or less) with his or her sibling (brother or sister). Thus in societies where kinship is an important determinant of behaviour, brothers and sisters are expected to present a common front to the world. It is important to emphasize here that we are discussing standardized behavioural norms and not private feelings or idiosyncratic behaviour. With this in mind we can see that the indulgent familiarity of the maternal uncle towards his nephew matches the mother's generous affection towards her child. What goes for the mother goes for her brother also. Equally, the frigid formality of the paternal aunt echoes the stern authority of her brother, the child's father. Moreover, the respect which informs the child's relations with his paternal relatives is here heightened by the sexual difference between nephew and paternal aunt. This aunt is in some sense a kind of female-father figure, just as the maternal uncle is in a sense a male version of the mother.

This interpretation assumes that institutions (such as the licensed disrespect and ragging between nephew and uncle) are not aimless social eccentricities, but function logically and coherently. So once we adopt this purposive, *functional* approach and set the problem in its *structural* context social behaviour makes sense without invoking hypothetical historical antecedents. Junod, it will be recalled, proposed that the maternal uncle's indulgent behaviour was to be explained by an earlier matrilineal (or 'matriarchal') phase which had left its mark on the now formally patriarchal BaThonga. This was a pseudo-historical theory for which there was no hard evidence. It was also, as Radcliffe-Brown observed, both unnecessary and unlikely. For in matrilineal societies where kinship is traced through women on the mother's side of the family, the mother's brother does not usually behave in this fashion towards his sororal nephew. Quite the reverse. Here a child belongs to his mother's clan, whose primary male representative and 'father figure' is the mother's brother. In such circumstances wives produce children for their brothers, and the essential family unit consists of a brother, sister, and sister's children. A man's heir is his sister's son and the relationship is thus fraught with strains which Jack Goody sees as inevitable between property-holders and heirs; the bond between uncle and nephew is in fact a direct counterpart of that between father and son in patrilineal societies.[15]

Subsequent criticism of Radcliffe-Brown's admirably clear analysis by Lévi-Strauss, Goody and Needham centres on his 'extension of sentiments' from primary (e.g. mother) to secondary kin (e.g. maternal uncle) and points to his exclusion of other arguably relevant relationships such as those between brother and sister, and husband and wife.[16] Although it would not be difficult to defend the extension-of-sentiments argument on psychological grounds, this is not really necessary, since Radcliffe-Brown's analysis can be presented (as it is here) without recourse to assumptions about the relative priority of relationships. The fact that not all societies that anthropologists call 'patrilineal' exhibit correspondingly warm relationships between sister's sons and mother's brothers does not necessarily invalidate the argument either; for, as we shall see later, definitions of what constitutes 'patrilineal' kinship (or 'matrilineal' for that matter) are seldom watertight. Other defences could also be invoked. Here it is sufficient to note that the analysis presented above offers a plausible interpretation of several distinct relationships by treating them not as unique isolates but as interlocking parts of a

15. J. Goody, 'The Mother's Brother and the Sister's Son in West Africa', *Journal of the Royal Anthropological Institute*, vol. 89, 1959, pp. 61–86.

16. C. Lévi-Strauss, 'Structural Analysis in Linguistics and in Anthropology' in C. Lévi-Strauss, *Structural Anthropology*, Penguin, 1972; J. Goody, *ibid*; R. Needham, *Structure and Sentiment*, University of Chicago Press, 1962. L. de Heusch, 'The debt of the maternal uncle: contribution to the study of complex structures of kinship', *Man*, 1974, vol 9 No 1, pp. 609–19.

larger pattern with a clearly defined structure. Functionalism assumes that to a significant extent things are what they do. Structure provides the framework in which functions are exercised. Changes in social structure are thus likely to be accompanied by changes in the function of component institutions. Similarly, when the functions of institutions alter radically we may expect to see corresponding structural changes.

DIFFUSIONISM: AN ALTERNATIVE APPROACH?

The linked analytical concepts of function and structure (introduced here in their rudimentary forms) developed naturally out of, and partly in reaction to, the historical, evolutionary approach; with them we have reached the central point of departure for most of modern social anthropology. But before we try to make sense of other people's mystical beliefs in the following chapters, there is one further method of interpreting cultural and social facts which we must identify and assess. This is the approach known as *diffusionism*, which remains part of the basic methodology of archaeologists and to some extent of historians. It depends on the simple and indisputable fact that ideas and cultural artefacts travel, hopping from continent to continent and distributing themselves about the world in the wake of migrations and along trade routes. Our mass communications make us take such processes for granted: we must remember that television and jet-travel have greatly expanded and accelerated the volume and intensity of such exchanges. The essence of diffusionism is that where you find the same or similar techniques you propose the existence of some form of cultural connection or 'borrowing', especially when, in the case of material objects, the similarities do not stem automatically from the raw materials used, and where they are reinforced by large numbers of parallel instances. The greater the identity in cultural forms, both qualitatively and quantitatively, the more they are likely to derive from a single common source. This of course is what inspired Thor Heyerdahl's dramatic Kon-Tiki expedition in which he sailed on a raft from South America to Polynesia, thus hoping to prove that he was following in the wake of ancient migration routes which could explain the cultural similarities he found between the two culture areas.[17] His more recent voyage on the *Ra* was based upon similar diffusionist assumptions. Few other diffusionists have been prepared to test their theories so directly or adventurously.

This method of looking at cultural objects, developed chiefly by German and American scholars at the turn of the century, assumes in its extreme form that complex and exotic techniques can only be invented once in the history of mankind. There are thus no cultural coincidences. All common forms share a single, unique source. Or, as the late Lord Raglan roundly declared (admittedly in a more restricted context): 'savages never invent or discover anything'.

In prehistoric archaeology the only 'hard' data are often material products, and extinct peoples and societies become identified by their material relics as for instance 'beaker-folk' or 'basket-makers'; such similarities in technology can then be used to establish links between different sites and their inhabitants. Typology becomes the primary means of identifying cultures and of dating them. Thus, where substantial quantities of the same material equipment or products are discovered, archaeologists tend to assume that they must have been produced by the same people. Similarly, where in different strata of the same excavation or in separate sites *discontinuities* in the styles of artefacts occur, these indicate that different manufacturing communities are involved. So those relics of past civilizations which defy time and weather become, in effect, visiting cards as well as trademarks, and provide the key to the spatial and temporal connections of various 'culture areas', each identified by a particular assemblage of objects and cultural styles. So strong is traditional archaeology's faith in the uniqueness of cultural forms and the rarity of innovations that it is prepared to go to inordinate lengths in the quest for similarities in design and style. Thus local styles which bear some slight resemblance to a powerful foreign prototype may be written down as debased plagiarisms and classified as 'degener-

17. T. Heyerdahl, *The Kon-Tiki Expedition*, Penguin, 1963.

ate' forms or 'skeuomorphs',[18] rather than evidence of an indigenous tradition with its own distinct characteristics.

One of the most ambitious and colourful of diffusionist theories is undoubtedly that advanced by the English anatomist Eliot Smith (1871–1937), a contemporary both of Malinowski and Radcliffe-Brown, who sought to explain the global distribution of mummification and other exotic practices. Elliot Smith traced mummification to Egypt, studying the crania of early Egyptian races. He chanced to find an identical skull in Cambridge which, to his surprise, came not from Egypt but from the Chatham Islands, near New Zealand. This conjunction sparked off his remarkable theory that from Egypt, where they had originated, an oddly assorted 'culture-complex' including mummification, sun-worship and large stone monuments had spread round the world. Later, after plotting further distribution maps, this interesting conglomerate was expanded to include the swastika design, the tattooing of women's chins, ear-piercing, head-deformation, serpent-worship, the deluge myth and *couvade*[19] – quite an assortment![20]

It is not difficult to see how this approach lays itself open to abuse and drastic criticism. Cultural items are torn from their natural social context and lumped together, in the most arbitrary fashion, with similarly uprooted, and hence distorted, elements with which they may have no necessary connection. The method can also be faulted by reference to that infallible test of relevance, 'so what?'. Even if it can be established beyond all reasonable doubt that certain cultural items were indeed originally developed in one place and thence diffused to another, by whatever means (not excluding industrial espionage), this may have no relevance whatsoever to their significance in the new environment. Goods, especially ideological ones, have a habit of being tampered with in transit: they are notoriously subject to sea-changes. Those

18. Archaeologists employ this term to refer to imperfect replicas, usually in another material, of a major style or cultural form. 'Neo-Norman' or mock Gothic would thus be marginal examples.

19. This word describes the practice, common in some societies, where when a wife is pregnant her husband behaves as if he were also.

20. This theory is advanced in Elliot Smith's *The Migrations of Early Culture*, Manchester, 1915.

who receive them in an already altered form may impose a further change in their identity and meaning. Take a very simple but nonetheless instructive example. In the installation ceremonies of the Divine King of the Shilluk tribe of the southern Sudan one of the most cherished items in the ceremonial regalia is now apparently a Scottish international rugby cap – one of the more exotic relics of the British colonial legacy in Africa. This borrowed item, no doubt bequeathed by some burly and well-meaning district commissioner, does not possess quite the same significance in this ambience as it had in its original context.

This diffusionist approach, which applies most readily to individual, concrete items of material culture, differs from the evolutionary method in the following ways. It seeks the origins of the present not in the past which is temporally distant, but in external contacts which are spatially remote. It is thus a kind of distributional history in space rather than in time – although in archaeology both chronological and spatial dimensions are involved, and is widely employed in modern geographical studies. Both the diffusionist and the evolutionary methods contrast with the structural-functional, which is above all contextual, and seeks at least the primary significance of the present in the present rather than in the past.

These three contrasting ways of approaching the same data can be conveniently illustrated by applying them to that contemporary social phenomenon: student unrest. When confronted with the difficult problem of explaining this the diffusionist will try to establish the movement's place of origin. He will then produce an account of the insidious spread of revolutionary propaganda from overseas following the well-established 'conspiracy theory' so often presented by newspapers and politicians in search of convenient scapegoats for present discontents. Your evolutionist, by contrast, will contend that these dangerous 'counter-revolutionary tendencies' are atavistic 'survivals' of primitive aggressive behaviour which, in line with socialist policy, should be cannalised in more productive directions. Finally, the structural-functionalist will rebut both these explanations. His solution will be to seek causes of unrest and frustration within the contemporary physical and social environment in which workers live. Since many of these are so patent and numerous, his difficulty will be to isolate those factors which seem to be most significant in promoting discontent.

When we examine a specific case from these different points of view it becomes obvious that they may all contribute to our understanding. Certainly, contrary to the opinions of some of their firmest advocates, they are not necessarily mutually contradictory. Whether in relation to Polish politics or other social issues, in our communications-obsessed world only a fool would claim that the diffusion of ideas and techniques is unimportant. And like the black writer, James Baldwin, few of us can resist the temptation of blaming the present – at least in part – upon the past. If this achieves nothing else at least it helps shift the burden of guilt. We are all structural-functionalists today, just as we are all in a way Freudians and Marxists whether we like it or not; but we must also recognize that we do gain additional insight into the significance of social phenomena when we know where they come from spatially and temporally. Like those who practise them, customs and beliefs have inevitably both a past and a provenance. No matter how ethereal they may seem, they do not exist in a timeless limbo but possess determinate antecedents in time and space. Our awareness of these other dimensions helps us to correct the conservative, *status quo*-maintaining bias which functionalism so readily fosters and which, if unchecked, can seriously distort our assessment and understanding of the dynamic forces animating particular societies. Social phenomena have a disconcerting habit of climbing up to positions of eminence from which they conveniently repudiate their humble origins; we must not be misled by this. Above all, functionalism must not be allowed to become a kind of contagious magic characterized, in Frazer's definition, by the confusion of effects with causes. Evolution (as a series of historical developments) and diffusion blend together to furnish the wider setting for particular customs and beliefs; they place the latter *in situ*, but they do not determine their meaning as functioning parts of a given contemporary social structure. In this sense the contingencies of space and time, as it were, issue blank cheques. Just as significantly, however, we are not entitled to infer the *origins* of social phenomena from their current functions. This tendency is the worst sin committed by over-enthusiastic functionalists.

Finally, in this summary and highly compressed review of our methodological origins, let us note how the French structuralism of Claude Lévi-Strauss, which enjoys such a vogue at present, stems directly from that of Radcliffe-Brown and Malinowski, and, in a sense, achieves a new synthesis between their styles of analysis and that of the diffusionists.[21] Of course this heady new movement has many other antecedents. There is an exciting dash of Hegel's dialectic and of every version of Marx; and Freud and Jung are clearly important influences, to say nothing of Durkheim. These are excellent ingredients for a cerebral cocktail, and Lévi-Strauss combines them brilliantly, producing what is in many respects an elaboration of Radcliffe-Brown's early version of structuralism. He sees man, especially 'primitive' man, as a rustic philosopher of great intellectual ingenuity and artistic brilliance, a wayward mentalistic beachcomber, endlessly improvising dazzling new patterns of culture from the flotsam and jetsam of other civilizations. These patterns, however, are far from arbitrary: they represent variations on a series of interconnected themes. The resulting 'structures' which can be discerned (at least by structuralists) dis-associate and re-form in exciting new transformations with kaleidoscopic ease. Structure exists at various levels of consciousness (or unconsciousness) and although its relationship to mundane 'reality' (the Marxist 'infrastructure' whose ultimate importance Lévi-Strauss periodically acknowledges) is often tangential and tenuous, it helps resolve such fundamental contradictions and antinomies as that between nature and culture, self-interest and the common good, and, more immediately, certain basic conflicts inherent in particular forms of social organization. Thus the elements of structure have to behave purposively, working at and overcoming basic human problems. As one follows Lévi-Strauss, or any of his leading adherents, down the misty corridors of thought, each offering access to a new and more profound level of structure, successive mysteries are revealed until, within the inner sanctum of the 'deep struc-

21. Cf. I. M. Lewis, *The Anthropologist's Muse: An Inaugural Lecture*, London School of Economics, 1973, p. 13. See R. F. Murphy, 'A Quarter Century of American Anthropology' in *Selected Papers from the American Anthropologist, 1947–1970*, Washington, 1976, p. 17.

ture', we encounter 'the human mind' (the usual translation offered by Lévi-Strauss's English supporters of his *esprit humain*).[22]

As Lévi-Strauss himself acknowledges, all social phenomena can of course be said to possess or exhibit 'structure' (i.e. some degree of orderliness and patterning), just as, with almost equal plausibility, they can be claimed to have some functional significance. The truth is perhaps that Lévi-Strauss's conception of structure has no greater intrinsic value than Radcliffe-Brown's – although it is made to carry a vastly more elaborate analytical superstructure. This, however, is surely not a matter for grave concern (except of course to ardent devotees) since the precise metaphysical status of the magic shibboleth is of much less interest than the insights which it has inspired. And, as I hope to demonstrate from time to time in later chapters, it is as legitimate to utilize Lévi-Straussian notions where these seem appropriate and fruitful as it is to derive inspiration from Freud – without necessarily being a dogmatic, doctrinaire Freudian.

Much the same is true, I think, of those related and predominantly American trends variously called 'New Ethnography', 'Ethnoscience', and 'Cognitive Anthropology'. As the last title implies, anthropologists of this persuasion concentrate upon categories of thought and native philosophies or theories of knowledge (which they often call 'conceptual systems'), drawing heavily upon linguistic theory and methods in an effort to achieve increasingly rigorous and exhaustive inventories of alien concepts and beliefs.[23] This development can only be welcomed when it inspires more scrupulous, subtle and sensitive scholarship in our description and analysis of other cultures. This, after all is the basic aim of our subject: the translation of culture. However, the danger evident in some of the work produced here is that, like diffusionism, it tends to examine particular cultural items without an adequate appreciation of their social context, and so may give a distorted picture of what are essentially social

22. For excellent introductions to structuralism see Edmund Leach, *Lévi-Strauss*, Fontana, 1970; and C. R. Badcock, *Lévi-Strauss Structuralism and Sociological Theory*, Hutchinson, 1975. J. Goody, *The Domestication of the Savage Mind*, Cambridge University Press, 1976, offers a searching critique. See also R. F. Murphy, *The Dialectics of Social Life*, New York, 1971.

23. An admirably representative collection of work in this style is S. A. Tyler (ed.), *Cognitive Anthropology*, Holt, Rhinehart & Winston, 1969. E. Ardener, 'The New Anthropology and its critics', *Man* (N.S.), vol. 6, 1971, pp. 449–67, is an interesting critique.

phenomena. It has been one of the traditional strengths of the structural–functional approach to explore the relationships between beliefs and the social nexus to which they belong, finding meaning not only in cultural form, but also in social content. With this in mind, in the following chapter, I begin my account of modern social anthropology by showing what illumination this approach brings to beliefs which at first sight appear to require a great deal of explanation.

Chapter Three

Misfortune and the Consolations of Witchcraft

Nothing distinguishes one community more sharply from another than its beliefs concerning the meaning of life, the position of men in the universe, and the ultimate significance of affliction and suffering. We all like to pretend that unpleasant things, and especially death, do not really happen – except to others (and preferably those we dislike). Yet when we are involved personally we are forced to acknowledge their existence and to try to understand them. Thus the ways in which we interpret and come to terms with these unpalatable facts of life reveal our deepest and most cherished cultural assumptions.

We may begin by looking closely at religious and philosophical beliefs which, at first glance, seem particularly remote and baffling, and to many simply ridiculous. Witchcraft beliefs provide the ideal starting point. While such beliefs enjoy a certain vogue in fringe cults in our own contemporary society, our dominant scientific tradition has persistently dismissed them as 'irrational' superstition, based upon an essentially mistaken view of the world, and thus quite unintelligible, except perhaps as a confession of ignorance. It is ironic that the present undiscriminating reverence for exotic mysticism risks misunderstanding such beliefs for the opposite reason; that of accepting them at face value uncritically and out of context. This new attitude assumes that beliefs in occult power are solidly based in a true and more profound understanding of ultimate verities. Few anthropologists share this optimistic view and I certainly do not believe in witchcraft. I make this declaration because one of my aims in this discussion is to show that we do not need to share other people's beliefs in order to understand them sympathetically: we can see the sense in beliefs even when we are convinced they are based upon false premisses. By following the functionalist approach pioneered by Durkheim and Radcliffe-Brown, we can appreciate that the most erroneous of assumptions may yet serve as a perfectly sound basis for a coherent and logically satisfying system of beliefs.

This appreciated, we can come to terms with the initially disquieting fact that the success and persistence of an ideology is, alas, no guarantee of truth. Its viability depends less on the final validity of its basic assumptions than upon its own internal logical coherence and appropriateness in the lives of those who acquiesce in or profess it. Truth and logic do not always walk hand-in-hand: like the fool and his money they are easily parted. And, as we shall see, even where they directly contradict the evidence of the senses, false beliefs may yet continue unabashed and display a quite remarkable resilience. Every self-respecting ideology develops its own complex defence mechanisms which cunningly conceal, or paper over, the glaring discrepancies and inconsistencies which inevitably arise between what *ought* to happen and what actually does. The elaboration of new countermeasures as an established ideology reacts to increasing pressure has, up to a point at least, the immediate effect of shoring up its shaky foundations and further entrenching its spurious validity.

ZANDE WITCHCRAFT

We shall take witchcraft beliefs, mainly in tribal contexts, as our point of departure for a wider-ranging general discussion of tribal religions. It should be appreciated, however, that exactly the same kind of analysis as we shall develop here could be made equally revealingly of practical, everyday communism, Christianity, the apartheid philosophy of white South Africa,[1] the delusions of the mentally ill, or, as Ernest Gellner so tellingly shows, contemporary linguistic philosophy.[2] So while our quest to understand the mysteries of witchcraft may take us deep into the inaccessible jungles of distant continents, we shall regularly encounter disconcertingly familiar images showing how close to home we really are.

1. P. L. van den Berghe, *Caneville*, Wesleyan University Press, Middletown, Connecticut, 1964.

2. Ernest Gellner, *Words and Things*, Penguin, 1968.

My text here is Evans-Pritchard's unrivalled study[3] of the witchcraft beliefs of the Zande people of the southern Sudan as he found them in the late 1920s and early 1930s living under the generally benign rule of the British raj.

Before we confront their beliefs we need to know something of their setting, but this will not take long to recount; I shall adopt the anthropologist's familiar if sometimes confusing practice of writing in the 'ethnographic present' tense. In the period under discussion, the Zande number about half a million and live mainly as cultivators growing maize, sweet potatoes, ground-nuts and some fruit; the presence of tsetse fly makes it impossible to keep cattle. Fishing, hunting, and the gathering of edible roots and berries also contribute significantly to the Zande diet. A homestead consists typically of a man and his wife (or wives) with their children, and in addition the families of a few other close patrilineal relatives. These small communities are usually situated close to rivers and streams, along the sides of which gardens are cleared from the bush. Settlements are not, however, permanent since the Zande are shifting cultivators, scratching a living in one place and then, when the soil is exhausted, moving on elsewhere to open new gardens and fields.

Politically, Zande society is hierarchically organized, although their traditional empire with its constituent kingdoms and chiefdoms has, naturally, been considerably affected by the imposition of European rule. But the aristocrats of the *Vongara* clan who supplied all the kings and most of the chiefs retain much of their status as a ruling élite.[4] In the present context, however, we need only note that one of a chief's most important traditional roles is his judgment in cases of witchcraft accusations brought before him. Here the veracity or otherwise of charges of witchcraft activity is tested by the chief's own oracle, which is credited with almost infallible powers.

3. E. E. Evans-Pritchard, *Witchcraft, Oracles and Magic among the Azande*, Oxford University Press, 1937.

4. For details see E. E. Evans-Pritchard, *The Azande: History and Political Institutions*, Oxford University Press, 1971.

WITCHCRAFT AND SORCERY

Before we can proceed further we have to grasp a fundamental distinction which the Zande draw between two kinds of occult power, the first of which we shall call 'sorcery' and the second 'witchcraft'. As the Zande see it, sorcerers are people who employ magical spells, rites and medicines to achieve their fell ends. Their malevolent apparatus is tangible and external to themselves. Witches, in contrast, do not need any of these aids; their power consists in their own innate psychic capacity to cause harm. Their weapon is malicious thought itself, not techniques which, in principle, can be detected and observed.

Zande witches are thus very different figures from the 'witches' in *Macbeth*, who in these terms are 'sorcerers'. But what is the basis of their psychic malevolence? Zande consider that this innate capacity has its seat in a distinct physical organ within the witch's stomach. Before they were colonized the Zande regularly carried out autopsies on the dead bodies of suspected witches, to see whether their bodies revealed any trace of the deadly 'witchcraft substance' (*mangu*) or essence in the small intestine. Red eyes to the Zande are also a sign of witchcraft, and red-eyed individuals are feared and treated warily. The propensity to engage in witchcraft is considered to be hereditary, passing from father to son and mother to daughter. Zande thus believe this power to be sex-linked and consider that it increases with age: children may be capable of bewitching, but the power is weakly developed in them; in mature adults it is more strongly realized. Finally, in addition to sorcerers and witches proper, Zande also recognize a related if less dangerous category of malevolent people whom they refer to as 'gall-bladder men'. These are bad-tempered, ill-disposed characters with the touchy disposition we imply by the word 'liverish'.

This distinction between witchcraft and sorcery (which, incidentally, is seldom drawn so sharply by other peoples) is neatly paralleled in the contrasting effects which Zande assume each to possess. Sorcery is considered the more deadly force; appropriately it is an upper-class phenomenon which affects persons of quality but is not employed between commoners. Witchcraft in contrast is thoroughly plebeian: princes and chiefs are neither accused of it nor attacked by it. Hence Zande conceptions of mystical malevolence mirror their hierarchical structure: other aspects of the social system are reflected in the fact that witchcraft is never suspected between closely related kinsmen. And – to us this comes as a surprise – witches are as likely to be men as women. Here at least sexual equality (of a kind) reigns. We shall return later to the problem of discovering who bewitches whom.

WHAT DOES WITCHCRAFT DO?

First we must ask what are the things that witchcraft and sorcery are believed to bring about. The answer is virtually every conceivable misfortune and illness. If your crops fail, or grow much less prolifically than your neighbour's, then it is due to witchcraft. If you have bad luck in the chase, if your wife is persistently flighty and difficult, if a chief favours your rival and ignores your requests for attention, then the cause is or may be witchcraft. If your children are stricken with a serious disease, if you or your wife fall ill, then again you suspect witchcraft. Even death is viewed by the Zande as the result of witchcraft. The Zande in effect maintain the pretence that people should never die; mortality, which they lament, they ascribe to witchcraft. This reluctance to accept death as a 'natural' and inevitable stage in the cycle of life recalls the doctrine set forth in the Old Testament and enshrined in orthodox Christian teaching. As St Augustine maintained, man's original state knew neither evil nor death: God did not create death, which was consequently contrary to the 'Laws of Nature'.

Despite this interesting parallel with our own cultural heritage, the emphasis and indeed the trust which the Zande appear to place in witchcraft as a prime mover seems bizarre and even absurd. Faced with such apparently perverse ways of thinking it is easy to conclude that they cannot possibly reason as we reason. For if they are so obsessed with witchcraft and sorcery, how can they possibly also comprehend those empirical chains of cause and effect which we take for granted and employ as the touchstone of rationality? Must we then conclude that the Zande are in these terms irrational, incapable of rational, cause-and-effect reasoning? The answer is emphatically no, for when they want to, the Zande are as down-to-earth and pedestrianly matter-of-fact as we think we are. Are we then to assume that the Zande and other people with similar beliefs in occult power are virtually schizophrenics, with their minds split between two irreconcilable ways of comprehending the world? Again the answer is certainly no.

As is so often the case, the source of our difficulties is not what we are discussing but how we are discussing it: it is we, not the Zande, who are at fault. For as closer inspection shows, the significant thing is that common sense and the mystical are invoked by the Zande at different levels of interpretation. They explain different things, or different parts of the same thing, and can thus coexist without creating deep conflicts in those who employ them with admirable discrimination and precision. In fact as we shall see, witchcraft (or sorcery) is generally invoked to explain *why* misfortunes befall particular victims, whereas *how* they occur is explained and understood in the prosaic matter-of-fact fashion we think of as being empirically true.

Take a typical illustration. If a man walking through the forest barks his shin on a tree stump this is caused not by witchcraft, but by carelessness. People should look where they are going. Suppose, however, that the superficial injury swells up and develops into an incapacitating leg wound. Such an unpleasant and unanticipated development radically changes the situation, and further and more profound explanations are clearly called for. Similarly, a bad workman cannot blame witchcraft for his poor craftsmanship. If an ill-designed and poorly constructed house collapses, how can you expect otherwise? If a canoe capsizes or sinks because it was manifestly badly built then no further explanations are required. The Zande do not expect things to work unless they are properly made. Yet when some well tried and normally successful technique fails, then clearly something is wrong, and you suspect witchcraft. An expert potter who sedulously observes all the taboos of his trade may find that a whole batch of carefully turned pots crack in firing. If his materials and workmanship were of their normal high standard, he is entitled to some explanation for this unexpected outcome.

From these examples it will begin to be apparent that witchcraft is invoked as a causal explanation of *irregularities*. It can also be seen that it provides a deeper cause than that supplied by ordinary, everyday reasoning. Further light on Zande explanation is provided by their reaction to suicide. Zande say that a suicide takes his own life 'because he is bewitched': 'witchcraft' killed him. But if you ask how the dead person died, Zande will explain the cause of death in terms (say) of hanging: hanging 'caused' his death. If it is then asked what drove him to this desperate end, Zande will refer you to the particular tensions and stresses of his life. It may be that he had quarrelled bitterly with his kin and could see no remedy for his plight. Here, of course, Zande are reasoning as we reason. In general, however, we would stop at this point and accept as an explanation that he killed himself because he found his personal circumstances intolerable and sought to escape from them. Zande, in contrast, do not stop here: there is still the question why, in all these circumstances, the suicide took his own life. People, after all, are often involved in disputes and difficulties with their relatives, but only a minority commit suicide. Thus where we might add that he killed himself while the balance of his mind was disturbed, Zande would say he did so because he was bewitched.

Hence Zande and other peoples with a similar witchcraft philosophy invoke the notion of witchcraft to explain *why* particular abnormal events occur to specific individuals. Their understanding of *how* they happen is the same as ours. Yet for them a description of the full circumstances of a misfortune or disaster is not sufficient in itself. There remains the more fundamental question of why it should befall a particular person at a particular time and place. This is something which we can only discuss vaguely in terms of chance and probabilities, or if we believe in divine determinism dismiss fatalistically as God's will. The Zande, however, are more honest and uncompromising: they do not dodge the issue since they maintain that accidents never happen.

If a Zande is severely wounded by a wild animal while he is out hunting, Zande will say that his injuries are the direct result of the animal's attack. But they hold it is witchcraft which singled out this particular victim for attack and made him the target of the animal's assault. They even describe this 'final cause' (or, if you prefer, 'last straw') action of witchcraft in terms of a vivid hunting metaphor. Witchcraft, they say, is the 'second spear'. What they have in mind here is the common situation that, while hunting, the quarry is first wounded by one hunter's spear but ultimately brought down by another spear thrown by a second huntsman. Here then is an explicit recognition of multiple or plural causation, with witchcraft (or sorcery) playing a final, and decisive, part.

Let us not forget, however, that witchcraft is by no means the excuse for all mistakes and misadventures. Certain things can never be blamed on or explained in terms of witchcraft. Lying is never due to witchcraft, nor can it excuse adultery; a thief cannot plead in mitigation that he was bewitched, for witchcraft is not recognized as a cause of theft. And although, as we have seen, witchcraft may be a cause of death, it is not the only one. In fact it does not enter the picture at all in those cases where people die as a result of deliberate assault or murder. Witchcraft thus cannot be easily applied to circumvent or violate customary norms of behaviour. On the contrary, it works within the framework of the Zande legal code and studiously observes all its provisions and prescriptions.

At the same time, it is not alone in the field: there are alternative mystical explanations of misfortune. Sickness may be considered to be a punishment inflicted for neglect of certain taboos. The Zande, in common with many other African peoples, believe leprosy is due to incest. Ancestral spirits also exercise a shadowy effect, punishing those who fail to pay them the requisite respect. The presence of these additional mystical agencies complements the non-mystical causes already examined and thus expands the range of explanation.

So, far from being obsessed by witchcraft and sorcery as the causes of every unkind stroke of fortune, the truth is that Zande recognize many overlapping and reinforcing causal agencies. This luxuriant multiplicity means, of course, that different parties will explain the same events differently according to their selective, subjective view of the situation. What I and my friends put down to evil witchcraft, my enemies are likely to attribute to incompetence or bad management. A good illustration, increasingly common in contemporary Africa, concerns success and failure in examinations. Those who fail or do poorly in an examination, or some other competitive test, find consolation in the wiles of witchcraft. They have not been permitted to show their true ability because of the malignant witchcraft of their rivals. The latter, naturally, are unlikely to accept this interpretation of the results; they have little sympathy for those who have performed badly due to their inherent lack of ability or inadequate preparation.

In this context the situation which arises when a person dies is very instructive. It will be recalled that except in cases of manifest homicide, death in general is attributed to witchcraft. But British administration made it impossible to charge someone openly with killing another by witchcraft. Witchcraft was no longer a recognized cause of death since the British authorities considered such beliefs as absurd as they were uncivilized. The Zande found this very perplexing and assumed, perfectly logically, that by suppressing sanctions against witches, the British were inevitably condoning and even promoting witchcraft activities! So they had to resort to indirect tactics. These usually consist of 'vengeance-magic' against the suspected, but unchargeable witch. Such counter-magic is carried out clandestinely. The only public sign that magical vengeance has been successfully practised against a suspected witch-murderer is the cessation of mourning by the family of the original victim. All these accusations, rebuttals and counter-accusations are largely covert and known in detail only to the prince or chief whose judicial oracle confirms or refutes all witchcraft-murder accusations; hence the same death appears in different guises to the various parties concerned. When, for instance, someone in our family dies, we assume that our bereavement is due to witchcraft. Others, however, assume the reverse. For them the death in our family is the result of their successful and fully justified vengeance-magic in return for an earlier killing in their family. So one killing, mystically interpreted either as the result of witchcraft, or of its antithesis vengeance-magic, cancels another and the slate is wiped clean.

Clearly everything depends upon the point of view that is adopted, and upon rival interpretations of the same events. Zande conceptions are sufficiently flexible to permit the selection of explanations according to one's position and interests. Contradictions which might seem likely to undermine the system have often the reverse effect. Consider the following sequence of events. A dies and his next-of-kin begin practising vengeance-magic against a number of suspects one of whom is B. B eventually dies, to the gratification of A's family, who regard his demise as a judgment. Not long after, however, they hear that the late B's family have stopped mourning. This shows that B's family consider that their vengeance-magic has in turn successfully accomplished its object. This assumes, of course, that B's death was not the consequence of A's vengeance-magic and that B was not a witch but the innocent victim of someone else's witchcraft. In these circumstances A's party resolves the conflicting information at its disposal by concluding that B's family are simply bluffing to hide their guilt. Evidence which could potentially threaten the whole system of beliefs in the efficacy of witchcraft is thus reinterpreted in consonance with the basic premisses which it challenges.

DETECTING THE WITCH

We now return to the specific issue of how the victim of misfortune sets about discovering the malevolent author of his distress. As one would expect, the Zande have many different oracular and divinatory techniques for detecting witches; only two of these will be considered here. The first is the séance with the 'witch-doctor', a magician, part of whose practice is detecting witches and providing vengeance-magic for the recently bereaved. From this perspective, the witch-doctor is clearly on the side of the angels and his business is highly legitimate. But there is a darker aspect for he is liable to be suspected of misusing his magical powers as a sorcerer or purveyor of evil spells and potions. We shall return to this point later.

In his socially approved role as witch-finder, the witch-doctor receives clients, listens carefully to their problems and in the divining sessions points to their probable origin. Good, that is to say successful, witch-doctors possess a well-informed knowledge of local gossip. This helps them to respond sensitively to their clients' suggestions and to furnish a diagnosis and accusation of guilt which is highly acceptable to the victim. A guessing game goes on with the diviner responding to the client's cues so that at the end of the consultation, the client departs with all his worst suspicions amply confirmed. Although this type of divination is clearly readily subject to manipulation, Zande are naturally disinclined to admit this; they regard it as a mystical process on a par with other oracular procedures where human bias is less obvious.

The second and most important divining technique involves an oracular substance (*benge*) which is credited by the Zande with possessing the power of distinguishing between contrary propositions and thus solving human dilemmas. It is a powerful alkaloidal poison, but the Zande do not see it as an ordinary poison but as an autonomous mystical power capable of issuing decisions which are taken very seriously indeed. The oracle is employed by administering standard doses of *benge* to a live chicken. The client then addresses the oracle: 'Oracle if such is the case, kill the chicken'. And in confirmation with a further chicken, 'Oracle if such is the case, spare the fowl', or vice versa. Verdicts are thus delivered by the mystical substance *benge* on the propositions which the client formulates to test his suspicions. If the outcome of this simple test with two chickens is not satisfactory, the questioner can resort to further tests with other fowls and doses of *benge* on a 'best out of three' principle or some other convenient formula. Vacillating individuals, requiring constant reassurance, would evidently need a large supply of chickens and of the *benge* oracular material. As Evans-Pritchard explains, 'in every Zande household there is a fowlhouse, and fowls are kept mainly with the object of subjecting them to oracular tests. As a rule they are only killed for food (and then only cocks or old hens) when an important visitor comes to the homestead, perhaps a prince's son or perhaps a father-in-law. Eggs are not eaten but are left to hens to hatch out.'

Since the Zande distinguish *benge* from 'ordinary' poisons and regard it as a mystical truth-drug, Evans-Pritchard [5] maintains that those who employ it as an oracle do not manipulate it deliberately. Nevertheless, there does seem to be ample latitude in determining how many tests will be conclusive in a given case. And even if this does not enable the desired result to be obtained convincingly, there are further possible ploys which are readily available. If, for instance, later events show an oracular verdict to have been wrong, those concerned may take the view that the original judgment was false because the oracle itself was bewitched! False prediction may also be attributed to the client's failure to observe taboos or other procedural shortcomings in the conduct of the oracular ritual. In the same fashion, if the witch-doctor offers advice which turns out to be wrong, you write him off as a quack and change your doctor. You do not condemn the whole of his profession, nor question the validity of the underlying mystical assumptions upon which it is based. After all, when our western doctor's diagnosis or treatment turns out to be ineffective we may regard him as a useless quack, but we do not also conclude that the entire system of medical science is erroneous. So in the Zande system, even when things do not turn out as they should, the ultimate effect is a reinforcement of faith in the efficacy of mystical power.

Yet we must not get their faith in witchcraft and magic out of proportion. Zande also freely recognize non-mystical causation and can be breezily matter-of-fact when they choose. However attractive its revamped image may appear to those disillusioned by the inadequacies of western scientific rationalism, the stereotype of the totally mystical tribesman remains as misleading and inaccurate as ever. Particularly in the early stages of field-work, the anthropologist is often much more naïve than the people he studies. It is not uncommon, for example, for anthropologists, noting meat and other sacrificial offerings placed before the gods, to ask, somewhat incredulously but with appropriate reverence:

5. A more recent study focuses specifically on oracles among the neighbouring and closely related Nzakara and demonstrates, however, that *benge* is subject to deliberate manipulation (A. Retel-Laurentin, *Oracles et Ordalies chez les Nzakara*, La Haye, Mouton, Paris, 1969). The continuing vitality of Zande witchcraft in the 1970s is testified by the Austrian anthropologist, Manfred Kremser's research.

'And will the gods come and eat the food you have prepared?'
Of course, the stock answer such questions receive is: 'You must
be joking. The gods are not like men. They do not eat food as we
do; they only consume the essence. How stupid you anthropologists are!' To drive this point home, let us leave the Zande for a
moment and consider the following experience of a research
student working in the Cameroon Republic. Penny Wright (to
whom I am indebted for this story) was attending a healing ceremony which involved the temporary burial alive of the patient –
in this case a child. After several hours of interment and long and
complicated ritual preparations, a series of oracular tests was performed to discover whether it was time to open up the ritual grave
and recover the cured patient. Receiving a positive answer, the
covering was hastily removed and the ritual experts and relatives
of the child anxiously pressed forward, peering into the pit to see
how the child was. Suddenly at this culmination point in the healing rite, the whole assembly became unaccountably convulsed
with mirth, and the puzzled anthropologist, note-book at the
ready, pushed her way forward to the front of the crowd. As she
soon discovered, the explanation for this unseemly merriment was
that when the priest directing the operations had solemnly in-
quired how the sick patient was, the child had irreverently blurted
out: 'I am bursting, let me out, I want to pee.'

We must now consider the procedures followed by the Zande
once a witch has been detected. Having divined the source of his
miseries, the bewitched victim reports to the chief's court, where
he submits his accusation for verification by the chief's own oracle.
If the accusation receives official confirmation, a messenger is sent
to confront the witch and to ask him with all due civility to cease
his evil influence. The standard reaction when you receive such
charges is to draw yourself up in a dignified manner and disclaim
all knowledge of the dastardly deed. This is done politely, and
you are careful to add that if anything unfortunate has happened,
it was certainly not deliberate, and you wish the sick person a
speedy recovery.

Here we encounter the intriguing problem of how much
witchcraft is considered by the Zande to be a conscious or unconscious process. In general the Zande stoutly maintain that

witches are conscious agents. Yet Evans-Pritchard records that he never met a Zande who admitted to practising witchcraft, although when pressed Zande might acknowledge that witchcraft substance could act on its own account, perhaps even against the conscious intentions of the person concerned. Evans-Pritchard's conclusions, which his data amply confirm, is, as might be anticipated, that the Zande are inconsistent in evaluating intention or volition in acts of witchcraft. While the accuser asserts that deliberate malice is involved, the accused protests his innocence, politely but firmly disclaiming any malevolent intentions.

THE NEXUS OF MISFORTUNE AND CONFLICT

Why all this politeness? All the parties are in close and fairly intimate contact and there is no point in gratuitously annoying and antagonizing people – especially since the oracles may have made a mistake. Now we reach the really interesting question: who are Zande witches? The answer is potentially everyone, but more particularly your neighbours, friends, and acquaintances – anybody with whom you have dealings, and especially those you envy because of their success, or fear because of your good fortune. If you are a commoner they will not be among the nobility, since you cannot hope to compete with them, nor will they be people living far away with whom you have no dealings. Unlike many other peoples, the Zande are refreshingly direct in their witchcraft. They accuse as witches those whom they hate and fear, and they do not readily accept substitutes. Here Zande clearly exemplify the principle, enunciated by Tacitus and endlessly repeated by modern psychiatrists, that it is a basic characteristic of the human mind to hate the man you have injured.

So it is evident that witchcraft (or sorcery) is a particular cultural conceptualization of envy and guilt: these are the emotions which it expresses and upon which it feeds. In common with these base emotions it receives general condemnation as an anti-social force which, by its very nature, is inherently immoral and despicable. Those who practise witchcraft are, by definition, in the wrong: if they had right on their side they would hardly need to descend to such mean tricks as witchcraft.

It also follows that witchcraft regularly appears in disputes which are outside the law. These typically concern matters which are either too petty to receive formal legal treatment, or too involved to be brought to court. They may, however, follow court cases when the unsuccessful party seeks to redeem his position by recourse to these extra-legal (and illegal) processes. There is thus clearly a close relationship between witchcraft (or sorcery) accusations, and aggression and social tensions. One of the most unambiguous demonstrations of this comes from New Guinea where the virtual abolition of tribal warfare achieved by relatively recent European rule has been accompanied by a marked increase in the incidence of sorcery accusations.[6]

Amongst the Zande, as we have seen, such disputes take place between neighbours who share many common interests but are nevertheless in frequent competition. And for a succinct description of that social nexus that fits the Zande like a glove we can go, for a change, to sixteenth-century Essex. The Puritan Elizabethan clergyman, George Gifford,[7] had this to say on the typical witchcraft setting:

Some woman doth fall out bitterly with her neighbour; there followeth some great hurt... There is suspicion conceived. Within few years after she is in jar with another. He is also plagued. This is noted of all. Great fame is spread of the matter. Mother W is a witch ... well, Mother W doth begin to be very odious and terrible unto many, her neighbours dare say nothing but yet in their hearts wish she were hanged. Shortly after another falleth sick and doth pine... The neighbours come to visit him. Well neighbour, saith one, do ye not suspect some naughty dealing; did ye never anger Mother W?

This brilliantly condensed vignette reveals clearly who is being attacked. The real victim, the actual target among the Zande and usually elsewhere also, is not the supposedly bewitched subject, but the accused witch (or sorcerer). This, after all, we ourselves acknowledge in our own world when we speak of 'witch-hunts' against communists in America, or counter-revolutionary capitalists in socialist states. And although we have generally ceased to

---

6. See P. Lawrence and M. J. Meggitt (eds.), *Gods, Ghosts and Men in Melanesia*, Oxford University Press, 1965, pp. 17–18.

7. From *A Discourse of the Subtill Practices of Devilles by Witches and Sorcerors* (1587) quoted in Alan Macfarlane, *Witchcraft in Tudor and Stuart England*, Routledge & Kegan Paul, 1970.

believe directly in witchcraft, the irrational charges levelled against coloured immigrants in Britain smack strongly of the witchcraft accusation. Certainly they impute to the accused a degree of mystical malevolence just like that implied in witchcraft charges. Since, moreover, witchcraft is inherently immoral and the witch is the epitome of evil, what better method could possibly be devised to discredit rivals and enemies? The accusation which expresses the righteous moral indignation of the accuser immediately puts the accused in the wrong; and that is especially satisfying when you want a scapegoat to blame, or when you wish to gain an advantage over an enemy. Further, since witchcraft represents a wanton defiance of commonly accepted standards of decency and propriety, the fear of being so accused tends to exert a constraining effect. It is dangerous to be too conspicuously successful, or to step out of line.

Now the witch naturally takes his form and character from the society which conceives him. Thus he attacks what people at a given time and place hold in highest esteem, and people's fears of witchcraft correspondingly reveal their deep-seated cultural pre-occupations. So leaving the Zande again and moving back to our own cultural tradition at the time of St Augustine of Hippo (354–430), we find the public orators and professors of late antiquity understandably fearful lest their memories might be stolen by witches. Memory-snatching was in these august circles a supposedly favourite trick of witches.[8] In Elizabethan England, it is recorded that the vicar of Brenchley in Kent who kept losing his voice during services blamed this on the malicious witchcraft of one of his parishioners. Unsympathetic members of the congregation remained unimpressed, however; they maintained that the source of the vicar's problems was the French pox![9] More generally in sixteenth- and seventeenth-century England and Europe, children, livestock, milk and crops were believed to be vulnerable to the witchcraft of jealous neighbours. Witches were also par-

8. P. Brown, 'Sorcery, Demons and the Rise of Christianity from Late Antiquity into the Middle Ages', in M. Douglas (ed.), *Witchcraft Confessions and Accusations*, Tavistock, 1970, p. 24.

9. K. Thomas, 'The Relevance of Social Anthropology to the Historical Study of English Witchcraft', in M. Douglas (ed.), *Witchcraft Confessions and Accusations*, Tavistock, 1970, p. 55. See also K. Thomas, *Religion and the Decline of Magic*, Penguin, 1973.

ticularly threatening to fertility and sexual potency. Those everyday things which are at once most vulnerable and most valued
are most readily menaced by that satanic subverter of brotherly
love and good-neighbourliness – the witch or sorcerer. Witchcraft
conceptions represent, as Monica Wilson has neatly expressed it,
the 'standardized nightmares' of the community, the horrifying
spectre of what it most fears and dreads, the sinister antithesis of
all its hopes and expectations.

Hence as the enemy of society the witch comes to be viewed as
the embodiment of all those dark forces which threaten cooperation, group cohesion, and the entire moral order. Blending indissolubly with the untamed forces of hostile nature, the witch
becomes the vicious foe of everything that society approves. In
this symbolism every virtue finds its corresponding vice. Fraternal
loving-kindness runs rancid in obscene incest. The bonds of
brotherhood are treacherously betrayed by ungovernable selfish-
ness and egotism. The cult of the ancestors is grotesquely desecrated by satanic, cannibalistic orgies at their shrines. Like a
dreaded vampire, the witch feeds illicitly on the blood of its
unsuspecting prey, the good citizens who go about their daily
tasks with cheerfulness and open-heartedness. Frequently, the
witch or sorcerer inflicts his final *coup de grâce* by tearing out his
victim's heart and ravenously feasting on it. Imagine then what
Africans in South Africa must think of the miraculous transplant
surgery of Dr Christian Barnard! For them Dr Barnard's achievements are like prophesies fulfilled. Modern technology and international publicity and acclaim simply confirm one of the oldest and
most widely-distributed suspicions on the African continent, that
the foreign usurper lives literally, as well as metaphorically, by
sucking the life-blood of his black subjects. In this context the remarks of a wise old West African (Bangwa) witch-doctor, compar-
ing witchcraft and modern science, seem eminently appropriate.
The ever-present anthropologist to whom we owe this quotation
(Penny Wright) was told: 'Just as native doctors here meet in
the witch bush to find new medicines, scientists in your place meet
in their witch bush to invent new things. They all sit together
with their "tigers".'[10]

10. This is the word used in the local Bangwa pidgin; the 'tigers' are actually leopards.

OTHER AGENCIES OF MYSTICAL ATTACK

We can now appreciate how accusations of witchcraft or sorcery establish a satisfyingly significant linkage between misfortune and enmity. As Evans-Pritchard succinctly sums it up for the Zande: 'Every misfortune supposes witchcraft, and every enmity suggests its author'. When we blame our ills upon someone we call a 'witch' we proclaim our own innocence at their expense. We appeal to all good men and true to rally to us and vent our outrage against the object of our fully justified indignation. So, in effect, we turn adversity to profit: we parade our infirmities and at the same time make quite sure that someone else suffers also.

Witchcraft and sorcery, which in any case few other cultures distinguish as sharply as the Zande, are not the only mystical responses to the experience of affliction in tense relationships. A less drastic course than either (or their more common hybrid form) and one preferred in certain contexts in many cultures, is to blame the injury sustained on a puckish nature-spirit or demon. Again the victim of affliction protests his own innocence, but in this case at the expense of a mischievous spirit rather than of a person. Such afflictions typically assume the form of 'spirit-possession', where the victim's illness is diagnosed as a form of bodily intrusion and possession by the disease-bearing spirit. Here spirits are credited with acting like pathogenic microbes which directly assail the human body and threaten its health by sapping its vitality and energy. (An alternative though sometimes co-terminous interpretation is in terms of 'soul-loss'. According to this theory of disease, which is strongly held in many societies, virtue, as it were, drains away from the stricken victim and his powers and health fail accordingly. Normal health can only be restored by recovering and replacing the missing organs or essence which have been abstracted.)

Spiritual afflictions of this kind are notoriously prevalent amongst women. So, for example, among the Muslim Somali of north-east Africa, married women are frequently prone to mysterious complaints which are diagnosed by the experts as possession by evil spirits. These latter are exceedingly demanding; treatment consists of discovering their requirements and agreeing to them on condition that the human victim is released from their power. It is a striking fact, by no means lost on the men who have to pay for them, that the spirits which so plague their women-folk have expensive tastes and invariably request such items as costly perfumes, jewellery, fine dresses, and delicious foods and sweetmeats. So the therapy really consists in spoiling the patient, while ostensibly meeting the demands of the spirit as revealed to the expert therapist. During treatment, the possessing spirit often communicates its demands by making the patient 'speak with tongues'. And although the spirit may have promised to remove its baneful influence once its requirements are met, relapses are very common. Indeed, it is not so much that the invading spirit is definitively exorcized from its human host, as that the host learns to live with her familiar who may make his presence felt whenever his mistress is in difficulties.

Thus some women, especially and significantly those who have difficult relationships with men, find themselves drawn into membership of clandestine women's groups which meet from time to time to honour their spirits. Here possession has been transformed from an undesired, unsolicited illness into an ecstatic religious experience, and the most committed enthusiasts are considered to be 'married' to their spirits who 'ride' or 'mount' their human hosts. Such celestial unions may compete with their earthly counterparts, and the idea that the spirits should sexually possess their devotees is by no means excluded. Spiritual congress of this kind is, in fact, found all over the world and throughout history – as the biographies of famous Christian and other mystics confirm – and occurs more often than is generally supposed in our own contemporary Western world.

This erotic association, frequently strengthened by the most militant cult leaders being free-living divorcees and prostitutes, confirms men's worst suspicions and prejudices about what their wives are *really* up to. Certainly it contrasts with the picture the women paint, in which the cult is an innocent healing rite designed to rehabilitate sick wives and thus enables them to resume their wifely roles with renewed energy and zest. It is consequently scarcely surprising that Somali men tend to be very ambivalent in their attitudes towards these women's ailments, especially since some impatient husbands find that the best cure is often a good beating ! But, at the same time, they also believe in the reality of these demons which their Muslim faith recognizes and explicitly describes in the Koran. The spirits, for their part, are said not to like men.

Why should women resort to such devious tactics? The reason is, I think, partly that in this particular society men rule the roost and women have a low status and few rights they can directly exercise. Divorce is common and easily obtained by men : women can only achieve it with difficulty. So with the legal dice against them, women are forced to adopt such oblique means of redress and appeal as possession 'illnesses'. Through the effects which it exerts on men, spirit-possession is in fact one of the most prized and successful weapons at the disposal of Somali women.

The element of feminist protest which can be discerned here is even more obvious in a kindred possession illness affecting women in the smart suburbs of Khartoum, capital of the Sudan. Here, exactly as amongst the Somali, possessed wives – or at least their spirits – regularly demand gifts from their domineering husbands including, sometimes, costly gold teeth. When they become possessed by their spirits, these demuré, purdah-confined ladies undergo a remarkable change. Their possessing familiars are sharp-tongued vipers which berate the women's husbands in a fashion that no self-respecting man could tolerate directly from his wife.

These are two examples of women in traditionally male-dominated societies using an indirect form of mystical attack. The possessed woman, like her bewitched counterpart, becomes the immediate centre of attention and care, and although she exerts pressure upon her spouse the latter is not assailed as radically as he would be were he accused of being a witch. It is one thing for a man to yield to his wife under pressure from a spirit, and quite another to be declared a witch. The point to make here, then, is that possession of this sort, which is very common in many societies, embodies the spirit of protest; those who 'speak in tongues' regularly adopt an appropriately shrill commanding tone.[11] This aspect of these cults is well illustrated in the classic nineteenth-century Fijian manifestation of flower power known

11. See I. M. Lewis, *Ecstatic Religion*, Penguin, 1971.

beguilingly as the 'Water Baby Cult'. There, in the early days of contact with whites, young men and minor chiefs excluded from positions of authority in the traditional establishment were suddenly and unaccountably seized by capricious water-spirits. They were thus inspired to assume flower names, and attracted a great deal of attention and interest – precisely, in fact, what they had previously been denied.

This example conveniently makes the point that it is not only women who are vulnerable to the attentions of these rebellious spirits. Socially disadvantaged men are also prone to similar afflictions; and in some cases, with a commendable absence of male chauvinism, both sexes of a depressed class or group may be equally at risk. Thus in caste-bound India the role of spirit-inspired priest or 'shaman', the onset of which is announced by a possession 'illness', is a career enabling low caste men to climb to positions of eminence and power. In this vein, Gerald Berreman [12] recounts the poignant success story of Kalmu, the blacksmith's son, whom he first encountered in 1958 as a thirteen-year-old drop-out from the village school. After a youthful marriage ended tragically with the death of his wife and two children, the grief-stricken Kalmu began to behave bizarrely and showed signs of being possessed by a powerful local deity. The deity speaking through this humble medium commanded sufficient authority to mobilize the local people into building a new temple for the god and a house for his servant. So Kalmu was launched on a highly successful career as a shamanistic seer and miracle-worker which enabled him to acquire both wealth and power and hence to compensate very effectively for the severe disabilities under which he laboured on account of his low caste origins.

To illustrate how the inequalities which underlie such possession afflictions are always and necessarily relative (rather than absolute), we may end this short list of examples by referring to the *Santeria* cult currently popular amongst Cuban refugees in mainland America. Despite their often middle-class origins, these uprooted opponents of Fidel Castro, who have never gained the support they anticipated would enable them to return in triumph

12. Gerald D. Berreman, *Hindus of the Himalayas: Ethnography and Change*, University of California Press, 1972.

to their native land, find consolation in the arms of the *Santeria* spirits, which are of partly African origin. Indeed, so successful and all-pervasive is this new syncretic religion amongst the refugee Cuban community that a widely ramifying economic 'support-structure' has mushroomed up in its wake. In Miami alone there are reported to be more than fifty *botanicas* – shops selling all the necessities of the cult – and there are also pet-shops specializing in the doves, chickens and peacocks which devotees require for the rituals.[13]

Such spiritual afflictions, then, are to be found in circumstances where other secular means of ventilating grievances or pursuing vital interests are blocked, or very restricted. In some circumstances both possession illnesses and witchcraft and sorcery accusations afford a protest which falls short of actually severing the relationships causing the cramping pressures. As has been indicated above, it seems possible to distinguish between these two aggressive strategies in terms of their relative severity. The possession attack seems on the whole to be a milder and less radically challenging assault than that conveyed by charges of witchcraft or sorcery. In a number of cultures where both mystical strategies are available we find that social inferiors employ possession against superiors whose ultimate authority they grudgingly accept, whereas witchcraft (or sorcery) accusations are reserved for challenging unacceptable authority.[14] Hence the mystical angles of the polygynous family triangle may assume the following shape : co-wives accuse each other of witchcraft, but do not accuse their husband. In their competitive interaction with their common spouse, they bid for affection and attention through the appealing medium of bouts of possession.[15]

Witchcraft and sorcery accusations, then, are often selected as the most effective and appropriate means of destroying relationships and discrediting rivals in a thoroughly nasty way. In many central African societies indeed, accusations of witchcraft (or sorcery) provide the normal and expected accompaniment to the break-up and dissolution of previously united kinship groups.

13. Mrs Joan Halifax-Grof, personal communication.
14. Cf. E. R. Leach, *Political Systems of Highland Burma*, Athlone Press, 1954, p. 181.
15. Cf. I. M. Lewis, *Ecstatic Religion*, Penguin, 1971, pp. 117-26.

Families too big to be happy, and whose continued existence as single units cramps ambitious junior members, fall apart with a rancorous outburst of witchcraft charges. So, in effect, such accusations of mystical malevolence may help to 'blast away' redundant or obsolete links in the social structure of a community, thus paving the way for healthy new growth. From this demolition-perspective we see that, paradoxically, witchcraft can play the maverick, exerting radical as well as conservative effects. Sometimes the accusers are not diehard reactionaries defending the existing order, but radical innovators seeking to change it. This, indeed, seems to be the dominant pattern in sixteenth- and seventeenth-century rural England, where the anonymous charity provided by the new poor laws represented a serious attenuation and curtailment of older sentiments of communal loyalty. The typical witch was now the poor neighbour, begging food and drink from people who had once been willing to acknowledge these claims, but did so no longer. In the new context, these were quite out of keeping with the times, for the poor had to change as well as everyone else. Charity did really begin at home and should stay there, with, moreover, an appropriately restricted definition of what was 'home' and what was not! So those who persistently demanded succour when they were no longer entitled to it and irritatingly pricked the conscience of the rich were particularly apt for denunciation as witches.[16]

In this period charges of witchcraft involving satanic pacts with the devil were freely employed by politicians to explain the otherwise puzzling success of their opponents. Cardinal Wolsey, like Anne Boleyn, was thus supposed to have bewitched Henry VIII, and Oliver Cromwell was accused by his enemies of being in league with the devil on the eve of the battle of Worcester – which he won. At the time of the Great Rebellion, the Calvinists believed firmly in the power of witchcraft, while the Catholic Royalists opposed the witchcraft persecutions. The Great Rebellion can be regarded in part as an anti-witchcraft movement, like those which sweep through traditional African societies in a utopian quest for a new world cleansed of sin and hatred. Witch-

16. See Alan Macfarlane, *Witchcraft in Tudor and Stuart England*, Routledge & Kegan Paul, 1970.

craft is often found hovering round the figure of the apocalypse.

These cursory snippets from our own past, for that alas is all there is space for here, at least show how the contemporary anthropological understanding of witchcraft throws new and (at least in some quarters) welcome light on what were until recently unusually dark and baffling corners of our history. Our 'witch-crazed' ancestors, as so many of the older school of historians are apt to paint them, were of course no more crazy and no more mystical than the Zande – nor were they any less rational. It is a cardinal error, and one to which intellectual historians are especially prone, to suppose that people can only think in terms of one set of assumptions. True some modes of thought are in certain circumstances and periods dominant over others; they may even hold the envied status of an official orthodoxy. But none are so pervasive, nor so completely satisfactory, that they rule out the need for other lines of explanation. In a later chapter I refer to the modern notions of witchcraft and satanism which receive such wide publicity today.

Chapter Four

The Natural Order

HONOURING THE DEAD

In the previous chapter I deliberately held open the question whether Zande witchcraft should be classified as 'religion' or as something different. This is an issue which we must now confront by considering what range of mystical activity the term religion includes and where its outer limits lie. We can usefully begin our discussion here by taking up a very important and characteristic religious theme: the ambiguity or ambivalence which is so often such a striking feature of mystical power. Take Zande magic for example. In itself it is neutral – neither good nor bad. It acquires a moral value according to the use made of it. Thus vengeance-magic launched against witches is a perfectly legitimate and morally acceptable course of action; but recourse to similar magical practices directed against honest, upright members of the community is bad and is in fact sorcery. It is the ends not the means which are decisive here.

This ambiguity comes out very nicely in a different way in the case of the religious concepts and behaviour of an East African people called the Lugbara, who live in Uganda.[1] These tribesmen have traditionally an uncentralized political organization in which the most significant positions are held by elders heading small locally-based clusters of agnatic kin. Such units, consisting of a few closely related families, contain between a dozen and sixty individuals who live together and cultivate under the direction of their elder, whose chief responsibility is the allocation and control of arable land. The elder's secular authority is very significantly reinforced by his monopolistic control of the relations between men and the ancestors. He is the custodian of the shrines at which offerings are made to the ancestors of the group which he leads. As the guardians of customary morality, the ancestors judiciously

1. See J. Middleton, *Lugbara Religion*, Oxford University Press, 1960.

appraise the actions of their descendants, punishing any who commit such 'sins' as flouting the elder's authority or threatening the harmony of the group over which he presides. Such sinful deeds include disrespectful behaviour towards an elder, fratricide, incest, and – naturally – impious neglect of the ancestors themselves. For these and other misdemeanours the ancestors are apt to inflict crushingly punitive illnesses and misfortunes. Hence, as in so many other traditional cultures, the victims of affliction are thus revealed as criminals; in contrast to the situation in Samuel Butler's allegorical novel *Erewhon*, it is not so much that sickness in itself is a crime as that it is a symptom and consequence of criminal activity. The underlying moral assumption is the smug conviction that the good and just prosper because they so deserve: lack of success is proof of immorality – there are no deserving poor ! This callous view of suffering which smacks strongly of the protestant ethic (epitomized in the complacent exhortation: God helps those who help themselves) has a very familiar ring and is clearly seen today in the attitudes towards the mentally ill held by all but the most enlightened members of western societies.

Here then, amongst the Lugbara, we see a thoroughly moralistic creed, based upon and administered by ancestor spirits, and applied for and to the benefit of the village elders. The ancestors rarely act on their own initiative: generally these avenging angels of justice are invoked by the local elder. Typically, it is in response to his self-righteous complaints about the failings of his local flock that the ancestors spring to his defence. Indeed one of the most compelling demonstrations of the elder's power is his claim to have called down ancestral affliction upon a morally negligent member. of his community. What the elder thus proclaims is that he has a 'hot-line' to the ancestors, that they are on his side and, in effect, do his bidding. As the ancestor spirits are such realistic replicas of living elders it is perhaps not surprising that they should work in such close and harmonious collaboration. Certainly we see here a very close relationship, of the kind envisaged by Durkheim, between society on the one hand and religion on the other. The religious or mystical order clearly supports the secular establishment, rather than opposing it as in some of the spirit possession cults we reviewed in the previous chapter.

That at least is the static picture. Now let us assume a more dynamic perspective and consider how this religion actually works over time in different phases of the life-cycle of the local group. Like their individual members, these tiny political units exhibit a cycle of birth, growth, and decay. As a group swells in size with natural increase of population and with new members joining it from outside, it eventually reaches a point where it ceases to enjoy an optimum exploitative relationship with its physical and economic resources. It becomes too big and unwieldy and no longer possesses sufficient land to satisfy the needs of all. Initially nothing succeeds like success: but eventually success exceeds itself, and decline and despondency set in. In this more fiercely competitive situation people quarrel more readily and more often, and the elder who had been such a paragon of gentle paternalism finds things increasingly difficult. The community he rules is no longer the united, happy family it once was. Factions form around a few pushing militant figures who begin to question the old man's waning powers.

On the mystical plane we find a sombre reflection of this unhappy state of affairs. The elder reacts violently to every action which he construes as an attack upon the dignity of his office and frantically invokes the support of the ancestors. Every case of sickness or misfortune is claimed by him as a judgement against the upstarts who dare to challenge the legitimacy of his rule. But in the end his efforts inevitably prove unproductive. After all, he is treading a very delicate path. There is a limit to the exercise of power, particularly when it takes the form of affliction and distress. Those who, as the Lugbara elder does, assume responsibility for the cruellest and unkindest strokes of fortune may provoke a dangerous backlash – which is exactly what happens. The elder's opponents and detractors claim that he has gone too far, that he has overstepped the bounds of acceptable discipline. The Lugbara assume that elders who abuse their position are witches, so the suspicion that he is a witch is broached and rapidly gains ground amongst the dissidents. The elder and his dwindling following claim that misfortunes are the judgment of the outraged ancestors; his opponents – led by those who covet his position – claim they are due to intolerable acts of malicious witchcraft, providing incontrovertible proof that their author is no longer fit to retain his exalted office. As this view wins general favour, the elder is denounced and discredited. One or more factions, under their triumphant new leaders, hive off to live elsewhere, leaving the old man with the shattered remnants of what was once a large, confidently prosperous community. The new leaders will in their turn suffer the same fate: but that is an irony of life which is not apparent to everyone.

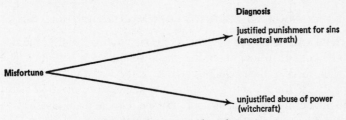

Diagnosis

justified punishment for sins (ancestral wrath)

Misfortune

unjustified abuse of power (witchcraft)

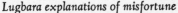

Lugbara explanations of misfortune

Amongst the Lugbara there are thus at least two alternative mystical theories of disease and affliction. One sees them as judgments inflicted by the ancestors: the other views them as the consequence of the envious spleen of anti-social, perverted witches. To return to our original point – the ambivalence of mystical power – the same misfortunes are open to two conflicting but ultimately complementary explanations. By ascribing unjustified adversity to the malice of witches, the Lugbara are able to maintain their central doctrine that the ancestors are just and good. Witchcraft thus disposes of the thorny problem of the existence of evil.

Finally, let us note that the inherent ambiguity exemplified here is even more obvious when the righteous indignation of established authority is *directly* expressed in mystical sanctions which do not require the intervention of a third party such as the ancestors. The best illustrations of this are in societies where the authorities bring defaulters to heel directly by the power of their curse. Amongst the Nyakyusa of Tanzania this power is known literally as 'the breath of men' and is clearly conceived of as a 'murmuring' afflatus, which marshals and expresses the public opinion of the community. Its basis lies, significantly, in 'pythons in the stomach' which are also the source of witchcraft.[2] More generally, the ambivalent obverse of the elder's curse is the evil-eye – one of the most condensed and concentrated forms of witch-craft. The distinction between the indignant glare of justified moral condemnation and the baleful gaze of malevolent envy is, obviously, tenuous and arbitrary.

WITCHCRAFT IN RELIGION: MAIN AND MARGINAL CULTS

Witchcraft is for the Lugbara, as for many other peoples, one side of a coin on whose other face the ancestors smile benignly. The main focus of their religious activity is the ancestors, with witch-craft and sorcery acting as subsidiary and opposed mystical forces representing disharmony and disorder. The Lugbara also believe in a single omnipotent deity as the ultimate creator of life and the dispenser of death. This highly ambiguous power also animates socially approved diviners, and is connected with their opponents, witches and sorcerers. In his benevolent aspect he is the source of rain and hence petitioned to alleviate drought, and also to prevent meningitis. In this fashion, the Lugbara deity represents certain general phenomena and inescapable universal afflictions such as death (which they also connect with witchcraft). But his import-ance is slight compared with that of the ancestors who, as the censorious champions of local morality, are the main religious cult of the Lugbara; and this central morality religion is, as we have seen, complemented by the marginal witchcraft cult.

How do these findings bear upon our earlier discussion of Zande witchcraft? While I certainly accept that the witchcraft beliefs discussed so far could be considered as a variety of religion, this Lugbara data and certain clues in Evans-Pritchard's account sug-gest that witchcraft (or sorcery) is only *part* of Zande religion.[3] They also have a cult of ancestors (or of the dead) which seems to be concerned with morality and to provide the anticipated antithe-

2. M. Wilson, *Good Company: A Study of Nyakyusa Age-Villages*, Oxford University Press, 1951, pp. 96–108.

3. E. E. Evans-Pritchard, *Witchcraft, Oracles and Magic among the Azande*, Oxford University Press, 1937, pp. 16, 215–17, 441, etc.

sis to their witchcraft beliefs; and there is further evidence of belief in a higher – if generally otiose – central deity. Thus, reviewing the Zande material in the light of our widening experience, we can again detect what may be seen as a main morality religion (the ancestor cult) co-existing with a subsidiary, or ancillary, marginal witchcraft cult.

One final point before we leave witchcraft – at least for the moment. In the Lugbara case, the ancestors make no bones about their direct administration of the moral code: if you do not toe the line they quickly bring you to your knees with a few sharp, salutary lessons. In other religions, however, the forces of order are more devious and underhand. Punishment affords them little pleasure and they seek to maintain an untarnished image of uncompromised benevolence. The problem therefore arises of achieving this enviable state and yet ensuring that sinners do not go unpunished. As the reader may already have guessed, the solution again lies in that endlessly resourceful answer to moral dilemmas – witchcraft. As, like Pontius Pilate, the ancestors gladly wash their hands of the sordid business of administering justice, witchcraft readily steps forward to take the necessary action, acquiring in the process an even more clearly defined moralizing character. The situation now is that witchcraft is only really effective against sinners. The righteous need have no fears. They are exempt from its noxious effects, for goodness is its own protection. By removing their normal protective cover from those who commit moral wrongs, the ancestors (or other central powers) deliver the guilty into the hands of their secret police – the witches and sorcerers. Again, we should note the interdependence and mutual necessity of the main and minor channels of mystical power.

The true significance of witchcraft is only disclosed when it is set within its full configuration of mystical forces; the same applies to ancestor cults. To discuss these, or any other religious forces, in isolation is to misunderstand them. Here successive interpretations of that classic case, the traditional Chinese ancestor cult, provide an object lesson. Despite a lingering tendency to see the Chinese cult of the dead as a simple and direct projection on to the mystical plane of the strict code of filial piety controlling the behaviour of sons towards their fathers, recent studies by Sinological anthropologists are increasingly adopting a wider cosmo-logical perspective which places the dead, where they naturally belong, among the other spirits and forces of traditional Chinese religion.[4]

MAIN MORALITY-RELIGIONS

In the Lugbara case it is easy to see the hand of Durkheim. Or at least, it is as if the Lugbara had read the great French social philo-sopher's work and devised a religion faithfully mirroring their social structure. However, many traditional societies with a similar secular structure have *very different* mystical concepts and religious beliefs. To emphasize the point that there is no simple, necessary, deterministic relationship between the forms of religion and society let us briefly examine the religion of the Nuer. Like the Zande they live in the southern Sudan and have been studied by Evans-Pritchard, so that at least the personal equation can be held constant in comparisons between these two cultures.[5]

As it happens, the Nuer have a social organization which is very similar to that of the Lugbara: so alike are they, indeed, that Middleton describes the Lugbara with virtually the same termino-logy as his teacher, Evans-Pritchard, uses in describing Nuer society. A case of forcing one set of data into another's mould to make them look alike? No; the most remarkable features of the two descriptions of religion are not their similarities but their dif-ferences. Although the two peoples share a similar type of political structure, their religious beliefs present a striking contrast.

Like the Lugbara, Nuer society is politically uncentralized and based on a segmentary system of interlocking patrilineal descent groups which will be discussed later in chapter 10. Thus, if we assume a simple deterministic relationship between the social and religious orders (as anthropologists all too often do), we can expect that Nuer religion similarly extends, as it were into the skies, its own secular lineage structure. The result would be an ancestor cult similar to that of the Lugbara. This, however, is not the case,

4. Contrast M. Freedman, *Rites and Duties, or Chinese Marriage*, London School of Economics, 1967 with the same author's *Lineage Organization in South Eastern China*, Athlone Press, 1958 and *Chinese Lineage and Society*, Athlone Press, 1966.

5. E. E. Evans-Pritchard, *Nuer Religion*, Oxford University Press, 1956.

for although Nuer ancestors do receive some attention from their descendants this pales into insignificance in comparison with the cult of the deity *kwoth* who is the unchallenged central focus of Nuer religiosity.

Kwoth is the creator and mover of all living things, vaguely associated with the sky and sometimes said to be like the wind. He is the source both of good and of bad fortune, the ultimate centre of the dynamism of the cosmos in man's experience of his physical and social world. In his role as creator and protector of the Nuer nation, he is sometimes addressed respectfully as 'father' and as 'owner' of all things. All that exists, having been created by him, is his property – his to withhold, to bestow, and eventually to reclaim. So Nuer readily acknowledge that when they pray and give thanks to *kwoth* with appropriate offerings they restore to him what is already his. Ideally they offer cows or oxen, saying sometimes with a mixture of petulance and resignation : 'God take your cow !' This is the pastoral idiom of sacrifice. In actual fact, all that may be offered may be a few strands of tobacco which, in many contexts, are assumed to suffice. Another acceptable substitute is the wild cucumber, the full-scale slaughter of an ox being reserved for occasions of serious distress when, as in some intractable illness, god's help is urgently sought.

To the Nuer, god appears both as lofty and remote, though omnipotent, while sometimes approachable and near-at-hand: indeed on some occasions he is felt to be too close for comfort and is earnestly beseeched to withdraw his presence and leave his people in peace. Above all, god represents the moral order of the Nuer world, rewarding the upright and just with success and prosperity, and visiting sinners with affliction and adversity. The most heinous offences are incest (i.e. sexual relations, and above all marriage, within the exogamous lineage), adultery (which contaminates all the parties involved including the innocent spouse), disrespectful behaviour towards one's relatives by marriage, and other transgressions of this sort. These sins may be seen to menace lineage identity and solidarity – the paramount Nuer virtues.

In his role as friend and protector of the Nuer universe, and more especially of its constituent lineages, god is seen in specific manifestations or 'refractions', which introduces the familiar theological problem of the one and the many. In the widest context, god is single and indivisible; in more parochial settings he appears in more familiar and less diffuse forms. The degree to which the entire godhead is evoked as a unitary spiritual conception depends upon the circumstances. God is all things to all Nuer; they see him with as many different faces as they divide their own society into separate kinship groups. It is thus possible, indeed common, for each of two rival lineages to claim, as the British and Germans did in the First World War, that 'God is on our side'. Each party singles out a different manifestation appropriate to its position: but ultimately both admit in a wider, more inclusive, context that there is only one god. Here Nuer theology seems to echo the thoughts of the ancient Sicilian philosopher Empedocles who spoke of god as 'a circle whose centre is everywhere and whose circumference is nowhere'. The extent to which the total, composite deity is called upon to explain an event depends upon its generality and universality. Great and widespread calamities, showing no respect for the divisions Nuer draw amongst themselves, clearly reveal the hand of god in his most omnipotent, transcendent form. Lesser and more particular disturbances can be ascribed to more immediate punishment for specific sins.

There is far more to Nuer religion than this cursory sketch can convey. My point, however, is that here we encounter a main morality-religion sustained by a complex and composite spiritual hierarchy which is a veritable fount of divine justice and retribution. One might well say that the Nuer sound as though they came straight out of the Bible – the Old Testament rather than the New. The organization of their religious concepts, god and his component spirit-refractions, certainly reflects the social order in a highly Durkheimian fashion. But, and this is a major qualification, the *nature* of the mystical powers involved, their shape and distinctive characteristics (or phenomenology) are *not* predictable from the social organization. Things would all be much easier for sociologists of religion if they were. The point, then, is that what the Lugbara achieve in one religious mode, the Nuer do in a very different style.

A final example of religion as a maintainer of law-and-order is provided by the Akawaio Indians of Guyana.[6] They are also a politically uncentralized people, but not based on lineage ties. There is no Chinese-box style articulation of segmentary groups; each small cultivating community situated on a river bank has a high degree of autonomy and is generally hostile towards its neighbours. In this case it is again not the ancestors who are important, but a rather diffuse constellation of nature spirits. These differ from those of the Nuer in that they do not fuse together into a single, all-pervasive deity. The diversity of the spirits thus directly parallels the Akawaio social order. But there is the same substantial caveat which we registered in the case of the Nuer : the particular *kind* of mystical powers which sustain the social order cannot be predicted from the social order.

As we have noted, the Nuer have fairly definite ideas about sin, certainly if pressed they would happily deliver a sermon on the subject. The Akawaio are less forthcoming. The spirits which are the focus of their religious concern are not regarded as being *directly* moralistic in such an explicit fashion as their counterparts among the Nuer. Yet they can be shown to be in some sense the *implicit* guardians of morality. For, like the Lugbara ancestors, they are held responsible for sickness and affliction, especially when they occur in contexts of social strife and conflict. In general, the Akawaio consider that breaches of the brotherly love which should inform relationships between members of the same community will attract the anger of the spirits, who then bring illness and adversity as punishments. Thus, to some extent in company with our contemporary psychiatrists, these Carib-speaking Indians trace the causes of illness to unsatisfactory and rancorous relationships within the community. The cure lies in identifying the disturbed relationship, making such reparation as seems appropriate, and so restoring peace and tranquillity. The spirits thus exhibit a praiseworthy concern for the psychological health of the community.

The trouble with this and other moralistic creeds is that they do not allow for the righteous manifestly *not* enjoying the fruits

6. A. Butt, 'Training to be a Shaman', in S. Warell, A. Butt and N. Epton, *Trances*, Allen & Unwin, 1966, pp. 39–60.

of their exemplary conduct. When, like Job in the Old Testament, the just are unjustly treated and disaster strikes a respected pillar of society, serious difficulties arise. How are these to be surmounted? The Lugbara solve this problem by appealing to witchcraft. How the Nuer cope with the same dilemma is not entirely clear from Evans-Pritchard's account. For their part the Akawaio Indians deal with the matter in what is, in effect, an inverted version of the Lugbara solution. As will be recalled the Lugbara trace the causes of unmerited misfortunes to those power-hungry elders who hang on to office, although no longer capable. The Akawaio are more extrovert. In probing the sources of undeserved distress they generally look outwards to the people across the valley, or over the hill. Each Akawaio settlement is a tiny republic whose patriotism bristles with hostility towards other, rival communities. The impressive sense of internal cohesion at the price of external hostility is epitomized in the ambivalent role of the shaman, or inspired priest, in each community. Through trance experiences stimulated by drinking tobacco juice, the shaman (or his spirit) flies into the skies to commune with the spirits, and discover and remedy the causes of affliction in his village. With these techniques the shaman guards and protects his human flock, interceding, when necessary, with the gods on their behalf. His external image offers a remarkable contrast to this picture of dedicated pastoral care. Externally, in his relations with other villages, he becomes the vehicle and focus for the xenophobic fear and animosity between rival communities. So, manifestly unjustified afflictions in one village are ascribed to the malicious witchcraft of the shaman across the river. Here again we can discern two contrapuntal mystical currents; each of which plays a major positive rôle on its home ground and a negative and malign one elsewhere. One village's benevolent deities are, in effect, another's malevolent demons.

From this perspective we can return again, and finally, to the ambivalence of mystical power which has caused so much unnecessary confusion in anthropological writing on religion, magic and witchcraft. Having defined witchcraft and sorcery as intrinsically evil, anthropologists are often embarrassed when they find them employed quite openly and without moral censure: indeed in some societies in New Guinea and west Africa, people positively exult in their prowess in these occult arts and enjoy a corresponding respect. It is these *positive* examples of what is generally taken to be a *negative* force that have given rise to such concepts as 'white' (i.e. good) witchcraft; they are part of our European tradition and lend a certain credence to Margaret Murray's exaggerated presentation of a satanic underground cult of evil co-existing with orthodox Christianity.[7] The examples we have reviewed enable us to see clearly that mystical power may assume many contrasting shapes and forms, but that what determines its moral evaluation is simply the purpose for which it is employed. Among the BaKongo [8] and many other African peoples, both chiefs and sorcerers are commonly considered to be capable of killing people by occult means, but only the former do so legitimately.

COSMOLOGIES

The data are piling up thick and fast, and it is time that we paused to examine how far we have travelled and which direction we should now follow. We began with Zande beliefs in witchcraft to explain particular misfortunes in tense relationships, one method of explaining mystically (and transcendentally) human misery and of rallying support and succour to the victim of misfortune. We saw too that however mistaken its basic assumptions might seem, this pattern of thought did make sense. At that stage we ignored other possible religious beliefs. Then, widening our focus, we looked at Lugbara witchcraft and the ancestor cult which complements and completes it. We saw that witchcraft could serve as a very important ancillary force subtly dealing with the manifest existence of evil. This led us to concentrate our attention on what we may term 'main morality' religions where, whatever their nature, the spirits involved act as the puritanical censors of traditional morality.

We then widened our discussion further, taking the Lugbara,

7. M. Murray, *The Witch-cult in Western Europe*, Oxford University Press, 1963.

8. W. MacGaffey, *Custom and Government in the Lower Congo*, University of California Press, 1971.

Nuer and Akawaio as examples to demonstrate how the same censorious moral role is played by different mystical powers: the converse is the same type of mystical power playing different roles in different religions. One community's kind spirits are, as we have seen, another's dreaded demons. Contrary to what is often supposed, especially by the more *engagé* workers in comparative religion, there is no cross-culturally valid catalogue of phenomenologically distinct kinds of beneficent or baneful powers. Mystical forces are judged by their fruits. While a given social system probably has a finite set of religious requirements under given conditions, these can be satisfied in many and perhaps even an infinite variety of ways. The social structure in a particular environmental setting creates, as it were, religious expectations. The specifications required to meet these can be readily elicited and catalogued. What cannot be deduced or predicted is precisely how the specifications will be met, nor which materials will be employed.

In this respect the relationship between society and religion can be compared to that between families and the homes they live in. Families of the same size and income have roughly similar functional requirements; having established these basic and essentially 'objective' requirements, however, it is obvious that they can be satisfied in different ways and styles. Taste is not an objective facet of family size. The same goes for religions. Every religion has to meet certain basic standards, but styles, designs and materials vary widely. Different societies of the same structural type have, evidently, contrasting religious tastes. Furthermore, to pursue this metaphor, having selected a particular spiritual décor and furnishings, those who live in it come to be influenced by its stylistic and symbolic properties as well as its more obvious functional or utilitarian appropriateness. And just as it has been designed to satisfy their requirements (not always necessarily with equal success), they come to find themselves serving its interests. So religions, symbolic systems, and ideologies develop a metaphysical life of their own and acquire qualities which stubbornly resist being reduced to mere reflections of the social order. Certainly there is at least always an important 'feed-back' effect between beliefs and society. To this extent, Marx's bold assertion, 'Man makes religion: religion never makes man', greatly oversimplifies the complex realities of the relationship between the social and religious orders.

Yet whatever the actual characteristics imputed to the mystical powers selected, seemingly arbitrary, for a given role, most religions appear to possess two complementary categories. One is charged with upholding the moral order, while the other equally essential class helps to explain inappropriate affliction. This is why it seems sociologically useful to distinguish between main and marginal cults. But, of course, religion is not only concerned with morality or finding consolation in adversity. Wider and more general problems in human existence and experience have to be brought within man's comprehension. Man needs to relate to, and therefore to interpret and understand, his climatic and environmental circumstances, and bring these into connection with his social and personal life. The term 'cosmology' or 'world-view' is a convenient shorthand way of referring to these wider, environmental referents of religion. Cosmology thus seeks to make sense of ecology. And here, as at more specific levels of religious conceptualization, we can again discern logical patterns and relationships. This leads us directly to the topic of symbols and their meanings.

THE WILDERNESS

We can conveniently begin with a widely drawn cosmological contrast, that between the secure realm of human habitation and activity, and the wild wasteland which surrounds and threatens it. With all its biblical and other evocative resonances (as for instance the 'enchanted forest' of fairy tales), the wilderness begins where the warm sphere of human interaction ends. The boundary separating these two domains is thus a function of a community's isolation and lack of effective communication with, and control over, its surroundings. Modern technology pushes our wilderness completely off the inhabited globe into space. This last-to-be-colonized region still retains some mystery and glamour as an unsubjugated never-never-land where, in science fiction at least, almost anything can happen. The drama of the space race derives very largely from this being the last wilderness left.

Those peoples with less elaborate technologies and a narrower range of effective communications and intercourse live much closer to the wild; for them, it is the antithesis of the mastered, lived-in realm of normal everyday social intercourse. This contrast between 'culture' and 'nature', as Lévi-Strauss phrases it (although both are of course cultural conceptions), can be illustrated by the Lele people who inhabit the Kasai region of the Congo basin in central Africa.[9]

The Lele are subsistence cultivators, growing maize, groundnuts, and raffia palms from whose fronds they weave mats which are used as a special currency – a rare case of money really growing on trees. Villages are sited in clearings in the forest, and these two opposed domains – village and forest – are strongly emphasized in Lele cosmology. The forest is important as a source of food, since some gardens are situated in it, and it supplies palm wine, fibre for making clothes, wood for house construction and also a variety of sacred medicines. It has sublime importance, however, because it is the scene of the hunt, itself as much a prestigious and sacred activity as a means of acquiring meat. So the forest has a sacred character too; men may go regularly into it, but women are not permitted the same ease of access. Every third day they are not allowed to enter the forest; and on all important religious occasions – at mourning, the birth of twins, the appearance of the new moon, the departure of a chief, in menstruation or child-birth – they may not enter the forest until special rituals have been performed by men.

Ultimately the forest is hallowed because it is the abode of spirits which haunt streams and their sources. These spirits of the forest are considered to control the fertility of women and to prosper men's hunting. All the beasts of the forest are under God's power though allocated to the Lele for food. Of these animals, water-pigs are those most highly charged with mystical power; they wallow in water, which the Lele believe to be the place of spirits, so the association is plain. Fish likewise are connected with the forest spirits, and thought dangerous to women: pregnant wives, for instance, should not eat fish. Certain bush-bucks

9. See M. Douglas, 'The Lele of the Kasai', in Daryll Forde (ed.), *African Worlds*, Oxford University Press, 1954, and *The Lele of Kasai*, Oxford University Press, 1963.

which, like spirits, sleep by day and move by night are similarly regarded as spirit-animals, so their flesh is forbidden to women.

Clearly the Lele world-view is built upon a series of structural associations and contrasts. There is a loose connection between men, forest and spirits, and they stand in collective opposition to the world of women which centres on the villages and the clearings. Women keep the home fires burning while their menfolk hunt and commune with sacred things. The land outside the village, but in the clearings on which wives grow ground-nuts, is in revenge mystically fenced off to men. In general, women and their activities are mystically potent, but also dangerous and threatening to men. The femininity of women threatens to pollute Lele masculinity: in common with our own and many other cultures, the Lele display a form of the Delilah-complex, although in their case the common association between women (as wayward creatures of nature) and the wild is virtually stood on its head. Before hunting Lele men abstain from sexual intercourse and avoid all contact with menstruating women. This, of course, is not to say that there will be no hunt-ball afterwards. The hunt has strong religious overtones, and it can only succeed if harmony and peace prevail. Disputes and enmity endanger it. If the hunt produces a great quantity of game this proves that the gods are smiling because all is well in the community. The hunt, indeed, is a spiritual barometer of brotherly love and communal affection, and, most significantly, ensures the fertility of women.

Here then we see how different social pursuits, areas of activity, and the distinction between men and women are woven together into a composite picture of the universe with a mystical connection between its components. The Lele view of man's place in the universe and of the boundaries of experience is mystical. Other tribal cosmologies exhibit analogous features some of which we shall consider later. The point to emphasize here is the extent to which man's view of his environment is affected by his technological mastery of it. There is a similar relationship between the individual and his surroundings which is suggested in a psychologist's perceptive formulation of the position: 'Part of the intangible boundary of the self is marked off by what we can control. When we can control, there the self is; when we are controlled, there the world is. Control is the capacity to alter objects and to determine experience.' [10]

SYMBOLS

A further element of Lele thought illustrates another common principle of cosmological logic or, if you prefer, of religious symbolism: tribal systems of thought, and perhaps all closed or relatively closed systems of belief, tend to exhibit a strong and, as it must seem to some, edifying concern for tidiness. An appropriate motto would be: tidiness is next to godliness. We have already seen evidence of this in Zande witchcraft beliefs with their eager concern to assimilate and 'naturalize' new information so that it is consistent with the basic assumptions which Zande take for granted. This striving after logical and formal consistency, even for symmetry (for there are certainly aesthetic considerations at work), is well shown in tribal taxonomies and folk natural history. They exhibit to an exaggerated degree that intolerance and sense of unease we all show when faced with information or experience which we cannot readily assimilate and 'make sense of' (as we say) by fitting it into our existing knowledge and categories. For the experimental scientist such discordances and incongruities are the spur to new discoveries and lead to the development of new theories – or so at least we like to think.[11] But for those with a relatively static model of the universe and more or less fixed expectations, the discrepancies are deeply troubling if they cannot be ignored or resolved by supplementary perceptual categories.

Consequently what does not fit neatly into existing experience is anomalous and apt to seem mystically dangerous. Such anomalies are like Bernard Shaw's conception of indecency, 'matter out of place'. All this is very abstract, so let us take a specific example by considering the significance of the pangolin for the Lele. The

10. A. D. Weisman, 'Reality Sense and Reality-Testing', *Behavioural Science*, vol. 3, 1958, pp. 228–61.
11. In practice established bodies of scientific theory show considerable lethargy and resistance to change as a number of philosophers of science have observed. See e.g. T. S. Kuhn's well-known work, *The Structure of Scientific Revolutions*, University of Chicago Press, 1970, and I. Lakatos and A. Musgrave (eds.), *Criticism and the Growth of Knowledge*, Cambridge University Press, 1970.

pangolin or scaly ant-eater, an animal rather like a hedgehog with a tail, is ritually dangerous to Lele women; but it is also the object of a male cult (notice again the sexual axis). Lele men who have produced sons and daughters are allowed to join the pangolin club, whose rituals concentrate upon fertility and success in hunting.

Why is the pangolin dangerous to women, and why is it associated with a male fertility cult? Lele describe the animal as follows: 'In our forest there is an animal with the body and tail of a fish, covered in scales. It has four legs and it climbs on trees.' Here are our first clues. The pangolin is a forest animal and at the same time a taxonomic enigma: it cuts across several distinct categories in Lele zoology just as it does in ours. Hence in company with other anomalous creatures of the forest it is dangerous to women. But what of its association with fertility? As it is partly in the same taxonomic class as fish and water-creatures, it is associated by the Lele with forest water and hence with the spirits of streams. Moreover, it is said to beget single young, unlike most other animals. This habit of mono-reproduction is explicitly compared by the Lele to human reproduction. Hence the pangolin suggests a link between animal and human kind. The force of this interpretation is further strengthened by Mary Douglas's observation that Lele women who produce twin births are compared to animals, since multiple births are characteristic of animals rather than of humans. Ideas of the parallel between normal multiple birth in animals and abnormal multiple birth in humans are widely distributed, and contribute to the significance of twins in many cultures.

For the moment let us simply note that natural history may have important ritual implications. Although not the only source of mystical power, anomalous phenomena are often given special treatment if they are difficult to classify. What does not fall into established categories from one angle may do from others; anomalies are always situational and relative, never, or very rarely, absolute. Detecting them is a tricky business, especially in unfamiliar cultures and languages. Despite the serious limitations to a general theory equating anomaly and mystical danger, there is respectable if sometimes ambiguous psychological evidence that what is *perceived* to be *unclassifiable* (and this is perhaps the crucial thing) is cognitively and emotionally disturbing.[12] Words and names, as we all know from everyday experience, possess magical power: naming and identifying experiences and things imposes some degree of control over them and gives at least the illusion of bringing them within our power. When we identify something we pin it down and are halfway to mastering it. So great is our faith in identification, that we often mistakenly imagine that when a problem is diagnosed it is solved. What seems initially unique and disturbing can become a well-known if regrettable fact of life shared with many others. Generalization is often, initially at least, a sound antidote to bleak despair.

SYMBOLISM

This desire to classify and categorize experience, and thus to render it manageable, seems to be present or implied in all schemes of symbolism. What is a symbol? Following the Oxford Dictionary, which is here a more lucid guide than my more abstruse colleagues, we can say that a symbol signifies something other than or complementary to itself; it can therefore be used to represent, express, or image things which are external to it but to which it is linked in an appropriate fashion. The crucial factor of associational appositeness relating a symbol to what it symbolizes is rarely seen directly and explicitly, although heraldry is replete with such purpose-built symbols. An excellent example, for which we know the explicit intention of the inventors, is the London School of Economics coat of arms which has a beaver as key figure. In the version drawn in 1921 by Sir Arnold Plant (then a student at the School), the beaver was selected to symbolize the School because 'it was understood to be an industrious animal with social habits'. It is not recorded whether those who designed this emblem were aware that 'beaver' is also slang for the female sexual organs.

So symbolism is a kind of sign language, or semaphore, a code only intelligible when you have the key. Symbols possess both intellectual and emotional (or affectual) efficacy: think of the sign of the cross, the Nazi *Sieg Heil*, the masonic handshake,

12. For a convenient summary see, S. Feldman, *Cognitive Consistency*, Academic Press, 1967.

Churchill's 'V-sign', or the more recent 'up yours !'; the more polyvalent, multi-facetted, or 'condensed' symbols are in their range of reference and meaning, the greater their mystical (or metaphysical) significance. As we saw earlier, a central godhead whose manifold characteristics can be all things to all men is more powerful than a more parochial and less versatile spirit. But how are we to interpret the symbolism of other cultures; how can we crack their symbolic codes? Eliciting and translating meaning accurately is difficult enough with explicit phenomena : how then are we to understand the implicit, inner significance of things whose nature depends on subtle allusions?

One solution is to assume that, since all men are in their most basic attributes ultimately alike and use similar mental processes, then they must mean the same things when they employ the same symbols and metaphors. One system of universal interpretation sees a phallus in every elongated object and a vagina or womb in everything round or circular. And if those whose symbols were thus explained hotly denied the interpretations, that would simply be further proof. The beauty of such methods is that they can never be proved wrong since, by ignoring what the people concerned themselves think, you have removed any empirical basis for testing the interpretations. There are other similar schemes of analysis. As is well known, Freud saw the Oedipus myth as symbolizing a son's desire to possess his mother and kill his father. But Fromm interprets it as a conflict between matriarchy and patriarchy; Jung sees it as a story of ethical conflict between laziness and duty; and Ferenczi argues that Oedipus himself is a phallic symbol since his name means literally 'swollen-foot'. As Annemarie de Waal Malefijt, from whom I borrow these examples, wickedly observes : 'If interpreters from similar cultural backgrounds cannot agree upon the meanings of symbols, how different must be the symbolic meanings assigned by people with different cultural experience !' [13]

The psychoanalyst J. A. Hadfield has brilliantly shown that the trouble with this type of approach, even with material from one's own culture, is that it is essentially arbitrary.[14] It assumes every-

13. A. de Waal Malefijt, *Religion and Culture*, Macmillan, New York, 1968, p. 177.
14. J. A. Hadfield, *Dreams and Nightmares*, Penguin, 1954.

thing, and this is the last thing the field anthropologist who tries to understand other peoples' symbols can afford to do. He must start with the explanations and commentaries which his informants *themselves* offer about their symbols. These must first be examined in the contexts in which they are usually employed, where they occur naturally, although subsequent generalizing discussion helps the anthropologist to improve his very superficial initial understanding. Learning the meaning of symbols is part of the anthropologist's practical semantics : discovering the meaning of words, noticing when their use is appropriate and when it is not. All this requires imagination, patience, considerable linguistic skill, but above all a rigorous respect for the facts. These must come first; fantasy can come later.

With these exhortations in mind let us now turn to examples of anthropologists trying to elucidate the meaning of exotic symbols. One of the most impressive of recent contributions is the meticulously detailed and subtly perceptive work of Professor Victor Turner [15] amongst the Ndembu people, who also live in Central Africa and not very far from the Congo Lele. The Ndembu fall within the so called 'matrilineal belt' stretching across Central Africa from the Congo into Zambia and Malawi and are cassava cultivators, living in what is now the western province of Zambia, close to the Congo border. Traditionally uncentralized politically, they live in small scattered villages, each composed of a number of matrilineally related men and their wives and children. Turner follows Radcliffe-Brown's classic analysis of the religion of the Andaman Islanders which was first published in 1922 and heavily influenced by Durkheim and the French school; he sees the luxuriantly rich ritual and symbolism of the Ndembu as providing socially integrative forces compensating for the lack of a unitary political structure. We need not take up the argument here : let us, instead, turn to the more interesting subject of the explanations offered by the Ndembu themselves for certain key symbolic motifs.

Before proceeding to details, however, we should note that the Ndembu are remarkably articulate in these matters. Contrary to

15. See V. Turner, *The Forest of Symbols*, Cornell University Press, 1970, and *The Drums of Affliction*, Oxford University Press, 1968. For a vivid New Guinea analysis, see G. Lewis, *Day of Shining Red*, Cambridge University Press, 1980.

those who claim that tribesmen always think concretely rather than abstractly, the Ndembu have an abstract general term for 'symbol' (*chinjikikilu*) derived from a verb used in hunting to mean literally 'to blaze a trail' (*ku-jikijila*). So a symbol is for them 'a blaze or landmark, something that connects the unknown with the known'. Things of this kind, Ndembu say, point towards or 'reveal' other things, using again a word employed in tracking and hunting. These associations by no means reduce Ndembu symbolism to the level of boy scout bush manoeuvres, for as with the Lele and many other peoples hunting is a sacred rite, pregnant with religious significance.

Turner claims that each Ndembu symbol makes visible and accessible to purposive public action basic elements in their society and culture. It is loaded with efficacious cultural and social associations, and these refer to natural and physiological facts of everyday experience. Here, as elsewhere, a given symbol may have a wide range of meanings. For example, white clay (*mpende*) may represent such apparently disparate ideas and things as: semen, ritual purity, innocence from witchcraft and, at its most abstract, 'togetherness with the ancestor spirits'. The same symbol is encompassing a wide range of conceptions which, at least in some respects, share a common, underlying theme. Take the tree the Ndembu know as *mukula*, a red gum. This is symbolically invoked in contexts in which it is connected with, for instance: matrilineal descent, hunting, menstrual blood, and the meat of wild animals. The link is a sticky red gum secreted by the *mukula* which coagulates quickly and is explicitly compared by the Ndembu to blood.

Consider now its contexts of use. At boys' initiation ceremonies, a *Mukula* log is put near the place where they are circumcised. As soon as the operation has been performed and while they are still bleeding, the young warriors are placed on this *mukula* log. Ndembu explain that the *mukula* here represents the wish of the tribal elders that the circumcision wounds should heal quickly and cleanly for, as they observe, the *mukula* gum coagulates rapidly to form what looks like a scab. Here the Ndembu employ a judicious mixture of Frazer's two cardinal principles of magical thought – association by contact and by likeness. The Ndembu go further, saying that in this context the red gum also represents masculinity, and the life of the adult male who, as hunter and warrior, will inevitably shed blood.

An even wider and perhaps more profound range of images is suggested by the *mudyi* tree. At girls' puberty rituals the novice, folded in a blanket, is gently placed at the roots of a slender *mudyi* sapling. Ndembu say that the sapling's pliancy stands for the girl's immaturity and youth: the tree is sometimes stated to be the novice's 'matrilineage', and its leaves her 'children'. The tree is also supposed to represent the growing maiden acquiring womanly sense or wisdom, and Ndembu sometimes say that she 'drinks sense as a baby drinks milk'. So, in a sense, this tree is the tree of life for Ndembu women. Fortunately, the Ndembu are generously prepared to share the secrets of this symbolism with us. They begin by observing that if you scratch the bark of this tree it immediately exudes beads of milky latex. And the 'milk tree', as they appropriately call it, represents in their minds, and just as readily in ours, a mother's milk and its source, her breasts. Following this train of thought, the tree also signifies a mother and her child and this Ndembu 'madonna image' is extended to include a matrilineal descent group, called literally a 'womb or stomach'. Casting this imagery into the past, the tree is also said to be the place where 'our tribe and its customs began'. So the milk tree becomes the seat of all mothers, the source of our ancestors and the place where they used to sleep. To be initiated beneath the fecund fronds of this tree, with these deep resonances of meaning, is to be made ritually pure or white. This sequence of interpretations is highlighted by a series of opposed associations: an uninitiated girl, a menstruating woman, and an uncircumcised boy are all alike in lacking whiteness. They are all unclean; and in the boys' initiation rites we find that the *mudyi* tree also has its part to play in the symbolism of circumcision. And when the whole gamut of richly charged contexts is reviewed, Turner concludes that the 'milk tree' represents in the symbolic life of the Ndembu their equivalent to Goethe's conception of 'eternal womanhood', an image which is peculiarly apt as their society is founded on the matrilineal kinship principle.

Red and white, the two colours so far mentioned, are joined by a third, black, to complete the Ndembu system of colour symbolism where the imagery reaches perhaps its most abstract level. Teasing out the meanings of symbols in their contexts with the aid of the explanatory commentaries of his informants, Turner suggests that white signifies health, strength, fertility, the blessing of the ancestors – indeed harmony in society and nature. Redness, on the other hand, which is associated both with the (destructive) shedding of blood and with the primordial ties of kinship in blood signifies at a more abstract level discontinuity, disharmony, and might acquired by, and displayed in, breaking the rules of order and harmony. It is thus in one configuration of refulgent meanings the sign of male aggressiveness and manly virtue. The last colour, black, is connected with the faeces and closes the circle since it is the colour of decay and of death.

ARE THERE UNIVERSAL ARCHETYPES?

None of the symbolic usages reviewed so far is very difficult to follow. It is of course true that the human body, its associated natural processes, and those of other living organisms, provide natural models that offer a finite range of symbolic themes which we can pick out in different cultures. However, the same symbols may convey quite distinct meanings in different cultural settings.

A very obvious example can be found in colour symbolism itself. In contrast to white, black is widely employed to represent evil, terror, darkness, decay, the appropriate colour for mourning – a range of depressing associations perhaps ultimately deriving from the alternation of night and day; we share these with the Ndembu and readily assume they are universal. Certainly all known societies distinguish between night and day and most consider night to possess sinister qualities (often connected with the suspension of regular social intercourse). However, we must not leap to conclusions too hastily. Whereas in most Christian countries black is worn in mourning, in most Muslim ones white is the funeral colour, yet Christian and Muslim conceptions of the nature of the after-life and the significance of death are broadly the same. Similarly, white is also the colour of mourning in traditional China and there are other less well-known cultures where black is an auspicious colour. The fact is simply that the two colours do not possess universal symbolic meanings shared by all the peoples of the globe.

With this cautionary illustration behind us we can now proceed to a more complex and interesting example. In our own folk symbolism and in those of a number of other cultural traditions, 'horns' convey a sinister, demonic association connected with illicit sexuality, as in the expression 'horny'. Traditionally at least, horns convey to us the notion of the cuckold – the unfortunate, unmanly husband whose wife's unsated sexual passion finds its outlets elsewhere. In that rich compendium of ethnographic treasures, *Shakespeare's Bawdy*, Eric Partridge tells us that the word horn stands for the penis in an extramarital adventure, as in the 'horn of adultery' or 'horn-maker' (causer of cuckoldry).

It so happens that amongst the Nuristan Kaffirs in a remote mountain valley of Afghanistan, 'horns' have this aggressive manly sexual connotation. But in this case they refer to licit, socially approved, marital sexual intercourse, to manliness in general, and are also directly connected with goats, the main livestock of the Kaffirs. Thus to be 'horned' among the Kaffirs is not to be meekly cuckolded. On the contrary, it is the proud assertion of belligerent warrior bellicosity, traditionally expressed in head-hunting raids against the surrounding Muslim population. In this culture a soft feeble person is said to 'lack horns': men who have proved their manhood in war and battle, as well as in their marriage beds, are entitled to sport ornately carved horns on their door-posts. Special 'horn chairs' are reserved for those who achieve the highest status in this fiercely competitive society.[16] (Most of these traits are shared by the famous Naga head-hunters of Assam whose evaluation of amatory success is, however, perhaps more ambiguous.) [17]

Of course in both our own case and that of the Nuristanis – horns express aggressive male sexuality. But, and this is the point,

16. See S. Jones, 'The Waigal Horn Chair', *Man* (N.S.), vol. 5, 1970, pp. 253–7.
17. See C. von Fürer-Haimendorf, *Morals and Merit*, Weidenfeld & Nicolson, 1967, pp. 85ff.

the contexts in which this is displayed are opposite to each other. We should misunderstand the Kaffirs completely if we simply imposed our folk symbolism on theirs.

Another instance of these elements combined in a slightly different way comes from a less remote and exotic source, the Sarakatsani shepherds of the Greek mountains studied by John Campbell.[18] Here our ethnocentric values receive a further jolt, since these pastoralists literally divide their sheep from their goats, associating sheep with men and goats with women. It is women, not randy old men, who are explicitly linked in herd-management and symbolism with goats and thence, following the more familiar male chauvinist logic, with the Devil. 'Women', the Sarakatsani reason, 'through the particular sensuality of their natures are inherently more likely to have relations with the Devil; and goats were originally the animals of the Devil which Christ captured and tamed for the service of man.' Sheep, in contrast, are God's creatures, and the ideal image of the men who tend them is naturally that of the Good Shepherd.

CONTRASTING PAIRS AND THE MEETING OF EXTREMES

So far we have concentrated on the meaning of specific symbols. But it is becoming increasingly plain that symbols do not stand alone and can be understood only in a wider context of associations and contrasts. The problems raised by this gregarious tendency, and particularly by the recurrence of paired contrasting symbols, become very evident when we consider a bodily product which receives symbolic attention in most human societies and provides extremely expressive symbolic material – hair. The stock psychoanalytic approach assumes a universal connection between hair and sexual virility, and it is certainly not difficult to find examples which fit this interpretation. There are, however, other and perhaps socially more interesting aspects to explore. One of these focuses on the contrast between short and long hair.

There is much evidence that, at least in the case of men, short cropped hair signifies the acceptance of discipline and compliance with authority, whereas long hair signals the exact opposite –

18. J. Campbell, *Honour, Family and Patronage*, Oxford University Press, 1964.

defiance of the established order. In our own world we find short-cropped convicts, crew-cut soldiers and service-men generally, monks and others equally 'under orders'. Long hair, in contrast, shows rejection of authority and is the preferred hair-style of rebels and revolutionaries the world over, of woolly-haired intel-lectuals, hippies, and others seeking freedom from traditional constraints and a world of exciting new potentialities. Both in its title, and in its contents, the highly successful musical, *Hair*, brilliantly epitomizes these associations. If we want to go further back in history (and are prepared to be suitably eclectic) we can find a similarly expressed contrast between Roundheads and Cavaliers. Confirmatory evidence comes also from the use of close-cropping to humiliate and discipline dissident rebels and traitors. When, at the end of the Second World War, France was liberated, those who had collaborated excessively with the Germans often had their hair cut off by the French Resistance. Similarly, at the time of writing, presumed traitors to the Catholic cause in Northern Ireland regularly have their hair shorn and are then 'tarred and feathered'. The compulsory haircuts forced upon the long-haired defendants in the indecency trial of the underground magazine Oz, are a clear example of the disciplinary message con-veyed by the cutting of hair. It is thus by no means surprising that a contentious current issue in British schools is the permis-sible length of boys' hair.

Animals are often also hairy (a fact adroitly exploited in Desmond Morris's book *The Naked Ape*), so that unkempt locks suggest some connection with animalkind as opposed to human-kind and thus, as Lévi-Strauss would argue, signify the contrast between nature and culture. It is easy to draw up a list of opposed attitudes and values, based on this antithesis, such as the following: [19]

American Middle Class	*Hippies*
orderly	spontaneous
planned	unorganized
instrumental	expressive
social	self-absorbed

19. Adapted from Stuart Hall, 'The Hippies: An American Movement', in J. Nagel ed., *Student Power*, Merlin Press, 1969.

reasoning	empathizing
individualistic	communal
pain-accepting	pleasure-seeking
prepared to postpone gratification	committed to the existential 'now'
routine	anarchic

And so we could continue. But we now have some understanding of the universality, or otherwise, of symbolic archetypes. I do not pretend that this hairy example [20] will stand up to intensive and searching cross-cultural scrutiny, since the elements in the contrasted pairs weigh slightly differently in different cultures; indeed, as with most linked social phenomena, one could find some cases of complete reversals (or in Lévi-Straussian terminology, 'transformations') in which, as the old phrase has it, the extremes meet. Notice, however, that contrasts of this kind, and such other obvious ones as right-handed/left-handed, head/heart (or loins), mind/body (another variant?), up/down, cold/hot, dry/moist, male/female occur very widely, although in a bewildering variety of assortments and with different meanings in different cultures. Lévi-Strauss has rendered social anthropology an invaluable service in emphasizing the significance of such contrasting motifs; although we need not go so far as him and turn our subject into an esoteric animal, vegetable or mineral parlour-game in which every card is a joker and can assume whatever meaning the player likes.

20. This example partly follows C. R. Hallpike, 'Social Hair', *Man* (N.S.), vol. 4, 1969, pp. 256–64.

Chapter Five

Myth, Rite and Eschatology

THE MEANING OF MYTH

Symbols achieve their most elaborate and compelling public currency in myths – those 'sacred tales' with which men seek to invest their lives with cosmic grandeur. A strong case can consequently be made for treating myths as the real 'soul-stuff' of social anthropology. As a sensitive classical scholar, Jane Harrison, long ago remarked in a passage which reflects the influence of both Freud and Frazer, 'myth is the dream-thinking of a people, just as the dream is the myth of the individual.' [1]

In this spirit myth frequently postulates a time before time, a kind of sacred prehistory, a drowsy surrealistic world in which the coordinates of time and space are suspended or shifting, and nothing is impossible. So the primordial dawn in which Australian aborigines set their creation myths is expressively described as the 'Dreaming' or 'Dream Time' which, as Stanner has put it, 'was, and is, everywhen'. The most famous of these myths comes from the Murngin aborigines and was described and analysed by Lloyd Warner;[2] it relates how the two Wawilak sisters were crossing the Arnhem Land bush during the Dream Time, collecting animals and plants as they went, and telling them that they would become sacred objects (i.e. totems) in the future. Having given birth by committing incest within their own clan, the two sisters and their children came to the sacred waterhole of Mirrimina, home of the mythical python, Yurlunggur. Here they stopped to camp, and the elder sister polluted the pool of the Great Python by accidentally allowing her menstrual blood to fall into the well. This action enraged the Python. When the women attempted to cook the animals and plants they had collected, each species leapt up and ran into the well. Then the snake rose from the water and

1. J. Harrison, *Prolegomena to the Study of Greek Religion*, Cambridge University Press, 1903.
2. L. Warner, *A Black Civilisation*, Harper, 1937.

swallowed the sisters and their children. Afterwards the earth was
covered by a flood. The terrifying noise of the snake's thunder and
the torrential rain attracted the attention of two Wawilak men
who, fearing that some calamity had occurred, set out to trace the
two Wawilak sisters. Eventually they picked up the tracks of the
Great Snake, and one of them said (evidently with a magnificent
sense of understatement): 'I think the sisters had trouble: I
think that maybe a crocodile or python has killed them.' Un-
daunted, the men continued their journey and eventually came to
the sacred well, where they slept. The two women appeared to
them in a dream telling them the story and the songs which they
had sung to keep the snake at bay. Thus the sacred mysteries were
revealed to mortal man to cherish and to celebrate in his rituals.
As the Murngin told Warner: 'We dance these things now, because our *Wongar* [Dream Time] ancestors learned them from
the two Wawilak sisters.' We shall come later to the relationship
between myth and ritual. For the moment we need only note how
this major aboriginal creation myth, in which the Python (representing the male elements in the society) is also the wet season
and swallows and regurgitates the dry season to bring plenty,
owes much of its sacred quality to its character as a cosmic dream.[3]

Myths and fairy tales (which are often discarded or borrowed
myths) are easily identifiable when they recount extraordinary
events and encounters between gods, spirits and mortals which
defy normal conventions of man's place in the universe and his
relations with his fellows. Paradoxically it is precisely the palpable
suspension of mundane 'reality' which enables myth to state
eternal verities. Myths proclaim great truths by telling great lies !
Central figures who are mortals must, even when capable of
miraculous feats, perform them at appointed times and places
within a logical chronological framework defined by dates; this
makes questions of identification more complicated. We are thus
led to ask: when does myth with dates become what we call
'history', a record, however partial or partisan of things that
actually happened? And, conversely, are tales which lack dates,

3. For a detailed analysis of the symbolism of the myth see L. Warner, *A Black
Cilivisation*, Harper, 1937; also R. Layton, 'Myth as Language in Aboriginal Arnhem
Land', *Man* (N.S.), vol. 5, 1970, pp. 483–97

although cast in the form of an unfolding series of sequential events, necessarily myths?

The problem is familiar to genealogists particularly in a literate or partly literate culture. The hagiographies of Christian and Muslim saints contain a bewildering mixture of fact and fiction from which it is difficult to disentangle the historical content. For example, the Somali pastoralists of north east Africa relate how certain of their founding ancestors sailed across the sea from Arabia on prayer mats. This is a myth statement which, amongst other things, celebrates the fact that the Somalis are fervent Muslims of long standing and maintain pretensions to Arab identity. Such plainly mythical passages are, however, regularly followed in the most elaborate genealogical stories (some issued as books) by extremely circumstantial accounts of their various 'descendants' down the centuries. Some of the characters are true historical figures, and finally we reach living men whose oral record of their fathers and fathers' fathers in part confirms the written versions. Royal pedigrees (or 'king-lists') regularly assume a similar character and present the same interpretative problems. Thus one of the most impressive royal dynasties, that of the former Emperor of Ethiopia, Haile Selassie, traces its origins to Menelik I, son of King Solomon and the Queen of Sheba.

Genealogies of this kind are rather like concertinas. At one end they are tied to God and immortality, and at the other to actual, living people. The first part of the story, providing a divinely instituted foundation for what follows, is pure myth; the last part is mundane fact. In the middle-ground of the story we find the two ingredients juxtaposed, and the chronicle of ancestors and events is frequently expanded or contracted as the past is reshaped to keep it up to date. Under stable conditions certain fixed names and points may occur in different versions of the same genealogy: but their very constancy may alert our suspicions and point to the highly selective character of tradition in its memory of the past. Total recall is not common in recollections of the past! Unfortunately the presence or absence of dates (and equally, of literacy), does not in itself tell us whether we are dealing with history or myth. Some myths achieve their effectiveness not by

setting their plot in a timeless limbo, but by endowing it with
every appearance of circumstantial accuracy. All significant
history risks becoming myth, particularly when selective representation of great events in mythical form is used by rival factions
to assert their separate identity, as in the recent history of
Ireland.

But if many highly significant myths masquerade as history
and thus lose the dream-like somnolence of the aboriginal Dream
Time, they retain another quality generally ascribed to dreams –
the airing and potential resolution of ambiguities and conflicts.
Myths thus invite analysis by the same methods which psychoanalysts have employed in the study of dreams. Freud called attention to the Oedipus myth as a universal human statement of the
tensions between parents and children in the elementary family.
He interpreted these as being primarily sexual, stressing the incestuous attraction between son and mother. For Freud recognition of Oedipal incest marked the transition from raw nature to
human society: it was, as Lévi-Strauss expresses it, 'the break-
through from Nature to Culture' – the great watershed separating
man from his hominid ancestry. Treating incest as an 'over-valua-
tion' or excessive manifestation of kinship, Lévi-Strauss notes the
widespread, perhaps universal, occurrence of myths involving
acts of primordial incest on a cosmic scale such as the myth of the
Wawilak sisters. At least in part these arise from man's attempt
to explain his own first beginnings. If the origin of family life is
traced back to a single primordial family or figure, reproduction
must originally have involved incest. Yet it is precisely the
abhorrence of mating between close kin that distinguishes man
from animals, and this is linked with use of marriage to weld
individual families and groups together into solid communities.
For this reason in-marriage is mystically outlawed. As Edmund
Leach, Lévi-Strauss's most lucid English interpreter, puts it: 'the
"First Man" should have had a wife who was not his sister. But in
that case any story about a "First Man" or a "First Woman" must
contain a logical contradiction. For if they were brother and sister
then we are all the outcome of primaeval incest, but, if they were
separate creations, only one of them can be the first human being:

thus the Biblical Eve is of one flesh with Adam and their relations are incestuous . . .' [4] Whence, of course, the Fall.

These themes which we saw in the Murngin myth are vividly presented in the creation myths of the Tukano Indians of Colombia, described by Reichel-Dolmatoff.[5] The Tukano recount how their creator deity, the Sun Father, committed incest with his own daughter at the time of Creation, an act which they commemorate in their *yurupari* rituals, which paradoxically proclaim 'the strict exogamous laws that are characteristic of the Tukano'. This incestuous cosmic coitus produced the *vaje* plant (*Banisteriopsis caapi*), a hallucinogen regularly used by Tukano shamans to achieve ecstatic visions which are explicitly compared to incestuous sexual intercourse. 'Hallucination and coitus are equivalent, not in the sense of procreation but rather as an experience full of anxiety, because of its relationship to the problem of incest.' Indeed, the Indians explain that they take the drug in order to 'return to the uterus, to the *fons et origo* of all things, where the individual "sees" the tribal divinities, the creation of the universe and humanity, the first human couple, the creation of the animals, and the establishment of social order with particular reference to the laws of exogamy'. But this sublime and highly valued experience, in which we might say that the Indians re-dream (or re-live) their creation, retains its incestuous connotations since, in penetrating the primeval womb, the drug-intoxicated subject identifies himself with a phallus entering his mother's womb. The Tukano visionary quest achieves its highest form in their eyes when its sexual quality is drowned (or as they literally say 'suffocated') in a mystic uterine union !

SOLOMON'S SEAL

In the case of the Tukano, as in Turner's analysis of Ndembu symbolism, the highly-informed anthropological exegesis seems clearly and very directly based upon an impressive body of first-hand evidence adduced by the people themselves. This is not

4. E. R. Leach, *Lévi-Strauss*, Fontana, 1970, p. 57.
5. G. Reichel-Dolmatoff, 'The Cultural Context of an Aboriginal Hallucinogen: *Banisteriopsis caapi*, in P. T. Furst (ed.), *Flesh of the Gods*, Allen & Unwin, 1972, pp. 84–113.

generally the case in the analyses of myth offered by Lévi-Strauss and other structuralists. They prefer to work, as it were, in the dark, undistracted by interpretations proffered by the people whose myths they investigate. Lévi-Strauss assumes the role of a universal psychoanalyst whose patients are myths, or, more accurately, that of an analyst who treats cultures as patients who expose their souls in their myth-dreams. Deep-seated conflicts of which the myth-makers may be unaware are brought to light and resolved – at least to the satisfaction of the immensely erudite and endlessly resourceful self-appointed therapist. But, of course, since the cultures concerned are left to live with their myths, Lévi-Strauss is denied even that minimum of practical self-validation which successful psychoanalysts enjoy when their patients' problems disappear after therapy !

Ironically, however, both the psychoanalyst's and Lévi-Straussian structuralist's interpretations may be equally arbitrary and problematic. Lévi-Strauss himself recognizes this, nonchalantly declaring that as long as he has something interesting to say it does not matter much whether he inspires the myths he studies or they inspire him. Thus, ultimately, the structuralist approach uproots myth from its socio-cultural context and treats it as a universal art form to be analysed and evaluated by whatever stylistic or aesthetic canons one chooses. No wonder the method appeals so strongly to literary critics for, in their field, the work of Empson (among others) has already thoroughly prepared the ground for the structuralist seed. Indeed, in many essential respects, structuralism returns the study of myth almost to the point at which it rested with Frazer and Jane Harrison, before Malinowski. I say 'almost' because, as will become clear, Malinowski's imprint goes deeper than is often supposed and because Lévi-Strauss's special virtue is to successfully subsume, and sometimes to transform, the work of his predecessors.

It was however Malinowski who taught us to regard myths pragmatically as 'charters' legitimating and justifying contemporary events, the past continually reinterpreted to validate the present. This behaviourist theory of myth as a mere adjunct to ritual and contemporary activities, a true epi-phenomenon of these, was accompanied by a characteristically scathing attack on those earlier writers who (in Malinowski's opinion) were so misguided as to treat myths as symbolic, intellectual (or cognitive), explanatory statements. Myth, Malinowski thundered, is not 'an intellectual explanation or an artistic imagery, but a pragmatic charter of primitive faith and moral wisdom'.[6] Despite these powerful assertions, Malinowski's view of myth as an anchor for contemporary realities implies an explanatory role and does not, and cannot, exclude symbolic imagery, just as a strongly functional element is implicit in Lévi-Straussian structuralism. It is indeed especially interesting to note that Malinowski's specific recognition of the role of myths in highlighting and mediating between conflicting social and cultural principles directly foreshadows Lévi-Strauss's emphasis on structural mediation and transformation. Malinowski illustrates this by showing how certain Trobriand myths explain and resolve disputes over land between locally resident people of low status and pushy high-status intruders. These rustic versions of what we might well now call the 'Developer's Myth' still 'contain the antagonistic and logically irreconcilable facts and points of view, and only try to cover them by facile reconciliatory incident, obviously manufactured *ad hoc*.'

We may envy Malinowski's forensic assurance, but we cannot fail to notice how close all this is to Lévi-Strauss. And there is an even closer (and readily understandable) parallel in Edmund Leach's analysis of Burmese politics (to which we shall refer later), and his avowedly 'structuralist' interpretation of the biblical accounts of King Solomon's ancestry. Leach [7] argues that the biblical picture of Solomon's claims to his kingdom reflects a major contradiction in the social structure of the ancient Israelites; in particular it expresses the tension between marrying within the group (endogamy) and marrying outside it (exogamy). The land of Palestine is given to Israel's descendants by God; but to retain their title to it the Israelites must preserve both their blood and their faith. Now the biblical stories make it clear that the population is not of one blood, but contains many different elements. While the Law requires them to practise endogamy, Israel's des-

6. B. Malinowski, *Myth in Primitive Psychology*, Kegan Paul, 1926, p. 23.
7. E. R. Leach, *Genesis as Myth and Other Essays*, Cape, 1969.

cendants often find it expedient to do the opposite, and the tension between the two types of marriage is, Leach maintains, a constant refrain in the stories surrounding Solomon and his antecedents. The problem troubles them deeply, and so the biblical tales keep harping on the difficulties of endogamy. Truth, as it were, will out.

The same texts from which Leach elicits this ingenious conclusion are, however, just as readily open to rival interpretations. Thus, where Leach detects an obsessive preoccupation with making the right marriages (and cooking the books to conceal improper unions), others (such as Pamment)[8] find that the dominant message is the more explicit moral that political power is a reward which God grants the righteous. On this reading (which will be familiar to readers of Dan Jacobson's novel, *The Rape of Tamar*), the central and crucial tension is between charismatic and established authority – between achieved and ascribed power. Of course, these are not necessarily alternative, mutually exclusive interpretations. Both messages (and many others) may indeed be encapsulated in the biblical accounts of Solomon's origins; the two kinds of interpretation can readily be combined as in John Braine's novel, *Room at the Top*, where the charismatic low-class hero wins fame and fortune by marrying (exogamously) the boss's daughter.

As I have already suggested, interpretation is particularly intractable when myth assumes the guise of history but we have no independent means of discovering (even in the broadest sense) what actually happened. We may establish the contemporary meaning and significance of a myth, but we are left in a tantalizing uncertainty as to what real events lie behind the myth. When we are fortunate enough to possess independent evidence enabling us to assess the historical content of a myth, we may be able to interpret similar myths where such evidence is lacking. Evidence fortuitously available in one context may provide a key to unlock other puzzles. In this vein, John Argyle has demonstrated that in parts of central Africa myths of kingdoms which unexpectedly discover legitimate heirs who were lost and presumed missing are actually standardized rationalizations for

8. M. Pamment, 'The Succession of Solomon', *Man* (N.S.), vol. 7, 1972, pp. 635–43.

dynastic usurpation.[9] The message they convey is that, far from being our long lost brother, the 'lost and found claimant' is in fact a foreign usurper who has wrested power from those who formerly ruled. This important discovery puts an entirely new complexion on a host of myths, including many from classical antiquity, and can even be applied to the Oedipus story itself. As in interpreting symbolism, we must beware of assuming that the same myth themes convey the same message in different cultural contexts.

Myths thus have to work hard to earn their keep. If they are to avoid demotion to the lowly status of fairy tales, they must say a great deal briefly and effectively; the principle of parsimony applies with a vengeance. Like symbols, the more meanings and nuances a myth conveys the greater its appeal and survival value. As with other works of art, the more general and universal its range of significance the better. Malinowski's conviction that myths exist simply to embellish ritual, a point of view vividly conveyed in Lloyd Warner's term 'oral rite' for the myths of the Australian aborigines, is an extreme example of the behaviourist position. Paradoxically it also leads to the communications theory of Lévi-Strauss and other structuralists, which sees myth as a form of sacred language, the most sublime of all currencies. And in support of this venerable view of myth as *logos* (or *mythos*) it is pleasing to cite one of the most articulate spokesmen of that remarkable philosophical people, the Dogon of the Niger. 'The Word', according to the Dogon sage Ogotemmêli,[10] 'is for every· one in this world; it must come and go and be interchanged for it is good to give and receive the forces of life.'

Without entering into the sterile debate as to whether myth or rite came first, we can safely say (*pace* Malinowski) that for the participants, myths are often very far from holding an epiphenomenal position. Frequently ritual is simply the enactment of myth, as in the major rituals of the Australian aborigines. If there were no myths there would in certain cases be no rites to celebrate. Perhaps the simplest and least misleading formula for the relationship which seems generally characteristic of these two

9. W. J. Argyle, *Oedipus in Central Africa*. University of Natal, 1971.
10. M. Griaule, *Conversations with Ogotommêli*, Oxford University Press, 1965, p. 137.

great dimensions of religiosity is this: myth is to ritual as music is to dance.

RITUAL

So far we have been concerned with mystical beliefs and concepts in relation to the social facts of secular experience. Now we must turn to what many people regard as the most obvious and significant aspect of religion – that dramatic enactment of the mystical which we call ritual. So we habitually describe whole religions or vast denominations by this active part of religious observance; we speak of the Catholic and Protestant rites, and use 'cult' as a synonym for religion. We have, in fact, direct etymological warrant for these usages, since the word 'religion' itself comes from the Latin *religio* meaning a 'bond', binding men to obligations and expressing a relationship. Although the hearts of the faithful must remain inscrutable, at least in public rituals the religious can stand up (or kneel down) and be counted. This, of course, is one reason why sociological studies of modern religions, and particularly of Christianity, are so much conducted in terms of figures of church attendance. Here some sociologists follow those enthusiastic preachers who proudly claim that if the churches are full on Sunday all is well with the world. It is perhaps not entirely fortuitous that this type of sociological study seems to be losing popularity as church attendance figures decline.

It is partly a reflection of this simplistic view that the word 'ritual' has become denatured and impoverished, although there are signs that it is currently being recharged with meaning. Until very recently, the adjective most associated with ritual was 'empty'. And this accords very well with our use of 'ritual' to convey the idea of non-utilitarian obscurantist mumbo-jumbo, performed by long custom without anyone knowing why. We tend to equate ritual with redundancy and to relegate it to the obscure world of folklore and superstition. Following Huxley and the more recent ethologists, we extend this usage into the field of animal behaviour to refer to repetitive and stylized gestures or actions which do not have immediate or obvious pay-offs by directly satisfying sex or hunger. So modern studies of animal behaviour are crammed with accounts of 'rituals' involving twin-finned homo-sexual sticklebacks, and other intriguing creatures.

In this desacralized sense the term 'ritual' has dropped back into social anthropology. Its career is ironically similar to that of the notion of evolution. This, as we saw earlier, started its life in what is now sociology and was quickly appropriated by Dar-winian biologists from whom, in turn, it was re-acquired by social scientists. But, having passed through so many different hands, it had lost much of its original lustre. And so it is with 'ritual'. Influential anthropologists such as Edmund Leach would like to write down (or off) the original sacred aspect of the term, and focus exclusively on the stylized, repetitive sequence of ritual elements. Part of the objective here is to emphasize the communi-cative nature of ritual, and at this point Leach joins forces with Lévi-Strauss.

All this seems perfectly reasonable. But while acknowledging that secular and sacred activities share many significant features, I would mark the distinction which separates them. In company with Gluckman it seems to me appropriate to refer to the secular as 'ceremonial' and to reserve the term 'ritual' for more full-blooded activities which, in the view of the participants at least, owe their efficacy to connection with a mystical power. For me, using the term ritual to describe actions, however casually or non-chalantly they may be performed, implies that they invoke and involve religious power in whose effectiveness people actually believe. Ritual thus is sacred, even if participants do not carry it out with the calculated reverence that social anthropologists would like. It is often asserted that all tribal cultures are equally ritual-istic – indeed it is one of the oldest and most popular assumptions about them. This lingering Frazerian evolutionary notion does not, however, stand up to close scrutiny; tribal societies exhibit wide variations in the dominance of ritual in daily life. Some tribal peoples, and by no means those closest to ourselves in material technology, are not rich in ritual. Secularism, in this respect at least, is by no means a monopoly of modern industrial society.

RITES OF WAY

The most widely distributed rituals mark basic and irreversible turning points in life common to men everywhere. Without distinction of race or creed people everywhere are born, grow to maturity, marry (at least did until recently), and eventually die. So universally (though with striking variations of emphasis) we find birth and naming rituals, rituals marking the attainment of adulthood, weddings, and funerals. Here, put at its simplest, we can see that ritual oils the wheels of life as the individual moves through the human life-cycle from the cradle to the grave. Such rituals, aptly christened 'rites of passage' by the brilliant Belgian sociologist Arnold van Gennep,[11] who carefully dissected out their component elements, effect transitions from one position or station to another. At one end of the cycle the conveyor-belt moves its cargo from death to life, and at the other back from life to death.

Initiation rituals (or 'coming-out' rites), sometimes applied to boys and girls, sometimes only to one sex, provide an excellent illustration of the effects and general significance of such transition rites. They remove those who are being initiated from the status of child and confer upon them the new position of marriageable adult. (This may be done in several, widely spaced phases including an intermediate period of excessively prolonged social adolescence.) To mark this fundamental transition socially and in a psychologically appropriate fashion, the novice is first physically separated from, and systematically divested of, his old position of child. He has ritually to put away childish things, and is frequently spirited off to a conditioning camp in the wilderness, that inexhaustible fount of mystical energy and renewal. There he is symbolically stripped of his old personality and enters a transitory limbo (an interesting condition some anthropologists call 'liminal'). Finally, purged of his old social personality, the new recruit is eased into his new position in adult society with an appropriate ritual accompaniment. Such radical changes of status, which in our modern world are accomplished (more or less) gradually by schooling, are in tribal conditions often achieved much

11. A. van Gennep, *Rites of Passage*, Routledge & Kegan Paul, 1960 (originally published in French in 1908).

more rapidly and with correspondingly more dramatic and searing rituals: and, so far as I am aware, there are no tribal societies which tolerate the equivalent of the modern 'school phobia'.

This whole process, as van Gennep shrewdly saw, usually involves these three crucial elements: the initial break with the old (thesis); the intermediate being nobody nowhere, a kind of 'waiting for Godot' (anti-thesis); and finally the culminating on-with-the-new (synthesis). So a common and widely distributed symbolism in such transition rituals is that of death and rebirth (or resurrection); one status and personality is extinguished and, after the necessary period of adjustment, a new one is created. As Lévi-Strauss (or his adherents) might put it, there is a dialectical relationship between the old state and the new; for the individual inevitably passes through both, and on becoming a man he cannot altogether forget having once been a boy.

The dangers of the liminal, threshold, or chrysalis stage between one fixed point and the next is perhaps best seen in the context of death – when life and death are harsh realities, not simply metaphors. In small, tightly integrated communities, an individual's death is not merely a source of deep grief to his immediate family and friends: it has a much wider and more disturbing significance. We can usefully recall Thomas Mann's observation that, ultimately, a man's dying is more his survivors' affair than his own. This may sound callous, but consider the issues involved. In small-scale tribal communities, and to a lesser extent in our own, a person who dies leaves behind not only physical property (often including wives) to be redistributed, but also a bundle of roles and statuses which have to be dismantled and reallocated before the breach in the social fabric caused by the death can be filled in. Death challenges the facile inadequacy of the comforting phrase that 'no one is indispensable'. We become aware of these implications when an important head of state, a Nasser or a Kennedy, dies; we tend to forget that in smaller communities individuals play a wider and richer range of social roles, so everyone is relatively important. Death becomes a kind of national calamity; this may explain why so many tribal societies seek, even more resolutely than we do, to deny its existence.

However, people do die, and their deaths have to be acknowledged, however reluctantly, and the consequences dealt with in as undisturbing a fashion as possible. Consider what has to be accomplished before the *persona* of the deceased has been finally re-deployed. The positions he held in the social structure have to be filled by duly appointed successors and, at the same time, he has to be invested with the new status of spirit, ghost, or ancestor. Funerals and mortuary rituals are thus required to initiate and carry through both processes. Frequently these transitions are not effected immediately after the death: the manifold responsibilities of the deceased may take as long to unfold and reallocate as the most protracted probate proceedings in western societies. Tribal mortuary rituals tend to be long drawn-out affairs, frequently spaced over several months, as the slow process of social readjustment proceeds. In the meantime, the spirit or soul of the departed has still to assume its definitive shape. Here we might notice that many cultures consider men to possess multiple souls, consistent with the constellation of positions which they hold in life and relinquish at death.

We may also note how this measured response to death allows ample time for what Freud termed 'the work of mourning' to proceed in this dignified and leisurely fashion. As Hertz has remarked with great insight, 'the brute fact of physical death is not enough to consummate death in people's minds: the image of the recently deceased is still part of the systems of things of this world, and looses itself from them only gradually by a series of internal partings. We cannot bring ourselves to consider the deceased as dead straight away: he is too much part of our substance, we have put too much of ourselves into him, and participation in the same social life creates ties which are not to be severed in one day . . . Thus, if a certain period is necessary to banish the deceased from the land of the living, it is . . . because the double mental process of disintegration and of synthesis that the integration of the individual into a new world supposes is accomplished in a molecular fashion, as it were, which requires time.' [12]

In the traditional cultures which I have in mind it is evident that what we may call *social* death follows *physical* death. In our

12. R. Hertz, *Death and the Right Hand*, Routledge & Kegan Paul, 1960, pp. 81ff.

modern welfare conditions, however, men often retire gracefully from active life, becoming socially dead while they are physically very much alive. Such precipitate action, especially when accompanied by a tax-dodging *pre-mortem* distribution of wealth and assets, deprives the immediate kin and dependants of any motive other than sentiment for caring for the aged. Premature retirement thus separates the social and physical aspects of death which are naturally conjoined: our attenuated mortuary rituals seem to reflect this brusque disjunction and make the brute fact of physical death even more grotesque and obscenely embarrassing. Physical death in the welfare state has, as it were, become an awkward afterthought. And those who have settled all their accounts in this world before they enter the grave have little cause to be remembered.

In other cultures the dead do not immediately assume the relatively predictable life of serene ancestor spirits, which is consistent with the fluid and unsettled situation they leave behind. Their fortunes and progress in the world of the dead tends to unfold in step with that of their survivors in the land of the living. One of the most direct illustrations of this is to be found among the Manus people of the Admiralty Islands where, according to Reo Fortune,[13] a man's dead father's essence is held to be immanent in his carefully cherished skull, which is placed in the rafters of the house to preside benevolently over the fortunes of his descendants. When, however, bad luck strikes his son and family, and especially when another death occurs, this ghostly paternal presence runs the risk of rapid demotion to the unremembered spirits of the dead, and the ultimate degradation of being transformed into a sea slug. This ignominious descent down the zoological scale, from culture to nature (as Lévi-Strauss might say), accompanies and reflects the dwindling attention paid to him by the living.

Sepulchral fragmentation and collectivization reaches an extreme form in the elaborate double burial services of the Merina people of Madagascar so vividly described by Maurice Bloch.[14]

13. R. Fortune, *Manus Religion*, American Philosophical Society, Philadelphia, 1935.
14. M. Bloch, *Placing the Dead*, Academic Press, 1971.

The Merina first bury their dead in temporary graves, where they may lie rotting for a period of at least two years. After the flesh has completely decayed, the skeletal remains are exhumed and wrapped in precious silk shrouds for final burial in the family tombs. These ancestral tombs are often extremely elaborate and costly, frequently larger and more expensive than houses, and form 'one of the most striking features of the Merina countryside', defining the territories of the various 'clans'. The secondary burial service (called *famadihana* and meaning literally 'turning over the dead') involves ghoulish rites in which the wives of the bilateral kin group dance frenziedly, tossing the frail corpses up in the air with macabre shouts of glee. This, Bloch argues, contributes to the final depersonalization of the dead as they lose their individuality and merge inseparably in the collectivity of undifferentiated ancestors entombed in the family shrine. Those kin who should have lived together under the benign shadow of the ancestral sepulchre but were forced by the vagaries of fortune to live in different places are at last brought together. And in death, if not in life, the eternal verities of Merina culture are fully honoured.

These examples display the close relationship between the fate of the dead and of the living. We can readily appreciate the distress and pity which a man who dies childless inevitably evokes in such circumstances. In communities which revere continuity but where immortality depends upon the fallible memories of the living, those who die without issue have no one to venerate them and cannot fully become ancestors. Having no direct heirs to cherish their memory or see to their spiritual wants, such neglected spirits are particularly sensitive and readily adopt a menacing posture towards the living; they become capricious demons, consumed by the cantankerous envy and spite which the living assume their unenviable state must engender. This baneful condition is to be avoided at all costs. Thus some tribal (and other) cultures resort to a kind of spectral spare-part surgery, taking great pains to provide artificial or proxy-heirs for the childless dead. This is one of the achievements of the true *levirate* (which we shall discuss later), which enables the dead man's widow to be taken over by his surviving brother (or cousin) so that the survivor can give her children in the name of the deceased. Such posthumous proxy-fathering ensures the posterity of the dead and grants him that most desired of states, benign ancestorhood.

So amongst the Ashanti of Ghana, Meyer Fortes tells us, 'it is a fixed principle . . . that every citizen at death must have an heir and successor, be it no more than a nominal one. What is primarily at issue is a person's status as lineage member, as parent or spouse, and as citizen.' [15] And Fortes goes on to show how the same principle applies to titles and offices which, if they are to continue, must always be anchored in a palpable, physical embodiment. This solicitude for the childless dead is, of course, a corollary of the ultimate value attached to group continuity, which the traditional Chinese found most comfortingly displayed in the sight of incense-laden smoke wafting serenely heavenward from well-tended ancestral shrines.

RITUAL, SOCIETY AND THE WORLD

So we see that ritual demarcates, emphasizes, affirms, solemnizes and also smooths over critical changes in social relationships. It is an all-purpose solvent, an inexhaustibly resourceful regulatory agent. It perpetuates that sense of continuity and changelessness to which so many traditional societies attach such importance. In the same spirit ritual can also be employed to encapsulate and dramatize duty, obedience, and obligation. Rites often convey rights; indeed in Ndembu both words are the same. The marriage practices of the Coorgs of southern India, to which we shall refer later, provide a convenient example. Amongst the Coorgs, a man has a pre-emptive right to marry his cross-cousin, a right which he often waives. This potential entitlement is commemorated in the wedding ritual by his aggressive intervention; he thus reminds the world of his rights. And many examples to much the same effect could be quoted from other sources.[16]

From the foregoing it becomes evident that ritual performances are likely to provide a convenient index, even a register of social

15. M. Fortes, *Kinship and the Social Order*, Aldine, Chicago, 1969.
16. M. Freedman, *Rites and Duties or Chinese Marriage*, London School of Economics, 1967.

relationships. No relationship implies no shared ritual; conversely, the more intensely entwined and interlocking relationships are, the more they are likely to be enfolded in a web-like cocoon of ritual. We might also infer a cut-off point, beyond which relationships are so intense that to endow them with additional ritual affirmation would seem both superfluous and wasteful.

In general, the ethnographic evidence suggests that those who perform collective public or 'communal' rituals do so because they share other highly valued interests. The composition of a ritual congregation is thus a rough and ready guide to the range of collaboration and commitment in a community. People here are standing up and may be counted. They wish to be seen. If old so-and-so is not at X's funeral or Y's wedding without good excuse, the absence is significant: it represents a gesture of disrespect, an indication that the missing guest is outside the bounds of current 'togetherness'. This, of course, is why people choose the most widely publicized rituals to stage dramatic 'walk-outs'. Unless they are willing to sink their differences, even if at a minimal level, hostile groups stage their own separate rituals. And this is reinforced by the widespread (and perhaps universal) understanding that hatred or malice in the participants automatically nullifies the mystical efficacy of their ritual communion. By the same token, direct acts of physical aggression committed in a sacred context are doubly heinous: murder in the cathedral, or, in the Muslim context, in the mosque.

Many anthropologists, following Durkheim and Radcliffe-Brown, see the principal function of communal ritual to be the 'expression' or re-affirmation of sentiments of collective loyalty. People assemble ritually, it is argued, *in order to* show and further reinforce their existing sense of identity and cohesion. It is reassuring to find that, in some cases at least, more sceptical participants offer similar explanations of such communal rituals. I recall, for instance, the comments of a Somali friend on the traditional Somali practice of clansmen gathering together to perform solemn rites at the tombs of their ancestors whom they regard as Muslim saints. It is generally believed paying such respect to ancestors ensures the fertility of women and livestock, and indeed general well-being and success. The ancestors, of course, sometimes reveal themselves in dreams at particular places; if such dreams occur in time of special hardship which is dramatically relieved following prayers and offerings to the ancestors concerned, new local cults are likely to develop. Somalis are great pragmatists and if the veneration of a particular saint at a particular place proves fruitful it will grow in strength and significance.

In this tradition, my friend told me, a clansman of his had announced that during extreme drought and famine, with his camels and sheep dying round him, he was suddenly confronted by an apparition of an ancestor, who bid him be of good cheer and assured him that his fortunes would soon improve. And so the herdsman took comfort and trustingly killed a sheep in honour of the saint, and lo and behold the weather changed dramatically, heavy rain fell, and in a few days there was plenty of water and abundant green grass, and his livestock began to recover. Milk was soon again available and fortune smiled. The good news of this timely ancestral intervention soon spread, and other members of the clan hurried to the spot where the ancestor had appeared to pay him cult. And so a shrine was built at which clansmen regularly assembled each year to engage in pious feasting and ritual revelry, and many were the tales of their ancestor's miraculous beneficence. The story is a familiar one.

It was only some years after this highly successful cult had been established, my sceptical friend told me, that the man who had reported the first encounter with the saint told other people what had really happened. It is necessary to understand that the most filthy, loathed and polluting beast in the Muslim scale of values is the pig, and of pigs the most acutely foul part is the teeth. Now, my friend assured me, far from having edifying visions of his ancestors, the initiator of the cult had simply buried a pig's tooth. Thus his clansmen had been innocently revering the most unclean object it is possible for Muslims to imagine. But, and this is the point of this sick tale, despite this extraordinary revelation that they were virtually worshipping the devil, the clansmen were confident that they had actually enjoyed prosperity and success as a result of their ritual communion there. According to my informant, all this showed that the benefits men *thought* they got by venerating their ancestors were *actually* no more than the pleasures engendered by pleasant company and feasting. It was the party spirit, not that of the ancestors, my friend explained, that kept such cults going.

This is all very Durkheimian. It is also strongly reminiscent of those sick jokes the most sophisticated Catholics enjoy telling at the expense of the Vatican to demonstrate how broadminded and enlightened they are. I must therefore emphasize that my informant was not a member of the elect, but a simple Somali policeman who really only half-believed his own interpretation and whose wider world-view needs to be established. My friend believes in the mystical power of certain saintly lineages, and told me how a man of his acquaintance had unwisely raped a girl of this clan and became mad in consequence. He also scoffed at reports then current (1962) of American and Russian cosmonauts travelling through space. These he dismissed as spurious propaganda, for the Koran talked of seven vaults, or layers, of heaven in the sky, and to imagine that man could ever penetrate these was as ridiculous as it was blasphemous. These facts illustrate once again how extremely difficult it is to determine and describe accurately what other people believe.

But this is a digression. Other anthropologists would carry utilitarian interpretation even further, urging for instance that sacrificial feasts are simply excuses for a good binge and their only real benefit is to fill people's bellies and to stimulate the circulation of goods. In an extreme example, Marvin Harris [17] has tortuously asserted that in India, by making the cow sacred, high-caste Hindus restrict their consumption of meat and so benefit less inhibited and less well-fed people of low caste. And with more calorific precision if not much greater plausibility, Roy Rappaport [18] has recently argued that the Tsembaga, a tribe of shifting cultivators in New Guinea, engage in pig-eating rituals to recoup protein deficiencies which they have incurred in moments of stress. This argument, unfortunately, does not explain why they also eat pork ritually when not under stress – unless, of course, we assume that they store up supplies of protein in order to meet

17. M. Harris, 'The Cultural Ecology of India's Sacred Cattle, *Current Anthropology*, vol. 7, 1966, pp. 51–66; *Cannibals and Kings*, New York, Random House, 1977.

18. R. Rappaport, *Pigs for the Ancestors*, Yale University Press, 1968.

future periods of stress! We are also asked to believe that pig-consumption and warfare are directly related adaptively to the physical resources of the environment, so that everything is done for the best possible demographic and dietary reasons. The Tsembaga, it seems, are conservationists of a very high order. Thus the ghost of Malthus rises somewhat unexpectedly in New Guinea. And with ecology as its slogan, there emerges a new anthropological cargo cult headed by Harris, Rappaport, Vayda and others of this persuasion and with ecology as its trendy slogan. They seem blissfully unaware that their enterprise is the old functionalist one under a different name and new management.

This school of anthropological interpretation might, I suppose, argue that the Nagas of Assam who regard their enemies' heads as sources of fertility and bury them in their villages, are *really* only over-enthusiastic utilizers of phosphate, which they employ, with perfect rationality, to improve crop yields. Their aims, presumably, would commend themselves to the zealous ecologist who would, however, perhaps feel that alternative sources of phosphate should be sought. These 'bread and circuses' theories of ritual (which assume that tribesmen always march on their stomachs), although not entirely misplaced, cannot furnish *total* explanations of extremely complex events and processes and their multiple causes. Ritual relates to the existing economic and social order in a way which is neither simple nor straightforward – nor, above all, is its thrust always in the same direction. In some societies ritual is employed in the best Durkheimian tradition to sacralize the establishment. So, for instance, in Europe we have still a lingering conception of kingship as a divinely endowed institution, and royal rituals designed to protect and enhance the majesty of the monarch's authority. In the ancient world, and some contemporary tribal societies, these conceptions are further elaborated in the office of divine kingship, where the sacred aura of regal legitimacy is such that the health of the king and the prosperity of his people are mystically entwined.

These ideas are ultimately part of the universal mystique of power and authority, and the leaders of the most avowedly secular modern states are by no means immune from mystical identifications of this kind. The U.S.A. is not the most secular modern state, but it is sufficiently secular to illustrate my point. American shares are liable to fluctuate with the President's pulse, and the exchange value of the dollar rises and falls as confidence in the President waxes and wanes. Indeed, the Watergate scandal was a godsend to all who seek to understand the mystique of power; it showed very clearly how the office of the American president is believed to be divinely instituted and inspired to such a degree that even its most unworthy incumbents partake of its sacred lustre and thus acquire a very special form of diplomatic immunity. The parallel with Frazer's divine kingship does not, of course, hold in all respects. American presidents are liable to assassination, but not because people believe that if they were allowed to die 'naturally' they would take to the grave all the vitality and life of the nation !

RITUAL REBELLION

Royal rituals which primarily protect and hallow the existing power structure may however contain rebellious episodes. Certainly rituals whose official aim is to celebrate entrenched political authority often seem to dwell perversely upon the dissidence and resentment which the exercise of power inevitably provokes. So, frequently, rituals ostensibly dedicated to the perpetuation of the monarchy contain passages in which the accepted order is turned upside down: the high and the mighty are ritually abased; the humble are uplifted; women queen it over men; subordinates of all sorts temporarily rebel. Elements of such licensed rebellion in the tradition of the medieval feasts of fools, as Gluckman [19] has noted, occupy a prominent place in the traditional harvest first-fruits festivals of many of the southern Bantu kingdoms. In these elaborate ritual sequences, the king is publicly mocked and insulted, women brazenly assume the roles of men, and the whole familiar world of established authority is turned head over heels – at least for a time. Paradoxically, from this ritualized rejection of the system comes peace, harmony, fertility and prosperity. Songs of hate and unedifying scenes of ritualized

19. M. Gluckman, *Order and Rebellion in Tribal Africa: Collected Essays*, Routledge & Kegan Paul, 1963.

violence achieve their apotheosis in a glorious paean of praise celebrating the existing order despite its habitual inequalities and injustices.

The inclusion of these rebellious passages within such estab-lishment rituals Gluckman sees as an institutionalized safety valve, relieving dissent and disaffection. Here he follows Trotsky and the later Marxists rather than the 'early' Marx himself. By periodically ritually rejecting the authority of leaders, subordin-ates find their subjection easier to accept. Their resentment is regularly dissipated, and hence neutralized. Thus the rituals which appear to challenge and attack the kingship actually strengthen it. As Georges Balandier succinctly puts it: 'The supreme ruse of power is to allow itself to be contested ritually in order to con-solidate itself more effectively' [20] – to *reculer pour mieux sauter* as it were. Gluckman extends the concept of ritualized rebellion to include the frequent real rebellions which changed the personnel in power rather than the structure of power itself. For one despotic régime simply succeeded another, leaving the inequality un-changed. Rebellions, in other words, are to be sharply distin-guished from revolutions, where the whole system really is changed.

We find this dialectical relation between the acceptance and rebuttal of authority not only in tribal conditions. It can be glimpsed in carnivals and student rags of the old type. A good example of the latter, I believe (and here I speak as a participant observer), is to be found in the traditional installation of the Lord Rector of Glasgow University. This office is in many respects anomalous: in an otherwise extremely undemocratic organiza-tion it is filled by election, and the rituals celebrating the victory of the successful candidate include riotous battles between students and menacing attacks on the university authorities as pressures which have built up in this hierarchical, stone-age uni-versity burst into the open in a ritual context. In the same tradi-tion, there are well-known ritual inversions when the authorities temporarily assume the roles of their subordinates and *vice versa*. Thus, on Christmas day, the troops are served with their plum-puddings and other seasonal delicacies by their commanding

20. G. Balandier, *Political Anthropology*, Allen Lane, 1970, p. 41.

officers: and we recall how Christ washed the feet of his disciples.

All these examples presuppose an acceptance, however uneasy, of the existing order, simply including a little healthy dissipation of rebellious resentment. In other cases what start out as genuine rebellions, with a revolutionary intent, end up emphasizing harmony and order, and are transformed into ritualized expressions of unity and cohesion. This is certainly the impression conveyed by the affair of the L.S.E. Houghton Street barricades in the winter of 1970. Houghton Street is a narrow and busy road winding through the complex of buildings which constitute the London School of Economics and Political Science. Students and teachers at the School, venturing from one building to another across Houghton Street, daily risked life and limb as they dashed bravely through the fast-flowing stream of traffic which used the Street as a short-cut. Following unsuccessful attempts by the School authorities to have the street closed to traffic and after a minor accident, a group of students decided to take direct action. A barricade was hurriedly erected and the road effectively blocked off. At this point the police naturally intervened and a remarkably good-natured series of exchanges between the two sides ensued until the barricade was removed, on the understanding that urgent consideration would be given to the request to restrict traffic in the area. (The street was provisionally closed in 1975.)

These are the mere bones of a little drama which was almost entirely over in a day. The real interest in the present context, however, is how what began as a specific action against traffic rapidly developed into a highly symbolic performance. To some extent at least (and again I write as a somewhat casual participant observer), it seemed to be quickly and quite undeliberately seized upon for an impressive display of L.S.E. *esprit de corps*. Certainly Radcliffe-Brown, had he been present, would have noticed the unusually emphatic flurry of L.S.E. scarves and other insignia and the manifest sense of euphoric solidarity and *camaraderie* which the occasion provoked. Radcliffe-Brown, I feel certain, would have gone on to argue that the whole episode should be seen as a pretext in which the students of an anonymous nine-to-five non-campus university sought to assert and strengthen their fragile sense of corporate identity. The more poetically (or philosophically) inclined observer might even have discovered hints of a search for an identifiable collective identity, even a soul. That this quest was cast in the highly charged symbolic idiom of territorial integrity would confirm the analysis.

If this interpretation seems far fetched we can turn for some circumstantial support to the authoritative though transient student periodical, the *Agitator*. The following passage published in it at the time is, to say the least, suggestive: 'Houghton Street in itself is not important. It is significant in its symbolic value: it is just one of the many areas in which we can challenge the legitimacy of authority . . .'

I am not arguing that rebellious activity is always successfully ritually cauterized, nor, indeed, that ritual expressions of dissent and insubordination are necessarily so satisfyingly cathartic that they leave no energy for radical revolution. We might, for instance, consider that such ritualized rebellions were frustratingly titillating and lead eventually to a greater and more fundamental cataclysmic explosion. Consider the case of pornography. Those who are for it claim that it performs a healthily cathartic function, allowing people to let off sexual steam, and thus reduces the incidence of rape, sexual assaults on children and other evils. To its opponents pornography simply aggravates and encourages sexual desire and promiscuity, and contributes to the general decline in moral standards. Exactly the same claims and counterclaims are made in relation to violence on television.

I mention these parallels not because I believe that either view has any claim to final truth, but to point out that the same kinds of argument are used here and in the analysis of ritual. Ritual may express, cathartically, the pent-up rage of the underprivileged: or it may convey the sanctimonious satisfaction of the establishment. It may even fulfil both functions at the same time.

HEAVEN ON EARTH: 'INSTANT' AND ESCHATOLOGICAL RELIGIONS

The debate we have just outlined raises two fundamental and far-reaching theories of religion. Assessments of the social significance of religion, whether tribal or universal, and whether

offered by anthropologists, sociologists, psychoanalysts or theologians always seem to include one of two contrasting interpretations. Either religion is held to compensate or palliate the lack of
real secular power, or conversely to complement worldly strength.

By a judicious selection of examples, it is easy to argue convincingly for either view. As with everything else of importance
in social life, the truth is that religion can serve in different circumstances completely different ends. To take an obvious example:
Christianity can be convincingly presented as a revolutionary faith
devoted to the raising up of the downcast and justice for all the
oppressed. Equally plausibly Christianity can be portrayed as a
counter-revolutionary, establishment religion irrevocably committed to turning the other cheek and to rendering unto Caesar.
Christianity would scarcely have lasted as long as it has without
such basic ambiguities. But, of course, it is not the only faith which
is so blatantly two-faced. Both these radically opposed facets are,
potentially at least, in most religions and receive appropriate
acknowledgement in Marx's admirably succinct (if seldom quoted)
general formulation : 'Religion is the general theory of this world,
its encyclopaedic compendium, its logic in popular form, its
spiritual *point d'honneur*, its enthusiasm, its moral sanction, its
solemn complement, its general basis of consolation and justification.' [21]

All religions postulate the existence of mystical powers in terms
of which men endow their surroundings with ultimate, transcendental meaning. But religions also relate to man's social world and
to the moral rules which are the foundation and precondition of
predictable and orderly social intercourse. All religions, I think,
seek to build a bridge between these two concerns and to associate
moral evaluations with mystical forces.

A *priori* there appear to be two alternative methods of achieving
this. One means is to postulate an afterlife in which both good
and bad will receive just deserts. This eschatological solution is
chosen by most universalistic religions in their traditional or official forms. In both Christianity and Islam the morally exemplary
believer of staunch faith knows exactly what he is entitled to

21. T. B. Bottomore and M. Rubel (eds), *Karl Marx: Selected Writings in Sociology and
Social Philosophy*, Penguin, 1963, p. 41.

expect, and so does the sinner. Their destiny in the future-life is alike secure. Ideally it would be gratifying if God's justice was not done only in heaven or hell, but also on earth as well. Then the upright and just might enjoy the fruits of their exemplary conduct in this life as well as the hereafter. This very human aspiration underlies the traditional Christian view that those saintly souls who display Job-like stoicism in extreme and unmerited adversity can expect correspondingly generous treatment in heaven. This sophistry, as I know from my own experience, is as common in Islam as in Christianity. The consoling assurance that, appearances notwithstanding, God is truly the soul of justice has naturally helped these 'pie-in-the-sky' religions to retain the allegiance of abused and ill-used followers. It has enabled intolerably ill-treated peasants to cling to that last refuge of the downtrodden – hope. In promising a heavenly haven, these eschatological religions provide an important escape-clause so present hardship can be endured with fortitude and faith – at least within limits.

Yet for the majority of mortals this is evidently not enough. The vicissitudes of life are too taxing, too uncertain, and too replete with manifest injustices. Hence, in both Islam and Christianity, witches and other malevolent powers have been invoked to elucidate misfortunes and calamities which the promise of celestial redemption fails to render supportable. Likewise in the other eastern religions, long-term fatalism and unswerving faith in providence are underwritten by short-term expedients. Even that celestial meritocracy Buddhism cannot satisfy the pressing demands of its impatient adherents. Thus, as Fürer-Haimendorf points out,[22] in the daily practice of Theravada Buddhism in Sri Lanka, there is a trade-off between the cult of local deities and the worship of the Buddha. Blessing acquired from a shrine dedicated to the Buddha is offered to local deities whose veneration promises an immediate return. In contemporary high-technology Japan, Shinto folk ritual important in the active stages of life is replaced by Buddhism in old age.

Much the same applies in the case of Hinduism, where the ostensibly fail-safe mechanism of *karma* proves an imperfect answer

22. C. von Fürer-Haimendorf, *Morals and Merit*, Weidenfeld & Nicolson, 1967, p. 205.

to many pressing human problems. The karmic doctrine that a man's fortune is totally and uniquely determined by his past conduct in practice leaves as many loopholes as dissatisfactions. Contrary to the theory presented in Hindu theological literature, *karma* is generally believed to be contagious. One person's bad (or good) *karma* can consequently cause (or avert) general accidents and calamities which affect third parties. While a man may shrug off misfortunes (or some of them) as the inevitable, if convenient, consequence of his innate karmic handicap, he is less eager to attribute his successes to *karma*. Nor, for that matter, is *karma* alone and unaided a sufficient or even common explanation of mishaps. In Hindu villages, as Ursula Sharma [23] reports, illnesses and injuries are frequently ascribed to personal malice, an ill-disposed deity, or some other local malign power. As we saw in the case of Zande witchcraft, different causes are invoked by different parties to explain the same events, so that the whole gamut of available mystical agencies may be involved at the same time. Thus, one's good *karma* may protect one from the malicious envy of neighbours – but this cannot be taken for granted. People of low caste explain their unenviable condition in terms of totally unjustified ill-fortune. Others see their plight less charitably : it must be entirely justified, and is thus put down to the evil deeds of previous generations. Through *karma* the sins of the fathers are thus visited on the sons with a vengeance.

What Buddhists and Hindus *actually* believe, then, is, as elsewhere, more interesting and significant than what they are *supposed* to believe. Even these complex and highly resourceful eschatological religions are constantly required to provide (or at least not to prevent the provision of) immediately accessible solace and comfort on terms which exonerate victims of affliction from personal responsibility. Man's search for self-justification is endless.

At first sight, tribal religions present a radical contrast. They hold out no promise of future delights or tortures. There is an afterlife, but in it the righteous do not luxuriate in celestial comfort while the unrighteous groan on the racks of perdition. As we

23. U. Sharma, 'Theodicy and the Doctrine of Karma', *Man* (N.S.), vol. 8, 1973, pp. 347–64.

have repeatedly seen, the fate of the departed is influenced by the attention they can attract from the living. Most importantly, it is emphatically in *this* life, *not* in the hereafter, that a man reaps the consequences of his actions and so confronts his conscience. Tribal religions are sustained by the confident understanding that the good and the just enjoy their rewards *now*, here on earth. There is no question of deferred payment or gratification, no never-never traffic with the almighty. Men wear their consciences on their sleeves in that success and good fortune are *ipso facto* proof of virtue, and misfortune evidence of immorality. And, as we have noted, where these rules are ignored and the righteous appear to suffer unjustly, having committed no wrong, society turns to witchcraft (or sorcery, or capricious demons) to find a suitable excuse for these exceptional circumstances.

All this presupposes that the store of good fortune and success is limited, inelastic, and inflexibly pegged at an arbitrarily low level. As Saul Bellow's novel *The Victim* [24] argues in its analysis of the symbiotic relationship between the archetypical Jew (Leventhal) and the Jew-baiter (Albee), success is always won at someone else's expense. My gain is your loss, and *vice versa*. Available resources do not expand infinitely to take up demand: they are already stretched to utmost limits (or so people believe). With this underlying conviction and their gaze firmly fixed on this life, rather than future benefits, such 'instant' tribal religions celebrate an intensely ethnocentric morality, and an inward-looking anthropocentric vision. The cosmos, events in nature, and particularly their impingement on human affairs through fortune and mishap, all unfold inexorably in response to man's behaviour towards his fellows. Nature, and the mystical forces which animate it, respond dutifully to whatever dramas occur in social relations. The human condition, in short, is the prime-mover, and man stands resolutely, if sometimes defiantly, at the centre of his world.

This surely is a profoundly humanitarian view of life, assuming that how men and women behave towards one another *now* is most important, since it is the major source of future happiness or despair. This insistence on the present goes with a disregard for history in the objective sense, and seems to promote a conception

24. S. Bellow, *The Victim*. Penguin, 1966.

of time as cyclical rather than linear. It is also conducive to the growth of those time-stilling myths discussed earlier in this chapter. Here the important thing is how this type of religion suits a world in which most social relationships are, as it were, of low range but high intensity. It is the product of a compact, enclosed community in which everybody is somebody and thus matters, with a correspondingly concentrated sense of moral identity and compassionate concern. It is, finally, the characteristic world-view of a small and threatened band, huddled together for mutual support and protection, and surrounded by environmental uncertainties and other hostile forces.

This we immediately recognize as the familiar picture of the ghetto mentality, the closed society, always on the defensive and consequently assuming that everything that it gains cognisance of is of direct strategic significance. Everything that is known to occur in the world is egotistically and narcissistically assumed to impinge on its fortunes, so man must react to every stimulus he registers. Everything in the world has some relevance, some deeper and more direct bearing than first appears – if only it can be discovered. There is no neutrality here: no *actes gratuites*. This intense 'tribal vision' is by no means restricted to tribal societies; it is potentially present in all human communities and is readily activated in small, beleaguered minority groups, and – more fleetingly, but not less significantly – in hostile confrontations between vast ideologically opposed blocs. Obvious modern examples are provided by the intriguingly ambiguous relationships between the U.S.S.R., the U.S.A. and China. In the curious interactions and probings which in our degenerate times pass for diplomacy there is a continuous undercurrent of suspicion which finds every act, every gesture, every speech, every word pregnant with deep strategic significance. Communications are conducted in a spirit which, following one of Freud's patients, we might say is dominated by 'omnipotence of thoughts'. Ultimately each supernation is convinced that every event, however insignificant, carries some implication which affects its own political advantage.

This intensely ethnocentric preoccupation has mystical overtones; if things go seriously wrong the cause must be either certain grievous moral lapses within the body politic, or sinister witchcraft-like subversion in which internal treachery and external aggression join forces. At the height of their involvement in Vietnam, many Americans came to regard their truly astonishing lack of success in the war as a sign that God was not, after all, unreservedly on their side. Some, indeed, seemed to interpret failure in such an unequal contest as a sinister omen of their own sinfulness and corruption. This response recalls the humble Lele cultivators of the Congo who regard their score in battle and the hunt as a register of the moral condition of the village. At a more parochial and personal level, we all experience cases where, when misfortune has struck those we disapprove of, we complacently say that they got what was coming to them; we are less ready to accept that our own afflictions are open to the same interpretation. Assumptions that the content and tone of people's relationships and interaction do actually affect their health, if not their fortune, are of course amply confirmed by modern psychiatry.

Again, if we turn to modern Christian theology, we find that many theologians no longer regard heaven and hell as physical realities in the traditional sense. Rather they represent states of mind, and feelings of elation or despair in the individual's relations with his deity. So as Harvey Cox, one of their most eloquent exponents, observes,[25] the radical 'death of God' theologians characteristically employ such key terms as 'immanence' and 'present actuality' and speak unashamedly of 'the Christ in the here and now'. 'Salvation,' they urge, 'must be achieved now, in our history, in this world, and so this history becomes itself a prophecy of the final and transcendent eschaton.'[26] These ideas destroy the old 'pie-in-the-sky' principle and return us to the instant religions of tribal societies. No wonder magic, witchcraft and demonic possession are again popular, indeed have had immense box-office success. The occult has returned to our world with a vengeance as we export Marxism and import oriental mysticism.

Other secular indications point in the same direction: the telescoping impact of modern communications does, in some sense,

25. H. Cox, *Feast of Fools*, Harvard University Press, 1970.

26. E. Schillebeecky, 'Some Thoughts on the Interpretation of Eschatology', *Concilium*, vol. 1, 1969, pp. 22–29.

promote a tenuous global awareness of the lowest common factors of the human condition. This vague and fitful (not to say highly selective) recognition of a common humanity condemned to life within the confines of a single and increasingly over-utilized world is more obvious in an overcrowded single nation-state. Particularly in countries whose social policies commit them to state welfare, the public increasingly recognizes the truth of the corner-stone of Keynesian economic theory, the inter-connectedness of things. So, in our strange new version of the closed society, we speak of our 'rights' to an appropriately generous 'share of the national economic cake', thus implicitly, if not explicitly, admitting that the 'haves' can only have (in whatever currency of good) at the expense of the 'have-nots'. And if our appetite for new goods should flag, it will be quickly whipped up by those licensed mechanisms for exciting mass envy and covetousness which we blandly call 'advertising' and 'public relations'. Notice also how credit facilities are urged upon us with blandishments that assure us that we can now want without waiting.

The irony is that in our modern world, we are increasingly dominated by principles that once seemed characteristic of primitive tribal societies. We thus confront the peculiar paradox that our massive advances in technology may ultimately re-establish a view of life and of the human condition which has more vital aspects in common with tribal than with universalistic religions. Again, it seems, the extremes meet, for simple and extremely advanced technologies produce the same effects: they provide environments where men become acutely aware of their interdependence and come to recognize that, if they wish to survive, they must link arms and confront nature with the full force of their common humanity.

Chapter Six

Patrimony and Patriotism

ECOLOGY AND TRIBAL ECONOMIES

Where life is regularly menaced by undernourishment, malnutrition, and starvation, the major preoccupation is necessarily and naturally sheer survival. 'Give us our daily bread' is then an urgent appeal for help, not the empty platitude it has become in our embarrassingly affluent society. From this tribal perspective the idea that over-eating could actually become a hazard to health seems at once inconceivable and obscene. From day to day and from season to season, the food quest must receive primary attention if basic subsistence needs are to be met. Life hangs by a precarious thread, and minor variations in climate, resources, or population can readily plunge a tribal community headlong into disaster. There is either too little rain or too much; desperate droughts are all too often followed by flood and tempest which cause even wider ruin and suffering. Ironically many delicate traditional demographic equilibria are strained further by critical increases in population following the introduction and diffusion of modern medical facilities. Inadequate traditional storage facilities and deficiencies in transport and communications drastically limit the beneficial effect of local surpluses in a bountiful year. The crippling impact of lean years is thus difficult to alleviate. Production, moreover, tends to concentrate upon a few major resources and this, combining with the other constraints mentioned, means that the economy as a whole can have little elasticity.

These negative characteristics, which make the study of traditional tribal economies a truly 'dismal science', are further aggravated by under-developed (or, perhaps better, over-specialized) tribal technology, which limits the productive capacity of a group and its utilization of the physical resources at its disposal. Production tends to be relatively homogeneous and the division of labour is, with rare exceptions, correspondingly curtailed. Although trade and exchange may be significant factors externally, they usually play a minor role internally and, with important exceptions discussed later, are largely restricted to subsistence and consumer items. These factors encourage specialized forms of capitalization and investment where temporary seasonal surpluses, or other windfalls that cannot be conveniently and safely stored, are converted into gifts and loans to the less fortunately placed members of the community. Practices of this sort assume such institutionalized forms as gift-exchange, tribute, ceremonial feasting, and other types of conspicuous consumption which we shall examine in the next chapter.

This vignette, which we shall enlarge and modify as we go along, deliberately paints a gloomy picture since, as we shall see, it errs in the right direction, and where the facts are more cheerful they make a pleasing contrast. That said, we must begin by exploring the complex web formed by the inter-relationship of economy, technology and physical resources. Here we confront that currently fashionable subject, ecology, which seeks to analyse man's adaptational response to his physical surroundings. The beauties of nature are of course a familiar theme in art, poetry and aesthetics generally. But our sentimental interest only sharpens into acute concern when, through the excessive ingenuity of our advanced technology, we find ourselves wantonly despoiling our environment. With their limited, or over-specialized, technical resources, tribesmen, on the other hand, are in constant danger of being destroyed by their environment. In our case nature appears to be losing and has to be actively protected from our depredations. In the tribal case nature has the upper hand. We might thus say that tribesmen are forced to be ecologists, although they are not necessarily conservationists. Certainly they have to be expert naturalists since their survival depends directly on such knowledge. Of course, what makes good ecological sense in the short term from a narrow, parochial perspective may make nonsense in a wider context. Be that as it may (and we shall shortly be in a better position to assess these matters), those who live close to nature are acutely aware of continuous and often excessive exposure to natural forces which, for the most part, their technology is powerless to control. Extreme cases, where the relentless pressures of precarious and supremely inhospitable conditions are glaringly obvious, help us to explore the constraints imposed by physical environment on economic and social life everywhere. Such conditions should enable us to determine the limits of environmental determinism.

ARCTIC HUNTING: THE ESKIMOS

The traditional way of life of that remarkable people, the Eskimos, provides an ideal point of departure. Although they now number less than 100,000 the Eskimos occupy an enormous expanse of territory, stretching from Greenland across arctic Russia into Canada and America. Their survival over the centuries under conditions of extraordinary severity continues to fascinate those who live in less exacting climates. As everyone knows, the Eskimos have survived as arctic hunters and fishers with a sinuous, resilient culture, stripped of all clutter and non-essentials, and peculiarly well-adapted to the harsh rigours of their habitat.[1] Many Eskimo tribes live on snow and ice-covered tundra where the temperature rises above freezing-point for only two or three months in the year, and where there are few trees to provide shelter or timber for house-construction or other purposes. Such cheerless conditions force the Eskimo to rely heavily upon stone, hides and animal bone and, of course, on snow and ice. Stone houses are usually only built along the edges of the sea, and the most widely used dwelling is the famous Eskimo igloo. Fuel for cooking and lighting is obtained from animal fat, principally seal blubber. Caribou (rather than mink) is the fur in which Eskimos wrap themselves, and their skin clothes are so well designed to conserve body-heat and protect their wearers that they remain unrivalled by modern substitutes. Their equally effective snugly-lined boots are kept soft and supple by being regularly chewed. Chewing her partner's boots (rather than eating them) is, in fact, one way a good wife demonstrates

1. This general account, which ignores regional variations amongst the various Eskimo groups, is based in the main on K. J. V. Rasmussen, *Intellectual Culture of the Hudson Bay Eskimos*, Gyldendalske Boghandel, Nordisk Forlag, Copenhagen, 1930; E. M. Weyer, *The Eskimos*, New Haven, 1932; K. Birket-Smith, *The Eskimos*, Methuen, 1959; D. Damas, 'The Diversity of Eskimo Societies', in R. Lee and I. DeVore (eds.), *Man the Hunter*, Aldine, Chicago, 1968.

affection for her husband. Ingeniously designed ivory slit-goggles to protect the eyes from the appalling snow and ice glare complete the Eskimo hunter's attire.

In his nomadic movements and hunting activities, two basic means of transport are employed. For inland movement the Eskimo depends heavily upon the sledge and dog-team which is used for crossing the ice, snow and tundra wastes. For fishing and harpooning sea-animals, he relies on the light, sealskin-covered kayak canoe which is stoutly built on a whalebone frame. These and other items of Eskimo material culture bear testimony to the skill and ingenuity with which the Eskimos have equipped themselves from extremely unpromising resources in desperate physical conditions.

In this impressive achievement we see the imprint of culture upon nature. In modes of livelihood and settlement patterns climate and the environment gain their revenge. All departments of life are strongly affected by the seasons. In winter, life is concentrated on the sea and its produce (especially the seal): in summer the emphasis is terrestrial and men live largely off land and river resources. Winter finds many Eskimos in long-houses made of earth or stone, or of brushwood and snow, concentrated in quite large settlements along the coast. Usually each house contains a joint or extended family and more distantly related kin. The long-houses are grouped round a central assembly hall, and each settlement displays a strong sense of moral identity and local patriotism. Disputes between members of different settlements may provoke fights and feuds, but not within a settlement, where there is a strong moral compulsion to settle disagreements peaceably. Instead disputing parties express their animosity in a 'song-duel', a battle of words, the outcome of which is judged by public opinion.

In this warm cooperative setting, there is a strong emphasis on sharing and pooling of rights and resources, and this happy spirit of open-hearted generosity reaches its climax in that much publicized Eskimo culture-trait – wife swapping. These sexual exchanges are an obligatory feature of community rituals and stress the moral solidarity of the settlement as a whole. All this is in keeping with the winter settlement being the scene of most Eskimo ritual. Masked dances, game-increase rituals, and shamanistic seances (in which contact is established with the powers that control the life of man and of game) are all held in this congenial setting. Winter, thus, is the season of social aggregation, of sociability and of celebration. At no other time is Eskimo life more expansive.

Summer presents a striking contrast, when everything that has just been said has to be virtually stood on its head. As the ice melts, and the Eskimos move back onto the land and cross the tundra in search of summer game, especially caribou, they leave their comfortable winter quarters, and split up into small, family groups. This is the season of dispersal and division, with family units forlornly trekking across the ice and camping in their own small temporary camps. Wider ties are now largely redundant and are mostly disregarded: for in this competitive hunting situation each family is largely out for itself. Whereas in winter a whole sub-tribe regularly assembles to hunt seal or whale, in summer most hunting and fishing is done individually. The sociability which is so pronounced a feature of winter life is suspended.

These seasonal shifts in Eskimo life are so marked that they were used by Durkheim's nephew and protégé, Marcel Mauss, to illustrate his well-known theory that the tone and content of social life generally is a direct reflection of the 'mass' or 'density' of human settlements. Mauss persuasively argues that the larger and more densely packed settlements are, the more intense and developed their social life.[2] As we now know only too well, this utopian theory fails to take adequate account of the terrible effects of urban overcrowding and other disastrous consequences of industrial settlement-patterns.

In fact the repercussions in Eskimo life of the flux of the seasons extend far beyond anything we have yet described. The food quest is hedged about with a most elaborate and far-reaching system of taboos which plays a major role in Eskimo religion. The guiding principle here was explained by an Eskimo to the great arctic explorer, Rasmussen, as follows: 'The greatest peril in life lies in the fact that human food consists entirely of souls. All the

---

2. M. Mauss and H. Beuchat, 'Essai sur les variations saisonières des sociétés Eskimos', first published in *Année Sociologique* 1904–1905, reprinted in M. Mauss, *Sociologie et Anthropologie*, 3rd ed., Presses Universitaires de France, Paris, 1966.

creatures that we have to kill to eat, all those that we have to strike down and destroy to make clothes for ourselves, have souls like we have; souls that do not perish with the body and must therefore be propitiated lest they revenge themselves on us for taking away their bodies.'

Fortunately, however, animals can be killed and utilized by the Eskimos provided they rigorously observe what Rasmussen calls the 'rules of life'. These rules are both voluminous and detailed but they are all based upon a very simple principle which takes us directly back to the environment and to the seasonal fluctuations of life. On no account and in no circumstances may marine animals be mixed with land creatures: so winter and summer activities must be clearly distinguished. Thus seals, walruses and whales must be segregated from contact with caribou and other terrestrial game: each defiles the other. Caribou and whale steaks cannot be eaten on the same day; caribou skins may not be cut or tailored while people are living on the sea ice, or when hunting walrus. Even seemingly venial offences such as eating frozen caribou steaks out of season are taken very seriously and invoked to explain sickness and misfortune. As soon as summer comes, summer foods may not be eaten until all the clothes worn during the winter have been discarded or changed. Thus dietary rules like many other aspects of life faithfully mirror the cycle of the seasons.

Neglect of any of the hundreds of mystical game laws not only threatens to afflict the individual sinner with sickness and suffering but, more seriously, also endangers the well-being of the community. Anyone who infringes these taboos becomes enveloped in an evil-smelling miasma which automatically repels game. Such tragedies, however, can fortunately be averted, or at least mitigated, if the guilty party will only confess his misdeeds in a public séance directed by the local shaman. Thus, deeply embedded in Eskimo religion, as in more mundane aspects of their life, we find the clear imprint of their harsh environment and of the manner they have adapted to it. In many Eskimo communities the entire population is divided into two categories – those born in winter, and those born in summer.

In so adroitly adjusting to their environment, the Eskimos have become its prisoners. Their economy, their social organization and their religion all bear the signs of their specific arctic adaptation. Perhaps the most compelling, and certainly the most poignant proof of this is the Eskimo practice of female infanticide when manpower, in the literal sense, is an absolute necessity for survival. This is not to say that the stark terrain on which the Eskimos live *determines* the character of their culture and social structure. Although it is indisputably shaped by the inordinate demands of climate and habitat, Eskimo culture retains its unique identity. Other ethnic groups (as for example, the Lapps), have come to terms with the same or similar physical conditions in other ways.

SEMI-DESERT PASTORAL NOMADISM: THE SOMALIS

Let us now move to the other environmental extreme – hot dry desert or semi-desert conditions. And here at least I can speak from first-hand experience on the adaptive response of the Somali pastoral nomads of north-east Africa.[3] These pastoralists rear sheep, goats, camels and cattle and also keep horses and donkeys, the balance between the various types of livestock varying according to regional ecological differences. In the predominantly dry area of the north of the Somali Democratic Republic, with which we shall be concerned for the moment, the principal stock resources are sheep, goats and camels.

On these barren stretches of the northern coast facing the Gulf of Aden and the Indian Ocean the annual rainfall seldom exceeds four inches. The most favoured regions of the less torrid highlands, especially to the west, receive as much as twenty inches of rain in a good year and cultivation, combined with pastoralism, becomes possible. In general, however, this is an extremely dry country in which water and pasture – the two basic necessities of life – are in short and fitful supply; their distribution plays a major role in grazing movements and settlement patterns. The rains, moreover, when they do fall are frequently very local, varying widely in their geographical and seasonal distribution.

In such conditions, particularly at the micro-ecological level, the

3. See I. M. Lewis, *A Pastoral Democracy*, Africana Publishing Company, 1982, pp. 31–89.

only certainty is uncertainty, so freedom of movement and flexibility of social arrangement are clearly advantageous adaptions. As a transient and variably distributed resource, pasture is regarded as a free gift from God, available in principle to everyone, and not 'owned' or parcelled out amongst the various Somali clans and lineages. Water, similarly, where it occurs naturally in abundant supply on the surface of the earth, is freely accessible to all. Where it is scarce and obtained by heavy labour, exclusive rights to it are asserted by those who make it available. Men and kinship groups maintain widely distributed rights to water, since this enlarges their range of grazing movement. In this nomadic flux wells, particularly the deep 'home-wells' at which camels water in the dry seasons, help to demarcate vaguely defined areas of influence and movement. There are certainly no fixed territorial units, but the clans whose population ranges from 20,000 to 100,000 do have loosely defined spheres of interest. These are rarely adhered to strictly, and men tend to take their stock to the greenest pastures within reach.

Such free access when demand regularly exceeds supply, leads naturally to recurrent competition and conflict. Prudence dictates that the individual herdsman must not move too far from his kin; their help may be vital in a confrontation with hostile tribesmen. Such support is provided by the highly flexible patrilineal kinship system which is the backbone of Somali social and political structure. As I shall explain later, this unusually large 'segmentary system' of clans and lineages which unite and divide with mercurial speed provides the individual herdsman with security while allowing him maximum freedom of movement and autonomy. The political organization of the Somali nomads is, as we shall see later, equally flexible and republican.

Ecological and strategic factors thus place an extreme premium on mobility. The Somali nomad must be always ready to up and go, fully prepared at all times to steal away in the night like the Arab bedouin he so much resembles. The lighter he travels the better, so material equipment is reduced to a minimum. The chief item is the nomad's 'tent', a collapsible framework of curved branch supports, covered lightly with skin, and woven-grass and fibre mats. This has to be sufficiently strong to withstand occasional torrential rain, and sufficiently light and airy to provide a cool shelter in the sweltering heat. This ingeniously constructed home can be erected and dismantled in a few hours and its component parts are readily packed on the backs of burden camels and carried from pasture to pasture with speed and ease.

The dismantled curved armature of the tent is mounted upside down on the camel's back where it forms a compendious U-shaped container. This grotesque basket, precariously perched on the camel's hump, is packed with all the nomad's light effects: provisions, milk dishes, pots and other household utensils, as well as mats, blankets, clothing and so on. Hens, chickens and small children are also cheerfully piled in, so that virtually every small item which cannot carry itself is neatly stored away and transported in this convenient container. Except for the sick and injured, adults do not themselves ride camels. Unlike the Arab bedouin, the Somalis decline to subject such a prized possession to the indignity of being ridden. They prefer to walk with their camels, solicitously leading their laden burden animals by hand as they themselves toil along on foot. In the old days, mounted warriors rode on horses, which are now rare (in this capacity they are to some extent replaced by motor vehicles).

Picture then, a family of a man and his wife (or wives) striding across shimmering dry plains, leading three or four burden camels, laden with the family's possessions, and enveloped in acrid clouds of dust kicked up by the flocks of sheep and goats, and the few milch camels they drive with them. As soon as local pasture becomes exhausted, such groups pack up their belongings and set off in quest of better grazing. Sometimes individual families move separately; at other times, especially when under the threat of attack, closely related families huddle together, move as a single unit and camp in close proximity when they reach their destination. Grazing encampments formed in this way are always transitory, lasting for a few days or weeks according to local conditions and reports from elsewhere. The availability of water and grass is not, of course, the sole determinant of movement: many social and strategic factors also play a critical role.

In comparison with the Eskimos, the Somali nomads are fortunate in being able to live off domesticated animals. Their basic diet consists of milk, imported rice (or grain – some of it grown locally), and meat. Yet meat remains a luxury and is largely reserved for special occasions. These include both times of festivity and of emergency. In fact, sheep and goats are most frequently killed in the dry seasons when milk is scarce, and their skins are then sold or exchanged for grain and other foods and necessities. The Somalis are thus one of those pastoral peoples who tend (although not exclusively) to sell livestock and their produce, not when they have a surplus, but when they are hard up. (The sheep-skins thus produced constitute one of the world's major supplies of Persian lamb.)

Despite the advantages which domesticated animals appear at first sight to confer, the Somalis are in fact just as much prisoners of their environment as the Eskimos. Living as they do symbiotically with their stock, the rhythm of life becomes dominated by the needs of their animals. Anything that affects the life of the flocks and herds affects man just as acutely. So seasonal fluctuations in the supply and location of water and pasturage combine with the feeding habits, water requirements, and powers of endurance of the different species of stock to produce two distinct herding units. The family group we have described is concerned essentially with sheep and goats, which in the dry seasons cannot safely venture far from water. These less hardy and less mobile creatures are usually herded together in a single, undifferentiated flock and referred to by the same generic term. (They can also, of course, be distinguished linguistically.) This herding unit, which for convenience we shall call a 'nomadic hamlet', is essentially the domestic family and includes all a man's unmarried daughters. Boys from about the age of eight, as we shall see in a moment, join the other main herding unit based on camels. With the small animals (as well as the burden and some milch camels), its correspondingly reduced range of movement, and the predominance of women in its human membership, the nomadic hamlet is considered both vulnerable and weak. Its more robust counterpart is the camel-camp, consisting of the grazing camels of closely related men under the charge of unmarried herdsmen and boys. This long-range, highly mobile herding-unit regularly roves hundreds of miles from permanent water in the dry seasons, owing to the remarkable endurance powers of that lord of the desert, the camel, which stores water in its stomach, not, of course, in its hump. The grazing camels can pasture in remote areas where there is grass, but no water, and which are quite inaccessible to the sheep and goats.

Life in the camel-camps is spartan in the extreme and epitomizes the dominant values of the Somali nomads. There, living mainly on milk and often little enough of that, boys are initiated into the art of camel-husbandry and taught those hardy virtues which are a prerequisite for survival in this inhospitable environment. Creature comforts are few; often there are few cooking utensils or none at all; the young herders sleep at night under the stars, huddled together by the rough-and-ready bush pens in the midst of the camels they spend their daylight hours vigilantly guarding. They are constantly on the alert against camel-thieves and enemy raiders, and are usually armed with spears and sometimes a rifle or two. In the dry seasons their lot is particularly unenviable. If, as is more than likely, the camels are grazing far from wells, they have to be brought back for watering at intervals of approximately fourteen days. So the sturdy youngsters which this tough life breeds patiently drive their herds, often of hundreds of beasts, covered from head to foot in the choking red dust of the plains as they move up the long weary trails to the wells. In time of drought weaker animals fall by the wayside, and their bones, picked clean by the hovering vultures, serve as a grim reminder of the delicate balance between the human and animal populations, and their scant natural resources.

The two pastoral units, the short-haul hamlet with the sheep and goats, and the longer-ranging camel herds, are thus far apart in dry seasons. The wet seasons' rains and succulent fresh grazing make the disparities between the two herding units less significant. Good grass is available for all the animals in the same place, and water is no longer a problem. So in these bountiful seasons, the grazing camels, in the charge of their lusty young herders, move back to the hamlets which contain so many marriageable girls in search of suitors. The coming together of the two herding units produces a marked expansion and renewed animation of social life. This is the dating and mating season, the time for ceremonies and rites, for political deliberations, for composing and reciting poetry, and for the exercise of public oratory – an art which the Somalis esteem and in which they excel. Spring, the main rainy season, is thus a time of joy and plenty. Grass springs up, stock bring forth their young, milk becomes abundant, and the whole relaxed rhythm of life reflects this welcome relief from the austere rigours of the dry season. Nomads who have become as gaunt and hungry as their famished, drought-stricken livestock, are now fat, well-fed and filled with renewed energy and enthusiasm for their exacting life. Spring and summer are for the Somalis the time of maximum concentration, when the density of settlement is highest and social life achieves its climax. In the harsh dreary months that follow, men recall the ease and abundance of summer and look forward hopefully to their renewal in the new year, counting their age in the number of summers they have lived to enjoy.

The dry seasons present a forbidding contrast. Grass and water rapidly become scarce; human and animal populations are driven to live on their slender reserves. As pressure on the dwindling resources builds up, so does competition, and quarrels over access to or precedence at grazing and water become increasingly rancorous and frequent. Soon fighting erupts and involves ever-widening circles of agnatic kin, until large lineage groups stand fully mobilized against their enemies and old scores are quickly called to mind. A trivial dispute over whose camels should be watered first quickly develops into a general fracas in which a few nomads are knifed, speared or shot and there is a renewed outburst of fighting between feuding clans and lineages. Fighting and war figure prominently in the long list of dry season scourges which the Somalis bleakly recount. Such adversity reduces men to predatory animals; those who cannot satisfy their own needs with the help of their close kin are driven ignominiously to beg succour from others. It is proverbially said that if you piously pluck a louse from the back of a wandering hermit he will turn quickly – not to thank you, but to demand alms stridently. Even sexual life is drastically affected. Men complain that they are far too busy and preoccupied with the survival of themselves and their livestock to even think of sex at this time, and often too hungry to have any appetite for it. Life as the Somalis know and value it reaches its lowest ebb.

Thus the seasonal extremes for the Somali nomads are the reverse of those of the Eskimos, this contrast fortuitously echoing that between their physical environments; the seasonal oscillation is just as marked and emphatic. War and drought are equated by the Somalis in proverbs and contrasted with peace and plenty or, as they more expressively phrase it, 'peace and milk'. Somalis, of course, are not as simple-minded as some anthropologists of the cultural ecology school; they recognize that fighting and feud are not restricted to the dry seasons, when the struggle for survival is at its most acute. Many of their poems muse sadly on the inevitability with which ease and plenty breeds a careless overweening pride, promoting rash and ill-conceived acts of aggression, savage battles that turn prosperity to desolation and despair. In company with many martial peoples, the Somalis see both the glory and the futility of war. As a well-known Somali poem, called by its translators the Rewards of Success,[4] puts it:

He who drinks joyfully from the cup of prosperity and owns a herd of milch camels

Will surely lose his good fortune as it is written.

The whole Hagar people were brought to ruin by the claim 'I am the King';

Oh men, pride brings disaster; let that be remembered!

Unlike Eskimo religion, Somali religion does not directly reflect these seasonal patterns of adaptation. Nevertheless both cultures bear the ineradicable imprints of their natural surroundings. Yet in neither case does the environment in any simple or complete sense *determine* social organization. In each, man seeks to overcome natural constraints and hazards, and finds himself forced into certain channels of activity which are shaped by environmental pressures; this inevitably gives nature a large say in his affairs. Ultimately, however, the specific adaptational response,

4. B. W. Andrzejewski and I. M. Lewis (eds), *Somali Poetry*, Oxford University Press, 1964, p. 108.

however strongly moulded by physical and climatic factors, bears
the firm, defiant trademark of the specific and unique culture of
the people. The Somalis remain as Somali as the Eskimos are
Eskimo. To say this is not to deny the importance of ecological
adaptation, but to suggest its limits.

SOUTHERN CULTIVATING SOMALI

The flexible loose-knit lineage structure of the Somali nomads is
admirably suited to their environment and their use of its resources although it is by no means the only possible response.
Let us now move further south and consider the instructive case of
the southern cultivating Somali. These people speak a distinct
dialect of Somali and live in the relatively fertile triangle between
the Juba and Shebelle rivers, the only continuously flowing rivers
of any importance in the Somali Democratic Republic.

In this region cultivation, chiefly of sorghum and maize, largely
replaces nomadism, although livestock is an important element in
the economy. Here, in striking contrast to what we have seen
amongst the nomads, there is a sharp and clearly defined assertion
of territoriality. Much larger, permanent political units steadfastly
guard their borders against hostile intrusion. Whereas amongst the
northern nomads, groups as large as 50,000 or 100,000-strong are
only mobilized on an *ad hoc* basis in the transient context of
belligerent confrontation, here such units are as enduring as the
contours of the landscape. Their political structure is correspondingly more complex and hierarchical than that of the nomads,
who rely mainly on government by a male chauvinist version of
general assemblies. Among the nomads there are big-men and,
sometimes, symbolic rather than politically effective clan-heads,
whilst here there are (or at least were until the Somali state recently abolished them) chiefs with courts and subordinate officials
in something like the fashion, if not to the same degree, of the
Bantu kingdoms of sub-Saharan Africa.

Revealing distinctions also occur in marriage practices. The
northern nomads prefer to contract marriages with distant lineages
outside their own kin-group, thus creating valuable alliances to
increase the range of access to pasture and water. Amongst the

southern sedentary Somali the preference is for marriage *within* the group. This, in part, reflects the structure of southern tribes which are heterogeneous conglomerates of many originally distinct clans and lineage fractions. They are essentially confederations and marriage within the tribe contributes to its cohesion and solidarity.[5] Here, then, we see a series of systematic differences between the northern nomads and the southern cultivators within what is broadly a single culture and amongst people who are historically very closely related; most of the southern Somali are actually of northern extraction and once had the same organization which still flourishes with such vigour among the northern nomads. It is an impressive example of differential ecological adaptation.

THE BORAN GALLA OF ETHIOPIA AND NORTH KENYA

The previous example emphasizes the formative force of environmental differences. The Boran pastoralists of northern Kenya redress the balance, and demonstrate once more the crucial significance of cultural differences in ecological adaptation. Much of their environment is the same semi-arid scrub land as that of the northern Somali. Indeed, the southernmost representatives of the Somali nomads actually live cheek-by-jowl with the Boran in northern Kenya, and we can examine different cultural responses to the *same* environment.

Like their Somali neighbours, the Boran herd sheep, goats, cattle and camels and divide these up into separate herding units in the same fashion. But they draw finer distinctions than the Somali and endow them with greater social significance. Boran livestock are separated into the following categories: lactating cows, dry cows, lactating camels, dry camels, and sheep and goats. This series represents a scale of values, beginning with the most highly esteemed stock and ending with the least esteemed. These. variably rated resources are apportioned within families according to the seniority of their members. The eldest son herds the milk-

5. Cf. I. M. Lewis, 'From Nomadism to Cultivation: the Expansion of Political Solidarity in Southern Somalia', in M. Douglas and P. Kaberry (eds), *Man in Africa*, Tavistock, 1969.

ing cows while the youngest makes do with the sheep and goats. Since each category of stock has different grazing and watering requirements and different powers of endurance, members of the same family are encouraged to disperse, each herding his kind of animal in those conditions which best suit it. It follows, consequently, that the territory of the Boran is divided according to different types of grazing, each browsed by the same kind of animals in the keeping of men of similar seniority and position in their families. Family loyalty is thus sacrificed to ranking by order of birth and to livestock grazing requirements. However, the dispersal of kin also has advantages. It minimizes sibling rivalry and, this being a case where distance does make the heart grow fonder, contributes to the wider sense of Boran patriotism. Brothers may be separated, but their fraternal affection and loyalties reinforce primordial dedication to the Boran motherland.[6]

Compared with the three million or so nomadic Somali, the Boran of course are a relatively small ethnic group, numbering only some 30,000. They are thus roughly equivalent in size to one of the smaller northern Somali clans. Bearing this in mind, there is still, however, a striking distinction in their degree of integration. Murder and feuds *within* Somali clans are almost as common as *between* them. But within the Boran nation bloodshed is a heinous sin, and fighting and feud are virtually non-existent. Aggression is turned outwards and tightly suppressed within the group. Lineage organization is also less significant in Boran social structure, which is dominated by attachments and associations based on age and generation (which we shall explore later). Note how cultural features which stress status differences based on age and generation exert a significant effect even within those units where we should expect to find environmental pressures at their most exigent.

Finally, we may note how both the Somali and the Boran in their different ways have evolved social organizations adapted to their physical surroundings, for historical evidence shows that both have survived over many centuries. It would be a bold man, however, who would care to say whether one represents a 'better'

6. P. T. W. Baxter, 'Distance makes the heart grow fonder', in M. Gluckman (ed.), *The Allocation of Responsibility*, Manchester University Press, 1972.

adaptation than the other, or who would exclude the possibility of other equally advantageous adaptations.

HABITAT, ECONOMY AND SOCIETY

These examples will perhaps remind us that those who travel light in terms of material culture and technology in the most taxing and unpromising environments are, inevitably, strongly affected by climate and other physical constraints. Yet, however limited their technological equipment may seem to us, they do not face nature unprepared. If nature peremptorily proposes, in the short run at least it is man who disposes. A particular technology obviously sets limits to what is feasible in extreme conditions, the more so since, having once reached this minimally viable accommodation with nature, few people have the energy and initiative necessary to invent and introduce innovations which radically transform the economy. Of course inventions are not totally excluded, even in the most arduous conditions where, indeed, our proverbial lore tells us, rather misleadingly, to expect them.

Nevertheless the knowledge and expertise required to make the most intensive extractive use of given resources is often very hard to come by. There is thus a charmingly romantic touch to the theories of Wittfogel[7] and his more recent anthropological followers, who suppose that, faced with a given ecological problem, man will tackle it in the most sensible and efficient manner. So, according to Wittfogel's well-known 'hydraulic hypothesis', a vast riverine empire comes into being because (or so he asserts) 'a number of farmers, eager to conquer arid lowlands and plains are forced to invoke the organizational devices which, on the basis of primitive technology, offer the one chance of success : they must work in co-ordination with their fellows and subordinate themselves to a directing authority'.

Although, of course, it is not offered as such, this sounds like a description of contemporary Israel; Israel illustrates how technological know-how is not, as Wittfogel supposes, equally available to all, and how bureaucratic organization may be a

7. K. A. Wittfogel, *Oriental Despotism*, Yale University Press, New Haven, 1957.

precondition, rather than a consequence, of developments of this kind. Where Arab bedouin have been content to live the austere life of wandering nomads for centuries, Jews from central Europe have, as is to be expected, larger and altogether different ambitions. They also possess both the social organization and the technology to realize these aims. Ambition (which is a cultural factor) is perhaps a more authentic mother to invention than necessity. Until, with the aid of foreign technology, the discovery of oil transformed camel-herders into Cadillac-drivers, the Arabs were generally content to live with the desert – in their own inimitable style. Techno-environmental forces are necessary but not sufficient causes of social organization.

Having entered all these caveats it is nevertheless convenient for descriptive purposes to distinguish three broad types of traditional economy (which the examples listed illustrate):

1. *Hunters and Gatherers*
   Eskimos; Bushmen; Pygmies of central Africa; Hadza of Tanzania; Siriono of South America; Australian Aborigines; Veddas of Ceylon, etc.
2. *Pastoral Nomads*
   The Arab bedouin; the Somali; the Galla Boran; the Fulani of the western Sahara; the Bakhtiari, Basseri and other Persian tribes; arctic reindeer herders such as the Tungus, Chukchi, Lapps, etc.
3. *Cultivators*
   (a) Shifting or 'swidden' cultivators, using the slash-and-burn technique to clear and fertilize fields in the bush: the Zande, Lele, Bemba and other central African peoples; the Zafimaniary; the Iban of Borneo; various Philippine peoples; the Trobriand Islanders; the Tsembaga of New Guinea; the Kachins of Burma with their *taunga* slash-and-burn system; most of the peoples of Indonesia (except Java), etc.
   (b) permanent, sedentary cultivators: 'dry' farmers relying on rainfall for the watering of their crops and 'wet' (irrigation) cultivators growing rice, etc.

These three economic types are extremely rough-and-ready and subsume a whole host of subsidiary categories and distinctions which are, in varying degrees and circumstances, highly significant; there is an important distinction between hoe-cultivation and plough-cultivation; short-range nomadism, involving regular 'transhumance' between summer and winter pastures (sometimes known as 'vertical nomadism' where these are at different altitudes), is very different from wide-ranging, large-scale nomadism. Equally significantly and despite their general tendency towards over-specialization, tribal economies combine elements from each of these three categories. We have indeed already encountered cultivators such as the Lele and Ndembu who hunt ritually – if for no other purpose; very few nomads are completely dependent on their pastoral resources, and many cultivators rely in part on pastoral products. There are thus many impure, but few pure, examples of our three archetypes.

While the general sweep of social evolution is undoubtedly from expansive hunting and gathering economies to intensive irrigation cultivation and ultimately (at least for the moment) to modern industrial societies, cultivation either preceded or coincided with the domestication of animals. In the order in which we have arranged them, our three types of economy or 'eco-system' do not represent specific stages in an evolutionary series. With our sedentary bias, we tend to look askance at those who, like nomads and hunters and gatherers, are characteristically of 'no fixed address' and correspond to the unsettling image of the gipsy; but we must not assume that our prejudices are evolutionarily well-founded. Nor indeed is the evolutionary thrust always and invariably in the same direction; some hunters (such for instance as the Siriono of South America or the Veddas of Ceylon) are agricultural drop-outs, and some nomads are lapsed cultivators. Other contemporary cultivators (such as the southern Somali) are, as we have seen, former nomads. Transitions in any direction between our three basic economies are possible.

SOCIAL IMPLICATIONS OF ECONOMIC TYPE

With these limitations, our simple typology can demonstrate how each type of economy has direct (though not universally predictable) implications for life-style and social organization. We shall not of course be able to establish one-to-one correlations between economy and society, but we shall at least be able to show how the range of social formations expands dramatically as we move from hunters and gatherers to cultivators.

Starting with our first category, then, we can say without much fear of contradiction (and that is very unusual in anthropology) that most hunters and gatherers have a loose-knit and generally flexible social organization. This consists usually of small 'hunting bands', rarely more than a few hundred strong, mainly people related by blood or by marriage. The persistent assertion that such bands are necessarily patrilocal has at last been discarded in the light of superabundant evidence to the contrary. In hunting and foraging, a band is, to an extent varying with population pressures, constrained by the movements of other bands and by surrounding sedentary peoples. Especially in relation to supplies of bush fruits, roots, game and water sometimes bands display some degree of territorial exclusiveness, although this is by no means always true.

We could not expect such conditions to lead to complex, hierarchical systems of government. Typically there are few or no clearly defined positions of leadership, and the maintenance of order depends, not on specialized agencies, but on kinship and other ties. Conflicts can be easily resolved by the parties simply separating and joining different bands. Here, as has been well said, hunters are prone to vote with their feet. As we have seen among the Eskimos, such flexibility and informality is adaptively advantageous, for it permits great freedom of movement. Men and women have few encumbrances and few impediments to living where and with whom they choose. Hunting bands thus have in their transient and regularly changing composition something of the character of hippy groups and communes which attempt to create a free-and-easy atmosphere of constant spontaneity.

These appealing characteristics are partly a function of their lack of intense interaction, as becomes apparent when attempts are made to settle hunters and gatherers in sedentary communities. Here Colin Turnbull's searing record of the terrible fate of the Ik represents an extreme case compounded by famine and starvation.[8] Less drastic examples also show how sensitive this pattern of life is to overcrowding. When at the turn of the century the gentle Chenchu hunters of Andra Pradesh were forcibly settled, although their material conditions improved, their manners deteriorated and the incidence of violent crime rose at an alarming rate.[9]

Hunters and gatherers are, as might be predicted, strong in specialized zoological and botanical knowledge; and the study of their expertise in these fields thus occupies a prominent place in what anthropologists have come to call 'ethnoscience'. Readers of Laurens van der Post will scarcely need to be reminded that those who live in this way are also exceptionally talented trackers. So effectively are these skills deployed that in relatively favoured environments hunters and gatherers live moderately well, as a number of recent studies show. The admirably detailed research carried out by James Woodburn amongst the Hadza hunters and gatherers of Tanzania shows that they 'meet their nutritional needs easily without much effort, much forethought, much equipment, or much organization'.[10] Dr Woodburn calculates that in only two hours work a day the Hadza are able to maintain a balanced diet which compares very favourably in its nutritional content with that achieved at much greater effort by neighbouring peoples. The Hadza are exploiting nothing like the full carrying capacity of their environment; they only eat a fraction of the available edible roots and berries. In this surprisingly pleasant land of locusts and wild honey, 'for a Hadza to die of hunger, or even to fail to satisfy his hunger for more than a day or two is,' we are assured, 'almost inconceivable'.

Such recent work shows that, in terms of their own standards, *some* hunting and gathering communities are far from being as precariously placed as the Eskimos. If it seems a little far-fetched to claim that people, living so successfully off the land, represent the original 'affluent society', perhaps we can agree that in their failure to exploit their natural resources more fully they are a special case of underachievers.

8. C. Turnbull, *The Mountain People*, Cape, 1973.

9. C. von Fürer-Haimendorf, *Morals and Merit*, Weidenfeld & Nicolson, 1967, p. 22.

10. J. Woodburn, 'Stability and Flexibility in Hadza Residential Groupings', in R. Lee and I. DeVore (eds), *Man the Hunter*, Aldine, Chicago, 1968.

Moving now to our second category, pastoral nomads, movement and mobility are key features in the adaptive process, as they are for hunters and gatherers. 'Flexibility' and 'fluidity' are, as we saw for the Somali, characteristics of nomadic life and social organization which cannot be ignored. Writers who generalize about these two types of economy invariably seize on this shared property to such an extent indeed that their descriptions of the two ideal types (or 'generative models', in recent jargon) merge indissolubly. Moreover, Spooner rightly says: 'Nomadism is an extreme form of adaptation which generates extreme degrees of instability of minimal social groupings and requires a high degree of fluidity of social organization. There are, however, no forms of social organization or other cultural features which are either found in all nomadic societies or found exclusively in them.'[11] Nomads however achieve more complex and varied patterns of social and political organization and much larger groupings – even if, as with the Somali, these are only fleetingly realized. This is partly no doubt on account of shared rights in livestock. If the fluidity of the nomadic life seems peculiarly well attuned to a free-and-easy 'republican' political organization in which one man is as good as another, it does not exclude less egalitarian arrangements, as the political organizations of the bedouin Arabs, Berbers and Tuareg (to name but a few) amply testify.

Cultivation boldly throws open the door, cautiously prised ajar by nomadism, to disclose an almost limitless vista of styles and types of social and political arrangement. Even the ostensibly unpropitious foundations of shifting cultivation can support complex hierarchical states such as those of the Bemba of central Africa and Burmese Kachin which we shall consider in a later chapter. Irrigation or 'wet' farming is sometimes the basis of some of the largest and most complex traditional empires, but by no means always. Cultivation is an enabling factor, making available much higher productivity and releasing more productive energy which may, or may not, be harnessed in the service of complex political enterprises. We cannot tie types of political organization to types of agriculture, but we can at least say that

11. B. Spooner, 'Towards a Generative Model of Nomadism', *Anthropological Quarterly* vol. 44, 1971, p. 208.

sedentary cultivation promotes, as one would expect, a strong emphasis on territoriality, the political aspects of which we shall explore later in this chapter.

Finally, let us note in passing that population density, that staple resource of the demographer, is at low levels at any rate a poor predictor of political complexity. Some centralized cultivating peoples are almost as sparsely distributed as hunters, and certainly no more densely concentrated than some nomadic peoples. At the other extreme, high population densities entail intensive cultivation, if not industrialization.

PRODUCTION AND CONSUMPTION: THE DIVISION OF LABOUR

We can now go more fully into the economics of tribal housekeeping. We first examine the division of labour in production. The most obvious and immediate basis for the allocation of different tasks is of course sexual differentiation, a foundation which seems so natural and appropriate that it has remained virtually unquestioned until the recent assaults made by women's liberation. Whatever may be the case in the 'horsey' counties of England (if we actually look at the attire the case is more than a little ambiguous), in tribal societies hunting is invariably a male prerogative, and often, as we have seen, carries important ritual allusions. Even outside the hunting shires we conserve this tradition when we expect the male head of the family (the breadwinner who 'brings home the bacon') to carve the Sunday roast his wife cooked. Likewise, if women are doomed to the ignoble tasks of hewing wood and drawing water, because of their very lack of male vigour they are freed from the heavy work of cultivation: clearing new land and ploughing, which is doubly a man's task because of the male connection with heavy livestock.

Cattle are often tended and milked by men, while small stock such as sheep, goats, and hens are the appropriate province of women. In some cases finer distinctions are made. Amongst the Somali the ideal is that camels, representing male property and the reserves of the lineage-group, are exclusively connected with men. Claiming that women would not know how to tend them,

men generously assume responsibility for the camels – although
this does not prevent them expecting their wives to take charge
of the burden camels which are the most cantankerous. The
Sarakatsani pastoralists of the Greek mountains, which we have
already cited, as described so vividly by John Campbell,[12] divide
their sheep from their goats in an unexpected way. Women tend
the goats and are considered potentially polluting to the sheep
which, following the symbolism of the Good Shepherd, are unambiguously the province of men. Particularly in menstruation
and childbirth women keep well away from the sheep which their
husbands so lovingly tend.

Specialist crafts (e.g. weaving, tanning, pottery-making, iron-
working, and certain trading activities) constitute a further, if
minor, element in the division of labour in tribal societies. Such
craftsmen very frequently work part-time only, and are often not
fully dependent on the sale or exchange of what they produce.
This minimal division of labour ensures that with few exceptions
every member of the community lives by the sweat of his own
brow. In traditional societies which combine a more elaborate
pattern of economic specialization with a rigidly hierarchical
political structure, part of the price of power is the duty to dispense lavish and frequent hospitality, on a scale befitting one's
rank, thus promoting redistributive consumption.

This levelling effect is strengthened by the difficulties of storing
surplus supplies which we have already emphasized. Even the
least perishable of traditional crops cannot be kept indefinitely.
Sorghum, for instance, one of the easiest grains to store, can at the
most be kept for about ten or twelve years in pit-granaries. Its
germination properties slowly decline and its taste also changes,
maturing in a way which does not appeal to all palates.

These factors tend to discourage individual food-hoarding and
foster an ethos of redistribution and reciprocity, stimulating those
with a surplus to transform it into social credit, by giving it away,
rather than leaving it to rot. Livestock, as we shall see in a
moment, are subject to the same benevolent dispensation.

It might seem that the obligation to share surplus provisions
with the less fortunate, however commendable in moral terms,

12. J. Campbell, *Honour, Family and Patronage*, Oxford University Press, 1964.

would discourage over-production. Our tax-shy businessmen regularly, if not always very convincingly, assure us that taxation has reached such a prohibitive pitch that there is no point in striving to increase their income. But increasingly high tax payments do not earn the taxpayer increments of prestige or security as they do in traditional societies, unless, of course, profits are turned into prestigious non-taxable charities.

In tribal conditions, where security is always (potentially at least) at risk, even small profits shared with other members of the community can be very significant. It is often precisely the need for ample and widely distributed security that makes the production of a surplus worth while. The more one produces the more one is expected to give away; the positive side of this equation is that the greater one's generosity the stronger and more comprehensive one's corresponding entitlement to support and succour in time of need. To his great credit, Malinowski was one of the first to perceive this clearly, and proclaim loudly and unashamedly the basic motto of tribal economics: you scratch my back and I'll scratch yours. Malinowski actually called it 'reciprocity', or 'give and take'.

In this fashion surplus production is invested in human relations, material wealth is transformed into social assets, creating chains of indebtedness which build up and maintain a circle of grateful clients or followers. Wealth and resources tend to be shared on this very rational (but not necessarily crudely calculating) basis of enlightened self-interest. The emphasis here is a little different from that in the nostalgic picture sometimes painted by theorists of African socialism or *Négritude*. There the pre-colonial state of Africa is presented as an idyllic Eden in which every man loved his neighbour as much as himself and freely shared his possessions with no thought for any return. There is a flavour of this in the 'community society' invoked by Leopold Senghor to express the essence of African life, and there is an attractive touch of a similar idealism in the *ujamma*[13] or 'togetherness' propounded by President Nyerere of Tanzania. If these utopian visions help to provide an inspiration for effective com-

13. The term comes from Arabic into Swahili and, unlike so many words that have become popular slogans, retains its original meaning.

munity development and progress in contemporary Africa they will have more than fulfilled their purpose. But we must not allow these excellent objectives to cloud our understanding of the personal profit motive in traditional economics.

LIVESTOCK AS CAPITAL, CREDIT AND INVESTMENT

The same provident considerations underlie other types of risk dispersal and insurance strategies in tribal economies. Amongst pastoralists the owners of large herds usually divide them up into smaller, more manageable units which they distribute for safe-keeping amongst poorer relatives and dependants. These poor relations are given the use of the livestock in their care, and some of the offspring. They may even get a small additional food and clothing allowance. The advantages of the arrangement to them are clear. What, if we put ourselves in the shoes of the rich stock-owner, are the advantages to me?

First, by dividing up my wealth among my kin I enable them to participate vicariously and to some extent directly in my good fortune. Through their dependence on my stock they identify with me and we are partners in a common and mutually bene-ficial enterprise. Second, the division and dispersal in different parts of the country of my livestock maximizes their chances of securing adequate water and pasturage, and minimizes the likeli-hood of their succumbing to drought and disease. These are con-siderable dividends for the investment I have made. The owner of ample livestock resources adopts a management policy which promises the best chances of success for his herds and also en-hances his personal social and political prestige. Generosity is indeed its own reward.

With this image of the tribal speculator in mind, we can pro-ceed to that baffling phenomenon rampant among east African pastoralists and known, since Melville Herskovits coined the term in 1926, as the 'cattle-complex'. Far from treating their cattle merely as sources of meat and milk, these pastoralists displayed an obsessive reverence for their stock, using them in marriage settle-ments to acquire wives and children, as compensation for injuries and death and as offerings to the gods and spirits. With these and a multitude of other social and symbolic significances, cattle represented the ideal prestige wealth, the measure of a man's substance and success. This obsession was frequently acknowledged explicitly – as amongst the Sotho-speaking peoples of southern Africa who with picturesque appropriateness call their cattle 'gods with wet noses'. With little regard for the quality of individual beasts, the herdsman sought to build up large herds since it was ultimately in numbers of cattle that his wealth was reckoned. According to Herskovits, the cattle-complex is to be viewed as a Veblenesque parade of excess wealth, making no sense in rational, hard-headed economic terms.

As we have already seen, however, this interpretation ignores the calculating shrewdness of pastoral policies which over-produce in good years to offset bad years, and which deliberately disperse livestock, to minimize their vulnerability to disease and drought and to maximize their access to grazing and water. All this is perfectly rational in the toughest economic terms. The same empirical principles encourage pastoralists sometimes to deliberately pursue a policy of over-stocking to destroy exuberant vegetation in which ticks, flies and other animal pests flourish. Again, veterinary evidence demonstrates that small, poorly fed stock are less vulnerable to disease, so that large, scattered herds of thin beasts are less at risk than smaller compact herds of better stock. Thus, contrary to Herskovits, the 'cattle-complex' is an entirely rational management strategy in the precarious and hazardous habitats in which so many pastoral tribesmen live.

Unfortunately, however, the stigma quite unintentionally conveyed by Herskovits lingers on, and has seriously misled many well-intentioned development 'experts' concerned with livestock improvement and pastoral betterment. Indeed, it seems that there are no limits to the irrationality of pastoralists, for some actually defy the laws of supply and demand! This has been the experience of some of the cattle-marketing boards recently established in East Africa. For to their amazement buyers discovered that when demand was greatest and prices offered to the pastoral producers were at their peak, supplies of stock actually declined. When the price offered was raised further to entice the producers to sell, sales dropped. The reasons for this are quite straightforward and have been partly touched on already. Pastoralists tend to sell stock in time of depression rather than boom: under favourable conditions, they engage in what might be called 'target-sales', where the object is to acquire a certain cash sum for tax payment or other specific purposes. Once this is achieved, the motive for selling stock diminishes or disappears, and this explains the response which the marketing organizations found so puzzling.

The impact of the 'cattle-complex' image has been even more unfortunate in the case of the most pastoral of all pastoralists: pastoral nomads. This characterization simply set the seal on the picture of 'nomadic negativeness' already firmly established in the minds of sedentary governments by the nomads' tedious belligerence and evasiveness, and their haughty rejection of schemes for their betterment. The response of nomads to piecemeal development schemes providing better watering facilities, grazing control, or pest-eradication seems all too often to confirm disastrously their reputation for wildly irrational behaviour. Even such a sober and authoritative expert on African ecology as Allan is driven to write: 'Nomadic pastoralism is inherently self-destructive, since systems of management are based on the short-term objective of keeping as many animals as possible alive without regard to the long-term conservation of land resources. The general picture . . . is one of steadily increasing stock numbers on progressively deteriorating land.' [14]

The implied irrationality here is, perhaps, no less (and no more) than is found in our attitudes to urban traffic problems and so many other disastrous consequences of the relentless and selfish pursuit of the 'fast buck'. It is a little ingenuous to expect precarious ecological niches to foster that wide-ranging humanitarian concern which, ideally, if not in practice, comes effortlessly in more affluent conditions. There are a number of traditional systems of pastoral nomadism (such as that known as *hima* in Syria and elsewhere in the Arab world) which include quite sophisticated conservation provisions in the form of emergency grazing reserves. More seriously, this negative assessment fails to stress how traditional patterns of ecological adaptation have often been thrown completely out of gear by indiscriminate 'develop-

14. W. Allan, *The African Husbandman*, Oliver & Boyd, 1965.

ments', usually introduced on 'expert' advice, which do not take sufficient account of relevant ecological and social factors. Uncoordinated agricultural development, including otherwise successful irrigation schemes, often severely curtails the grazing and watering resources of nomadic populations and, in drought years, may contribute substantially to spreading famine and death. The introduction of veterinary services and the provision of wells must be accompanied by grazing control, and livestock culling and marketing arrangements. Otherwise the inevitable consequence is over-stocking, over-grazing, and serious soil-erosion. Carefully coordinated planning, on the widest possible regional basis, is therefore essential.

As the international development agencies are coming to realize,[15] pastoral nomadism is the only viable (and under optimum conditions productive) economy for substantial tracts of the earth's surface; every effort must be made to understand the complex nomadic eco-system, and to preserve and promote its most productive aspects in ways which do not do irreparable damage to the wider ecology.[16]

The terrible devastation wrought by the catastrophic drought in sub-Saharan Africa (especially in the Sahel and Ethiopia) in 1973–4 is a desperate reminder of the precariousness of the pastoral economy and of the urgent need for concerted international pastoral development programmes. Although the price in human suffering has been high, this disaster may ultimately inspire a more imaginative and ecologically sophisticated approach to the survival and development needs of pastoral peoples.

BUSHMEN BORROWING

The pressures to share and distribute wealth which we found in the 'cattle-complex' are equally evident in hunting and gathering societies. Consider the Bushmen of the Kalahari Desert. Within the loose-knit bands which are the principal social units of Bushmen society great stress is placed on the sharing of food, particu-

---

15. See Food and Agriculture Organization, *Expert Consultation on the Settlement of Nomads in Africa and the Near East*, F.A.O. R.P. 20, Rome, 1972.

16. T. Monod (ed.), *Pastoralism in Tropical Africa*, Oxford University Press, 1975.

larly meat from such large animals as kudu, hartebeest, springbok and ostrich. Animals of this size are not hunted individually: they are stalked and killed by parties of three or four hunters and, as each animal is too large to be consumed at once by the party, it is shared out amongst virtually all the members of the band.

Other hunting practices reinforce these tendencies. The primary responsibility for the division of the game rests with the owner of the first arrow which is considered to have killed the prey. But this is not necessarily the hunter who shot the arrow, for arrows are regularly lent and given. As Lorna Marshall so persuasively demonstrates, the giving and receiving, and the lending and borrowing of arrows thus disperse and distribute claims to meat.[17] They are really like meal-tickets distributed at random among the population. Each hunter carries in his quiver a bundle of potential claims to meat, so that the fruits of his success automatically benefit others, just as their hunting prowess benefits him. Again, in this elaborate Bushman archery etiquette we see the familiar motif of risk minimization.

REAL-ESTATE AND REALPOLITIK

All this mutualism, however, is not a simple, communist system of property rights. The communist–capitalist property dialectic will not take us far in understanding the realities of traditional society. We shall get much further if we talk about 'rights' rather than 'ownership'. Individual tribesmen enjoy certain automatic or 'natural' *rights* to most of the things they need. But these rights are rarely if ever absolute. Usually they are rights within rights, that is, rights limited by the concomitant interests, entitlements, and rights of others in the same possession. The individual's rights over his land and livestock, and their produce, even over his wives and children, are subject to the contingent constraint of the rights (potential if not actual) of others, to the same goods. Consequently a man may not dispose of many of the resources he 'possesses' without the consent of other members of the group. Utilization of resources depends on a person's social identity, for rights to property cannot be divorced from social relationships or from social obligations and duties. If therefore we follow Proudhon in regarding property as theft, we have to recognize that there is honour among thieves in this case. Conversely property relations serve as an index of social relations. Access to, control over, and disposal of resources are tied to social status.

Ultimately this is true in all societies. Even in our world, status considerations, including those based on colour prejudice, affect the workings of neutral market principles which, some economists still claim, govern the distribution of goods and services. It is not necessary to be a share-cropper or a shareholder to appreciate that many items of property are subject to multiple interests. Even the term 'freehold' is sadly misleading, as those who have experienced compulsory purchase orders know – the most freely held property is not actually free from the claims of others. Equally, in most modern industrial states the 'right' to sell one's labour is not a right but a privilege fully accorded only to full citizens. Aliens require work permits, which, as we know, can be revoked for political reasons. There is nothing surprising in this. What is surprising is to imagine that economic rights and interests can be exercised independently of political considerations. Everywhere the status of guest is an honoured one, but not if guests overstay their welcome. The laws of hospitality are not infinitely elastic, and the lingering visitor quickly becomes an unwelcome alien. Aliens by definition have political loyalties elsewhere. They are thus not entitled to participate fully in the economic life of their hosts and are expected to return home as quickly as possible, when required.

By the same token, those who choose to relinquish their nationality are in a sense committing social and political suicide, and risk losing their possessions with their citizenship. Wherever our sympathies may lie, it is this ruthless sociological logic which explains why Russian Jews emigrating to Israel are callously stripped of their major assets before they are allowed out. There are equally good tribal precedents for General Amin's similarly harsh treatment of Asians who leave Uganda. To say this is not to condone these practices, but to set them in their correct perspective.

Wherever we turn we find the same story. Political loyalty and commitment is the price which, willingly or not, must ultimately be paid for economic rights, both in highly centralized hierarchical societies and in informal egalitarian communities. Moreover, and as we should expect, the greater the pressure on local resources the more stringently economic participation is made conditional upon full political commitment. Conversely, where resources are abundant, but manpower is scarce, this closed-shop policy can safely and advantageously be relaxed. This supply-and-demand approach to the problem is over-simplistic, since it ignores the cultural setting in which these principles are applied. However, it will serve to introduce discussion of tribal property relations and rights.

GOD'S LITTLE ACRE: THE 'TERRITORIAL IMPERATIVE'

Let us begin with rights to land and follow our threefold typology of hunters and gatherers, nomads, and cultivators. In contrast to earlier misconceptions, recent research shows that some, though by no means all, hunting and gathering communities exercise territorial rights over resources. Within these areas monopolistic rights to fruit, berries and roots are asserted. Variations in the abundance of such fixed resources between different band territories may thus provide a motive for changing group allegiance. Game, in contrast, is a mobile resource, less tied to particular locations, and therefore territorially based bands need not logically claim exclusive jurisdiction over it. Hunting rules thus regularly allow the hunter to pursue his quarry even outside his own territory.

Amongst nomads, as we have already seen with the Somali, grazing is often (though not invariably) treated as a public good, freely available to all, on first-come first-served principles. Rights to water are, as the Somali again demonstrate, more exclusive and specific, especially where it is in short supply. Here the principles of Adam Smith, Marshall and the neo-classical economists are all honoured. The value of water and the circumstances under which access to it is granted depend on its scarcity and the labour expended in its production. Those, normally kinsmen, who collaborate in excavating and maintaining a well share rights to its contents. Thus the primary moral community of producers are also the principal free consumers. Watering-rights are correspondingly extended in other nomadic societies where the bounds of common moral identity stretch much further than they do in the highly atomized Somali structure. Amongst the Somali, where moral obligation normally stops at close kin, there is in the dry seasons a thriving trade in water. Enterprising entrepreneurs, with the aid of relatives or hired labourers, dig out large ponds, line them with cement and wait for the rains. Then the water is poured into old petrol drums and carried by truck into the most arid regions, where it fetches a pretty price.[18]

Our final economic 'type', cultivators, as we have already stressed, have an open door to a much wider-ranging and more intricately developed system of rights to territory. Shifting (or 'swidden') cultivators might be expected to have a flexible pattern of land tenure, since several years' cultivation exhausts a field and it is of no value until, some twelve to twenty years later, the undergrowth has regenerated sufficiently to be cleared and cropped again. This almost carnivorous assault on the terrain is very explicitly recognized by the mountain peoples of Vietnam, described so graphically by Georges Condominas, before their recent gruesome fate.[19] They speak directly of 'eating the forest' and reckon time spatially in terms of the areas they have successively devoured in shifting cultivation. Thus time for them is (or rather was) always magically restored as the forest reclaims its own. Generally, then, shifting cultivators assert rights to standing crops, thus claiming the fruits of their work in clearing the ground, planting, and tending the growing crops.

Whether or not rights are also asserted over abandoned fields which are regenerating seems to depend in part on the crops grown, on the time required for the soil to recover its fertility, and on demographic factors such as population pressure. Scarcity of land is conducive to the maintenance of tenurial claims, but it by no means follows that abundance of land ensures the abandon-

18. In the dry season of 1974 a forty-four gallon drum of water was fetching the equivalent of £3 or more.

19. G. Condominas, *Nous avons mangé la forêt*, Mercure de France, Paris, 1957.

ment of continuing rights. Thus the Burmese Kachin,[20] who do not always have sufficient land, maintain rights to old fields and operate, in effect, a system of fallowing. On the other hand the Iban of Borneo assert specific rights to their disused land although they have more than enough.[21]

Before we leave this expansive type of agriculture, I should stress that the slash-and-burn system is not an inefficient or profligate use of land. Studies by agronomists in central Africa, south east Asia and elsewhere have shown how this process of hacking gardens out of the bush, and fertilizing with the ashes of the cleared timber, provides as high crop yields as can be obtained on the same soils with modern fertilizers. Typically several different crops are grown in the same garden. In the gardens of the Hanunóo of the Philippines, Conklin [22] found areas of under three acres containing forty separate varieties of crops growing simultaneously! Taken in conjunction with its other characteristic features, this inter-cropping has led swidden farming to be described aptly as a system in which 'a natural forest is transformed into a harvestable forest' – and, we might add, retransformed back again. Recycling is integral to this pattern of agriculture in which man's intrusion into his natural environment is kept to a minimum.

Sedentary cultivators occupying a fixed territory clearly require a system of land-tenure to regulate the use of cultivable ground, and, if they are wet-farmers, a complex system of irrigation control. Arable land is parcelled out amongst the constituent units of the community and it is only by membership of these that a man is entitled to till the soil. In some cases – by no means necessarily those with the least elaborate systems of government – such rights are less to specific plots permanently fixed on the ground, than to a reasonable proportion of what the tribe as a whole has under its jurisdiction. This reflects the shareholding character of rights to land; the tribe as a whole resembles a trust, or corporation, managing estates which are parcelled out amongst its component divisions – wherever these happen to be. But there is one

20. E. Leach, *Political Systems of Highland Burma*, Athlone Press, 1954.
21. J. D. Freeman, *Report on the Iban*, Athlone Press, 1970.
22. H. C. Conklin, *Hanunóo Agriculture: A Report on the Integral System of Shifting Agriculture*, F.A.O. Forestry Development no. 12, New York, 1957.

important proviso. Effective residence *within the tribal territory* is an important condition for entitlement to land. A man may leave the group temporarily, and while he continues his original tribal identity retain the land rights that go with it. But if he definitively renounces his tribal identity, his rights to land normally lapse, and revert to the section of which he was once a member and ultimately to the tribal estate in its entirety. This reversionary principle emphasizes the character of the tribal territory as trust land, as do the restrictions which, traditionally at least, affect the sale of land. Rights to land, except of the most superficial kind, cannot be sold by one member without the consent of his kin, neighbours and ultimately the tribe as a whole. Equally aliens can only acquire land rights with such consent and on condition that they become adopted members of the tribe.

Adoption, the formal process of extending citizenship to alien immigrants, reveals clearly how the acquisition of economic rights and benefits goes with the assumption of political obligations. The southern Somali offer a convenient illustration. Here the new settler swears publicly his new allegiance, explicitly renouncing his former clan (or tribal) identity. He solemnly undertakes to make common cause with his protectors, to fight on their side, and to support them in every possible way. Compensation for life and injury is assessed and paid in standard units of camels, so the new clansman agrees to pay his share of any commitments to which his brothers become liable, and they in turn accept equal liability for his actions. If he is killed by another clan, they will seek vengeance and compensation for his dependents. And in keeping with the genealogical idiom in which Somali political loyalties are stated, the new clan-member forgets his own ancestors and adopts his host's pedigree. In practice such new citizenship has at first a provisional character. Time, active participation in the life of the community, and intermarriage gradually cement the relationship, and the adopted member and his sons become indistinguishable from other members of the clan. So the economic and political bond is finally sealed.

Because of the political character of rights, each tribesman in agricultural communities like the southern Somali has rights of use, not of absolute possession, to land. Each tribesman is a shareholder in a corporation whose members' rights are always limited by the rights of others, including their own heirs and successors. The interests of posterity are not neglected. The detailed arrangements by which property rights are administered and apportioned vary enormously. In tribal kingdoms the king is typically regarded like a company chairman managing the land as a whole as a trustee for the ancestors. Subsidiary chiefs and headmen answerable to him execute similar functions within their political divisions. The king is hailed as 'owner' of all the tribal land, but ideally he is rather the chief trustee of an inherited patrimony whose integrity and continuity is guaranteed by the watchful scrutiny of the ancestors.

Loyal subjects, community members by birth, cannot be denied cultivating rights within the kingdom; if they dislike the immediate administrator of the land on which they live they are in principle free to move within the tribal territory, attaching themselves to the local officials elsewhere. In some kingdoms or tribal chiefdoms, where kings install or confirm the appointment of subsidiary chiefs, the subsidiary chiefs are granted power over *people* rather than over *land*. Although, as in the saying, the people go with the land, their rights are protected independently of their attachment to immediate overlords. Their allegiance to the king at the centre of their political universe is mediated by a hierarchy of intermediary chiefs and headmen, but the rights of ordinary tribesmen to cultivate land remains an automatic entitlement, often independently vouched for in the idiom of kinship.

This is vividly seen in pre-revolutionary Ethiopia where, traditionally, two distinct categories of land rights were firmly distinguished. One, known in Amharic as *rist* consisted of inalienable *usufruct* rights to land, based on kinship (traced cognatically) and thus part of every individual's endowment by birth. The second (*gult*) approximated to the medieval benefice or fief, and implied the right to tax and rule those who lived on a specific portion of land. (These two separate rights may be held concurrently by the same person or institution, such as a monastery.) *Gult* rights were freely bestowed by the reigning Emperor (or King of Kings), on such subjects as he chose, including, frequently, hereditary nobles. They played a vital role in the complex Ethiopian political system.

The Church, lords and titled Ethiopian provincial governors appointed by the Emperor had the traditional right to administer and tax those who held *rist* rights in the estates allotted to them as *gult*.

This system in which farmers enjoyed guaranteed hereditary rights to land in several *gult* estates independently of their overlords, has important differences from that common (though not universal) in European feudal society where the peasant's only title to land was his fealty to his master. In Ethiopia, kings might come and kings might go (as indeed, in certain periods, they have done with bewildering frequency), but the humble peasant's rights to land went on for ever, protected by the strongest kinship bonds which the Amhara recognize. And, as will become apparent when we examine this kinship system in more detail, the ties based on descent and marriage involved here are conveniently elastic and flexible. Each Amhara peasant enjoyed a considerable range of choice in his selection of farm land and few Amharas were condemned to live as tenants or share-croppers, and fewer still were completely landless.[23] Of course the situation is very different in the case of the conquered non-Amhara peasantry. Members of other ethnic communities could usually only achieve parity of tenure by assuming Amhara identity – a process which we shall discuss later.

The connection between kinship and rights to land is equally fundamental in politically uncentralized segmentary tribal organizations where genealogies are the foundation both of claims to land and of political identity. Here those who live and farm together form a political unit whose solidarity is reinforced by common descent from the same ancestor. Again the tribal estate is divided up into portions of land which, as the Tiv of Nigeria well illustrate,[24] are distributed among the component kinship groups and managed by their leading members. In this example, land and lineage march together in perfect harmony at every level of social aggregation. The tribe is both a distinct land-holding unit and a group of brothers, all ultimately descended from the

23. A. Hoben, *Land Tenure Among the Amhara of Ethiopia: The Dynamics of Cognatic Descent*, University of Chicago Press, Chicago, 1973, p. 9.

24. P. Bohannan, *Tiv Farm and Settlement*, H.M.S.O., 1954.

common eponymous founder, Tiv. Through this shared ancestry, every individual Tiv enjoys an axiomatic right to live and farm somewhere within the tribal area.

PATRONAGE, CLIENTSHIP AND ECONOMIC DIFFERENTIATION

We have so far treated economic transactions and interests as a subsidiary (if reinforcing) aspect of intense, tightly-woven social and political relationships; and we have stressed economic homogeneity. Before we conclude this examination of the socio-economic nexus, we must briefly consider how, with a more elaborate division of labour, economic differences become at once the basis of and justification for striking socio-political cleavages. Here it is not economic identity, but its opposite, differentiation, that promotes social integration. We shall review two examples.

The first is the ancient central African kingdom of Rwanda as it existed prior to and following the imposition of Belgian rule in 1916. This state had traditionally a threefold caste structure, based on ethnic distinctions, which, as we shall see, happened to coincide, quite fortuitously, with clearly observable physical differences in the population. At the top were the giant Tutsi, an aloof culturally distinct élite of pastoral aristocrats whose traditions recorded that they had conquered Rwanda and established their dominion over the local Hutu cultivators. Although they only formed some 15 per cent of the total population, these patrician pastoralists used their prowess as warriors and superior military technology to lord it over the docile Hutu cultivators who made up most of the remaining 85 per cent. The final and smallest element, both numerically and in physique, were the Twa pygmy hunters – authentic 'black dwarfs' in this stratified, plural society.

The ruling Tutsi aristocrats acted as patrons to both the Hutu and Twa. The client Hutu supplied their noble lords with grain and helped the Tutsi to husband their prestigious cattle. Hutu became cattle-hands for noble Tutsi patrons and so participated vicariously in the dominant and infinitely superior pastoral world. While Hutu supplies of grain and labour freed the Tutsi rulers to pursue their manly martial activities, condescending patronage relationships might include the lending of cattle to loyal clients. The would-be client sought Tutsi patronage with the eloquent plea: 'Give me milk; make me rich; be my father'. Thus the great Tutsi–Hutu divide was bridged by economic transactions which benefited both sides and which were institutionalized through mutually binding, though not irrevocable, patron–client ties. These bonds between superior and subordinate cut deeply into the ethnic solidarity of the Hutu, who were partitioned into clusters of dependants attached to different Tutsi overlords. The Hutu sought some relief by playing off one Tutsi patron against another. There was also a certain wry satisfaction for the Hutu in contemplating the sad plight of those déclassé Tutsi who had lost all their cattle, and become 'poor whites' pathetically clinging with exaggerated emphasis to the last vestiges of their superiority. Above all, or so it seemed to the Belgian anthropologist Jacques Maquet working in Rwanda just before the final phase of Belgian rule, the Hutu had been conditioned to an almost unquestioning acceptance of Tutsi domination.[25]

In the transitional phase before independence (achieved in 1962), when the Hutu were encouraged to participate in the new representative institutions, the old Tutsi diehards became ardent African nationalists pressing for immediate self-government. Their position was very similar to that of the white Rhodesians. They sought to achieve independence before their traditional ascendancy had been significantly eroded. But this very understandable attempt to preserve the old order failed. In November 1959 the Hutu rose violently against the Tutsi and, after savagely massacring thousands of them, seized power. The Twa, significantly, tended to support the Tutsi.

INDIAN CASTE

The immense potential for social differentiation which economic specialization offers is nowhere more logically or elaborately realized than in the Indian caste system. Unlike the situation in Rwanda and many other stratified societies where power is held by

25. J. Maquet, *The Premise of Inequality in Ruanda: A Study of Political Relations in a Central African Kingdom*, Oxford University Press, 1961.

a minority, here, despite considerable regional variations, the high castes and their numerous sub-divisions are generally in the majority. Partly for this reason, and because of its very distinctive cultural (and especially ritual) features, and the way in which hierarchy is assumed to be the natural order of things, many scholars insist that caste is uniquely Indian and Hindu, and does not exist elsewhere.[26] The same, of course, can be said of any social institution. But whether we accept this parochial view or not (and we shall return to the issue later), the fact is that over three hundred million Hindus see human society as a composite structure of five interlocking but rigidly demarcated divisions. These are ranked as follows:

1. Brahmins: priests
2. Kshatriyas: rulers and warriors
3. Vaishyas: merchants and farmers
4. Shudras: artisans, labourers, craftsmen and servants
5. Untouchables: barbers, washermen, sweepers, night-soil removers etc.

The first three categories constitute the so-called 'twice-born',[27] and with the Shudras make up the traditional four estates or *varnas* of Vedic literature. The untouchables stand alone, and at an appropriate distance, but in practice form an indispensable part of the fivefold caste complex. Throughout the Hindu world, people belong to one of these five categories, with everything that implies, by virtue of their birth within a particular sub-caste or caste (*jati*). There are thousands of different castes and sub-castes, all in principle associated with a particular occupation. You name it, and some caste does it. Thus, as a Brahmin farmer teleologically explained: 'Caste arose because one man alone cannot do all the work himself. One person cannot do the work of a teacher, farmer, priest, smith, soldier – he would never have time. Therefore differ-

26. See, for instance, E. Leach (ed.), *Aspects of Caste in South India, Ceylon and Northwest Pakistan*, Cambridge University Press, 1960; L. Dumont, *Homo Hierarchicus*, Paladin, 1972.

27. These 'clean' castes participate in initiation, second birth and religious life generally. Their fragile purity is easily polluted by contact with members of the 'unclean' categories. See H. N. C. Stevenson, 'Status Evaluation in the Hindu Caste System', *Journal of the Royal Anthropological Institute*, vol. 84, 1954, pp. 45–65; for a comprehensive etymological assessment of the term 'caste', see J. Pitt-Rivers, 'On the word "Caste"', in T. O. Beidelman (ed.), *The Translation of Culture*, Tavistock, 1971.

ent castes were created to perform these different tasks.' [28] Different occupations, however, also imply different ranks or statuses. So as another Brahmin explained: 'Low castes came into existence because some tasks, like sweeping out latrines or skinning dead animals, are dirty and repulsive: ordinary people do not wish to associate with those who do such work, and therefore separate castes were formed.' The argument from necessity seems here to possess an almost irrefutable logic.

Caste, of course, is much more than simply a special case of closed-shop trade-unionism. As well as enjoying a monopoly, at least locally, in a particular occupation, each caste or caste division is rigidly endogamous and possesses its own distinctive culture (or sub-culture) and even sometimes language. Caste barriers, particularly in the two critically sensitive areas of intimacy – sexual intercourse and food-sharing – are stressed in a ramifying calculus of degrees of contact and pollution, to protect and preserve ritual purity. Many studies (most impressively perhaps that of Adrian Mayer) [29] show how this imparts an extraordinary Kafkaesque complexity to daily life, since the most subtle nuances in relations between different castes are invested with immense significance. It is not simply a question of; would you allow your daughter to marry a . . . ? Minutely detailed rules regulate who and in what circumstances may smoke together without fear of pollution; which castes may accept water, in their own or other vessels, from which; how, and with what degree of deference, and at what physical distance members of different castes should greet and approach one another.

So amongst the Nayars (Nair) of Travancore, as an English observer recorded in 1834, 'untouchables hid themselves in ditches or climbed up trees to prevent atmospheric pollution; if a Nair accidentally met one of them on his road, he cut him down with his sword with as little compunction as a noxious animal'. For an untouchable, consequently, the time taken on a journey depended on the actual distance and also on the number of high-caste people encountered *en route*. Today in Travancore, as elsewhere in India, caste distinctions are a very sensitive subject –

28. U. Sharma, 'Theodicy and the Doctrine of Karma', *Man* (N.S.), vol. 8, 1973, p. 363.
29. A. C. Mayer, *Caste and Kinship in Central India*, Routledge & Kegan Paul, 1960.

they are supposed to have been abandoned or assimilated to class differences. Still, however, when the low-caste labourer comes to his high-caste master's house for instructions he leans deferentially on the gatepost while the master remains comfortably seated on his distant verandah, much as in the old days the Nayar landlord shouted his orders from the same safe distance.

Dietary rules and practices provide a ready, though not infallible, guide to caste identity and status. At one end of the spectrum of purity and privilege, the Brahmins are fastidious vegetarians and should even avoid eggs. At the other, the servile and labouring castes eat both eggs and meat. The type of meat consumed is an equally critical diagnostic: those who eat pork rank lower than those who eat mutton; and, where the cow is truly sacred, those who eat beef rank lowest of all. Life-styles correspond to menus. The possessions, manners, customs and ritual observances of each caste are typecast and reflect its position in the five-fold hierarchy. Here, naturally, both today and historically, there is room for manoeuvre and dispute over the precise placement of particular castes and sub-castes on the basis of these manifest symbols of status. Social climbing is discouraged by the higher castes, and, in theory, the lower castes are not allowed to ape their betters. High-caste Hindus always watch for the behaviour which in colonial Africa, European settlers formulated in the stereotype of the presumptuous 'cheeky native' who 'does not know his place and has to be taught it'. In many parts of India the lowest castes are traditionally forbidden to have houses with tiled roofs or of more than one floor. Here as elsewhere outward appearances should reflect inner states. The social hierarchy of caste should be faithfully mirrored in the proportions and character of material possessions. Just as on some American university campuses the president or chancellor should have the biggest and best car, so in India the high castes are naturally entitled to a much grander and more ostentatious way of life than their subordinates.

This elaborate concern for one's image and its protection from defilement follows logically from the mutual dependence of the castes in relationships based upon such a thoroughgoing division of labour. In a world where job-demarcation is a religion, castes of different occupation and status are utterly dependent upon the goods and services of others to survive. The typical Indian village thus contains members of many different castes, and is in effect a rustic department store with goods and services provided by expert caste specialists. Transactions, of course, are not of the cash-and-carry type. On the contrary, such inter-caste exchanges (whether of goods or services) are characteristically embedded in social relationships and, as in Rwanda, often formalised in binding patron-client attachments (called *jajmani*). High-caste villagers own the land which is worked for them by their labourer clients, or by the clients of their tenants. Specialist craftsmen supply their services to higher-caste patrons in return for regular remittances of grain, animal produce, clothing and other items. Purely ritual services are provided on the same basis at births, marriages, funerals and other occasions by Brahmins, and by low-caste ritual specialists. Everyone makes his distinctive contribution to the common good.

What could be a more perfect example of Durkheim's 'organic solidarity' based on the division of labour? Of course, and this we must finally emphasize here as elsewhere, access to the necessities of life stems from effective membership of the community. And whether between equals (intra-caste) or superior and subordinate (inter-caste), relationships, as Dr Johnson observed of friendships, require to be tended carefully and kept in constant repair.

SOCIAL CHANGE, URBANIZATION AND TRADITIONAL TIES

The connection between belongings and belonging, which we have followed throughout this chapter, is nowhere more evident than in the response of traditional groups to changing economic and social conditions. In the Third World generally, modernization may challenge traditional ties of tribe, caste or kinship, but it seldom succeeds in overthrowing them completely. More typically these 'primordial' forces show resilient adaptation to new conditions. With increased economic and political competition, there is more to gain and lose; this encourages people to fall back upon, and where necessary modify, familiar and trusted principles of association. Moreover, the new urban centres, whether in Asia or Africa, throw people of different background together on an un-

precedented scale in conditions of reduced rather than increased
security, and life is often more arduous and uncertain than in the
villages. Think of conditions in a city like Calcutta.

The townsman is encouraged to seek support and security in
caste or tribal ties, and urban welfare associations are formed on
these bases. Such 'voluntary societies' – membership of which is
usually as *involuntary* as that of trade-unions – regularly function
like Christmas savings clubs and assume the roles of banks in
supplying their paid-up members with loans and credit. They are
thus often referred to as 'rotating credit' societies by anthropologists. These economic functions, appropriately reflected in
the Creole term *compin* (a corruption of the English 'company')
used in Sierra Leone, both promote and sustain the political interests of the groups they serve. What in one context (or stage of
development) operates as a simple savings or benevolent society,
in another becomes a political pressure group or even party.[30]

Of course the situation is complicated, especially at the top and
the bottom of the social scale, by the coexistence of new class
identifications which cut across the traditional barriers of caste
and tribe.[31] The most successful and ambitious economic and
political entrepreneurs ingeniously exploit new and old types of
relationship to suit their interests in different contexts. The paradox is that in the modern national setting, the 'worst pedlars of
tribalism', as one African leader has put it, are usually among
the articulate educated élite which also supplies the most fervent
nationalists.

The present situation in India is equally full of irony and
paradox. While the government seeks to encourage inter-caste
unions by offering cash inducements to those who marry outside
their own caste, members of the so-called 'backward classes' (those
of inferior caste) are entitled to special statutory benefits, specifically designed to offset their handicaps. This places people of low-

30. For a useful comparative account of such associations in contemporary West
Africa, see K. Little, *West African Urbanization: A Study of Voluntary Associations in Social
Change*, Cambridge University Press, 1965.

31. For excellent discussions of these factors in contemporary Africa see P. Lloyd,
Africa in Social Change, Penguin, 1971 and P. Gulliver (ed.), *Tradition and Transition in East
Africa*, Routledge & Kegan Paul, 1969. For analyses of Indian trends see L. Dumont,
Homo Hierarchicus, Paladin, 1972, pp. 264–86 and S. Epstein, *South India: Yesterday, Today and
Tomorrow – Mysore Village, Revisited*, Macmillan, London, 1973.

caste origin in a quandary. They naturally want to escape from the stigma of their inferior status, but by so doing they risk losing those special benefits to which their adverse birth specifically entitles them.

The socio-economic foundation of these continuities (which are far from being mere anachronistic 'survivals') is especially clear in the case of urban migrant workers who cannot count on living permanently in the cities where they sell their labour. Such people are not fully committed to urban life and return at intervals to the villages, where those who are fortunate retain land rights, and to which they intend to retire eventually. Here the problem is to live successfully with one foot in both camps. The urban migrant who stays too long away from home risks being forgotten. To counteract this danger, the prudent town worker welcomes all his country cousins when they visit the city, and takes care to send home regular presents and other tangible assurances of the strength of his abiding devotion. So whether he is an Irish navvy, a Chinese or Cypriot restaurateur in London or New York or a Bemba tribesman on the Copperbelt in Zambia, the transient urban migrant becomes a remittance-man, carefully cultivating his rural expectancies with an eye to the future. Nostalgia for the 'old country' and sentimental attachment to its quaint customs thus conceal an element of shrewd, if not crudely calculating, self-interest. This continuing attachment to one's place of origin is partly responsible for the reputation for shiftlessness and unreliability which dogs less successful migrants.

The assertion of ethnic identity is one way of staking and maintaining economic claims. Thus while the clothes he wears, the food he eats, and the way in which he lives may conform to an urban pattern this does not signify that the townsman has renounced his traditional identity in his social and political commitments. Appearances here can be very misleading. And with this cautionary reference to the deceptive and therefore best discarded notion of 'de-tribalization', we end this brief excursion into the economic aspects of ethnicity.

Chapter Seven

Exchange and Market

THE EXCHANGE OF GIFTS

Gifts, as we have just seen, regularly sustain attenuated social relationships which distance threatens to sever. The giver gains a return in the continuance of a valued connection to which he is, for the time being at least, unable to make any more direct contribution. By the same token, those who desire to create new relationships can exchange presents and thus establish the unquestioning mutualism characteristic of morally binding social ties.

As we know from our own experience, the distinction between 'gifts' and 'loans' is often arbitrary and imprecise, since both imply debts. And where ingratitude is an unattractive vice, altruism is a precious virtue. The most seductive gift of all is the 'free gift' – a give-away phrase suggesting that this is indeed a rarity, if not a complete illusion. We awkwardly acknowledge this and the implicit obligation to 'repay' or 'return' a gift (and thus to accept a commitment) when in our prudish fashion we stigmatize embarrassingly inappropriate presents as 'bribes'. It requires little reflection to appreciate that the difference between acceptable 'gifts' and improper 'bribes' depends upon arbitrary and delicately poised cultural conventions which, moreover, vary according to context. In common with most of the world, we accept that before and after the conclusion of an important international treaty it is perfectly proper for heads of government to exchange presents as signs of 'good will'. Members of the British public are, apparently, happy that the prime minister who has secured entry to the European Economic Community should receive a substantial prize as 'Statesman of Europe' – at any rate if the award is quickly passed on to a charitable cause. But we object strenuously when public servants are caught accepting gifts clearly intended to secure special favours. These standards of national public morality are in the main limited to cultures which have been profoundly affected by the Protestant ethic. Even then, scandals such as the Poulson case in England and Watergate in America show that these lofty ideals are easier to preach than practise.

While Western exponents of this tradition have been quick to condemn public affairs in the Third World as a jungle of iniquity and corruption, they have also shown a marked reluctance to disburse aid to countries not prepared to make an acceptable return. Indeed, I recall hearing an American ambassador state publicly and with engaging candour that when his government offered aid to developing countries it did not do so without expecting an appropriate response. Whatever may be said (or not said) by their spokesmen, the same applies to bilateral aid provided by the Communist bloc, France, and other countries. In the simplest and most direct terms, the price of aid is often trade, with the donor country, in commodities and at tariffs which are to its advantage. Here we glimpse a recognizable transformation of the medieval meaning of aid – a tribute demanded of a subordinate by a superior. No wonder then that 'aid without strings' should be such an attractive and rare prize; or that in the neo-colonial era small nations may retain some semblance of independence only by strenuous juggling to balance the aid secured from one major bloc against that from another. No wonder also that 'self-help' should provide so attractive a rallying-cry for leaders of the poorer developing countries.

At a more humble level, if no less poignantly, the anthropologist is constantly exchanging gifts with the people he studies. He may be acutely sensitive to the burden of demands made upon him for help and 'presents' of all kinds, both while he is actually carrying out his field-research and when he has returned to the security of his own home. But he should not forget how much he receives in return: his whole livelihood depends on peddling information and knowledge given by his informants and friends in the community he studied. It seems to me that the anthropologist's subjects might be said to have placed him in permanent indebtedness. Whether or not he actually realizes this is another matter. Let us, however, leave the anthropologist to search his own conscience and come to more immediate and general examples. We are all familiar with reciprocity in buying rounds of drinks in bars, in repaying (as we say) hospitality, and in 'returning' presents. We know too that the returns we make should equal, or better still exceed what we have ourselves received. For, as our traditional religious lore assures us, it is more blessed to give than to receive.

THE KULA

These passing references to our own experience (of which we shall have more to say later) serve to introduce the two most florid examples of institutionalized gift-exchange in the annals of ethnography. First we examine the Kula of the Trobriand Islanders, described in Malinowski's classic *Argonauts of the Western Pacific*,[1] the work which launched modern social anthropology, as we saw earlier.

The Trobriand Islands are flat coral outcrops (the largest only thirty miles long) to the east of New Guinea, and form part of an extensive chain or archipelago stretching to the Solomon Islands. In this idyllic South Sea setting, the Trobriand Islanders, who are swidden cultivators, live comfortably on the abundant produce (principally yams) of their fertile gardens. Although some coastal villages specialize in fishing and others in particular local crafts (e.g. making stone tools, wood-carving, or decorating pots), cultivation is the dominant Trobriand economy and, according to Malinowski, the Islanders spend at least half their working lives in the lush gardens. These keen horticulturalists conscientiously produce far more than is required to meet their immediate subsistence needs – which will come as no surprise after the last chapter. Part of the surplus is given as tribute to local leaders and chiefs, and part in fulfilment of kinship ties to the grower's sister's or mother's husband and his family, in which, in this matrilineal society, he has a direct interest. Any remaining excess may be left to rot as publicly as possible in the Veblenesque tradition of conspicuous waste. Competitive displays of yams in the style familiar from English agricultural shows are a regular event and earn the most successful gardeners coveted prizes which, however intang-

1. B. Malinowski, *Argonauts of the Western Pacific*, Routledge & Kegan Paul, 1922.

ibly, enhance their standing in the community. In the wider inter-village arena, challenging displays and exchanges of garden produce enable one group to seek satisfaction for a wrong done to it by another and, according to the outcome, hence serve as an alternative or prelude to actual physical retaliation.

But not all the energies and interests of this exuberant people are concentrated on the land. They are also, as the title of Malinowski's book is meant to indicate, intrepid voyagers, sailing from island to island in their ornately decorated outrigger canoes. Such expeditions are undertaken partly for trade but above all in the Kula. This, the point of the present discussion, is an extremely elaborate system of gift-exchange, linking the Trobriand islanders with the inhabitants of most of the surrounding islands. Malinowski's preliminary description runs as follows: [2]

The Kula is a form of exchange, of extensive, inter-tribal character; it is carried on by communities inhabiting a wide ring of islands which form a closed circuit... Along this route, articles of the two kinds, and these two kinds only, are constantly travelling in opposite directions. In the direction of the hands of a clock, moves constantly one of these kinds – long necklaces of red shell, called *soulava*. In the opposite direction moves the other kind – bracelets of white shell called *mwali*. Each of these two articles, as it travels in its own direction on the closed circuit, meets on its way articles of the other class and is constantly being exchanged for them. Every movement of the Kula articles, every detail of the transactions is fixed and regulated by a set of traditional rules and conventions, and some acts of the Kula are accompanied by an elaborate magical ritual and public ceremonies.

On every island and in every village, a more or less limited number of men take part in the Kula – that is to say, receive the goods, hold them for a short time, and then pass them on. Therefore every man who is in the Kula, periodically though not regularly, receives one of several *mwali* (arm-shells), or a *soulava necklace* (necklace of red shell disks), and then has to hand it on to one of his partners, from whom he receives the opposite commodity in exchange. Thus no man ever keeps any of the articles for any length of time in his possession. One transaction does not finish the Kula relationship, the rule being 'once in the Kula, always in the Kula', and a partnership between two men is a permanent and lifelong affair. Again, any given *mwali* or *soulava*

2. B. Malinowski, *Argonauts of the Western Pacific*, Routledge & Kegan Paul, 1922, p. 81–3.

may always be found travelling and changing hands, and there is no question of its ever settling down, so that the principle 'once in the Kula, always in the Kula' applies also to the valuables themselves.

All this sounds like some extraordinary costume-jewellery stunt: at first it is difficult to divine the motives that might explain why people are not merely willing but actually eager and proud to engage in the proceedings. Part of the answer is to be found in the wider implications of these curious exchanges, as Malinowski himself states: [3]

The ceremonial exchange of the two articles is the main, the fundamental aspect of the Kula. But associated with it, and done under its cover, we find a great number of secondary activities and features. Thus, side by side with the ritual exchange of arm-shells and necklaces, the natives carry on ordinary trade, bartering from one island to another a great number of utilities, often unprocurable in the district to which they are imported and indispensable there.[4] Further, there are other activities, preliminary to the Kula, or associated with it, such as the building of sea-going canoes for the expeditions, certain big forms of mortuary ceremonies and preparatory taboos. The Kula is thus an extremely big and complex institution, both in its geographical extent, and in the manifoldness of its component pursuits. It welds together a considerable number of tribes, and it embraces a vast complex of activities, inter-connected and playing into one another, so as to form one organic whole.

The assessment offered in the last sentence here is an excellent example of Malinowski's holistic 'functionalist' approach. Our present concern, however, is strictly with the Kula he so graphically described. Implicit in these quotations and in his account as a whole is the point, perceptively developed by J. Singh Uberoi,[5] that the Kula is a *political* institution. In its external form, Kula exchanges provide the Trobriand Island trader with a friendly agent and host in hostile communities overseas where his reception would otherwise be, to say the least, uncertain. One does not, however, trade directly with one's Kula partner: business is not combined with pleasure, or at any rate friendship.

3. B. Malinowski, *Argonauts of the Western Pacific*, Routledge & Kegan Paul, 1922, p. 83.

4. Thus green-stone for axe-blades is obtained from Morua Island to the east, rattan and bamboo from Fergusson Island, and clay from the Amphletts to the south.

5. J. Singh Uberoi, *The Politics of the Kula Ring*, Manchester University Press, 1962.

From a less utilitarian point of view, these *external* exchanges are a source of *internal* prestige. Those who sail together on a Kula expedition to a foreign island are all rivals, both in business and prestige. Each individual is out for the best bargains both in trade and in the Kula, and to return home laden with prizes which outshine those of his compatriots. The internal Kula, which again is normally conducted between those who are not already kinsfolk, has also strong political aspects. Chiefs and other leading 'big-men' have more Kula partners than commoners, and Kula networks of prestige underwrite and reinforce rank and power. Significantly Malinowski observes: 'Gifts are brought to the man of superior by the man of inferior rank, and the latter has also to initiate the exchange.'[6] Singh Uberoi succinctly sums up: 'Having thus crossed the seas as an ambassador of peace and protector of internal trade, a given Kula valuable then moves down the political scale, and remains for a time in the hamlet or village of its temporary owner ... Here it acts its part among persons who are closely bound together by ties of descent and common residence. When the next expedition calls from the next island, the Kula valuable will again launch forth into inter-island relations. And so on, round the ring.'

As we see clearly even in this brief account, the Kula transactions are very special and quite distinct from ordinary, everyday trade or barter. The latter, called *gimwali* by the Trobriand Islanders, has the familiar disparaging connotations of commercial transactions. The Kula objects themselves (collectively called *vaygua'a*) are prestige goods, true collector's pieces, often with their own individual pedigrees and histories. Each type can, indeed *must*, be exchanged for the other, but neither can be converted into any other currency or commodity. These ornaments cannot be transformed into consumer goods: they exist only for display and dispatch to a partner. And while their temporary possession confers honour and esteem they are often too heavy and cumbersome to be sported as decorations.

There is thus some point in Malinowski's comparison of the Kula valuables with the Crown Jewels in Edinburgh Castle (even if the latter do not normally circulate quite so freely). But a more

6. B. Malinowski, *Argonauts of the Western Pacific*, Routledge & Kegan Paul, 1922, p. 473.

apt analogy might perhaps be found in those cups or trophies so strenuously competed for in sports or racing and held by the winners only until the next competition. This would be consistent with the element of playful rivalry which features prominently in the ambivalent bond between Kula partners and makes these partnerships resemble formalized joking-relationships. However this may be, it is evident that the Kula 'valuables' are intrinsically useless and owe their unique value to their symbolic significance as exchange counters, or tokens. As Singh Uberoi rightly says, it is not simply that their exchange serves to extend the boundaries of the political group, so ensuring 'the regular maintenance of vital trade'. Rather, he argues, the Kula exchange itself symbolizes 'the reciprocity which sustains a society at home, as well as that which maintains its vital alliances abroad'. Hence for those who give and receive them, the 'ultimate social importance of the Kula valuables' is perhaps that they 'represent to the normally kin-bound individuals of these small stateless societies the highest point of their legitimate individual self-interest, and also the interest of the widest political association in which they participate'.[7]

Before we leave the Kula we must note that modern studies in the Trobriand Islands themselves and in New Guinea[8] show that it is only an unusually elaborate form of an institution generally characteristic of the region. The most specific feature of the Kula is its association, in the Trobriand Islands at least, with a more formalized and rigid pattern of political organization than elsewhere. More typically in New Guinea, competitive ceremonial exchanges of this kind, involving shells, pigs and other valuables, are employed by those who hold or aspire to the position of big-man, a precarious role in these fiercely egalitarian societies. Indeed, the wider social and economic implications of such political exchanges are so pervasive that, as Andrew Strathern insists, if we wish to understand conditions in the New Guinea highlands

7. J. Singh Uberoi, *The Politics of the Kula Ring*, Manchester University Press, 1962, p. 160.

8. H. A. Powell, 'Competitive Leadership in Trobriand Political Organization', *Journal of the Royal Anthropological Institute*, vol. 90, 1960, pp. 118–45; A. Wiener, *Women of Value, men of renown: new perspectives in Trobriand Exchange*, Austin, University of Texas Press, 1976. A. Strathern, *The Rope of Moka: Big-men and Ceremonial Exchange in Mount Hagen, New Guinea*, Cambridge University Press, 1971 and P. G. Rubel and A. Rosman (eds.), *Your own pigs you may not eat: a comparative study of New Guinea societies*. Chicago, University of Chicago Press, 1978.

'we must focus on competitive processes'. And in the Mount Hagen area in which he worked, a big-man compared the local ceremonial exchange system (called *moka*) to a 'card game. Now it comes to us and we win. Later it passes to someone else; and so it goes round'.

Here, as in general, prestige and power *within* one's own community are enhanced by successful confrontations with equals *outside* it. Thus rival feasts (or fights) between posturing big-men confirm and consolidate their reputations as community leaders at home. A leader's internal position is delicately linked to the respect he enjoys in the company of peers outside his own group. If the outside world takes him seriously, so, sooner or later, will his local followers. Similarly, academics 'display' their brilliant erudition in fierce intellectual 'exchanges' in seminars and conferences, and in learned 'debates' in scholarly journals. Esteem acquired in these external competitive encounters builds a scholar's reputation and advances his career within his own institution. It is thus not surprising that the leaders of rival groups should develop a curious mutual sympathy as they glower hostilely at each other, eye-ball to eye-ball – for, like the American and Russian heads of state, each opponent 'understands' (only too well) the other's 'difficulties'. Both realize that their authority over their followers depends on how effectively they appear to square up to each other. The trick is perfected by certain wrestlers: to exchange impressively vicious blows without seriously harming one's opponents. The danger is that one big-man may forget the unwritten understanding that it is all a game.

THE POTLATCH

This brings us to our second and seemingly more bizarre example of pervasive, institutionalized gift-exchange – the celebrated Potlatch of the Indians of the north-west coast of America and Canada, whom most people associate (correctly) with totem-poles. These poles were the most tangible and enduring symbols of Potlatch power. Their proud, magnificently carved animal and other designs were the crests or emblems of the Potlatch titles of their owners. The word 'potlatch' itself means 'giving', and the most detailed accounts of this institution refer to that found among the Kwakiutl Indians at the end of the nineteenth century. By this time, the Kwakiutl had been thoroughly affected economically and politically by European colonization, and even the best and most detailed accounts by early ethnographers (such as Boas) are nothing like as rich or vivid as Malinowski's luminous description of the Kula. There has been much speculation about the aboriginal (or 'pre-Contact') form and function of the Potlatch, and an associated tendency to view it historically. Although this does not compensate for the lack of Malinowskian depth, it does offer an interesting perspective on how systems of gift-exchange alter with their wider environment.

The Potlatch was essentially a feast or party, including, as all good parties should, the presentation of gifts to all the guests. It seems originally to have been a general-purpose transition ritual (or celebration) held to set the seal of public recognition and approval on such significant turning points as birth; naming; puberty; marriage; initiation into secret societies; peace-making between hostile groups; rescue, ransom or freeing of prisoners of war; death and other similar occasions. It was connected particularly with the assumption, both by individuals and groups, of honorific positions and titles either through inheritance or by achievement within the Kwakiutl community. The most important Potlatches were given by the chiefs of tribes or the leaders of local kinship groups for guests from other groups. The prestige thus acquired depended, naturally, on the generosity of the hosts, and a careful tally was kept of who received what – the recipients were expected to return the compliment and would lose face if they did not give as good as they had got. Such Potlatch party gifts were worth having. They included the celebrated Indian 'Coppers' – impressive copper trays or shields some two feet in length and bearing the engraved crest of their original owner; bark-cloth blankets (later replaced by the cheaper Hudson's Bay traders' woollen blankets); precious seal oil; and even canoes. The quantities involved, especially once the new trade blankets were widely available, are staggering. The largest Potlatch in the records up to

1849 featured 320 blankets. But this was a mere bagatelle compared with the 33,000 blankets distributed at the biggest Potlatch recorded between 1930 and 1949.

Between 1837 and 1924 the total Kwakiutl population declined dramatically, largely as a consequence of exotic European diseases to which the Indians had no immunity. Many hereditary titles thus fell vacant at a time when the Kwakiutl had achieved an unprecedented level of affluence, through the new opportunities for fur-trading and seasonal employment in the lumber and fish-canning industries. Indians of noble family were now allowed to hold more than one Potlatch title at a time, new 'Eagle' titles were especially created for the *nouveaux riches*, and – an even more daring innovation – for the first time women were permitted to enter the lists. Combined with the abolition of traditional warfare, these new opportunities for social mobility added zest to the aggressive, competitive character of the Potlatch. 'Be my guest !' is after all both an invitation and a challenge. So, as the Kwakiutl explicitly acknowledged, where before they had fought 'wars of blood' now they waged 'wars of property'. (The same transition from physical violence to fighting with wealth is recorded in Strathern's study of the *moka* exchange system in the Mount Hagen area of New Guinea. In the Trobriand Islands, cricket has been enthusiastically adopted as a civilized substitute for warfare.[9]) The Kwakiutl had become reckless capitalists, addicted to gambling for extremely high stakes, including staking Coppers, some of which were in fact already lodged in ethnographic museums. Rival contenders for a title waged viciously competitive Potlatches often ending in the bankruptcy of the unsuccessful candidate. The most extreme of these 'rivalry' Potlatches achieved their climax in an orgy of wanton destruction. Coppers which were treasured family heirlooms were smashed or thrown into the sea, and thousands of blankets liberally soaked with precious seal or candle-fish oil were burnt to dust. Even houses were sometimes razed to the ground in these epic feats of conspicuous destruction. The Kwakiutl evidently had money to burn.

These arresting affairs catch the imagination but, inevitably, leave a somewhat nihilist impression. We must not lose sight of

9. See H. A. Powell, 'Cricket in Kiriwina', *Listener*, September 1952, pp. 384–5.

their positive aspects. While their prestige and political implications are quite clear, it is also possible that, prior to the advent of European trade and industry, some guests at some feasts were actually hungry – or at least, if they were not, they came in the hope that their host's menu would include attractive items not available at home. In this vein a number of recent 're-evaluations'[10] of the Potlatch suggest that, although the Kwakiutl certainly enjoyed rich and varied supplies of foods prior to colonization, they were not all equally available in all seasons to all the population. The Potlatch may therefore have alleviated temporary local and seasonal food shortages. It is highly debatable how much this was a really significant feature of the Potlatch.[11] A less controversial feature of the Potlatch is that after prohibition by the whites had driven it underground, its clandestine continuance served as a vehicle for Kwakiutl nationalism.

THE GIFT INDUSTRY AT HOME

Highly coloured though the Potlatch and the Kula may seem, they strike a familiar chord, particularly at the Christmas season. Few of us, however, perhaps realize the full extent of gift-giving in Western societies. Here are some statistics referring to the situation in Britain, taken from an important pioneering study by John Davis.[12] In 1968, £1,140·8 million, or 4·3 per cent of all consumer expenditure in Britain, was devoted to the purchase of gifts, defined as items which once purchased were then involved in further exchanges.[13] £659·7 million (or 1·8 per cent of all manufacturers' sales) was realized by the sale of British made gifts, produced by 120,000 workers on a total wage-bill of £115·7 million

10. For instance S. Piddocke, 'The Potlatch System of the Southern Kwakiutl: A New Perspective', in E. Le Clair and H. K. Schneider (eds), *Economic Anthropology*, Holt, Rinehart & Winston, New York, 1968. The standard earlier study is H. Codere, *Fighting with Property*, Augustin, New York, 1950.

11. See, for instance, P. Drucker and R. Heizer, *To Make My Name Good: Re-examination of the Southern Kwakiutl Potlatch*, University of California Press, 1967.

12. J. Davis, 'Gifts and the U.K. Economy', *Man* (N.S.), vol. 7, 1972, pp. 408–29.

13. Promotional gifts, self-liquidating offers and 'free-gifts', estimated to be worth between £250 million and £340 million in 1967, and not usually involved in further exchanges are excluded in these statistics as are also 'business gifts', and gifts to charities (see Davis, op. cit., p. 412).

and using raw materials worth £193·2 million. As Davis says:
'Even though these figures are underestimates, and cover only
part of the total supply of gifts, they are considerable: the value
of manufacturers' sales is greater than sales by the ship-building
and marine engine industry, and approaches the total sales from
coal mining. In this sense gifts are five times more important in
the economy than all nuts and bolts and screws; forty-five times
more than cement; eighty-six times more than glue.'[14] Expenditure
on reciprocity was equivalent to one-fifth of that spent on food,
one-third of that spent on housing, and half that spent on clothes.

We may also note the strenuous efforts of manufacturers in the
toy and gift industries to combat seasonal fluctuations in their
trade (highest at Christmas); they have been most successful in
the case of die-cast metal model cars, which now sell throughout
the year. Another attempt is the production of naked dolls, with
outfits of clothes intended to be collected in the following months.
The greetings cards industry faces the same problem, and is busily
engaged in inventing new occasions for card-sending – with some
success. It is now possible to purchase in Britain cards bearing the
message 'From my budgie to your budgie'. Here, a trade journal
sagely remarks, 'inarticulateness on the part of the sender is an
important factor in greetings card sales. The verse must express
what the sender wants to say . . .'.[15] The development of cards,
especially Christmas cards, sold for charities has intensified the
commercial producers' drive to open up new markets. This is
vigorously pursued by the Special Days Promotions Committee,
composed of representatives of the greetings cards, cosmetic and
florists trade associations. Perhaps their most notable achievement
to date is the dedication of the second Sunday in October to
grandmothers. Further progress in this direction seems destined
to be frustrated by the attenuated kinship ties of modern urban
societies: how much easier it would all be if the industry were
operating in tribal conditions!

Greetings cards are one of the most unambiguous products of
the gift industry since, almost by definition, they cannot be consumed by the buyer. A few lonely hearts may send themselves

14. J. Davis, op. cit., p. 412.
15. *Retail Business*, vol. 34, 1960, p. 1028.

St Valentine's Day cards, but this can only account for a minute proportion of the cards sold. They are made to give and to be received; their exchange has much the same character as that esoteric 'mystical exchange of off-prints' in which academics engage, sending copies of their seminal works only to those colleagues of whom they approve or seek to influence and from whom they expect a return. None of these curious developments would have surprised Freud. As Ernest Jones recalls, he once jokingly suggested that the most convincing sign of the public acceptance of the new mental science would be the appearance in Viennese shops of special gifts 'for all stages of the transference'!

There is also evidence that sales of gifts in Britain are relatively independent of general market conditions. They may indeed vary inversely, the trade remaining steady or even increasing when sales of other goods decline in times of financial stringency and economic crisis. Such conditions may in fact encourage people to regard 'gifts' as an indirect way of purchasing desirable commodities. So, for instance, I buy my cousin a shirt or tie for Christmas in the expectation that he will reciprocate in kind.

Summing up, therefore, we can agree with Davis that there is indeed evidence of transactions in Britain (and in other industrial societies) forming what we might call a special 'gift economy', with rules and customs different from those of the market economy. Goods are transferred into this gift category from the market, from domestic production, and even by theft and pilfering (having, as we say, 'fallen off the backs of lorries'). More significantly still, it can be shown that the proportion of gift goods in the United Kingdom is of much the same order of magnitude as in traditional societies (such as the Hausa of West Africa, and the Siane of New Guinea) for which comparable quantitative data are available. Such comparisons may surprise us but they would not have surprised Marcel Mauss. In his brilliant *Essay on the Gift*[16] Mauss like Malinowski insisted upon the universal significance of gift-giving; he provided many of the original insights which are now enshrined in the currently fashionable approach

16. Published in French in 1925; English translation: M. Mauss, *The Gift*, Routledge & Kegan Paul, 1969. For some valuable recent thoughts on gift transactions, see R. Firth, *Symbols, Public and Private*, Allen & Unwin, 1973, pp. 368–402.

that treats all social relationships as exchanges, and achieves its most popular and specific middle-class expression in 'encounter groups' expressly formed for this purpose. We are not far from the world of the Potlatch and Kula. But before we attempt to place these exotic phenomena in the most illuminating perspective, we must deal with the more general question of currency.

CURRENCIES

Modern money represents, in the standard view of economists, the ultimate in perfection, the final achievement in a long and arduous evolutionary struggle in which crude and impossibly cumbersome means of exchange are replaced by ever more efficient and more comprehensive procedures. So we have moved from barter to banks and from kind to cash – and beyond. The most primitive or 'pre-currency stage' (to adopt Mrs Hingston Quiggin's quaint phrase) is illustrated by such oddities as the famous 'silent trade', in which retailers trustingly deposit their goods unattended at the road-side and passers-by simply help themselves, leaving an appropriate equivalent. (Mrs Quiggin transports her readers to West Africa to witness this curious spectacle. In fact they need go no further than many newspaper stalls in modern London.)

Economists generally dwell on the excruciating difficulties of direct exchange of commodities; they demonstrate the short-comings of barter by such poignant little tales as the hungry hatter who wanted meat from the butcher, but the butcher was not interested, for he already had a hat and needed shoes. In the absence of general means of exchange (and also, by implication, of credit) neither could help the other. Such discrepancies in de-mand led to more comprehensive and abstract units of account and exchange in the form of a generally accepted currency which could buy more than one commodity. Initially recourse was had to graduated amounts of precious metals such as silver and gold, various commodities being assigned 'values' in terms of weight equivalents. But this was still an elaborate and inconvenient pro-cedure. A further improvement was thus the adoption of actual coins of 'intrinsic' or 'face' value containing an equivalent amount of precious metal and thus, as we would say, 'worth their weight in gold'. Another leap forward was the issue of promissory bank notes which dispensed with the tedious business of carrying heavy money about. Finally, at the very summit of monetary perfection, cheques and other credit facilities were introduced, making transactions even smoother and easier. Such credit, Einzig wittily observes, was a 'substitute for a substitute'.

Drawing largely on our own ethnocentric history, economists tell us money has thus come to assume its modern form, providing a standard of value, a unit of account, a store of wealth, and above all an all-purpose medium of exchange, universally accepted in payment for every good and service. In principle at least, money can buy anything and everything. It is the all-purpose facilitator and open sesame, the completely comprehensive solvent and converter, possessing complete and pure liquidity. No wonder the idea that money 'talks' enjoys such wide circulation. Some indeed would even say it 'sings'; and I have heard rich Egyptians speak of its fragrant smell. Those natural philosophers, the Dogon, share this warm appreciation of liquidity. They believe that their cowrie shell currency was originally employed to exchange words as well as things; so that those who possessed no cowries were actually speechless.

Note that although we may enjoy the benefits conferred by this total transactor, we do not always take full advantage of them. Just as we share the tribal penchant for gift exchange to a surprising degree, so too we indulge in an unexpected amount of barter. It has recently been estimated that up to 50 per cent of international trade in the non-Communist world is conducted by barter for lack of acceptable foreign currency. Currency (and the economy in general) is subject in all modern states (whether socialist or not) to a high degree of state control: it is issued by national banks who also control its exchange rate. Even in our daily domestic transactions there are innumerable instances which show that we often bitterly regret the liquidity of our all-purpose money and seek to make it less perfect and more specific. Thus, we have found it necessary, or at any rate advantageous, to invent a whole series of 'special-purpose' currencies which are specifically designed to limit ordinary money's liquidity, to make it less negotiable. Typical examples are: gift-tokens; book-tokens; luncheon vouchers; trading stamps; and, in times of acute scarcity, rationing coupons. Moreover, specially attractive goods may develop into supplementary commodity currencies when they are in exceedingly short supply. Obvious examples are: nylon stockings in Europe during the Second World War; butter in Germany during the 1922 slump; and, the classic case, cigarettes in prisoner-of-war camps. The 'fringe benefits' earned in business and usually paid in kind rather than cash (such as the company car, house or other facilities – including call-girls) provide a further instance of commodity currencies utilized to supplement money salaries. (They might also of course be regarded as further examples of barter.)

In all these cases potentially distinct economic nexuses are created, which are to a varying extent, sealed off from the all-purpose currency transactions of our market economy. At first sight the ever-expanding range of credit transactions – by cheque, book entry, credit-card etc. which in the Keynesian era represent the ultimate in economic achievement – seem to have the reverse effect. They are presented as discoveries specifically designed to expand and increase liquidity, taking the 'waiting out of wanting'. The blurb introducing these particular credit facilities sets out to capture the client's enthusiasm with a brisk exposition of the classical evolutionary theory of currency – from kind to cash, and from cash to credit. As we have seen, currency becomes more and more ethereal – and eventually so intangible that its actual location and accounting raises metaphysical as well as computer problems.

We have seen that credit, or at least indebtedness is at least as old as currency. Credit cards introduce a further special-purpose money used mainly for prestigious transactions, such as wining and dining friends at expensive restaurants, buying substantial gifts and other luxury goods. In North America, where credit facilities are most developed, cash transactions are increasingly despised. Only poor bums actually pay cash, and credit is a measure of status.

TRADITIONAL CURRENCIES AND SPHERES OF EXCHANGE

These cursory references to some complexities of our own monetary practices offer a convenient perspective from which to view more exotic tribal currencies. In the previous chapter we noticed the widespread use amongst pastoral peoples of livestock as a medium of exchange and store of wealth in various transactions, including marriage-payments and blood-money; blood-money was, in the opinion of Einzig,[17] the ultimate origin of money, which, he argues, began as a unit of exchange and account in payment of reparations for death and injury in inter-tribal wars. Commodity currency is employed among the Somali nomads who operate on a camel-standard, with sheep and goats as small change. Livestock, and paper and coin currency are used interchangeably, with the former (and particularly camels) acting as high units, especially appropriate for prestigious or ceremonial transactions. A man's life is valued at a hundred camels and a woman's at fifty, with conventional money equivalents which, appropriately enough, vary to some extent with the cost of living. Thus the number of camels actually required may be considerably less than the number stipulated, and will in any case depend upon their age and sex. For injuries other than death a complex tariff, graduated according to the severity of the resulting impairment, stipulates the damages that can properly be claimed. A standard smaller unit, regularly employed here in the assessment of substantial damages and also in the collection and division of full blood-money, is the awkward figure of thirty-three-and-a-third camels. This, obviously, is purely a unit of account, which is paid in other currency, such as sheep and goats, or Somali shillings.

This mixed commodity and coin currency is not a recent development, since the Somali nomads have for centuries participated in the wide market-based trade economy connecting Ethiopia and Arabia. While coins and paper money are almost invariably used in the direct purchase of food, clothing and other goods in shops and markets, they may also supplement prestigious transactions where payment is primarily in camels. Equally, camels

17. P. Einzig, *Primitive Money in its Ethnological, Historical and Economic Aspects*, Pergamon Press, 1966.

and other livestock and their produce are regularly sold for cash. This multi-currency situation does not give rise to separate transactional spheres or contexts, each requiring its own special-purpose money, and conversions between one currency and another present little difficulty. Here, as among East African pastoralists, generally,[18] 'the use of cash as a medium of exchange does not displace cattle, since these continue to be depositories of value which earn superior interest by bearing calves and solidifying capital'.

The woven raffia cloth currency of the Lele of Kasai operates in a more restrictive way, according to Mary Douglas.[19] Here the commodity currency is inanimate, inedible and not self-producing and has at first glance more of the qualities of modern money – although it is used as clothing and may wear out. Produced by men and used in a similar fashion to cattle as a prestige currency, it is ultimately backed by (and thus, as it were, issued against) rights in women which, in this African gerontocracy, are monopolized by the elders. The restrictions placed by the Lele on its free convertibility and potentially all-purpose use serve, Douglas argues, to preserve this structure of privilege. Social pressures inhibit men from buying and selling raffia, so that the young wage-earners who are paid in francs find difficulty in converting these into the traditional prestige currency.

There is much variation in the extent to which traditional currencies such as salt blocks, copper and gold dust, iron and other metal pieces, and the ubiquitous cowrie and other shells are or were special-purpose moneys valid only for specific types of transaction. The impersonal, pervasive exchange attributes to which we are accustomed are most pronounced in transactions *outside* a local community or between economically specialized and socially differentiated sections within it. Regional trade involving such currency, as well as direct barter, was especially significant where markets were highly developed institutions organized in chains or networks at different centres on different days of the week as they were in parts of Africa, central America, and China. This

18. H. K. Schneider, 'Economics in East African Aboriginal Societies', in E. LeClair and H. K. Schneider (eds), *Economic Anthropology*, Holt, Rinehart & Winston, New York, 1968.

19. M. Douglas, 'Raffia Cloth Distribution in the Lele Economy', *Africa*, vol. 28, 1958, pp. 109–22.

convenient arrangement still flourishes in contemporary Ethiopia.

It does not follow, however, that the presence of markets necessarily implies the complete monetization of the economy. And the
same currency which in external trade is used for impersonal,
'one-off' transactions may be used in a very different way within
one's own community. This, for instance, is the case with the Lele,
who cheerfully exchange raffia cloth for goods with foreign tribes
but cannily confine its internal use to prestige transactions. Likewise subsistence goods may be sold to strangers, but they are given
free to kin and friends. Again we see the social context imparting
a distinctive character to those transactions which we call economic. Transactions will be most clearly distinguished where each
category or context has its own special-purpose currency. The less
universal money is in purchasing power and exchange function,
the more clearly defined the distinctions between different types
of transaction.

Such distinctions often assume a tripartite pattern, as Raymond
Firth showed long ago in his pioneering analysis of 'spheres of
exchange' in the Polynesian island of Tikopia.[20] The first category
here is the use of food and other subsistence items as rewards for
small services and goods of low value. Next comes more important
transactions in which bark-cloth, coils of sinnet cord and pandanus
mats are used to acquire specialist craft services. The third and
most prestigious nexus concerns transactions with highly prized
possessions such as bonito-fishing hooks (made of shell), cylinders
of turmeric (used for decoration), and canoes – all things usually
held and controlled by chiefs and thus associated with power.
These three sets of goods are normally employed in socially separate contexts; there is no all-embracing medium between the three
spheres of exchange. It is thus, Firth assures us, impossible to
express the value of a bonito-hook in terms of a given quantity of
food; such exchanges are never made and would be regarded as
'fantastic'. However, it is possible to express the approximate
exchange value of a canoe as a bonito-hook, a coil of thick shark
cord, a bundle of bark-cloth and a quantity of food.

A similar pattern of contextually distinguished exchanges, involving goods of different kind and value and with no common

20. R. Firth, *Primitive Polynesian Economy*, Routledge & Kegan Paul, 1939.

denominator for mutual evaluation and conversion, has been well described amongst the Siane of New Guinea where Salisbury [21] again found three transactional nexuses, concerned with sub- sistence goods, 'luxuries', and 'valuables' respectively. The first class are derogatorily described by the Siane as 'nothing things' (an expression recalling the 'nothing-man' or un-person who is the antithesis of the successful political leader or big-man) and include the freely and gladly rendered 'help' which kinsmen offer each other as a matter of course. 'Luxuries' include such 'small things' (here again we follow the local pidgin) as tobacco, palm oil, pandanus nuts, salt, stone axe-blades, palm wood for spears and certain imported European items. All these are owned indi- vidually and exchanged between friends, often in the form of hospitality, without reference to kinship obligations. At the top of this hierarchy of goods and transactions stand the special 'valuables' used only in ceremonial competitive exchange (*gima*) between exogamous groups led by big-men and referred to by the Siane as 'things' – with the implication that these really signify. The transfer of a woman as wife from one group to another is part of this category. Apart from women, these treasured valuables include scarce cassowary feather head-dresses, ornamental stone axes, dog's teeth necklaces, bird of paradise plumes, certain rare shells, and the ubiquitous New Guinea prestige commodity – pigs.

The significance of scarcity as a source of value and purchasing power implicit (and sometimes explicit) in this Siane scheme is illustrated by their treatment of European currency as it has become available through their increasing modern trade and em- ployment. At first, while European coins were still a rare novelty, they were treated as 'valuables' and so assimilated. By the 1950s, however, when some Siane were working as indentured labourers for European concerns, pound notes were considered 'valuables' and shillings and other coins had been demoted to the 'luxury' category. This assignment of notes and coins to these two separ- ate and relatively autonomous spheres naturally reduced the liquidity of the cash acquired by the Siane, since as treasures pounds could not in principle be converted into mere 'luxury' shillings. But, at the same time, the use of European money in

21. R. Salisbury, *From Stone to Steel*, Cambridge University Press, 1963.

external purchases naturally threatened the traditional barriers dividing the three categories. Less ominously, the replacement of their traditional stone axes by more efficient steel axes has revolutionized Siane food production, reducing the time spent on subsistence activities. This has prompted a great expansion of ceremonial exchange, and, as elsewhere in New Guinea and in the classical case of the Potlatch this development has been reinforced by the abolition of traditional warfare, which has stimulated an increased demand for valuables – which the supply of pound notes helps to satisfy. At the same time, the value and 'price' in pounds of traditional valuables has increased with scarcity and inflation and the standard rate of marriage payments has risen sharply. These trends are typical of the way the price of traditional valuables rises with the influx of all-purpose Western money.

The destructive impact of all-purpose money in breaking down the traditional barriers between readily available subsistence and scarce non-subsistence goods in such a 'multi-centric' economy is clearly seen amongst the Tiv people of Nigeria. In the early 1950s erosion had proceeded much further than it had in the period described among the Siane. Like the Siane, the Tiv traditionally had three spheres of exchange. The first comprised subsistence and commercial trading in chickens, goats and sheep, calabashes, baskets, pots, beds, chairs and other household utensils and equipment. The second involved such prestige items as slaves, cattle, horses, ritual positions, cloth, brass-rods, medicines and magic. The third and most highly esteemed concentrated on *people* rather than *things*, especially rights in women and children, but not slaves who were treated as non-people.

The traditional Tiv ethos assumed that like should be tendered for like or, better still, converted into goods of a higher order. Hence conversions upwards (true promotions) from the first sphere to the second, or from the second to the third were strongly approved. Downward conversions were firmly discouraged, and only resorted to in emergencies. Following European colonization, the substitution of money in many transactions, and above all its compulsory adoption as the only legal means of acquiring wives, made conversions between consumer and more valuable goods easy and, in terms of the traditional values, attractive. The ultimate effect, however, was disastrous. The Tiv found a ready cash market for their subsistence foods and other products, using the money acquired to buy valuables and ultimately women. But the supply of women was limited and hence their price soared with demand. The net result of this inflation was that it became more and more costly to marry and less and less easy to live off the land. The Tiv were the victims of both their own traditional economic snobbism and the monetization of their economy. No wonder they were driven to bitterly 'curse money, the Europeans who brought it, and the Ibo traders it brings'.[22] The belief that money is the root of all evil has, deservedly, wide currency.

The three categories of transaction each with its special-purpose currency (or set of goods) evident in these examples can be simplified into a dichotomy between subsistence and non-subsistence goods (compare the old distinction between utilities and luxuries). Luxuries are inevitably less readily obtained than utilities, their supply is limited and often uncertain, and they confer prestige and power on those fortunate enough to possess them. The crucial role of scarcity and unpredictability in supply is seen in David Riches's recent study [23] of the economy of a contemporary Eskimo community at Port Burwell in Canada. In this case, ironically, it was the introduction of all-purpose European money that gave rise to two separate spheres – one based on credit, the other on cash. In both the unit of account is the same – Canadian dollars.

The Eskimos work mainly for a cooperative with its own official retail store which is the only local shop. Payments for fish, furs, or handicrafts supplied to the cooperative are credited to the producer's account, as are cheques in payment of regular or casual work for the cooperative, state welfare, and family and other allowances. Members of the community derive subsidiary cash income from services provided or goods sold directly to visiting Canadians. The cooperative store supplies consumer goods, including rifles and ammunition for hunting. Certain luxury goods – such as fashionable clothes, confectionery and liquor – are not

22. P. and L. Bohannan, *Tiv Economy*, Longman, 1969.

23. D. Riches, 'Cash, Credit and Gambling in a Modern Eskimo Economy', *Man* (N.S.), vol. 10, 1975, pp. 21–33.

available locally, and are obtained externally – in the course of journeys, from mail order firms, Canadian visitors, or supply ships calling at Port Burwell in the summer. The supply of luxuries is scarce and uncertain, and they can only be bought with cash, which further enhances their glamour.

Apart from the minor sources, the primary supplier of cash is the cooperative store itself. But, and here is the rub, the supply of store cash is doubly restricted: first, there is not enough ready cash to meet the total local demand for it; second, available cash is not freely disbursed, since the ease and extent of issue varies with the state of each client's account. The greater the deficit in a client's account, the poorer his prospects of obtaining a cash advance. In these circumstances most people are perpetually short of cash and, whenever they are in a position to do so, charge articles to their account.

The internal 'local store goods sphere', as we may call it, thus operates principally on credit, while the external luxury trade depends on cash, and both are intimately connected, since the main source of cash for external luxuries is supplied by the co-operative store credit. The two contexts are also linked by another very important activity – gambling. This assumes two forms. Gambling with cards (usually a form of rummy) where success depends on skill as well as chance is restricted to the permanent settlement. Here the stakes consist of cash and/or bullets. In the smaller hunting camps where cooperation is at a premium, gambling with a spinning-top is more dependent on chance alone. The stakes in this case consist usually only of bullets. Rifles of various calibres are used in hunting, and ammunition for the heavier weapons is more costly and sometimes less readily available locally than that for the lighter arms. The store maintains large stocks of ·22 bullets which are sold at two cents each and usually bought in boxes of fifty. Heavier calibre ·222 and ·308 bullets cost between twenty-five and thirty cents each. In spinning-top gambling the following equivalents apply:

five ·22 = one heavy bullet = 25 cents

These rates reflect the scarcity of and demand for heavy ammunition. Ammunition of various calibres may be pooled in a single stake. Both types of gambling clearly distribute supplies of bullets and cash amongst the community, in the case of cash bridging the cash–credit spheres. Players with cash stake it to gain prestige, those without it stake bullets in the hope of winning money. (Players who lose all their stakes in a game are most appropriately described by the term applied to a man falling through thin ice.) Cash remains a scarce and highly prized resource. Because the money supply is totally inadequate, cash not credit functions as a status symbol and is thus given honorary local status as a special-purpose money protected from ordinary transactions.

We may now return to a final glance at the Kula and Potlatch. From our new perspective, we can see the Kula valuables are an extreme form of a 'special-purpose' currency operating in a rigidly defined nexus of prestige and power where their exchange creates and maintains relations of inequality. If Malinowski is correct, the uniqueness of the system lies in the absence of conversions of the kind we have encountered elsewhere. This appears to be the hall-mark of the exclusive and unique status accorded to the Kula valuables by the Trobriand islanders; they are intrinsically quite useless. By contrast (with the partial exception of the Coppers), in the Potlatch it is by withdrawing commodities (canoes, oil, blankets etc.) from ordinary use, by restricting their circulation, that value is created. The ultimate expression of this process is their final, conspicuous destruction. This is the most complete and irreversible conversion on which there is no going back. It is, as Georges Gurvitch has eloquently put it, a transition from 'having to being', and hence, we might add, the socio-economic equivalent of the mass–energy equation in physics.

TRIBUTE

Thus we come naturally to tribute, which is a symbolic statement in tangible terms of loyalty and submission. Tribute binds its recipient to its donors, setting up and maintaining the relation-ship of mutual dependence between superior and subordinate. Indebted as he is to his tribute-bearing followers, the superior must make an appropriate return. So among the Kachins of Burma, who have an acute understanding of these transactions, those who pay tribute are considered literally to possess debts (that is credit) against the account of the chiefs who receive it. And amongst the Ethiopian Amharan peasantry, the payment of tribute (in grain, salt bars, Maria Theresa dollars etc.) is traditionally regarded as a privilege confirming their (*rist*) title to land, for which people are quite prepared to die. In this idiom, when the hospitable largesse which they considered a chief owed them was not readily forthcoming, Bemba used to say : 'We will shake the tree until it gives up its fruit.'

Those who tender tribute have at the very least a right to overall protection and hospitable largesse. The crucial questions all follow from this. What are the local, culturally and historically specific expectations on each side? How are they honoured in practice? To what extent does the client derive benefit from his subordination? What proportion of tribute is converted into resources of direct value to the subordinate classes? And, connected with these, how clear-cut and unbridgeable is the distinction between those who give tribute and those who receive it? Finally, to what extent are differences in the character and quality of tribute, and the rules governing its return related to social and cultural distinctions between the two parties?

In pursuing this last question we shall touch on some of the others in a provisional and schematic way, returning to them in later chapters on political institutions. If we place variations in such transactions along a spectrum of increasing complexity and indirectness in the relation between the tribute paid and the return received, the exchanges typical of New Guinea big-men are at the egalitarian pole. These aggressive Melanesian leaders rise above their clansmen and neighbours by their enterprise in procuring gifts (which must be returned at equivalent rates) and in organizing feasts at which their accumulated stock is generously disbursed. They have to give and give again to cling precariously to their unstable and constantly threatened dominance. As with the rotating ritual offices characteristic of Latin American peasant society, in these fiercely egalitarian conditions men pay dearly for the privilege of leadership and risk losing more than they gain in the process. A more formalized structure of leadership and exchange exists among the Trobriand Islanders, where free-floating power has hardened into a hereditary endowment, and tribute has acquired a dominant place in the broader category of gifts. Here the chief stands at the centre of a web of redistribution, acting like some rustic captain of a cottage industry, or in Malinowski's phrase a tribal banker, directing the economic affairs of his followers. A further step takes us to the more hierarchical system of Tikopia where in theory if not always in practice chiefs are entitled to a more pervasive managerial role.[24]

In the more elaborately organized kingdoms of east and central Africa and, *a fortiori* in the vast Ethiopian empire, we find populations sometimes of millions rather than thousands presided over by a redistributing chief (or king or emperor), who is regarded as a public servant, conscientiously shouldering the terrible burdens of his high and responsible office and rendering his tribute-bearing subjects a bountiful return in public feasts, protection, the settlement of disputes – good government and care in the widest sense. Here the ruler is, in theory at any rate, ultimately a trustee, paternalistically administering a great national estate for the benefit of all. But of course there are trustees and trustees, and who is to determine the appropriate rate for the job? As their relative affluence in all kinds of wealth demonstrates, the rulers of some tribal chiefdoms and states have unquestionably enjoyed a much higher standard of living than their subjects while still operating within this redistributive rubric. Impressed by the tribesman's entrenched land rights and viewing things from the capital, some studies of African kingdoms present an unduly rosy picture of chiefly generosity and beneficence, minimizing the potentially crushing impact of compulsory tribute, *corvée* labour service, and other exactions. So, for example, it is not always easy to reconcile Gluckman's memorable portrayal of the pomp and splendour of kingship amongst the Lozi of central Africa with the levelling egalitarianism that he insists makes the king in essence a man of the people and of the soil which he has himself to till and sow.

Evans-Pritchard offers a very different assessment of the balance of privilege in the traditional Zande state. He states clearly and

24. R. Firth, *We, the Tikopia*, Allen & Unwin, 1936 and *Social Change in Tikopia*, Allen & Unwin, 1960.

unequivocally that the ruling Avongara élite, whom he describes as an 'exclusive caste', took 'no part in the production of food, other than the killing of an occasional beast, and relied for the necessities of life on the labour and tribute of commoners'.[25] Perhaps the most tangible benefits commoners received in return were spears (used as a currency in marriage payments, as well as in battle) and female captives from the many wars into which they were led by their bellicose rulers. The balance of advantage between tributary and chief is equally plain in the great traditional west African empires. The 'Black Byzantium' which Nadel [26] invoked to convey the intricate system of economic and political inequality in Nupe fits, with suitable modifications, the Hausa states, the famous Ashanti federation, Dahomey, Benin and the Yoruba kingdoms.[27] In these cases a wide gulf in economic resources and power is founded on and maintained by the tribute system, as it is in the Shan states of Burma and in other traditional Asian polities.

Only the largest of these traditional states are strictly comparable with the classical despotic empires of the East or those of the Incas and Aztecs of the New World. But whatever their size, they all belong at the extreme 'redistributive' end in our rough-and-ready spectrum of types of exchange. Here the balance of economic advantage is so overwhelmingly tipped in favour of the ruling redistributive élite that many social anthropologists share the feudal historians' anxiety to find justification for the spoils and privilege of office in the services provided by the aristocracy. Extreme inequality may prompt apologists to extreme rationalizations, as for instance, when it is argued (as it often has been and still in effect is in South Africa) that the primary beneficiaries of slavery are slaves !

Any worthwhile assessment of the profit and loss account between rulers and ruled in such highly stratified caste conditions must include a careful, quantitative examination of the management of resources *over time*, preferably in bad as well as good

25. E. Evans-Pritchard, *Witchcraft, Oracles and Magic among the Azande*, Oxford University Press, 1937, p. 16.

26. S. Nadel, *A Black Byzantium*, Oxford University Press, 1942.

27. For accessible accounts of these west African states see D. Forde and P. Kaberry (eds), *West African Kingdoms in the Nineteenth Century*, Oxford University Press, 1967.

seasons. One of the most illuminating and well-documented cost-benefit studies is Scarlett Epstein's analysis[28] of the flow of goods and services between land-owning farmers and their Untouchable labourers in the villages of Mysore province in southern India. This inter-caste *jajmani* relationship, mentioned in the previous chapter, is assimilated into a kinship tie, the dominant land-holder addressing his client farmhand familiarly as 'old son'.

The non-Brahmin farming caste themselves participate in the actual work of cultivation, as Brahmins often do in other parts of India. In bad seasons each land-owner's share of the crop is no greater than the annual reward due to each of his Untouchable clients. In good seasons the Untouchable labourer again receives the same amount, but the owner receives his bad-season share *plus* all the surplus. This unequal distribution of profit in bountiful years enables the farming caste to sustain a superior life-style in which generosity and conspicuous consumption play an important role. Hence, Epstein says, '... it was the expectation of good harvests which induced the master to accept in bad years a share equal to the annual rewards his labourers received, whereas the continued threat of bad harvests induced the Untouchable labourers to accept a reward which did not vary according to the labour performed or according to the abundance of the harvest.' What promised security for the Untouchables provided limited and intermittent prosperity for the land-owners. Since a similar pattern of dependence appears elsewhere in rural India, we may conclude that in Indian villages generally survival was the crucial issue; therefore land-owners had come to adopt a system of production aimed at meeting their needs in lean years rather than short-term profit. In traditional systems of redistributive exchange, the ultimate test of good faith and paternalistic *noblesse oblige* is the extent to which the lowliest can count on support and succour in time of need. When drought and famine strike what help can the peasant expect from his master? What, in such critical circumstances, have his regular payments of tribute secured? Unfortunately these are not academic questions; they are vital issues

28. S. Epstein, 'Productive Efficiency and Customary Systems of Rewards in Rural South India', in R. Firth (ed.), *Themes in Economic Anthropology*, Tavistock, 1967.

which the endemic poverty and insecurity of many Third World countries pose with increasing insistence.

PEASANTS

The commonest tribute-paying category in world history is that generally known as the 'peasantry' – a rural proletariat producing their own food and feeding others as well. 'Peasants', on this definition, belong to the more complex traditional empires or modern states, which are larger and have more political and economic differentiation than 'tribal' societies in the strict sense. The precise location of the transition point between tribesmen and peasants, however, is as difficult to determine as that between the corresponding traditional political systems. Most anthropologists and sociologists, like historians, would probably emphasize the hierarchical web of economic and political exchanges in which peasants produce food, while relying on others for some goods and services. They are not self-sufficient subsistence cultivators, and it is their dependence on others in the wider politico-economic system that makes them vulnerable to exploitation, creating in unfavourable conditions chronic insecurity. Whether they live by tilling the soil, fishing, or even by selling their labour, peasants are forced to exchange a substantial proportion of their produce to meet their own subsistence and other commitments.

This economic and political cleavage, separating the peasant from society around him, is further reinforced to varying degrees by cultural distinctions. Generally, it is at least possible (although not always very enlightening) to distinguish between the peasant sub- or 'folk' culture and the sophisticated culture of the dominant élite who possess a monopoly of knowledge and learning. In literate cultures, the distinction coincides broadly with that between those who can and cannot read and write. Where urban centres exist (as many would argue they must for these contrasts to hold good), this distinction corresponds to that between country and town. All these contrasts are implied in Robert Redfield's well-known dichotomy between the 'little' and the 'big' tradition.[29]

29. R. Redfield, *The Little Community*, University of Chicago Press, Chicago, 1955.

But the extent to which we can usefully aggregate common features characteristic of folk tradition everywhere, and so create a cross-culturally valid 'culture of peasantry', is another matter – and one to which we shall return in a moment. This is all the more pertinent today as the term peasant has shed its traditional pejorative connotations to become, in the Che Guevara style, the revolutionary rallying cry of oppressed masses.

In traditional circumstances before the industrial revolution, in Europe, Japan, China, and the Spanish and Portuguese colonies in America, the peasant masses were – as in our Indian and Rwandan examples – linked to their politically dominant masters through specific, mutually binding relationships. These relationships, usually institutionalized in the form of patronage, were as we have seen many-sided (or 'multi-stranded'): the economic component was only one element in a comprehensive connection with far-reaching social and political implications. And, as we have been insisting, the saving grace of this obviously exploitative 'lop-sided friendship' (to use Julian Pitt-Rivers's expression) was the measure of protection, however limited, that the peasant derived from it. So long as traditional values held sway, the patron was bound to extend his patronage to his client, and to do business with him rather than with someone else. Modernization and fuller involvement in a monetized cash economy have had varying impacts on such traditional protective devices, as we shall see.

First let us frankly recognize that no people mentioned in this book now exist as a hermetically sealed economic and political isolate, whatever the case when anthropologists first studied them. All participate, to varying degrees, in wider economic and political systems which are in turn involved in the vast market system of international and largely monetized trade. However reluctantly, or eagerly, they are all engaged in market transactions employing all-purpose money. In this sense all tribal societies which retain a significant rural base are now peasant societies – some, of course, more so than others. Even if the first intrusive European traders utilized local special-purpose currencies, colonization rapidly created a demand for cash with which to pay the foreign usurper's head or poll-tax (in some areas deliberately imposed to encourage tribesmen to sell their labour), to purchase exotic new commodities (often initially as status symbols), and, as we saw amongst the Kwakiutl and Siane, as a means of expanding traditional ceremonial activiṭies.

In some cases, this was achieved by turning a traditional cultivated plant into a cash crop and expanding production, as with American cocoa, Ethiopian coffee, or Asian rice, or new crops for which a world demand existed, were introduced, local subsistence cultivators simply becoming peasant farmers. Elsewhere, and especially in the more highly exploitative European colonies with their substantial settler populations, cash was obtained by selling one's labour either to European plantation farmers (as in India, south-east Asia generally, Oceania and parts of Africa) or to European industries such as the copper and gold-mining concerns in central and southern Africa and Latin America. The consequent growth of wage labour promoted an increased demand for agricultural produce in the markets which local peasant farmers met by expanding production. Cash-cropping for the external market, rivalling the European plantations, also grew up where it was allowed by the colonial authorities. At the exploitative extreme, 'dual' colonial economies thus developed; the subsidiary, supportive and partly monetized peasant sector produced food for the labour force of export industries whose profits passed in the main to shareholders in the metropolitan state. Clifford Geertz has convincingly demonstrated how such a pattern of exploitative extraction in Dutch Java was underwritten by the astonishing elasticity of traditional wet rice cultivation, which provided an almost limitless supply of food for the rapidly growing labour force.[30]

This is perhaps an extreme case. Yet it is an irony of history that what we optimistically call 'the march of progress' or 'modernization' which willy-nilly transforms subsistence cultivators into peasants also regularly aggravates the plight of *existing* peasant producers. This unfortunate outcome is especially marked in the capitalist states of contemporary Latin America, although it also occurs in communist states, where the collectivization of individual peasant farms has replaced one set of masters by another

---

30. C. Geertz, *Agricultural Involution: The Process of Ecological Change in Indonesia*, University of California Press, 1970.

with more exacting standards and more sophisticated measures of efficiency. Peasants are casualties not only of capitalism. Wherever the intensification of commerce creates new demands on them, they face two alternatives. With the aid of new farming techniques, or simply by working harder, they must obtain higher yields. Failing that, they have no option but to consume less and exchange more. Like the Cossacks in Tsarist Russia, Latin American peasants who are fortunate enough to own land, often hold pathetically tiny small-holdings (*minifundia*) and are compelled to supplement their return from these meagre resources by working for large, cash-crop enterprises. Such 'penny capitalists', as Sol Tax writing of Guatemala calls them,[31] thus regularly supply an important part of the labour force on the large *latifundia* estates and plantations often owned by banks or property companies.

Such conditions aggravate the peasant's fatalistic dependence on forces totally outside his control. Eric Wolf observes:[32]

... when the peasant arrangements for the exchange of commodities become part of the market system, the market affects not merely the peasant's produce, and the goods and services he can command with it, but his very factors of production as well. It may attach prices not merely to pots and ploughshares and potatoes, but also to land and labour, the two factors which grant him a measure of autonomy in a context of asymmetrical relationships.

Such limited anchorage as these afford is, moreover, further eroded by the exorbitant claims made by rapacious money lenders who are only too anxious to help the peasant when he desperately needs ready cash. No wonder what is so inadequately described as 'peasant indebtedness' bulks so large in accounts of peasant life.[33]

The peasant's miserable lot is aggravated by his powerlessness, chronic insecurity, and risks which jeopardise his very existence. These capricious forces figure strongly in what many anthropologists take to be the characteristic 'peasant world-view', which has

31. S. Tax, *Penny Capitalism*, U.S. Government Printing Office, Washington D.C., 1953.
32. E. Wolf, *Peasants*, Prentice-Hall, 1966, p. 48.
33. See, for instance, R. Firth and B. Yamey, *Capital, Savings and Credit in Peasant Societies*, Allen & Unwin, 1964.

been most succinctly delineated by George Foster [34] in terms of the 'image of limited good'. Drawing on his own experience in Mexican villages, Foster considers that the peasant sees his position 'as one in which all of the desired things in life such as land, wealth, health, friendship and love, manliness and honour, respect and status, power and influence, security and safety, exist in finite quantity and are always in short supply'. Such a view of the world, moreover, well accords with the highly egalitarian and competitive character of life in communities where there is much rivalry and conflict between independent households linked by dyadic (person-to-person) relationships of friendship, marriage, and fictive [35] rather than true kinship. Ties of the same sort connect individual families and groups of families to powerful patrons *outside* the local community.

The wide variation in the structure of peasant societies demonstrates, however, that there is no specific or uniquely 'peasant' social organization. The various kinds of faction or 'coalition' which Wolf distinguishes [36] occur in many different forms and combinations and do not readily lead to any simple typology of peasant societies. The vigilant reader will also have noticed how the spectre of 'limited good', which Foster finds haunting peasants, is just as familiar to tribesmen, and under appropriate conditions to all men everywhere.[37] Here, as in other milieux, the crucial factor is uncertainty. We have stressed how tribesmen typically confront captious and hostile environments, yet those of peasants are scarcely much better: and the potential benefit of the few additional amenities which they may possess is diminished by their correspondingly more acute economic and political insecurity.

These are unpalatable facts of life – not bizarre fantasies – and, as a number of recent studies affirm, influence the response of peasant communities to development opportunities in ways which

34. G. Foster, 'Peasant Society and the Image of Limited Good', *American Anthropologist*, vol. 67, 1965, pp. 293–315.

35. This is usually known by the term *compadrazgo* meaning co-parenthood (i.e. the relation between a parent and his child's godparent) which is employed in the Catholic countries of southern Europe and Latin America. See below, p. 236.

36. E. Wolf, *Peasants*, Prentice-Hall, 1966, pp. 81ff.

37. Cf. pp. 148–51.

are perfectly sensible and easily comprehended if one knows the local situation adequately. Here, as in so many other contexts where international 'experts' recoil in baffled bewilderment, the inadequacy lies with them rather than their clients. Those who doubt this should consult Sutti Ortiz's sensitive analysis [38] of decision-making among Indian peasant coffee-farmers in Colombia. 'Peasants,' she reminds us, 'are not endowed with a different soul or a different perception of the world from ours.' Hence, 'if they behave differently, if they shy away from recommended policies it is because they are either less informed about certain events, or perhaps better informed about the realities of their physical, social and economic world than we are'. As R. H. Tawney long ago observed: 'Civilized people are disposed both to underestimate the part played by economic rationalism in primitive society and to exaggerate that which it plays in their own.'

ENTREPRENEURS

Recent developments in the Mysore villages referred to earlier throw interesting light on how people react to and take advantage of technological and economic changes, and thus show the crucial significance of that archetypal innovatory figure, the entrepreneur. In one village where traditional *jajmani* ties were strong, the introduction of irrigation farming entailed the replacement of wooden by iron ploughs. The maintenance and repair of the new ploughs required correspondingly more skill and labour. This consequently greatly increased the work of the village blacksmith who, not unreasonably, asked his patrons for an appropriate increase in his traditional reward. Although they were producing larger harvests with the new equipment, the farmers refused this request on the grounds that the blacksmith's customary return was sufficient. However, the blacksmith, as persistent as he was enterprising, continued to press his case, and eventually an ingenious solution was found. The blacksmith recruited a younger relative from another village to carry on repairing the old wooden ploughs while he devoted himself to the new machines. On this understanding, the high-caste farmers agreed to pay their forceful

38. S. Ortiz, *Uncertainties in Peasant Farming: A Colombian Case*, Athlone Press, 1973.

blacksmith in cash for maintenance and repair work on their new equipment. Since both farmers and blacksmith were now working within the cash economy the farmers, like capitalist entrepreneurs, were now prepared to pay extra for a new service associated with higher crop yields.

In this case the impetus for change seems to have come mainly from the blacksmith, whose highly successful further business ventures (including building work) showed his personal energy and initiative. New technology has a crucial role within the framework of the wider money economy in disengaging people from traditional relationships and freeing them to branch out in new directions; this is further seen in the development of sugar-cane farming in the same region of India. Since this was a new crop, land-owners and labourers were prepared to experiment, and ultimately to accept novel agricultural methods. The constraints which discourage the application of new techniques to traditional crops were absent, and farmers found no difficulty in employing labourers on a daily cash basis. And, as with capitalist enterprises in general, the size of the labour force varied with wage rates and marginal productivity. As Epstein puts it: 'Since the problem of the subsistence for the village population was taken care of by the system of hereditary labour relations, a ... farmer could operate in spheres outside the customary system like any "rational" employer in an industrial society: he attempted to maximize his returns by equating marginal returns with marginal costs.' [39] Professor Epstein goes on to make a point of cardinal importance in development planning, that people often respond more favourably to an entirely novel source of food or wage labour than to an expansion or intensification of existing and all-too-familiar subsistence techniques. However, such radical initiatives only pay off sometimes, and it is not easy to forecast when they will succeed.

The entrepreneur is by definition an innovator who can turn a situation of unfulfilled potential demand to his profit. His originality, for which he seeks the highest possible reward as compensation for his risk and ingenuity, lies in perceiving an unexploited

39. S. Epstein, 'Productive Efficiency and Customary Systems of Rewards in Rural South India', in R. Firth (ed.), *Themes in Economic Anthropology*, Tavistock, 1967, p. 239.

opportunity, in seeing his chance and taking it. And if the entre-preneur is the apostle of marginal profit, it is entirely appropriate that we often find him in a socially marginal position. For his genius lies in forging a link, which he then seeks to monopolize, between previously unconnected circuits. The successful entre-preneur brings together goods, services and people in a happy and mutually satisfying conjunction, so far as possible on his own terms. As we have already observed, this job specification applies with embarrassing accuracy to the social anthropologist. It is also frequently encountered in the academic world at large. There, 'inter-disciplinary' or 'cross-disciplinary' activities offer consider-able scope to those who are prepared to strike boldly from the security of one subject across frontiers into another – ideally one that their own professional colleagues find difficult yet esteem. Successful brazen entrepreneurial strokes may actually produce new hybrid disciplines like economic history, social psychology, or trans-cultural psychiatry.

As our Indian example suggests, a really successful entrepreneur needs to be able to discard traditional inhibitions and moral im-pediments – either by operating in a new medium (such as money) or in a novel social context. It has often been observed that those at the apex and the lowest point of a hierarchical system are both in a sense less committed, less loyal, and hence more open to new opportunities than the mass of society in between. So it is some-times argued that the mercantile élite in contemporary Britain had more to gain and less to lose than the public at large by entry into the European Economic Community. Those at the top are peculiarly well placed to forge profitable links with their counter-parts elsewhere.

So, to return to tribal examples, the New Guinea big-men who only achieve prominence by their skill as manipulators are the very epitome of the entrepreneur; when colonial rule swept them into the wider money economy they responded in the way we would anticipate. Amongst the Siane and in other New Guinea communities, big-men became bigger by mediating between their followers and the new authorities, engaging, at the same time, in more and more elaborate ceremonial exchanges. European rule in Africa and elsewhere placed the leaders of traditional hierarchical tribes in much the same position. Initially, and subsequently particularly where the British applied the formula of 'indirect rule', chiefs became mediators in the new colonial economic and political order. The most ambitious and least scrupulous, and also those most willing to chance their luck, sought to maximize their personal profit from their role as go-betweens, bridging the awkward gap separating their traditional culture and values from those of their new rulers. Since the colonial authorities were at the start largely ignorant of the local social structure and system of values, chiefs could often exert considerable leverage. In the long run, as we shall see in a later chapter, they were liable to be caught in the middle of the ensuing tug-of-war between the European authorities and the mass of tribesmen.

In tribal and peasant societies, as elsewhere, ethnic minorities[40] with their own introvert culture and morality – including the crucial factor of mutual trust – have, like the Jews in Europe, specialized in speculative entrepreneurial services, cleverly initiating, as Barth puts it,[41] 'bridging transactions' to exploit 'points in an economic system where the discrepancies of evaluation are greatest'. The point at issue is very simple. It is much easier to extort high rates of profit from people to whom one is in no way morally bound. Kinship and friendship discourage, if they do not altogether prevent, more extreme exploitation. These factors are by no means a monopoly of traditional societies. By way of conclusion here we should add, as I hope the foregoing discussion clearly indicates, that we may assume universalistic economic principles and hence endorse the 'formalist'[42] rather than 'substantivist' approach (the latter assuming that economic transactions are inevitably qualitatively different in traditional and industrial societies). As we have sought to emphasise, politics and culture everywhere colour economics; market principles nowhere operate in a free state.[43]

40. For an interesting analysis of many examples, see A. Cohen, *Two Dimensional Man*, Routledge & Kegan Paul, 1974.

41. F. Barth, 'Economic Spheres in Darfur', in R. Firth (ed.), *Themes in Economic Anthropology*, Tavistock, 1967.

42. See eg R. Firth (ed.), *Themes in Economic Anthropology*, Tavistock, 1967; E. LeClair, 'Economic Theory and Economic Anthropology', *American Anthropologist*, 1962, 1179–1203; R. F. Salisbury, *Vunamimi: economic transformation in a traditional society*, Berkeley, University of California Press, 1970.

43. The classic statement here is K. Polanyi, C. W. Arensberg and H. W. Pearson, *Trade and Market in the early empires*, Glencoe, Free Press, 1957. See also M. Sahlins, *Stoneage Economics*, Chicago, Aldine, 1972.

Chapter Eight
Vital Statistics: Marriage and Kinship

MARRIAGE AND KINSHIP

Men, as we have seen, regard women as the highest form of good, the most precious of all currencies. Women are the means of payment for the highest price that can be paid. Women have a unique value as the source of men's posterity. The reproductive function is regulated by marriage which ensures that men relinquish their sisters in exchange for those of other men, following that unmistakable mark of humanity – the incest prohibition. Marriage makes woman the characteristic, indeed primordial, go-between and the natural target for the ambivalent attributes ascribed to the professional mediator; this is reflected in the stereotypes assigned to the female role by different cultures.

Our first concern is to distinguish between marriage and its consequences. Marriage directly establishes affinal relationships between the kin of the bride and groom; ideally it also produces offspring and hence provides the ideological principle of 'descent', that is, socially recognized common parentage or 'blood relationship'. Marriage thus gives rise to the fundamental social unit of two siblings, one of whom is married, the spouse and their child:[1]

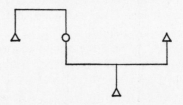

If descent through the father is stressed, children take their identity from him rather than their mother. Yet, at the same

1. In kinship diagrams, triangles represent males and circles females. Ties between siblings (brothers and sisters) are represented by⌐⎯⎯⎯⎤, and marriage by ⌊⎯⎯⎯⌋

time, they are also matrilaterally related by 'blood', as we would say, to the mother. Their patrilineal affiliation makes them in addition affines of their mother. Where descent through the mother is emphasized, the converse applies, producing a system of matrilineal kinship in which a child is at once both *affinally* and *patrilaterally* related to his father and to the father's kin.

The difference between kinship and affinity can be easily understood in our terms. In English we distinguish 'mother', a kinswoman, from 'mother-in-law', an affine, and imply *inter alia* that the corresponding norms of behaviour vary. So in English kinship, kin are related by descent, affines by marriage. Different cultures, and more significantly perhaps, individuals in different situations, stress one relationship at the expense of the others. Sometimes a man turns to his mother's patrilineal clan, appealing to their common matrilateral relationship. In other circumstances, the affinal rather than the blood relationship is emphasized.

Among the Gisu of Uganda, people are closely related by marriage and distantly connected by descent, and marriage relationships take priority for, as they forthrightly put it : 'in affinity there is no kinship'.[2] The Jaffna Tamils of Sri Lanka are even more absolutist. In their view marriage unites a bride with her husband in the fullest possible sense, making the couple indeed 'of one flesh'. Here the bride's position is the same as that of the children she will bear her husband. As they do, she takes as her first name her husband's last name and she is just as much part and parcel of her husband's substance as they are. Marriage severs her relationship with her own kin. Both the wife and her children have no bodily connection with her brother and his kin. They are not blood relatives, not kin, merely affines. For a woman Jaffna marriage is literally a transubstantiation.[3] The Wik-Mungkan Aborigines of Australia, according to David McKnight,[4] have arrived at a more balanced appreciation of the ties which flow from marriage. They cherish both the affinal and matrilateral re-

2. J. La Fontaine, 'Gisu Marriage and Affinal Relations', in M. Fortes (ed.), *Marriage in Tribal Societies*, Cambridge University Press, 1962.

3. K. David, 'Until Marriage Do Us Part: A Cultural Account of Jaffna Tamil Categories for Kinsmen', *Man* (N.S.), vol. 8. 1973, pp. 521-35.

4. D. McKnight, 'Sexual Symbolism of Food among the Wik-Mungkan', *Man* (N.S.), vol. 8, 1973, pp. 144-209.

lationship, treating their *elder* mother's brother as a kinsman, and his *younger* brother as an affine.

DESCENT

In its widest sense descent simply means to be related through a common ancestor. It is important to distinguish recognized or *de jure* descent from unrecognized or *de facto* descent. Recognized descent covers common ancestral origins which are known, respected, and employed for a variety of purposes; descent may become a basic principle of social organization on which many vital rights, duties and interests turn. It may even be extended to include people who are strictly not true kin. By a convenient fiction, they may be transformed into kinsfolk and assimilated within the community's common ancestry. Since they are treated as kin they become kin. To take a more tenuous case, British children sometimes call close friends of their parents 'uncles' and 'aunts', and these honorary relatives respond in the appropriate manner. In a much less casual way, the Catholic institution of god-parentage (*compadrazgo*), modelled upon the 'holy nuclear family' (Father, Son, and Blessed Virgin),[5] turns potential friends and allies into spiritual or ritual relatives. Baptism (or confirmation) establishes two relationships of approximately equal importance between godparent and godchild, and between godparent and parent (*compadres*). Friends are made by persuading people to assume a kinship (or quasi-kinship) role.

These themes are nowhere more brilliantly or subtly explored than in Mario Puzo's masterpiece *The Godfather*. As the wise old mafia leader and 'godfather', Don Corleone, explains as he lectures his negligent pop-star godson, Johnny Fontane: 'Friendship is more than talent. It is more than government. It is almost the equal of family. Never forget that. If you had built up a wall of friendships you wouldn't have to ask me for help.' There is no question of Don Corleone refusing help, for the constant flood of requests he receives from his vast circle of godchildren and their

5. See S. Gudeman, 'The Compadrazgo as a reflection of the natural and spiritual person', *Proceedings of the Royal Anthropological Institute*, 1971, pp. 45–72 and J. Pitt-Rivers, 'The Kith and the Kin', in J. Goody (ed.), *The Character of Kinship*, Cambridge University Press, 1974, pp. 89–105.

relatives is a flattering tribute to his power and honour. Don Corleone is only too ready to be of service and feels grievously offended if those who are entitled to his help do not request it.

Conversely, actual, existing and traceable kinship connections may be taken little notice of or ignored. Many people in small in-bred communities are *de facto* kin without knowing it or choosing to emphasize it. British people can readily explore their pedigrees at Somerset House, and then discover that their relatives are far more numerous than they had supposed. Few people actually do this, suggesting that, unlike many tribesmen, they are not very descent-conscious.

Yet extended kinship ties are still very much alive and play a significant role in many European peasant societies and in immigrant communities in industrial cities. Such minority out-groups enjoy a well-earned reputation for 'clannishness'; ties of common descent can, as we have already seen, provide a base for highly successful enterprises in the formally anonymous world of modern commerce. Family firms of merchant bankers are a good example, to say nothing of such world-famous kinship businesses as the mafia.[6] In a world of cut-throat competition, where no one is to be trusted, it is appropriate to rely on the most natural and binding of all human ties.

MARRIAGE

Whatever weight kinship is asked to bear and however it is traced, its ultimate source is marriage. Here there are two contrasting opinions, one expressed by George Bernard Shaw, the other by the Catholic Church. Shaw argued that marriage exists to legitimize sex – of course he was writing before the use of birth control became widespread. More far-sightedly, the Catholic Church maintains that marriage exists to legitimize children, to provide legitimate heirs and successors and to securely establish their social identity. In this case tribal societies and our own recent experience suggest that the Catholic Church is right and Shaw wrong. Marriage is concerned above all with children; we shall

6. See F. A. J. Ianni, *A Family Business: Kinship and Social Control in Organized Crime*, Routledge & Kegan Paul, 1972.

consider its other functions later. But how to choose partners? Who is appropriate? What restrictions, if any, are placed on personal choice?

Assuming that unions between the closest kin are excluded by incest prohibitions, there are basically three possibilities:

1. One can marry whom one likes.
2. One must marry *outside* one's own immediate group.
3. One must marry *inside* one's own immediate group.

The second policy (out-marriage, or exogamy) is common when the members of a group are already strongly united and feel little need for further social integration. It is less profligate and more economical to win friends and influence people elsewhere. In many different cultures this policy is rationalized in the motto 'we marry our enemies', which evokes such images as the romantic stranger, marriage by capture, and even rape. What Kate Millet[7] aptly calls 'the old phallic fantasy of shoot and screw' is, alas, much nearer the mark than the poetic exhortation: 'Make love not war. Lay, not slay.' In the spirit of the former rather than the latter, lineages and clans are often, although not always, fiercely exogamous, taking brides from those they habitually fight. Where this is so, we frequently find that in-marriage is discouraged by a definition of incest that precludes marriage within the group.

The incest taboo applied in this way promotes out-marriage rather than outlaws sex. Sexual intercourse, and more especially marriage, between primary kin such as siblings, or parents and children, would doubtless 'complicate' family life as many anthropologists, unconsciously following St Augustine, have argued. This helps to explain why, in certain lineage-based societies, sexual relations between a man and the wife of another member of the lineage are treated as a form of incest, subject to strong 'group-wife' prohibitions.[8] The self-denying ordinance forbidding mating with one's own womenfolk makes them available to the men of other groups. The exchange of women between groups

7. K. Millett, *Sexual Politics*, Hart-Davis, 1971.
8. J. Goody, 'A Comparative Approach to Incest and Adultery', *British Journal of Sociology*, vol. 7, 1956, pp. 286–305.

enables marriage to serve both the reproductive and alliance interests of the parties. In keeping with this objective, sexual intercourse may be tolerated or condoned where marriage is absolutely forbidden. To those who regard sex as sinful this may sound strange, but we have to remember that incest is always relative.

The crime of incestuous in-marriage is regularly subject to automatic mystical sanctions which immediately strike the guilty parties; they may be dangerously contagious, and threaten innocent people. In Africa leprosy is widely believed to be the consequence of incest. Not all tribal societies invoke mystical sanctions to discourage endogamy. Some rely on more prosaic sanctions. The Somali nomads, for example, prohibit marriage between closely related kin because they consider it divisive and disruptive. Those who infringe this rule are subject to fines and strong moral censure : mystical penalties only become significant in the case of improper liaisons – which are regarded with horror – between primary kin.

Out-marriage, then, is an extrovert and expansive policy which creates valuable ties outside one's own group or community. The northern Somali nomads deliberately marry their daughters to men of distant lineages to establish alliances with hostile or potentially hostile groups. But, as we have seen, the southern, cultivating Somali prefer in-marriage. In their sedentary cultivating economy there is less need for far-flung connections, and marriage is (in this case at least) employed to knit together tribal segments of heterogeneous origin.

This brings us to the third matrimonial strategy where marriage within the community is so strongly valued that out-marriage is prohibited. In principle this applies to the various divisions of the Indian caste system – although in practice there are variations. In theory each caste's ritual purity is preserved by the rigid rule of in-marriage. And fear of leprosy, the automatic sanction which in Africa threatens those who marry inside their own group, here hangs over those who contemplate marrying outside it. Many Muslim societies follow a less exacting form of endogamy, strongly favouring marriage between the sons and daughters of brothers (known as patrilateral parallel cousin marriage). This preference is so strong that a man possesses a pre-emptive right to marry his father's brother's daughter. She is not free to marry any other suitor unless and until her cousin has renounced his claim. The traditional Maori penchant for endogamy was rationalized in terms precisely opposite to those invoked by the Somali nomads to discourage it. 'Marry your sister,' the Maori proverb sagely advises, 'that you may [safely] assail each other.' 'Sister' here refers to women of the same clan, excluding true sisters and first-cousins with whom marriage is prohibited. By implication, it is desirable for clan-mates to marry since when they quarrel their being kin will restrain them. Marital stability is in the Maori view enhanced by kinship.

What can we say about the general effects and implications of endogamy and exogamy? Because of the inherent ambiguities of marriage, endogamy can either shore up weak in-group ties, or, conversely, diminish the stifling grip of ties that are already too demanding for comfort. It can bring people together (as in the southern Somali case) or separate them; it can unite a group and disassociate them from others. In many patrilineal Muslim societies patrilateral parallel cousin marriage seems to lead to a concentration of property and other interests at the family level and so reduces the otherwise overpowering claims of wider descent obligations. This view, which is explicitly stated in many Muslim cultures, is close to that of the Tswana, who although not Muslim favour this form of marriage (as well as several others), arguing that it keeps the bridewealth cattle within the family. Thus a Tswana proverb pleads: 'Child of my father's younger brother, marry me, so that the cattle may return to our kraal.'[9]

From a slightly different perspective, exogamy and endogamy may, paradoxically, produce similar results. Either can emphasize group identity and exclusiveness. The exogamic motto declares in effect: 'We are those who do not marry each other – this is our distinction.' The endogamic manifesto proclaims: 'We are those who do not marry anyone else.' Each statement has the same effect: it defines the limits of group solidarity in terms of marriage.

9. I. Schapera, 'Kinship and Marriage among the Tswana', in A. R. Radcliffe-Brown and D. Forde (eds), *African Systems of Kinship and Marriage*, Oxford University Press, 1950, p. 151.

MARRIAGE PREFERENCES IN EXOGAMY

Where exogamy is the rule we often find certain preferential patterns of marriage which limit the range of alliances. Two of the commonest preferred unions are:

Matrilateral cross-cousin marriage in patrilineal societies:

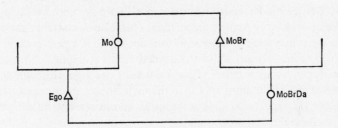

Patrilateral cross-cousin marriage in matrilineal societies:

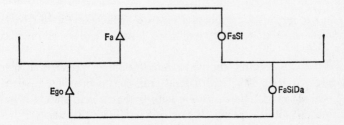

Why are these unions so popular? Part of the answer lies in the advantages they provide. The first capitalizes on the warm relationship common in patrilineal societies between the sister's son and his mother's brother. A man marries the daughter of his favourite maternal uncle and anticipates that the marriage payments will be reduced in his favour. The maternal cousin is a kind of bargain bride, and this matrimonial policy reinforces a highly valued matrilateral connection.

Much the same applies to patrilateral cross-cousin marriage in a matrilineal society, when a man marries his father's female heir. This commends itself to fathers in matrilineal societies when they wish to pass property on to their own sons, rather than their sister's sons, and thus circumvent the rule of matrilineal inheritance. Here the matrilineal principle is deviously respected, for the son is granted access to his father's possessions (or some of them) because his wife is a properly qualified heir. He is custodian rather than outright owner, but his children, who are genuine matrilineal descendants of their maternal grandfather, are legitimate heirs and successors.

Despite these attractive features, not all peoples with patrilineal descent systems practise matrilateral cross-cousin marriage, nor is it the only form of marriage in societies where it is preferred. We have already noticed, for instance, that patrilineal Muslim societies favour patrilateral parallel cousin marriage, although not exclusively. The same applies to the matrilineal case: some matrilineal societies and some matrilineal unions do not follow the patrilateral cross-cousin pattern.

ALLIANCE THEORY

We can go a little further and venture – briefly and with trepidation – into that rarified realm of kinship known as 'alliance theory'.[10]

Here we examine the wider implications of preferential marriage patterns. Take matrilateral cross-cousin marriage in patrilineal societies. The basic rule here is that a man should marry into his mother's people. If this rule is followed regularly it will produce connections between the groups involved which is represented schematically in the diagram opposite.

In this 'wife-flow' chart, group D supplies wives to C which gives wives to B which gives wives to A, and so on. The minimum number of parties required here is three. But, since there is no theoretical limit, the pattern is essentially open-ended, uniting a whole series of distinct patri-lineages. In technical jargon this system is known as *asymmetrical alliance* or *generalized exchange*.

10. For an unusually lucid introduction to this and other central topics in kinship theory see R. Fox, *Kinship and Marriage*, Penguin, 1967. A wider treatment of marriage than is possible here can also be found in L. Mair, *Marriage*, Penguin, 1971.

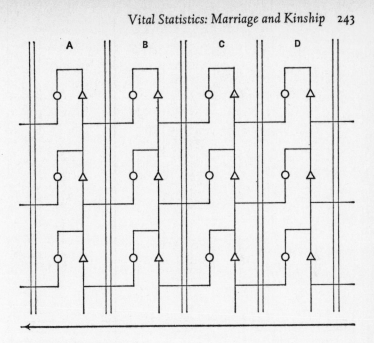

The first term perhaps best conveys the point that here groups do not reciprocate directly: some are always supplying women to their allies, while others are always receiving them. If the act of wife-giving is associated with high status, then the alliance relations between the component segments can also express a hierarchical order, following the direction in which women move. This arrangement can thus represent social stratification – or, as some would hold, create it. Examples of this are to be found in widely scattered societies in south-east Asia, Australia and South America, though rarely in Africa. Numerous counter-instances show that there is no inherent superiority attached to the role of wife-givers: indeed in many cases (including the hypergamous unions associated with Hinduism) the reverse is true.

This pattern contrasts markedly with that resulting from systematic patrilateral cross-cousin marriage. In this anti-Oedipal pattern a man marries his father's sister's daughter and the wife-flow chart is as follows:

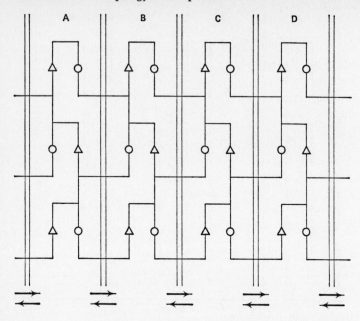

Here A supplies a bride to B in one generation, and receives a bride in the next. This pattern, usually known as *symmetrical exchange* (or *delayed direct exchange*), resembles an alternating current of electricity (just as *asymmetrical alliance* is comparable to a direct current). It is only one generation removed from direct sister-swapping which, as we shall see, is from many points of view the simplest form of marriage. Theoretically, only three parties are again required to complete the pattern, although in practice there are often more groups involved. Other things being equal – an unlikely condition many kinship theorists take for granted – this continuous ebb and flow of women weaves a closer textured tapestry of relationships; it is an alliance device of shorter range and lower capacity than the asymmetrical system.

GROUP MARRIAGE

Implicit in alliance theory is the notion that tribal marriages are contracted between groups rather than individuals, and involve a ramifying series of corporate interests and rights. In this respect, even in the most egalitarian societies, they have many of the characteristics of dynastic unions in European history. In such traditional societies as the Somali, where feud and blood-money are central institutions, girls may be thrown in as bonus offerings in the settlement of outstanding blood-debts. It is not simply that these women are mere chattels, pawns distributed as largesse amongst men, as they were among the ancient Irish or in parts of central Africa. There is also an understanding that these marriages will help to staunch the blood that has been shed, and that through their children the rival lineages will share new common interests. Marriage is acting as a pacifier and restorative.

More evidence of the corporate nature of marriage is found in such widespread institutions as leviratic marriage, widow-inheritance, and sororal marriage. In the first and second of these, a wife, on her husband's death, passes to his nearest appropriate kinsman, often a younger brother; of course this right may be waived, and a widow may marry outside her husband's group.

We can illustrate the levirate by reference to the biblical story of Judah and his sons, Er and Onan in Genesis, 38.

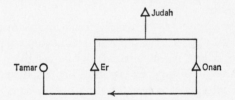

On Er's death, Onan was instructed by Judah to take Tamar, his brother's widow, and raise up children for his dead brother. Knowing that the offspring would not be his own, Onan disobeyed this command and deliberately spilled his semen on the ground, an act of 'onanism' which so angered God that he struck Onan dead.

In the full levirate the man who inherits his kinsman's widow is considered simply to be standing in for his deceased kinsman; if he sires children these belong not to him but to the man he has replaced. Marriage here transcends death, and the new man is merely a proxy-husband. In the less emphatic form, widow-inheritance, children of the second union belong to the new husband.

Where leviratic marriage and widow-inheritance are perfectly proper forms of marriage, illicit sexual relations between a married woman and her potential inheritor while her husband is still living involve incest. Here we encounter the 'group-wife' prohibition discussed earlier; part of its seriousness is that such actions amount to wishing that one's senior kinsman was already dead. The knowledge that group wives are potential heirs imposes severe constraints on all contact between men and their kinsmen's wives.

The converse of the two preceding forms is the sororate, where a widower is entitled to a replacement bride from the same family or lineage. A younger sister is usually drafted into taking her elder kinswoman's place; as might be expected, the strength of the widower's claim to a substitute spouse varies with the duration of the marriage and the number of his children; the longer the period of the union and the greater the number of children, the less the widower's entitlement to a replacement bride. Nevertheless the existence of this right demonstrates again that marriage is a union not simply between individuals but between the representatives of groups.

These specialized forms of marriage conveniently introduce the distinction between a child's physical father (*genitor*) and his social father (*pater*). The difference is clearly seen in the following anecdote. A sceptical inquirer was attending a spiritualist séance at which a medium was demonstrating his standard ploys. The medium asked the sceptic to test his powers by asking a taxing question. The man concerned was delighted to have this opportunity of, as he thought, exposing the fraudulent medium and so posed the following question: 'Where is my father at this moment, and what is he doing?' After a few moments the medium replied: 'This evening your father is drinking in the Golden Eagle bar.' At this the sceptical questioner burst out laughing, saying: 'Nonsense, my father died seven years ago.' 'Ah,' said the medium, 'the man who married your mother *may* have died seven years ago, but your father is sitting . . .'

The roles of *genitor* and *pater* may thus not coincide, they may be formally and officially vested in different persons, a man having sexual access to the wife of another who is the social father of any children that result. This separation between physical and social procreation corresponds with the results of ethological research on animal behaviour. These show clearly that the paternal role derives from relationships with the mother, rather than directly with the children. This distinction enables us to understand bizarre marital arrangements such as 'ghost-marriage' and 'woman-to-woman' marriage. Ghost-marriage, as the diagram

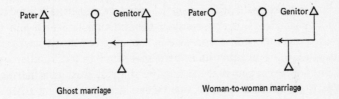

Ghost marriage   Woman-to-woman marriage

shows, resembles leviratic marriage in that heirs are provided for a man who has died childless by his widow taking a lover. The dead man remains the *pater*, while the lover is the *genitor*. In woman-to-woman marriage, a barren woman may acquire children through another woman to whom she acts as *pater*, the *genitor* being the second woman's lover. Clearly fertility and legitimacy are the issues here and they do not always coincide.

This suggests a valuable perspective for analysing tribal matrimony. The rights at issue in marriage can be divided conveniently, although not exhaustively, into two categories. The first, which may be called 'uxorial', relate to a woman's role as sexual partner and general helpmate – to bed and board. The second, which we can analogously call 'genetricial', refer to her role as a mother of children, to her fertility. A man may hold uxorial rights in a woman, including rights of exclusive sexual access, and yet not enjoy concurrent genetricial rights in her. In societies where descent is traced matrilineally through women, children belong to the mother's and not the father's descent-group so husbands by definition cannot exercise genetricial rights. Control of reproduction remains firmly vested in the mother's matrilineage, where it is exercised by a woman's brother. We shall examine the dynamics of this situation more fully when we discuss matrilineal descent *per se*. For the present we need only note the contrast presented by patrilineal societies, where a husband generally, but not invariably, holds both uxorial and genetricial rights in his wife. As we have seen, the proxy husband in leviratic unions has only uxorial rights in the widow, whose fertility remains the property of her deceased partner.

MARRYING

Much has been said of the *effects* of marriage, but little of how it is established. Let us now consider the transactions which join a couple together as man and wife in the alliance context we have emphasized. The most immediate procedure is for families or groups to exchange women, and the simplest way of achieving this is for two men to exchange sisters. Sister-exchange marriage has a satisfyingly primordial flavour, and is still practised in such widely separated societies as those of the Australian Aborigines, the Tsembaga of New Guinea (where 'package-deal' marriages take place with the exchange of several sisters at the same wedding), and a number of Indian communities in both North and South America. The Tiv of Nigeria formerly practised this institution and lament its passing. We may also note that Israel Sieff and Simon Marks, the founders of Marks and Spencer, exchanged sisters. In Arab societies two pairs of patrilineal parallel cousins are sometimes married at the same wedding, an arrangement valued for more than its mere economy; this amounts to sister exchange at one remove.

In most cases marriage is more indirect, requiring complicated matrimonial transactions which we can classify under two main heads: 'bride-service' and 'bride-wealth or price' (and/or dowry). In bride-service the groom works for his father-in-law, as in the Old Testament Jacob did for Laban and thus earns the right to the daughter's hand. This procedure is followed by the Bushmen of the Kalahari, the Bemba of Zambia, and sometimes the Amhara of Ethiopia, but is not widely reported.

BRIDE-WEALTH OR PRICE

Instead of offering his sister or his labour, the groom and his kin most commonly make a series of gifts to the kin of the bride. The first missionary and government reports of these practices emphasized their commercial character. Women, it was generally argued, were being treated as chattels, bought and sold like other market commodities. Here, perhaps, we may detect a lingering ethnocentricism, inspired by memories of European matrimonial practices in earlier centuries. In the seventeenth century, after all, there was a brisk trade in European women who were imported for sale as wives to the colonists of the New World. In 1620, for example, 150 'young and uncorrupt' imported girls were sold in Virginia for between 100 and 150 pounds of tobacco each (i.e. between £15 and £22). These European transactions were viewed in a much more charitable light by at least some of the clergy. A Virginian pastor, the Reverend Weems, was moved to write: 'It would have done a man's heart good to see the gallant young Virginians hastening to the waterside when a vessel arrived from London, each carrying a bundle of the best tobacco under his arm and taking back with him a beautiful and virtuous wife.' [11]

So in African and other colonies it was generally left to anthropologists to challenge with their more informed and sympathetic reports this thoroughly commercial interpretation of tribal marriage payments. They emphasized the multiple interests in play, pointing out the complex and enduring rights (and duties) that were redistributed in these transactions. Women were not, they argued, being bought and sold like cattle or other commodities; they were being exchanged in complicated and on-going transactions, forming binding relationships that had little if anything in common with market transactions. It was therefore wrong to speak of 'bride-price': a more neutral term such as 'bride-wealth' was appropriate. To stress the social and political aspects is not of course to deny the existence or significance of the economic. It is, however, somewhat ironic that those anthropologists who insisted that women were more than mere chattels should now be de-

11. Quoted in R. Chalmers, *A History of Currency in the British Colonies*, 1893, p. 6.

nounced by feminists as male chauvinists who failed to appreciate correctly how degrading the position of women was.

The truth of course is that it is all a question of emphasis; the emphasis between economic and non-economic considerations varies from society to society and, in some respects, even from marriage to marriage. That said, let us leave this semantic dispute and turn to the facts. Marriage payments are characteristically made in prestige wealth. Among pastoralists, the traditional currency is livestock, especially horses, cattle or camels, which are also employed in settling blood-debts. Rights in wives are thus negotiated in the medium used in transactions involving men's lives. To an increasing extent marriage payments now include money and other modern forms of wealth. The actual rates fluctuate with the overall socio-economic conditions, although attempts have often been made to maintain a standard rate of exchange between women and other valuables. Some dramatic changes in bride-wealth values have followed the introduction of western education. This largely reflects how women's education has lagged behind men's in the developing countries, as elsewhere. Often, then, the demand for educated brides far outstrips the supply and in most cases, the fortunate fathers of educated girls are not slow to exploit the situation. I vividly recall the scramble over the initial intake of pupils at the first girls' intermediate school in what was then the British Somaliland Protectorate. Something resembling a gold-rush developed, most of the girls' fathers receiving a host of rival bids, and offers of marriage gifts soared to astronomic heights. Jean La Fontaine records parallel developments among the Gisu,[12] and many other examples could be quoted.

DOWRY

Similar fluctuations with supply and demand occur in a more familiar marriage transaction, the dowry, which was formerly widely employed in Europe to enhance a girl's marriage prospects, as it still is in India, Sri Lanka and parts of the Mediterranean. In contemporary Cyprus a scarcity of marriageable men has led to a

12. M. Fortes (ed.), *Marriage in Tribal Societies*, Cambridge University Press, 1962; see also J. L. Comaroff (ed.), *The Meaning of Marriage payments*, Academic Press, 1980.

marked increase in the dowry, which is now expected to include the couple's house, which was formerly provided by the husband and his family.[13] Dowry is sometimes, in effect, a kind of 'groom-price' or 'groom-wealth'. Frequently it also becomes an advance settlement or allotment of a daughter's hereditary portion from her father's estate. Here it is primarily the woman (or her family) who seeks to conclude as prestigious a match as possible.

In the Hindu caste system, ambitious families endeavour to marry their daughters to husbands who have higher status, wealth, or power – if possible, all three. Brides are regularly advertised in the newspapers with alluring descriptions of their personal virtues and the magnificent dowries which go with them. The daughters of high-caste families find it easier to fulfil the Hindu ideal of the marriage of equals. But, for many of the rest, marriage is aptly described as caste endogamy tempered by hypergamy, that is 'marrying-up' slightly above one's station. As Nur Yalman [14] states the position for the Kandyan Sinhalese, 'women may have sexual relations with equals and superiors. They may marry men of higher ritual status. But they must not fall below. Men, however, may do as they like: even if they have sexual intercourse with women of lower castes, this does not matter much. They may deny or repudiate all connections, and in any case they can keep low women as "concubines".'

This male chauvinist logic is familiar, but it must not obscure the point that dowry is usually offered as compensation for the lower status of the bride. Where both families enjoy the same position no dowry may be needed. Many poor families cannot, in any case, afford to pay worthwhile dowries and thus cannot secure advantageous unions for their daughters. In societies where bride-wealth is required impoverished families are similarly unable to contract any but the meanest of marriages. Such despicable unions are known expressively in South Africa as 'take and squat: donkey marriage', a characterization widely shared elsewhere. Amongst the Somali, the corresponding marriage gifts are so insignificant that they are known simply as 'food', as they are

13. P. Loizos, 'Changes in Rural Property Transfer among Greek Cypriot Villagers', *Man* (N.S.), vol. 10, pp. 503 –23.

14. N. Yalman, *Under the Bo Tree: Studies in Caste, Kinship and Marriage in the Interior of Ceylon*, University of California Press, 1967, p. 177.

no grander than the obligatory sharing of food with any guest.

Poverty brings together societies where bride-wealth and dowry are the rule; this may serve to remind us that the standard marriage in many cultures includes *both* prestations. As John Campbell[15] says of the Greek Sarakatsani shepherds, dowry frequently serves to 'complement the wealth with which the new family is or will be endowed by the husband's family . . . each side contributes one of its members and a certain amount of property'. The balance between the two types of marriage gift varies, as we shall see, to some extent (although not invariably) with the way descent is traced and its social and political implications.

MARRIAGE TRANSACTIONS

How are the settlements agreed before or at marriage actually rendered? The answer is most frequently in instalments – on the 'never-never'. The recipients are not necessarily keen to have the total amount in a lump sum. They are more likely to want to keep the account open and at least part of the debt outstanding: this ensures that the recipients will always be able to exert leverage on the donors should the occasion arise.

What are the marriage gifts for? What do they do? In the case of bride-wealth they convey rights in the wife from her kin to her husband's. They also represent a tangible public statement of the marriage transaction which they announce and solemnize. Now, as we have seen, in societies in which descent is traced, patrilineally, through men, the husband acquires those rights in his wife's fertility which we have labelled 'genetricial'. In matrilineal societies where descent is traced through women, these rights are not conveyed with the wife to her husband's group. They remain where they began, with the woman's natal kin. Here it is the husband's sexual services, his potency, that the wife's group acquires.

Certain consequences follow from these differences. Where the wife is her partner's equal or superior in status (that is, hypergamy is not involved), marriage payments (in the form of bride-wealth) should be higher in patrilineal than in matrilineal societies. If the wife is found wanting either as a loyal companion or source of children, it is understandable that the husband should be entitled to some redress. In many patrilineal systems, either failing may constitute adequate grounds for divorce, and/or the replacement of the defaulting woman by a sororal substitute; alternatively, the husband may legitimately recover part at least of his original bride-wealth. The appropriate proportion depends in large measure on the number of children, if any, produced by the wife. Here there is a clear conception of an equivalence between the rights in the wife's fertility and the gifts made by the husband's side at marriage. Cattle beget children, or at least are expected to: to a significant extent, bride-price is actually child-price.

We can now examine more closely the full implications of marriage in patrilineal societies. Often the rights transferred from the wife's to the husband's kin are so comprehensive and so firmly grasped by the recipients that even illegitimate children belong to their mother's husband and not to her lover. They belong to their *pater*, not their *genitor*, and the *genitor* can only claim them by paying substantial damages to the *pater*. Such a vehement protection of the father's rights may be expected in particularly strong and binding forms of marriage, directly reflecting the valuable and inclusive rights the husband has acquired. We are not speaking of individual marriages, but of marriage as a normative institution; we might expect that high marriage payments, patriliny and stable marriage would all be interrelated, forming one of those rare functional complexes which so delight social anthropologists. This conclusion was drawn by Max Gluckman [16] from his classic comparison of marriage and descent among the Zulu of southern Africa and the Lozi (Barotse) of Zambia.

The Zulu are a patrilineal people with high marriage payments and stable marriage, divorce being extremely rare. At marriage the husband and his kin acquire monopoly rights in his wife's fertility. This is emphasized in some of their ancillary marital institutions, for example, the levirate, the sororate, ghost-marriage, and

16. M. Gluckman, 'Kinship and Marriage among the Lozi of Northern Rhodesia and the Zulu of Natal', in A. R. Radcliffe-Brown and D. Forde (eds.), *African Systems of Kinship and Marriage*, Oxford University Press, 1950.

woman-to-woman marriage. All these, as we have seen, are specialized unions which underline the collateral and corporate character of marriage. Zulu men are polygynists and aspire to more than one wife, particularly favouring marriage with two or more sisters. Such unions are highly prized, for, as the Zulu declare, sisterly love will overcome the jealousy that inevitably accompanies polygyny. This concern to maintain harmonious relations between co-wives is part of the wider traditional emphasis on marriage as, in principle, a permanent alliance relationship between groups.

The Lozi of central Africa present a nice contrast. Their kinship system is bilateral rather than patrilineal, relationships traced on the mother's and the father's side being accorded more or less the same weight. Marriage payments are small in comparison with those of the Zulu and marriage is unstable. Where the Zulu encourage sister marriage, the Lozi abhor it. They hold sisterly love and loyalty in too high esteem to subject it to the painful hazards of polygynous strife. The unavoidable frictions of co-marriage, they maintain, would spoil the natural harmony between sisters. While the Zulu husband is the complete master of his wife's fertility whoever impregnates her, his Lozi counterpart does not acquire full genetricial rights in his wife. If she takes a lover, the lover is legally entitled to his natural (illegitimate) children. Here the *genitor* rather than the *pater* has priority.

This contrast between the patrilineal and strongly wedded Zulu, and the bilateral and weakly married Lozi, confirms the conclusion which we had already deduced from first principles. It is also supported by data from such other patrilineal peoples as the Tswana, Shona, Ngoni, Nuer and Romans – to cite a few well-documented examples. The Shona, indeed, resemble the Jaffna Tamils mentioned at the beginning of this chapter in that a woman sheds her own clan identity at marriage and assumes her husband's.

But before we conclude that we have discovered a *bona fide* law relating type of descent, marital stability and marriage payments in an eternal and invariant triangle we have to recognize, however reluctantly, that not all patrilineal societies fit this picture. This is disconcerting, and it would be gratifying if we could find plausible excuses for the exceptions which did not jeopardize Gluckman's promising hypothesis. Unfortunately this is not possible. There are a large number of patrilineal systems which can never be reconciled with this simple formula. There are many patrilineal societies, past and present, where marriage does *not* involve the transfer of women as wives in the fashion of the Zulu and Nuer. In such cases, wives retain significant ties with their own natal kin and these residual loyalties are frequently acknowledged in ritual. So, for example, among the patrilineal Coorgs of southern India a crucial passage in marriage rituals involves the disposal of twelve 'pieces of gold'. These are actually only pebbles: but what they represent is very real. The bride takes eleven 'pieces' with her, leaving one behind with her own family. This is much more than a remembrance: it expresses her continuing rights in her natal family, her sheet anchor or insurance policy which entitles her, if her marriage founders, to return home. The ceremony signifies that Coorg marriage does not terminate a woman's membership of her own patrilineal group. The same point is made, perhaps even more eloquently, in the marriage ceremonies of certain regions of pre-revolutionary China: when a bride left her parents to marry, she dropped a lock of hair which was then attached to the half-open door 'to signify that while she has been sent away the house is not completely closed to her'.[17]

SOMALI MARRIAGE

Let us now examine marriage amongst the patrilineal Somali nomads, since this is one case which does not fit Gluckman's hypothesis. We may even be able to suggest a more plausible hypothesis relating descent and the stability of marriage. The Somali are by any reckoning at least as patrilineal as the Zulu and Nuer and, although impressive marriage payments are made, marriage is highly unstable.[18]

Let us begin with the principal transactions involved in

17. M. Freedman, *Rites and Duties, or Chinese Marriage*, London School of Economics, 1967, p. 23.
18. Cf. I. M. Lewis, 'Marriage and the Family in Northern Somaliland', *East African Studies*, no. 15, East African Institute of Social Research, Kampala, Uganda, 1962.

marriage. There are in fact four: a betrothal gift (*gabbaati*); bride-wealth (*yarad*); the dowry brought by the wife (*dibaad*); and *mahar*, the bride's personal dower. The *mahar* is the essential Islamic component in marriage: no Muslim union is complete without it although in material terms it is usually the smallest prestation. Its nature and value – perhaps a piece of jewellery, several hundred Somali shillings, or a few sheep and goats – must be stipulated at the time of marriage, and agreed by the bride in the presence of witnesses and of the officiating Muslim priest. It need not, however, be actually transferred by the groom to the bride before or at the wedding. It may be, and indeed often is, only handed over if the marriage ends in divorce. It is essentially a divorce surety, guaranteeing a divorced wife a small settlement. Though this dower is often paltry and nominal, this transaction and the accompanying Muslim rites unite a couple as man and wife and give the husband full genetricial rights to his partner.

The *mahar* transaction relates primarily to the personal aspects of marriage: it unites two individuals without reference to, and without establishing links between, their collateral kin. But marriage among the Somali nomads is much more than a mere joining together of individual spouses. This core has a wider context, of alliance relationships between lineages. All the other marriage transactions relate to this wider conception. The initial betrothal gift gives the suitor pre-emptive rights in his fiancée. If he subsequently marries someone else, he forfeits his *gabbaati*. If the girl and her kin default, they are liable to pay damages to the slighted suitor and his kin. Assuming that neither side falters, the next issue concerns the amount of bride-wealth which the girl's kin are prepared to accept. Long and delicate negotiations ensue resulting, if the conclusion is favourable, in an agreed and minutely detailed settlement. The main component consists of camels, ranging in number from a half a dozen to over a hundred, with cash and other ancillary gifts. Such prestige items *par excellence* as horses, rifles and ammunition may be included. Whatever its components this substantial bride-wealth includes contributions from a wide circle of kin, who thus demonstrate tangibly their appreciation of the union as an alliance with their group.

The same holds true at the receiving end: an equally wide

range of kin on the bride's side receive a share of the in-coming *yarad*, emphasizing their collective commitment. They have to decide the character and quantity of the dowry (*dibaad*) which the bride will take with her to her husband. This, as might be expected, varies with the bride-wealth and their assessment of the desirability of the match. A minimum display of good-will requires that the bride should be equipped with burden camels, laden with the supports and mats which form the nomadic tent, and other domestic utensils, as well as a flock of sheep and goats to provide milk for the children with which the couple will surely be blessed. Some milch camels are usually also included: even some of those received in bride-wealth may be directly returned. By sending a generous dowry, the bride's kin parade their munificence and their pleasure. In practice, this return prestation ranges in value between about a third and a half of the original bride-wealth. Any subsequent gift from the wife's kin during the marriage is viewed as 'dowry', again illustrating the on-going character of the relationship.

In the eyes of God and man *mahar* makes a marriage. But it does not set up the continuing affinal relationship between lineages which are part of any satisfactory union. If a couple elope, marrying secretly in defiance of their parents' wishes, no affinal connection is created and neither side has any collateral claim on the other. Hence, if the wife dies, or is childless, the groom has no sororatic rights at all; in the event of her husband's death the widow is free to marry as she chooses, and her husband's kin have no claims over her. The bilateral, collective ties of what is considered a proper marriage reinforce the union of the two individual spouses, and the rights and obligations on each side reflect the character of the various marriage prestations. Despite these ramifying connections, however, and this is the point of our example, Somali marriage is not stable. One might argue that Somali marriage is the frail, brittle thing it is, *because* of these strong collateral pressures between actually or potentially hostile lineages. Marriage transfers the immediate custody of a woman from her father and brothers to her husband, but it does not transfer her allegiance. So, in the inevitable tug-of-war between her spouse and her kin, her kin regularly take precedence.

The Somali nomads, then, contradict Gluckman's hypothesis. They are a patrilineal society in which, where substantial marriage payments are made, a man can gain full genetricial and uxorial rights in a wife without her completely relinquishing her own kinship identity. Throughout her life a Somali woman retains her natal lineage membership; if she is killed by a third party, it is the duty of her natal kin rather than of her husband to seek vengeance or compensation. The husband may assist, but it is not his primary responsibility. He has no direct claim to her blood-money (or at least not to the full amount), and has to content himself with a (sororatic) replacement bride from his dead wife's lineage. On the same principle, if his wife commits serious wrongs or offences which require substantial damages, these are the responsibility of her kin rather than his.

The requirements of patrilineal descent, then, are met by a form of marriage in which a woman retains her own lineage identity and is not herself completely absorbed in her husband's group, although full uxorial and genetricial rights in her are transferred to her husband. The wife thus retains a legal personality independently of her husband, which being the responsibility of her own kin provides an enduring insurance in times of difficulty and marital discord. All this is fully compatible with unstable marriage as long as the *pater*'s legal rights over his children are safeguarded. Women can come and go, as long as their children remain in their father's lineage. Gluckman has supposed that if someone holds complete or substantial rights in an asset (in this case a wife) this implies that he must do so for ever. Control of the means of reproduction does not imply permanent rights which cannot be relinquished, or that the person in whom they are held belongs totally and unambiguously to the holder. In patrilineal societies of the Somali type married women have important, if secondary, rights as citizens of their own lineages.

The ethnographic data include at least two different types of patrilineal system, each with a corresponding kind of patrilineal marriage. One type, represented by the Nuer, Zulu and others, transfers women in marriage to the lineage of their husbands lock, stock and barrel; marriage in this type is usually stable. The other type, represented by the Somali, Arabs generally, the Tiv,

Tallensi, Fulani and many others, does not transfer women completely and marriage is not stable, in this respect resembling matrilineal marriage. In general the fragility of marriage is at least in
part a function of the extent to which wives retain strong ties
after marriage with their own natal kinsfolk, or achieve by
other means significant extra-marital independence. So stated the
proposition becomes almost self-evident.

PLURAL FAMILIES

Whatever its stability, marriage everywhere produces the basic
nucleus of family structure – a woman and her children. Until
recently it was assumed in Europe that the paternal role of the
husband was essential, so-called 'matricentric families' with only
a 'visiting' husband or 'boy friend' being regarded as odd and
anomalous, or more charitably as 'deprived'. Yet whether or not
there is a regularly resident male head, all families are 'matricentric'. Consequently where polygyny is normal and a man is
married to several wives at the same time, each wife and family
frequently has its own house or quarters, its own gardens or field
and granaries, and its own livestock. These dispersed resources
are jealously guarded against encroachment and form the nucleus
of separate patrimonies for each uterine group of children. Not
all the polygynous family's property is parcelled up in this fashion.
Major resources in land and livestock are often managed on a cooperative basis as a single unit. Among the nomadic Somali, each
uterine family has its own flock of sheep and goats and, probably,

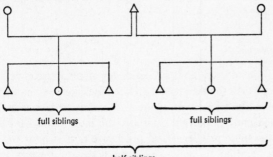

its caravan of burden camels, while the grazing camels that form the group's largest capital are managed as a single unit.

The children of the matricentric family are full siblings (as long as polyandry is not practised in combination with patrilineal descent), since they share common parents, and are half-siblings of the other children of the polygynous family group. As the diagram illustrates the closest kinship tie is between full siblings. This is directly acknowledged in a special relationship often found in patrilineal Bantu-speaking societies between a boy and his 'cattle-linked sister'. The cattle a girl brings to her family as bride-wealth are used to enable her full brother to acquire a wife. This practice harks back to direct sister-exchange.

Such uterine or matricentric families are often called 'houses' or 'hearths', and are also referred to more evocatively as 'breasts' and 'wombs'. Their descendants refer back to maternal origins as a basis for political cooperation or cleavage. All this is familiar: we employ the same imagery, and appeal to the same sentiments when we speak of our 'motherland', or use the word 'metropolis' (literally, 'mother-city').

Where descent is reckoned matrilineally, the distinction between full and half-siblings loses much of its importance. In this case half-siblings, each following his mother, belong to different lineages and clans. Ties traced through their common paternal ancestor exist *outside* the framework of matrilineal descent; they cannot serve as points of differentiation as opposed matrilateral connections do in patrilineal systems. They may, on the other hand, link separate matrilineal groups, although again alliance on this basis is given less weight than that based on matrilateral ties in patrilineal societies.

POLYGYNY

Conspicuous display and the desire for as many heirs as possible encourage men to take more than one wife. They say in Nuristan: 'A wife is like a field; you plant seed in more than one field.' The older and more important men are, the more wives they tend to have. But these privileges and prizes are not without cost. They increase familial tensions, not only between co-wives but also between the husband and his sons. Conflict centres on competition over women and over the use of family property to acquire wives. The family head's latest marital adventures may seriously inconvenience his unmarried sons when they are desperately seeking brides but cannot find the necessary bride-wealth.

Co-wives are usually ranked in the order of their marriage to their common spouse. Typically the first wife keeps the keys of the family chest or money box. Her authority as first lady over her younger co-wives is to some extent counterbalanced by the family head's disproportionate interest in his later and younger partners. The legal superiority of the first wife is reflected in the privileged position which her children assume on their father's death. Not all societies of course practise primogeniture, but generally the children of the first wife receive a larger share than their half-siblings. Such preferential treatment tends to exacerbate the problems of polygyny, and the rancorous rivalry and strife between co-wives. Despite these difficulties, however, a man's first wife may herself urge him to marry another wife, to increase the female labour force, to provide companionship, but above all to enhance her status.

This is the traditional fashion. But in the developing countries today there is a general, but not unambiguous, trend towards monogamy. Several factors are involved. Christian missionary teaching and European practice have taught that polygyny is a barbaric and primitive custom. There are also new economic disincentives. Women nowadays have larger and more expensive tastes, the cost of bringing up children and sending them to school is rising, and wives chafe more than they used to at the idea of sharing their man with another woman. All these discourage polygyny, especially amongst the educated élite. Old customs, however, die hard, and there are still some powerful influences working in the opposite direction. Partly as a consequence of sexual discrimination in education, leading African politicians often have difficulty in finding a wife who can be both society hostess and politically significant partner. An uneducated wife with important political connections in the hinterland may be essential to an ambitious man's career, but he also needs an attractive and suitably qualified partner for his urban social life. Here we again encounter the interplay between countryside and town which is such a significant factor in contemporary Africa. Polygyny is an obvious way of meeting these equally important rural and urban interests. This new pattern of polygyny is particularly well established in West Africa where many such marriages now involve 'bush wives' and 'frock wives'.

POLYANDRY

Polygyny, St Augustine held, is unfair to women and polyandry renders paternity uncertain. Polyandry is less common than polygyny and seems, on the whole, better suited to matrilineal than to patrilineal conditions. Consider, for instance, the traditional organization of the Nayar warrior caste of Malabar in southern India. The Nayars combined polyandry and matriliny with great success; they were divided into local matrilineal groups, most of whose men were regularly away on military service while their sisters remained on the family lands at home. Each matrilineal group of sisters was led by an elder brother, home from the wars, who managed the estate and controlled the family. Such matrilineages were married collectively to other matrilineages of the same caste and the girls of one group were all 'wives' to the men of another. The husband here was little more than a stud male, impregnating women who received many different men. The men, home on leave, had rights of sexual access but little more. They possessed uxorial rights only in a vague, collective sense and, of course, genetricial rights were not relinquished by the matrilineages.[19]

BILATERAL DESCENT

We have already used such terms as patrilineal and matrilineal kinship and we must now examine the main types of descent in more detail. Convenience and familiarity suggest that we begin with the widest, most comprehensive, and least exclusive system of

19. See K. Gough, 'Changing Kinship Usages in the Setting of Political and Economic Change Among the Nayars of Malabar', *Journal of the Royal Anthropological Institute*, vol. 82, 1952, pp. 71–88 and C. J. Fuller, *The Nayars Today*, Cambridge University Press, 1976.

reckoning descent and move to less inclusive systems. We begin, then, with *bilateral* descent, which more or less describes our own system and exists in some degree in virtually all societies. Here socially significant descent is traced equally through male and female ancestors at every generation. All those who trace descent from a common ancestor, through male or female links or a mixture of both, are regarded as kin. Those who share such descent form a bilateral *descent group*. Descent groups are *ancestor-focused* units and include all those who happen to be descended from a particular common ancestor.

If we pick out all the descendants of several collateral ancestors (thus tracing the corresponding descent groups) we find that some people belong to more than one group. Bilateral descent groups, in other words, overlap, and the further back we go the greater is the degree of shared membership among different groups. Bilateral descent is thus rather like those much advertised 'package-deal' club-subscriptions where, by a single transaction, one becomes a member of a host of different clubs. None of these, of course, are very exclusive. Lack of exclusiveness is a price one has to pay for the automatic multiple-membership which bilateral descent provides.

Such bilateral, cognatic or 'ambilineal' descent groups (as they are sometimes called) can thus be pictured as a series of intersecting cones or overlapping triangles, as the diagram shows:

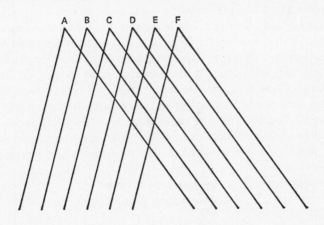

In principle one belongs to as many groups as the ancestors from whom one traces descent. One can identify with the group that offers most advantages in a given situation without infringing one's membership of the others. This flexibility is particularly attractive in times of stress and difficulty. If a particular group exhausts its local resources through growth of population or as a result of some calamity, its members can turn for help in many different directions. This elasticity in cognatic descent facilitates demographic adjustments to ecological and climatic inequalities; it works advantageously in communities in isolated and precarious geographical niches – as in small overcrowded Pacific islands or in the flood plains of the Zambesi river inhabited by the Lozi. This has encouraged the determinist view that bilateral descent is a direct response to such conditions, but quite different systems of descent can also be found *in the same physical conditions*, and cognatic descent also flourishes in environments which lack these demographic pressures and uncertainties.

Bilateral descent also offers the possibility of forming more ephemeral and more individually specific social units known cumbersomely but conveniently as 'ego-centred kindreds'. Here certain degrees of kinship (as with English 'first', 'second', and 'third' cousins etc.) provide a recognized stock of potential allies in times of need, both for regular subsistence tasks and when the security of life and property is threatened. Each group of full siblings has a unique circle of kin. The ego-centred kindreds of those who are not full siblings overlap and intersect – especially if they are close relatives. People are pulled in contrary directions through their loyalties to different and potentially opposed kindreds. These ramifying connections exist in all societies, but the recognition and emphasis they receive varies widely. Where descent is truly bilateral, the kindred regularly coexists with the more inclusive and enduring ancestor-focused cognatic descent group or 'ambilineage'. The ambilineage serves corporate on-going interests which, in principle, exist in perpetuity. The kindred endures only for the life-span of the individual whose transient needs it serves.

Bilateral descent, as we have been stressing, enables one to keep options open. Open-ended cognatic descent groups can be made more exclusive and specialized in their membership by restrictive clauses. This can be achieved in two contrasting ways. One is to adopt a more rigid and uncompromising definition of the kinship connections that confer legitimate membership, as by weighting paternal and maternal ties differently. Ultimately this procedure destroys cognatic descent, leading to more restrictive types of kinship which we shall discuss presently. The other less radical device consists simply of additional limiting qualifications independent of descent. The commonest of these is a residence requirement, associating people with particular ambilineages according to their domicile. While a person is still a potential member of several cognatic descent groups, his first allegiance is to the group owning the land where he lives. Not all the members of the group necessarily live in the same locality: the less active or committed may live elsewhere while those who do live locally form a residential core and active quorum in matters affecting the joint interests of the group. The combination of joint residence and descent, of kith and kin, provides a more secure base for corporate interests and patriotism than kin alone, and this enhanced sense of unity is reflected in the fact that such local units are frequently exogamous. Localized ambilineages thus play an important role in the social organization of many societies. We have already seen them amongst the Lozi of Zambia and shall restrict our examples here to the Amhara of Ethiopia and the Maori of New Zealand.

AMHARA AMBILINEAGES

The significant kinship unit amongst the Christian Amharas of the Ethiopian highlands is a cognatic descent group called *beyt* ('house') some eight to ten generations in depth. It consists of between fifty and one hundred and fifty people who hold ancestral (*rist*) rights in common land a mile or so square in a particular parish. The group is in practice usually exogamous, and those cognates who reside on its territory form the active core, one of their number being their joint representative. The rights of non-resident members may lapse after two generations' absence, like those defined by the recently coined British concept 'patrial'.

Since the land they occupy is also held in fief, these locally based cognatic ambilineages form, in effect, kin-based political segments within the complex Amhara political system. But although they are mobilized in land disputes concerning the interests of their members, they display only a small degree of corporate unity. Membership in a particular *beyt* is not exclusive; it is one of a number of rival attachments to different cognatic groups. Thus there is flexibility and the opportunity for choice and successful social mobility both in land-rights and the loyalties and allegiances these entail. So, 'most men are able gradually to increase the size of their landholding as their household grows and matures. Men who gain political prominence acquire additional land more rapidly.' [20] Under endemic competition for status and land, each Amhara peasant seeks to exploit his cognatic ties at the inevitable expense of group solidarity. In time of need he therefore turns to his personal, ego-centred kindred rather than his local ambilineage. A man's ultimate security consequently depends upon his immediate kin, brothers, sons, and paternal and maternal cousins and nephews.

THE MAORI HAPU: FICTION AND FACT

The Maori *hapu*, to which we now turn, is a cognatic land-holding unit. A man is potentially a member of as many *hapus* as he has ancestors. But he cannot be everywhere at once; so, as with the Amharas, he lives and farms on the land of one particular group. Usually this is the community in which his father lived, since, while maternal and paternal ties theoretically carry equal weight, in practice paternal ties take precedence. Actual communities, then, are composed largely of patrilineally related men. If the anthropologist ignored the Maori's own self-image or 'folk-model' (which is cognatic) and simply described what actually happened, he would classify this system as 'patrilineal'. A similar discrepancy between the official blueprint and the actual composition of groups occurs amongst the Hadza hunters and gatherers of Tanzania. The structure of Hadza groups (to the extent that they exist) is in fact

20. A. Hoben, *Land Tenure Among the Amhara of Ethiopia*, University of Chicago Press, Chicago, 1973, p. 9.

based upon bilateral kinship ties, although the Hadza themselves consider that they trace descent *matrilineally*.

If principles are treated so cavalierly what weight can we attach to them? The answer is to be found in a dynamic analysis of how the same people respond to situations of hardship and scarcity. This will become clear if we compare the response of the Maoris and Mae-Enga of New Guinea to different demographic pressures. The Mae-Enga present themselves as firmly patrilineal.[21] How-ever, many of those who live and farm together in the same community are actually cognatically related. In times of crisis the picture changes dramatically. When the population of a local group outgrows its resources and shortage of land becomes serious, a purge of non-patrilineal kin is mounted. Relatives who were welcome before are transformed overnight into undesirable aliens. Those who are not genuine patrilineal patriots scuttle back to their own paternal homes. So in emergencies fiction becomes fact and precept practice. Exactly the same applies in the reverse direction among the Maoris. Here if land becomes scarce in his father's community, a man makes a bee-line for a less densely populated village where his cognatic connections guarantee him a friendly reception.

These examples show how facile classifications of whole societies under a particular descent label can be very misleading. When we compare kinship in different societies we must therefore always specify its functional implications in various contexts and con-ditions. The functional significance of the same descent pattern in different societies varies widely, so widely in fact that some com-parisons are misleading or meaningless, unless they are carefully controlled. This cautionary warning becomes all the more impor-tant as we turn to the more specific and limited types of descent in terms of which societies are often glibly categorized.

DOUBLE DESCENT

Hitherto we have seen how options can be reduced by ancillary restrictive clauses independent of descent. In cognatic (or bilateral) descent we trace relationships indiscriminately through both male

21. M. J. Meggitt, *The Lineage of the Mae-Enga of New Guinea*, Oliver & Boyd, 1965.

and female ancestors at every generation. Let us now exclude one set of ancestors in each generation and stick to male ancestors on the paternal side and female ones on the maternal side. The result is *double* (or *dual*) *descent*, a truncated and diminished version of cognatic descent. Looked at from the other end of the spectrum of types of descent, it is simply a combination of patrilineal and matrilineal descent.

Under such conditions every individual has dual allegiance to a patrilineal and to a matrilineal group. There must be some division of labour between his two identities if a schizoid situation is to be avoided – at least this seems to be implied in practice. For example, among both the Yakö of the Cross River region of Nigeria described by Daryll Forde[22] and the Yap Islanders of the Pacific studied by David Schneider[23] patrilineages form localized land-holding groups, while matrilineages are dispersed and provide diffuse attachments between the members of different communities. Matrilineal identity thus tends to cut across patrilineal divisions, and reinforces a higher level of social integration.

Yakö villages are divided into wards, each occupied by men of the same patriclan (*kepun*). This unit is exogamous and conducts its communal rituals in a ward assembly house. Its members belong to many different matriclans; matriclan identity thus links men of separate and potentially hostile patriclans. These extra-territorial connections have both a material and a spiritual significance: livestock and other movable wealth are inherited matrilineally, and each matriclan is a ritual congregation with a spirit shrine and attendant priest. Significantly, the matriclan spirits are believed to be more powerful than those of the patriline.

Matriclan identity is of great importance, and indeed is arguably more important than patriclan membership. A man pays bride-wealth to his wife's matriclan rather than to her patriclan. Similarly, if a man is murdered, compensation is paid to the matriclan and not the patriclan. Here maternity is more honoured than paternity. Indeed, in the case of homicide, the offended matriclan

22. D. Forde, 'Double Descent among the Yakö', in A. R. Radcliffe-Brown and D. Forde (eds), *African Systems of Kinship and Marriage*, Oxford University Press, 1950.

23. D. Schneider, 'Double Descent on Yap', *Journal of the Polynesian Society*, vol. 71, 1962, pp. 1–24.

may claim a woman in compensation from the killer's matriclan. If this woman bears children they belong to the offended matriclan and not to their mother's matriclan, thus replacing the dead man. This seems to be overcompensating, for if the dead man had himself lived to produce children they would have belonged to his patriclan but not to his matriclan; they would have taken their mother's matriclan identity.

In systems of dual or double descent, each person is a member of two separate kin groups. A man's children are his patrilineal descendants, but they also take their mother's matrilineal affiliation and are thus her brother's heirs. A father is a mother's brother to his sister's children and has binding responsibilities towards these nephews as well as to his own patrilineal heirs.

From this system we come to unilineal descent where descent is traced primarily in one direction only, either patrilineally or matrilineally. Under patriliny a man's children are his heirs and successors, whereas under matriliny his heirs are his sister's children. Since men rule the roost almost everywhere, in patrilineal systems the ruling sex also confers citizenship. In matrilineal systems this does not occur, and some interesting problems result.

MATRILINY

Where descent is traced matrilineally, through women, the men nevertheless monopolize all the positions of power; a man's closest relative is his sister and his most immediate heir and successor (after his brother) is her son. In such circumstances men must seek control of their sisters, and their sisters' children. A sister's marriage is of crucial concern to her brother, for the marital relationship which ensures the perpetuation of the matrilineage may compromise the sanctity of the bonds between brother and sister, and between mother's brother and sister's son. Husbands must not come between siblings except within well defined limits. Matrimony must not jeopardize matriliny. Ideally marriage should always give way before the over-riding interests of matrilineal kinship. Now the closer a brother lives to his sister and her husband, the more easily he can keep a watchful eye on their relationship, and ensure that marriage is kept in its proper place. Hence where the married couple live is always a crucial issue in matrilineal kinship systems.

The simplest way to safeguard the sibling bond is for brothers and sisters to live together in the same place and to allow men in from outside to impregnate the women at convenient intervals. It is not easy, however, to construct human societies in the image of stud-farms, although the traditional system of the Nayars came pretty close. Here the basic property-owning groups were bevies of sisters living on family estates, led by elder brothers who had completed their military service. In this martial society the women of each kin group within the caste or sub-caste were ritually married to the men of another corresponding group. When these men were home from the wars, they would visit their 'wives' to discharge their role as procreators. Matrimony was whittled down to a bare minimum. The 'husbands' possessed few rights, beyond generalized sexual access to their 'wives', and owed correspondingly few obligations to the women or their children. Those husbands currently visiting a pregnant wife should make some token contribution towards the expenses of her confinement, but little more was required. Under these conditions each matrilineage perpetuated itself without the marriage relationship threatening the more highly valued bond between siblings. Marriage existed to legitimize impregnation rather than sexual intercourse. That marriage was indeed a threat is clearly seen in the changes which have occurred amongst the Nayars over the last two centuries. With the abandonment of their traditional martial role under British rule and other economic changes, marriage has become stronger, binding specific individual spouses together and creating a clearly defined family unit with an accompanying decline in the significance of matrilineal descent.

This tussle between fraternal and uxorial affection is more equitably resolved in the traditional matrilineal system of the Ashanti of Ghana. Here again brothers and sisters live together under the same roof. But both are married to spouses in adjacent households only a stone's throw away. This enables the husband, who is much more than a mere impregnator, to visit his wife and children regularly – usually at least once every day. The woman, too, is much more of a wife than her Nayar counterpart, preparing her husband's food and seeing to his other wants with proper wifely solicitude. In the evenings children cheerfully ply back and forth between the matrilineal homesteads of their parents, bearing steaming bowls of food, which epitomises this happy balance between the potentially competing interests of matriliny and matrimony. A wife may even eventually live with her husband while of course remaining within visiting distance of her brother. The highly successful development of matrilineally based cocoa-producing companies in the modern cash economy is an impressive testimony to the high survival value of this harmonious system.[24]

The Dobuans of Melanesia strike a slightly different and at first sight more generous balance in the tug-of-war between matriliny and matrimony. They have adopted a kind of commuter *connubium* in which the visiting spouse can be either the wife or husband. Usually both partners alternate periods of residence in their own and their spouse's matrilineal village during the year, or they may operate an annual rotation of residence. In contrast to the situation among the Ashanti, this transhumant marriage is fraught with tension and difficulty. The incoming spouse is invariably treated as a most unwelcome intruder and, however well-intentioned, is a prime target for accusations of sorcery. Here in-laws receive no respect and are unceremoniously treated as outlaws. Because of this or other reasons, the Dobuans evidently feel menaced by marriage; they protect the integrity of the matrilineage by denying those who marry into it respect or affection.

Here we see again how difficult it is to whittle matrimony down to mere procreation. Few impregnators are as easily fobbed off as Nayar husbands once were. Strange though it may seem in western Europe, men want more than sex, and make demands on their wives which matrilineal societies find excessive and difficult to handle. One possibility is to grant these favours on condition that the husband comes and lives uxorilocally with his wife's group where he can be kept in his place. Under this dispensation, the women of the matrilineage live together as a residential and property-owning unit and are joined by their husbands. In return

24. See P. Hill, *Migrant Cocoa Farmers of Southern Ghana*, Cambridge University Press, 1963.

the women's brothers have to live with their wives and are hence separated from their sisters and sisters' children. Here the husband has, as it were, got one foot in the door of his wife's matrilineage and, if her brothers do not look out, he may usurp their place. The intrusive husband is likely to be treated coldly by his wife's sisters and, especially, by his wife's brothers when they visit their home. So among the Yao of Malawi where most marriages conform to this uxorilocal pattern, the incoming husband is derided (rather significantly) as a lecherous old billy-goat. Frigid receptions are, however, a poor substitute for direct action. To safeguard the interests of the matrilineage, therefore, the Yao allow eldest brothers to break the marriage residence rule and encourage them to bring their wives to live with them in their own home. This privilege ensures that the manager of the family estate is at hand to watch over his sisters, their husbands and their children, and to see that matrilineal interests are properly served. Here the recent conversion of the Yao to Islam, which is essentially a patrilineal religion, provides the heads of matrilineal family groups with convenient additional justification for breaking the rules and practising virilocal marriage.

In uxorilocal marriage the cost of keeping the women of the matrilineal core group together with their children is the dispersal of the majority of their menfolk; virilocal marriage has even less to commend it. If wives leave their matrilineal homes to join those of their husbands, their brothers are left to produce children for other men. The senior generation of men of the matrilineage live together on the maternal estate, but their heirs are elsewhere and the children they themselves sire do not belong to them. From the viewpoint of the maternal uncle, there is a danger that his sister's children, living with their father, may become too attached to him and thus alienated from their true kin. This difficulty can be offset by the sister's children living with their maternal uncle when they reach puberty and become ripe for marriage. Where this procedure (known as the 'avunculate') is followed, the nephew will marry and settle down in the village where his inheritance and succession rights lie. Under these arrangements a man in effect lends his sister to another on the understanding that he can redeem his male heirs when they reach maturity – a rather specialized division of labour! So the regular gifts made by a Trobriand islander to his sister's husband forcibly remind the latter of his obligation to surrender his children to their official 'owner'. In this fashion a senior man will eventually surround himself with his younger brothers and also with more distant matrilineal heirs.

Finally we must note that if both the women and the men of the matrilineage are dispersed by marriage in different local communities the matrilineal system loses much of its force. In many central African 'matrilineal' societies today the typical local units consist of fathers, sons, and brothers living patrilocally with their wives, and passing on land and sometimes other kinds of property patrilineally to the next generation. Here there is a thorough dilution of the matrilineal principle. Yet matrilineal connections may still play a significant role in providing cross-cutting ties between separate local communities which help to limit or prevent inter-village strife. In such conditions people find themselves in a web of conflicting loyalties. Residential and *de facto* patrilineal interests pull in one direction, while the more comprehensive inter-village matrilineal relationships pull in the other. This ostensibly 'matrilineal' central African organization is in practice virtually indistinguishable from the 'dual descent' system of the Yakö, and equally close to the increasingly common bilateral structure which threatens to engulf us all in a dreary uniformity of kinship organization. To say a society is 'matrilineal', 'patrilineal' or whatever is to say very little, unless we specify in detail the *relative* significance of kinship in the total social system.

So much then for the probably exaggerated 'problems' posed by matriliny whose features are not entirely negative. We should note in passing that although uxorilocal and virilocal residence both create difficulties, they do separate those who hold property and power from those who will inherit it – a situation which many of those locked together in intense competition under other descent dispensations would dearly love to achieve. Of course every system of descent creates problems, but some seem more intractable than others. That said, however, it is clear that the difficulties in matrilineal systems stem directly from the conflict between male domination and citizenship traced through women.

If women were to seize political control, making matriliny matriarchy, or to employ artificial insemination, things would be very
different.

KINSHIP TERMINOLOGY

Although in tribal societies there is usually no lack of kinsfolk,
it does not necessarily follow that there is an elaborate range of
kinship terms. In many cases the more relatives there are, the
smaller the number of kinship terms required to describe them.
This, indeed, is the characteristic feature of *classificatory* kinship
terminologies, where a few primary terms such as 'parent', 'child'
and 'sibling' elegantly and economically categorize a large array
of distinct and in principle distinguishable relatives. Here the
terms which describe close familial relationships are also applied
in a warm, open-hearted way to more distant connections.
Whether this should be seen as an 'extension' of the basic para-
meters of kinship, or as the selective use of intrinsically elastic
kinship terms applicable to 'close' and 'distant' kin without prejudice to their ultimate meaning, is an issue that need not detain
us here. Nor need we go into the complex algebra developed by
anthropologists who specialize in the comparative study of kinship terminology. For our present purpose it is sufficient to note
four useful categories of terminology based on the terms applied
to the close collateral kin of an individual's (ego's) parents.

If I refer to my father, my father's brother and to my mother's
brother by the *same* kinship term, then the leading principle is
clearly *generation*, which is the name anthropologists use for
this pattern (1 in the diagram).[25] If the two collateral relatives
are referred to by the same term (as in English and Amharic)
and thus differentiated from my father, then the system is known
as *lineal* (2 in the diagram). If my father and one uncle (not both)
are described by the same term this is known as *bifurcate merging*
(3 in the diagram). Finally, if there are three separate terms, one
for each category of relative, we call the system *bifurcate collateral* (4 in the diagram).

25. This pattern, which tends to be associated with bilateral descent, is mainly found
amongst speakers of the Malayo-Polynesian languages.

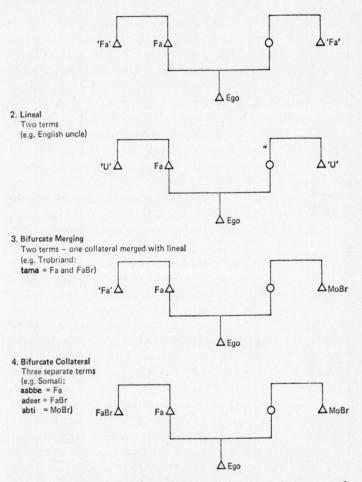

1. **Generation**
   Single inclusive term

2. **Lineal**
   Two terms
   (e.g. English uncle)

3. **Bifurcate Merging**
   Two terms – one collateral merged with lineal
   (e.g. Trobriand:
   tama = Fa and FaBr)

4. **Bifurcate Collateral**
   Three separate terms
   (e.g. Somali:
   aabbe = Fa
   adeer = FaBr
   abti = MoBr)

More generally, as Radcliffe-Brown long ago demonstrated, kinship terminology and behaviour (at least in part) reflects three major guiding principles. The first is known as the 'unity of the sibling group'. A single term often refers to siblings of either sex. If I stand in a certain relationship to one person then, in principle, my relationship with his siblings is the same, and theirs with me.

This principle may of course be affected and modified by the relative seniority of siblings as we have seen in the case of the Wik-Mungkan.

Our second principle is the 'unity of the lineage group'. Here an external lineage (other than one's own) to which one is connected through a relative is treated as a single, undifferentiated group, and all its members stand in the same common relation to oneself. Generational distinctions are ignored and elided. All are treated in the same fashion as the person to whom I am related. So, for example, in a patrilineal society I may treat *all* the members of my mother's patrilineage as maternal relatives of the same type and call them by the same kinship term. From my perspective their common properties are more important than their differences.

We come now to our third principle, that of generation, which is familiar to us in the form of the 'generation gap'. We tend to think ethnocentrically that this striking cleavage between the old and the young is unique to our own disintegrating society. The truth is that such generational cleavages occur in all societies and exhibit two broad and readily comprehensible trends. In general, relations between the members of immediately succeeding generations (such as between father and son) are marked by constraint and tension. This reflects the exercise of authority by the senior generation over the younger; the young only acquire property and power at the expense, and eventual retirement or death of the old. As John Middleton coolly records of the Lugbara, 'A man loves his father but he waits for him to die.'[26] This conflict of interest is often minimized and controlled by conventional respectful behaviour, which accentuates social distance and reduces stressful interaction.

Between members of alternate generations (such as grandparent and grandchild), the absence of direct competition for control of wealth and power encourages amicable relations. This is the basis of the proverbial indulgence which grandparents display towards their grandchildren, and the strong identification which is frequently acknowledged explicitly. Children may be named after or in honour of their grandparents, or considered to reincarnate them. Often grandparents and grandchildren refer to each

26. J. Middleton, *The Lugbara of Uganda*, Holt, Rinehart & Wilson, 1965, p. 27.

other by a single reciprocal kinship term which means in effect 'person of alternate generation'. This cross-generational solidarity is perhaps one of the most striking features shared by kinship systems which differ markedly in other respects. An impressive recent demonstration of this was the Chinese Cultural Revolution, with Chairman Mao acting as a universal grandfather figure to the revolutionary young, benignly inspiring them to discipline the intervening parental generation. Freud's Oedipus theory of intra-familial conflict, though cast in a sexual idiom, rests ultimately on the same basic facts.

These patterns of friendship and competition between genera-tions may be systematically employed in the social structure of communities. This is the case for example in village organization and settlement structure among the Kaonde tribe of Zambia, who live near the Ndembu. Each Kaonde village is divided into two halves, with those of the same or alternate generation on one side confronting their opposite numbers of proximate generation on the other. The diagram shows a typical village which I surveyed in 1960. This physical separation by generation is explained by the Kaonde as following from the shame and embarrassment of the relations between mother's brother and sister's son in this

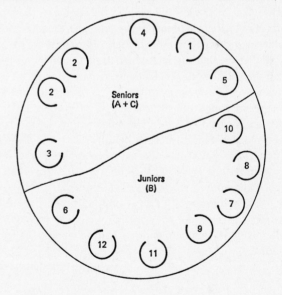

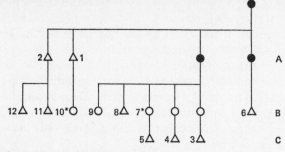

* 7 and 10 had their husbands living with them.

matrilineal society. Those who hold authority and those who are heirs to it are kept primly apart, and whichever half of the village contains its headman is the senior. When the headship passes from maternal uncle to nephew, the junior half becomes senior and the senior junior, so power in villages oscillates between the two constituent parts.

GENERATION AND AGE-SETS

More pervasive groupings may be based on the principle of generation. The Galla-speaking peoples, the largest ethnic congeries in north-east Africa, are probably the supreme example. Here men are traditionally recruited by generation into 'sets' or 'streams' to which they belong for life and which are a fundamental building block of the social system. Like sons sent to schools or colleges patronized by a family over generations, Galla of the same generation progress through the successive age-linked roles of life in an orderly and predictable way. The main stages are as bachelor warriors, married family men, political leaders and judges, and ritual officiants. Each generational peer group elects its own leaders, who assume political control of the tribe as a whole when they reach the appropriate stage. The stages are formalized into 'grades' arranged on (usually) a five-point cycle. In principle each set occupies a given grade for a period of eight years, after which they all move up a grade, so political control changes hands every eight years.

Ideally, sons are initiated into their generation set, whatever their actual age, when their fathers are in the reigning grade, five stages and forty years further on in the system. At the same time the fathers reach full social and political maturity exactly when *their* fathers, who are ideally sturdy octogenarians, are retiring and being replaced by *their* grandsons. To achieve this, marriage is delayed so that sons will be of an age to be initiated approximately forty years after their fathers. Ideally, then, an infant is initiated into the same set as his father along with the sons of other men of his father's generation. Then he marries and has children just before he and his set enter the reigning grade some forty years later. Finally, another forty years later he and his companions retire gracefully from active life.

The practical difficulties of actually working this *gada* system do not concern us here. Note how *gada* membership cuts across clan and age-set lines and thus contributes to the overall solidarity of tribal political units.[27]

This brings us directly to the use of age as a basis for role ascription. The Galla expect their citizens to accept increasingly responsible roles as they get older, in common with the Lele of the Congo and many other peoples to whom we referred earlier. Unlike ours, most traditional societies are gerontocratic in that as men grow older they receive increasing prestige and power. There are practical limits to this attractive doctrine which are pithily summed up in a terse Coorg saying: 'The wisest is eldest.' As a principle of social grouping, age is most pervasive in those societies where individuals are systematically grouped together in age-sets. Here those of an age, rather than of a generation (although the two concepts blur at the edges), go through life as a staunchly loyal team of fraternally united comrades. Their mutual loyalties, which are reinforced by their competition with parallel age-sets in the same age-grade and their opposition to their seniors and juniors in other grades, link men (and sometimes also women) who may be divided by kinship, place of residence or other significant social ties. The important integrative potential which they thus offer is probably most fully and certainly most aggressively exploited in the militaristic cultures of the traditionally

27. See A. Legesse, *Gada: Three Approaches to the Study of African Society*, Free Press, New York, 1973.

predatory pastoralists of east Africa – the Masai being a prime example. The great conquering Zulu hero, Shaka, is generally considered to owe much of his remarkable military success to the army he organized on a basis of age-regiments.

On the other hand the Nyakyusa of Tanzania, who take the principle of age organization to what might seem its logical conclusion, are not generally known for bellicosity. They believe that those who belong to the same age-set are so closely bound together that they should form a separate local community. The basic form of Nyakyusa settlement is an age-village; kinship ties and rights in movable property (mainly cattle) are dispersed rather than combined with residence. The conflict of loyalties which this unusual arrangement produces, as their ethnographer Monica Wilson[28] reports, has wide repercussions in other aspects of their life and is even reflected in their witchcraft beliefs. The ideal is that neighbours in an age-village should generously share food and other resources, but the most coveted foodstuffs – milk and meat – come from cattle which are owned agnatically by people who do not live together in the same village. Inequalities in wealth in livestock, in wealth lying outside the control of the village, are consequently a common source of envy. It is thus easy to understand that Nyakyusa witches should be considered to possess an insatiable appetite for meat and milk.

28. M. Wilson, *Good Company: A Study of Nyakyusa Age-Villages*, Oxford University Press, 1951.

Chapter Nine

Power at the Centre

We live in a pervasively and self-consciously politicized age and culture. Everything for us must now possess a political dimension, and if something does not already have one, it is not long before one is discovered for it. We glibly talk about business politics, educational politics, the politics of the mass media, academic politics, family politics, environmental politics, and even of sexual (or sexist) politics. The spectrum of protest politics is truly vast and all-embracing : any disadvantaged group or category, we now concede, owns rights to self-expression which can only be realized through the politics of liberation. Further evidence of this generalized and indiscriminate politicization is to be found in the increasing use of such essentially political words as anarchist, revolutionary, radical, liberal, progressive, reactionary, bourgeois, imperialist, and fascist as terms of approval or abuse in our personal relations – often outside a strictly political context.

We have come a long way from the sedate world of formal political parties. In those halcyon days politics referred to the well-regulated and ideally good-tempered competition for power between the properly appointed national parties whose legislative activities at Westminster or Washington exhausted the conventional political domain – this, after all, was the result and aim of the hard-fought battle for universal suffrage. Then it was only the big battalions that fully qualified for the honour of the title 'political', and fringe activities could be safely ignored. Now everything counts, and in some respects the more unusual and specialized the issue the better. The repertory of acknowledged contemporary political activity runs from ecologists through animal rights and anti-seal-culling activists to a whole series of other pressure groups, with the traditional political parties trailing along behind and desperately seeking to recover some of the action. In the process, obsolete political terms and concepts are revived, as in contemporary Britain where the representatives of both labour and capital have talked of regulating their mutual dependence by means of a 'social contract'. In an atmosphere in which entrenched inequalities are increasingly questioned the contractarian spirit is again in the ascendant. The purist political scientist would no doubt warn that where politics becomes so all-embracing and inclusive it becomes everything and therefore nothing. For the anthropologist, however, the prospect is encouraging. For increasing recognition of the political in our *own* society helps us to appreciate how politics in non-industrial societies is often embedded in other social institutions and thus implicit rather than explicit. (This will hardly surprise advocates of the conspiracy theory of power.) But what then is politics? The simplest and for our purposes perhaps least misleading answer is that politics is concerned with the making of (policy) decisions which affect how people order their affairs and control their resources. How such decisions are arrived at and by whom; how those who make them are appointed, controlled and replaced; the limits within which they act; the nature of their authority and power – all these are central issues in politics.

We need not agree unreservedly with Samuel Johnson's characteristic assertion that 'no two men can be half an hour together, but one shall acquire an evident superiority over the other'. Yet from our everyday experience we do know that in most political situations, whatever the ideological aims or political culture of those involved, some people exert more influence than others. However informal and democratic the proceedings, and however *ad hoc* or ephemeral the relative positions of those concerned, human groups never lack leaders and followers. (It is partly because of this and through their dedication to spontaneity that communes in European industrial cities tend to be extremely unstable.) This admitted, the more traditional European view of politics and government tends to take for granted, however, the existence of universally institutionalized political inequality and the existence everywhere of hierarchically organized states. The conception of the state as the global political norm obdurately refuses to wither away. In its old form, this ethnocentric tradition treats the history of mankind as the achievements of monarchs and ministers, lesser breeds simply acting as foils or extras. It was in this spirit that the earliest missionaries, explorers, and colonial officials in Asia and Africa were accustomed to hail any unknown party of tribesmen they encountered with the peremptory request: 'Take us to your leader. Lead us to the Chief.' And where there actually were chiefs and traditional kings, even if they resisted colonization, at least the situation was familiar and could be handled according to well-understood principles. One could always 'go to the top' as the expression has it.

This élitist assumption was one of the corner-stones of the British policy of indirect rule, which was applied first in India and then in Africa, where its most eloquent apostle was Lord Lugard,[1] the pioneering administrator who in 1890 negotiated the first British treaty of 'protection' with the BaGanda and so founded modern Uganda. This administrative principle was actually an economy measure to use local indigenous institutions where there were not enough expatriate officials to go round. It formed part of a wider colonial philosophy which showed respect, however distantly and paternalistically, for the traditional institutions of the colonized. (The French and Portuguese, in contrast, had a more direct approach, usually destroying traditional chieftaincies and kingdoms, and then moulding their new subjects in their own image – an acculturative process which they called 'assimilation'. In practice these theoretically opposed national policies sometimes amounted to much the same thing.)[2]

The British policy of recognizing existing local authorities and attaching them in a subordinate capacity to the colonial superstructure ran into difficulties in regions where no chiefs could be found. The absence of traditional rulers seemed at first a startling aberration; according to the accepted wisdom, proper tribesmen the world over had chiefs and respected them. Those who did not admit to any must therefore either be obdurately concealing their leaders from their new masters, or be the most anarchic of savages in desperate need of the civilizing benefits of European rule. Fre-

1. This policy is expounded in his classic: F. D. Lugard, *The Dual Mandate in British Tropical Africa*, 1922.

2. For a thoroughly comprehensive assessment of colonial policy in Africa see Lord M. Hailey's masterly *African Survey*, Oxford University Press, 1957.

quently the colonial office in London simply refused to accept that
in some places there were no indigenous authorities, and exhorted
its functionaries to search more diligently. So, for example, at the
beginning of this century the few harassed expatriate officials in
the British Somaliland Protectorate were bombarded with dis-
patches from their superiors in Whitehall urging them to find the
'golden stool' which, by analogy with the Ashanti, would enable
them to discipline the unruly Somali nomads. Our hardened and
much better informed men on the spot already knew to their cost
that there was, alas, no Somali golden stool, or anything remotely
resembling it, possession of which could provide effective control
over their quarrelsome subjects. It took the colonial office a long
time to accept the unwelcome truth that in this and many other
comparable cases there were no chiefs in the conventional sense.

Political theorists and political scientists have been almost
equally slow to recognize the theoretical and practical significance
of the anthropological discovery of the 'non-state' (as W. J. M.
Mackenzie calls it). Now, however, most social scientists who
study politics share with anthropologists the view that the state
simply occupies one broad band on a vast spectrum of types and
styles of government and political system, running from highly
centralized structures at one extreme to un- or de-centralized
systems at the other. And at all points along the continuum (for
it is a continuum) from 'maximum' government to 'minimum'
government, different kinds and degrees of centralization and de-
centralization can be realized in a rich diversity of cultural forms.
No culture or historical period, however unique the texture and
colouring of its political life, has a monopoly of a particular degree
of hierarchy or of republican egalitarianism, its opposite. And, as
we all know, those who at one period obey tyrannical rulers may
subsequently refuse to live under any but the most democratic
government. Within the same cultural tradition polities often
change dramatically. Indeed the history of political thought combined with the findings of comparative political anthropology
suggests that the antithesis between what medieval historians call
the 'descending' (or despotic, centralist) theory of government and
its opposite, the 'ascending' populist, democratic tradition, are in
some sense universals of human experience. Thus the regular

oscillation between centralized and uncentralized political organization which Edmund Leach [3] discovered in Highland Burma is far from being a limited or unusual phenomenon. We are acutely aware of this perennial tension between the centre and the periphery as we recoil from the inhumanity of anonymous over-centralization and long nostalgically for what we take to be the cosy simplicity of small-scale, participant politics.

LAW AND ORDER

This brings us to our final preliminary point: the relationship between politics and law and order, and between community and culture. As the history of decolonization reminds us, in the last analysis politics is concerned with freedom – with self-determination and full autonomy. To enjoy complete sovereignty a political community must be able to conduct its own internal and external affairs without interference. Within the limitations imposed by its external environment, it must have the capacity to go its own way. In the words of Kwame Nkrumah: 'It is far better to be free to govern or misgovern yourself than to be governed by anyone else.' It is arguable whether many modern states are actually fully autonomous in this sense. It is obvious that defence and other inter-state alignments and alliances limit and abridge sovereignty. This is partly what was at issue (and remains largely unresolved) in the debate over Britain's membership of the European Economic Community.

The power to determine external policy implies the authority, the will and the ability to maintain internal order. You cannot expect to be treated as a politically mature sovereign body abroad unless you can satisfactorily manage your affairs at home. So, Schapera's [4] classical formulation runs, political organization is 'that aspect of the total organization which is concerned with the establishment and maintenance of internal cooperation and external independence'. This definition recognizes that, despite our traditional and admirable doctrine that the judiciary and bureaucracy should be separated from politics, in the final analysis

3. E. R. Leach, *Political Systems of Highland Burma*, Athlone Press, 1954.
4. I. Schapera, *Government and Politics in Tribal Societies*, Watts, 1956, p. 218.

governments not only legislate but also, while they retain effective power, possess the means to enforce their legislation. The seventeenth century anti-monarchist English philosopher, John Locke, who is the main intellectual source of this doctrine of the 'separation of powers', had no illusions about the ultimate sanction of government. 'Political power', he declares in his second *Treatise on Government* (1690), 'I take to be the right of making laws, with penalty of death, and consequently all less penalties for the regulating and preserving of property, and of employing the force of the community in the execution of such laws, and in defence of the commonwealth from foreign injury, and all this only for the public good.'

All this follows directly from the elementary principle that unity is strength. Internal disaffection and disorder threaten external cohesion, while internal harmony and accord tend to be encouraged, within certain limits, by publicly recognized external dangers.

States strenuously resist external interference in their internal affairs. Thus the refusal of Ian Smith's Rhodesian régime to recognize the jurisdiction of the British Privy Council was based on the correct assumption that to do so would amount to admitting an infringement of Rhodesian sovereignty. For precisely the same reasons South Africa could not accept that the International Court had the power to pronounce authoritatively on her (illegal) claim to control Namibia. In the same vein, those who in the ghetto areas of Ulster maintain internal discipline with such barbaric ruthlessness can legitimately claim that they are well on the way to forming separate political units. No wonder also that 'law and order' is so sensitive an issue in the United States. If you have achieved self-control you are in the running for self-government.

This double-faced connection between policy-making and social control, commemorated in English in the etymologically cognate words 'police' and 'politics', is clearly displayed in many tribal political structures. This is one reason why anthropologists so often speak of 'politico-legal' institutions or offices; and where political and legal boundaries are shifting and hard to define rigidly, they invoke the convenient term 'peace-group' for the largest community whose members are sufficiently united to be able to settle their internal disputes peaceably (although they may not always do so). This way of defining a political group, which emphasizes the law and order aspect, is particularly appealing where formal political offices are difficult to identify. It goes without saying that our 'peace-group' is someone else's war-group, since we will obviously be prepared to defend our fragile unity, if need be by force. This paradoxical but entirely logical equivalence is directly recognized in the language of some American Indian groups where the term the anthropologist translates neutrally as 'tribe' means literally 'to fight against external foes'. Political solidarity, to reiterate, presupposes the capacity to combine to protect joint interests. In this sense every state is a police-state.

The boundaries of political and legal authority do not always coincide. There are frequently many different levels of political alignment and legal identity, some of which overlap and intersect without exactly matching. There is also the crucial point, as we shall see, that political boundaries do not always duplicate cultural frontiers – and here we broach the question of the relationship between community and culture. Like modern states, some traditional political units are pluralistic in that they include several culturally distinct communities. Equally, cultural differences may be employed to accentuate and justify political distinctions – indeed some are invented expressly for this purpose. Although the term 'nation-state', a hangover from the irredentist nationalism of the nineteenth century, is firmly established in the vocabulary of international relations, many modern states are manifestly not united nations, since they lack a single, comprehensive national culture. By the term nation, following the best anthropological authority we understand, of course, a culture-unit (a point to which we shall return in the next chapter). In this sense although the Arabs form one nation they do not all live together in one state: while the Jews, who are at least as widely dispersed, do at least possess only one state, expressly founded on the basis of their Jewish nationalism as the sole repository of their ethnic destiny, and which, moreover, contains a dissident Arab minority. These cases remind us of the true complexity of the connections between political (and economic) interest, legal obligation, and cultural identity. There are many ways in which these three elements can be combined.

These and other issues are best explored by reference to specific ethnographic examples. So we now consider three traditional African states whose political structures are well documented in some historical depth, and which conveniently illustrate different degrees and styles of centralized authority. We choose those of peoples we have already met in other contexts – the Bemba of Zambia, the Amharas of Ethiopia, and the BaGanda of Uganda – which, ranged in this order, represent successive steps towards political centralization. In each case, as in European history from feudal to recent times, the locally dominant historical trends are in the same direction. Each state thus recalls our own historical experience, displaying a familiar process which we here pick up at a point well along the line of increasing centralization in exchange and redistribution sketched out in our discussion of tribute in chapter 7 (page 221). There our emphasis was primarily economic. Here we stress (wherever possible in historical perspective) the scale of political unity, the degree of cultural homogeneity, the kind and character of centralized control (and especially the balance between sacred and secular authority), and the comparative anatomy of administrative, judicial, fiscal and military organization. While scarcely exhaustive, our three cases are sufficiently representative to introduce a wider and more theoretical assessment of the logistics of centralized power. In the following chapter we complete our analysis of traditional government by concentrating on uncentralized political organization, and we explore the relationship between centralized control and modes of dispute-settlement and attempt to identify some formative forces which promote the development or decline of centralized rule.

DIVINE KINGSHIP AMONG THE BEMBA

The matrilineal Bemba are traditionally one of the three most prominent peoples in the modern state of Zambia (formerly Northern Rhodesia), the other two being the Lozi of Barotseland and the Ngoni. When Audrey Richards was carrying out her pioneering field studies in the early 1930s, the Bemba numbered a little over 100,000 (today their strength is approximately 250,000) and lived widely dispersed over a large area of poor soil at a density of under four persons per square mile (less than that of the northern Somali nomads). In this unpromising environment the presence of the tsetse fly virtually rules out cattle-keeping, and the traditional economy is based on shifting cultivation, with the *citimene* system of slash-and-burn cropping, and finger millet as the principal crop. Gardens seldom retain their fertility for more than four or five years, and villages, which regularly contain from thirty to forty houses and families, move almost as frequently. Despite their mobility, however, villages remain grouped in wider regional units through their ritual dependence on a chief. Traditionally chiefs hold fixed titles – those of the original incumbents – and their ritual domains, taken collectively, form the Bemba state presided over by the king or *Citimukulu* (styled 'Paramount Chief' by the British), drawn from the aristocratic crocodile clan. All the Bemba share the same culture and language, and ultimately trace their origins to the ancient Luba kingdom of the Congo, from which they claim they split off to settle in their present territory some two hundred and fifty years ago. It is on this basis, as the descendants of the original pioneers and founding settlers, that the crocodile clan are held to be undisputed leaders throughout Bemba territory. As a commoner explained, the royal family are named after the crocodile because 'they are like crocodiles that seize hold of the common people and tear them to bits with their teeth'. (This statement recalls Locke's ironical condemnation of absolute monarchy, which he says is as if men protected themselves against polecats and foxes 'while being content, nay think it safety, to be devoured by lions'.)

Most chiefs belong to this powerful clan, and each controls the people in his territory from his ritual capital, where he holds court as ruler, judge, and tribute collector. The king at the centre has a dual role – as chief of his own central chiefdom and as head of the nation. He controls his own district and receives tribute labour from it rather than from subordinate chiefs. Before British interference, all the chiefs relied on the tribute they were given to support their priestly advisers (the *bakabilo*) when the latter attended court (and helped to dispense justice), to entertain their subjects hospitably, and to support a personal following of retainers, body-guards (and in the nineteenth century a small militia), musicians and others. The Bemba have a well-deserved reputation amongst their neighbours as fierce warriors, and sought every opportunity to extend their territory, a chief's prestige being closely related to the size of the region under his dominion and the number of his followers.

The major chiefdoms are linked to the kingship in a fixed order of precedence, which in practice operates as a promotion cycle. Ambitious and successful chiefs are promoted to increasingly senior chiefdoms and hope ultimately to obtain the paramouncy itself. Their relative ranking is expressed in the language of kinship, so that whatever the actual relationship of the incumbents may be, they refer to each other according to the relationship between their offices. The pattern linking the various chiefships is that established by their original founders, each successor inheriting his predecessor's name and kinship position. This system of 'perpetual' (or 'positional') succession, like that of the Petrine doctrine in the Roman Church according to which each pope assumes the legal personality of St Peter, perpetuates the original distribution of power within the kingdom. Here Collingwood's famous phrase about the past being encapsulated in the present applies with remarkable force; political time is held still in frozen immobility as the original hierarchy of authority continues for ever.

What goes for chiefs and king applies with equal force to commoners. All Bemba follow an emphatic (matrilineal) version of Roman law in succeeding to the name, spirit and kinship position as well as to the property of their predecessors. An heir thus assumes the total social and spiritual personality of those who went before him, identifying himself completely with them, totally absorbing them and being in turn absorbed by them. In this fashion, as the culmination and continuation of all his predecessors the present *Citimukulu* can say: 'When we spoke to Livingstone' or, going back over two hundred years, 'When I came from the Congo'. This is a very strong use of the royal 'we' and one that annihilates the conventional restrictions of time and place.

The component chiefdoms are also locked together in a fixed cycle of ritual, a mystical chain reminiscent of the Elizabethan 'chain of being', in which the king, aided by his priestly councillors, acts as initiator and plays the principal part. The king presides over the rituals which open each phase of the agricultural cycle, the clearing of the bush for cultivation, the planting of seeds, and the first-fruits harvest ceremonies. He thus rules through ritual, inaugurating and regulating the entire seasonal cycle. Here, to revert for a moment to the theme of an earlier chapter, ritual not only oils the wheels of life but actually sets them in motion. In times of national calamity (for which he may be held responsible through neglect of the stringent taboos he must observe) he launches a chain of propitiatory sacrifices: and in times of prosperity (for which he seeks to reap the credit) he performs the 'great prayers' of thanksgiving in which he displays the beneficence of his reign in all its splendour.

As the sole repository of the cumulative power of his predecessors who first reigned, the *Citimukulu* is saluted as 'Owner' or 'Father of the Land', and is expected to nurture and cherish his people, generously sharing with them the blessings he derives from the sacred relics (*babenye*). As in the classical divine kingships, the health and wellbeing of the king and of his subjects are inseparably conjoined. If he falls ill or suffers injury or misfortune, the life and prosperity of the nation are threatened: hence he must be protected with the utmost vigilance from all contact with disease, death or pollution.

This mystical identification of people and kingship is familiar since we share a similar tradition of divine rule, vestiges of which linger on, often in unsuspected ways; for instance it is still a criminal offence in Australia to hold a funeral on our monarch's birthday. For the same reasons we expect our royalty to spend a disproportionate time visiting the sick in hospitals, although we no longer speak openly of bringing patients to be 'touched' for the 'king's evil' – a treatment applied (apparently with some success) to Samuel Johnson when he was brought to London at the age of three to be healed by Queen Anne's miraculous touch. Similar expectations, no less potent for being unstated, underlie royal visits to disaster areas.

So much is common ground between ourselves and the Bemba. But the Bemba ask much more of their divine rulers. The king and his immediately subordinate chiefs are required to perform ritual sexual intercourse with their wives at regular intervals for the good of the country. These solemn acts of national intimacy (one is tempted to say of public privacy) are arranged by the priestly councillors, and take place in the special ritual house which is always the first building to be erected in a chiefdom and is known significantly as the 'place of tribute'. This is the most efficacious way by which the king's royal energy is released to empower his people and fructify their land and crops. But the heat so produced to 'warm' the country, bringing life and fertility, is potentially dangerous and is consequently hedged about with protective ritual prohibitions and precautions which are administered with fastidious care by the *bakabilo* priests who 'keep the king divine'.[5] Like lesser chiefs, the king cannot in fact perform the essential rituals of kingship effectively without the collaboration and support of the *bakabilo*, who may scold him and, if they consider it in the public interest, withhold their cooperation. So constrained, the king symbolizes the nation and his emotional life and moral conduct directly affect its wellbeing. In the same Frazerian tradition, in the old days when the king was near to death he was ritually strangled by his faithful councillors to prevent his taking the vitality of the country with him into the grave. Even so his death was a national disaster. The land had lost its lively 'warmth' and had grown 'cold' – it was 'broken into pieces'.

The *Citimukulu*'s traditional supremacy rested upon his unique status as a god in human form. From the middle of the nineteenth century, however, just before British colonization, the advent of Arab slave traders introduced a vital new element – fire-arms. While not conclusive, the available historical evidence suggests that the crocodile chiefs increased their grip on their subjects by force of arms, appointing loyal warrior leaders as 'king's men', and thus adding a new secular dimension to their formerly dominantly ritual power. Under these conditions, the king's executioners killed his enemies and savagely mutilated those who were unwise

5. A. Richards, 'Keeping the King Divine', *Proceedings of the Royal Anthropological Institute*, 1968, pp. 23–36.

enough to offend him or violate his property. At this time, Audrey Richards argues, the paradox of the all-powerful benign ruler who was also ruthlessly merciless began to be more clearly perceived by his subjects.

Subsequent developments point to the tension between the priestly councillors, as representatives of the people and the potentially autocratic king. British administration undermined some of the traditional perquisites of chiefly office – discouraging tribute labour, which smacked of slavery – but confirmed the special status of the king as a salaried 'Paramount Chief' with recognized (though diminished) judicial and other powers. On the other hand, the chief was now expected to be the premier spokesman and exemplar for modernizing innovations which the Northern Rhodesian administration sought to introduce. If these proved unpopular, as the maintenance of village cleanliness and the construction of hygienic latrines usually did, the chief was placed in a difficult position. Where the views of his people and the administration were in conflict, he could only side with his people at the expense of his credit with the administration. The 'progressive' and cooperative chiefs who won administrative laurels were often regarded very differently by their subjects. As in other colonial territories, this new and more complicated situation produced by the encapsulation of the Bemba kingdom within the wider system of British overrule disturbed the traditional redistributive nexus between ruler and ruled, and encouraged chiefs to pursue their own interests. In the early 1930s, with the suppression of tribute and only a minute stipend, the *Citimukulu's* position was such that his advisers often melted away from court hearings because there was no food for them. The king could scarcely be blamed if he sought new avenues to wealth and power.

In the meantime ordinary tribesmen flocked in large numbers as migrant labourers to the newly opened European mines on the nearby Copperbelt. As much as 60 per cent of the tribe's able-bodied manpower was often away with, as can be imagined, drastic consequences for the traditional cultivating economy. But there were compensations. This early urban experience gave the Bemba a headstart in modern political activities, and goes far to explain the strong Bemba component in President Kaunda's government, which has been a frequent source of embarrassment and has led to a number of serious political crises. At a more parochial level, in LuBemba itself these and other modern influences have exacerbated the growing cleavage between the ordinary peasant cultivators and the aristocracy. And the extent to which the *bakabilo* are regarded as representing an effective check on chiefly despotism was dramatically illustrated immediately before independence, when, in the new language of political condemnation to which he had become accustomed, the reigning *Citimukulu* urged the departing colonial rulers to dismiss his councillors because they were 'not progressive'! His position had evidently become similar to that of the Tutsi aristocracy in Rwanda who, it will be recalled (p. 190), had pressed the Belgians for early independence as soon as they began to feel the threat of Hutu competition.

PRESTER JOHN'S EMPIRE: AMHARA AUTOCRACY

The Amharan-Tigrean empire[6] of Ethiopia presents a very different picture. Here, under much more difficult circumstances, much more is asked of secular government. Bembaland would form only a tiny province or district of the sprawling, unwieldy Ethiopian empire; and the power of its monarch, even if he is a kind of god, pales before the actual might of Ethiopian kings. In Ethiopia we are concerned with a highly complex system of government where mystical features are still significant but where ultimately rule is, and has for centuries been, based on force of arms. At once the oldest, largest, and most cosmopolitan of Africa's traditional empires, Ethiopia is a conquest state containing a unique diversity of peoples and language-groups, a true mosaic of cultures and social structures, occupying over 400,000 square miles and numbering some twenty million people. Its present boun-

6. For an excellent brief introduction to Ethiopia's cultural history, see E. Ullendorff, *The Ethiopians: An Introduction to Country and People*, Oxford University Press, 1965 and also D. N. Levine, *Wax and Gold: Tradition and Innovation in Ethiopian Culture*, University of Chicago Press, 1965; the best concise history remains A. H. M. Jones and E. Monroe, *A History of Abyssinia*, Oxford University Press, 1935. For a uniquely informative analysis of Ethiopian politics and government before the 1974 *coup*, see C. Clapham, *Haile-Selassie's Government*, Longman, 1969. See also J. Markakis, *Ethiopia: Anatomy of a Traditional Polity*, Oxford University Press, 1975.

daries, which owe much to the audacious conquests of Menelik in the last century, would be even more far-flung had not the Italian, French and British colonizers greedily laid claim to portions of the surrounding littoral at precisely this period. Known since the middle ages in Europe as the mysterious Christian kingdom of Prester John, Ethiopia itself had the good fortune to escape foreign colonization until the brutal Italian invasion of 1935, when the great powers stood back and pusillanimously allowed Mussolini to seize his short-lived East African empire, thus revenging the stunning defeat inflicted by the Ethiopians on an earlier generation of Italian imperialists at the battle of Adowa in 1896.

Prior to 1896, the Italians had been infiltrating from a foothold on the Eritrean coast and were intriguing between the two leading Ethiopean figures of the times – the Tigrean emperor Yohannes IV (1872–89) and Menelik II, king of Shoa in the Amhara heartland. Control over the import of fire-arms, mainly from the Turks, had long been a crucial factor in Ethiopian affairs, and Menelik prudently acquired large quantities of weapons and ammunition from the French and Italians. After the unexpected death of Yohannes in a battle against the forces of the Sudanese Mahdi in 1889, Menelik succeeded him as emperor and the Italians concluded a treaty which they claimed (wrongly) made Ethiopia their protectorate. Further arms and money poured into the country, but when the Italians attempted to press their claims Menelik mobilized his forces against the European invaders and routed them at Adowa in 1896. Over eight thousand Italians were killed outright and another four thousand of their native soldiers: almost two thousand prisoners were later released by the Ethiopians.[7] This was one of those exceptional colonial encounters proving by default the accuracy of Hilaire Belloc's famous lines:

> Thank God that we have got
> The Gatling gun and they have not.

This astonishing African victory over a major European power was made all the more impressive by the surprising humanity with which many of the Italian captives were treated. Its shock

7. A detailed reconstruction of the battle, written shortly after it was over by Augustus B. Wylde, the British vice-consul for the Red Sea, is contained in his book, *Modern Abyssinia*, Methuen, 1901.

effect upon the prestige of Italy was such that it has been held responsible by some political historians for the rise of modern Italian nationalism. It was in this spirit that, speaking for many of his countrymen, in his old age Gabriele d'Annunzio urged a young fascist soldier departing for the 'African war' of 1935 to wipe out this humiliating memory of which he could still feel 'the scar, yes, the shameful scar, of Adowa'. Whatever part the ignominy of Adowa played in the rise of fascism in Italy, it was this victory and the consequent grudging recognition of the other European powers which, combined with Ethiopia's biblical association, gave her exalted international status as the first sovereign African Third World power. This unique reputation, increased rather than diminished by her gallant though unavailing resistance to the vicious fascist onslaught of 1935, goes far to explain how the very name Ethiopia has acquired such magical potency throughout the colonized world. So, in South Africa, Ethiopia is the rallying cry by means of which hundreds of African separatist churches seek to express their frustrated quest for dignity and autonomy. And in the West Indies the ex-slave masses formed the Ras Tafari movement which takes its name from the personal name of emperor Haile Selassie before his coronation and treats him like a god and his country, Ethiopia, as heaven on earth. This movement developed in the early 1930s from the evangelical teaching of the Jamaican Negro and Black Power pioneer, Marcus Garvey (1887–1940), who in 1918 founded the United Negro Improvement Association, advocating the mass migration of American Negroes to Africa as a return to the Ethiopian homeland, and coined the famous slogans: 'Africa for the Africans!', and 'One God, One Goal, One Destiny'.

The same circumstances, in conjunction with Haile Selassie's personal genius for politics, lie behind Ethiopia's leading role in Pan-African affairs and made Addis Ababa the natural headquarters for the Organisation of African Unity and for the Economic Commission for Africa. Not, of course, that all this is without irony. Traditional Amhara attitudes towards foreigners in general and Blacks in particular are as arrogantly ethnocentric as those of their Hamitic and Arabic-speaking neighbours to the north and east. Some found it even more paradoxical that in an era of liberation movements and Maoist republics, Africa's leading spokesman should have been an emperor.

But behind these contemporary events stretches a long, turbulent history. We have already indicated the setting: the cultural and ethnic pluralism which Ethiopia shares with its much more recently formed neighbouring African states. The Semitic-speaking Tigreans and Amharas who have effectively dominated Ethiopian history since at least the fourth century, when they embraced Christianity, stem from a fusion of local Cushitic (or Hamitic) stock with South Arabian immigrants who settled along the Red Sea coast in the first millennium B.C. The Tigreans occupy the northern provinces of Tigre and Eritrea (where the Tigrean and Eritrean nationalist movements are based) which contain the ancient capital of Axum. For over five hundred years, however, the Amharas of Begemdar, Gojjam, and Shoa provinces to the south have provided most of the country's rulers. Both ethnic groups live in the normally well-watered central Ethiopian highlands and plateau, where they grow the indigenous cereal *teff* as well as wheat, barley and, in drier areas, maize and millet. These peoples are the Cossacks (rather than Samurai) of Ethiopia, providing a peasantry, who own horses, plough their own fields with an ox-drawn plough, and keep cattle, and a fief-holding military aristocracy. In the hotter, lower-lying southern regions of the country where the false banana (*ensete*) is the chief crop, the hand-hoe replaces the plough. Here live the Semitic-speaking Gurage,[8] the Cushitic Sidama, and further to the south-west the Kaffa, Janjero and other tribes.

But the largest ethnic group in Ethiopia are the Cushitic Galla, who may number as many as ten million and stretch from the barren Boran plains in the extreme south to well north of Addis Ababa. Their present distribution is the result of massive sixteenth-century invasions from their southern pasturelands into the central highlands, where the enfeebled armies of the Christian kingdom could do little to check their advance. Ultimately they possessed the numerical advantage, and with their unconventional sudden attacks and ambushes outmanoeuvred the more ponderous if better equipped professional Ethiopian forces. Both sides used

8. See W. A. Shack, *The Gurage: People of the Ensete Culture*, Oxford University Press, 1966.

cavalry, and the royal armies had a considerable supply of fire-arms (mainly matchlocks). But these were not of much use against the guerrilla tactics of the Galla, whose traditional military organization (based on age and generation groups) was peculiarly well suited to this type of war-fare. The inability of the Christian forces to deal more effectively with the Galla invaders (over whom they nevertheless later re-established their ascendancy) reveals the perilous condition to which the kingdom had been reduced by centuries of conflict with Muslim states of the principally Cushitic populations on the eastern and southern flanks. Indeed, only the death and defeat of the great Islamic conqueror Ahmad Gran (1506–43), the *Imam* of the Muslim state of Adal whose capital was the ancient city of Harar, finally saved the Christian state from extinction. The Muslims, who had thus indirectly contributed to the success of the Galla incursions, were in their turn also affected adversely by them, and were never able to regain their former might.

This great population upheaval, the most significant and far-reaching in Ethiopia's recent history, was followed by important technological and cultural changes. Although their traditional economy, typified by that of the Boran (page 166) was based on pastoral nomadism, many Galla who settled in the rich arable lands of the central highlands became cultivators and Christians and are increasingly indistinguishable from the surrounding Amhara whose language and culture they have adopted. It is thus not surprising that some authorities should consider the present imperial family to be in origin more Galla than Amhara. Not all the Galla, of course, adopted Christianity. Some still adhere to their traditional religion[9] while others have adopted Islam, following the example of their close relatives and neighbours the Somali, of whom some 750,000 live in the eastern province of Ethiopia; Islam is also the religion of a high proportion of Tigreans and other peoples in Eritrea.

Today although Christianity is still the official state religion, Islam can probably count at least as many adherents. Nevertheless, the Christian culture of the Amhara-Tigreans provides the

9. See K. E. Knutsson, *Authority and Change: A study of the Kallu Institution among the Macha Galla of Ethiopia*, Etnografiska Museet, Gothenburg, 1967.

locally based core civilization and the strongest vehicle for a comprehensive Ethiopian nationalism transcending the many separatist traditions; Amharic is the main language and opportunities for social mobility to the highest positions in the state are encouraged by the bilateral basis of Amhara kinship. At the same time, since religion and ethnicity do not necessarily coincide, religious differences can contribute to unity as well as to disunity within the state. We must also appreciate that, despite the religious conflicts of the past, in their local versions, and especially in their shared syncretic cults, Christianity and Islam possess a common stock of elements which can make for harmony as well as discord.

As the empire has expanded its centre of gravity has moved steadily southwards from the earlier northern capitals to the present city of Addis Ababa which was established by Menelik in the nineteenth century. As we know from internal historical sources in the ancient liturgical language, Ge'ez, and in Arabic, together with contemporary reports down the centuries by Portuguese and other foreign visitors, for the last five hundred years the pattern of Amhara rule has followed that of a military occupation. Newly conquered peoples were forced to pay tribute to their Amhara rulers, while their leaders, if they proved sufficiently pliant and loyal, might be incorporated within the Amhara administrative system. Some traditional chiefs became local authorities like their counterparts in British Africa; others were exiled and counted themselves fortunate if they were given posts elsewhere. Senior local officials were almost invariably Amharas and other Amharas settled directly amongst the vanquished. As far as land and other profitable resources – such as ivory, animal skins, gold, incense, and slaves – were concerned, the Amharas were rapacious asset-strippers. Title to the conquered land immediately passed to the Crown and was then parcelled out in *gult* estates among the military officers and soldiery who had seized it. Some might be given to the Church as benefices, while other allotments were bestowed on dignitaries whom the reigning emperor wished to reward for their services, and some remained as part of the vast private resources of the monarch. There were always eager claimants for fresh supplies of tribute and plunder.

This reallocation incorporated the conquered communities as tribute-paying tenants or sub-tenants on their own traditional lands. Under a benevolent Amhara governor and reasonable landlords, the local tribesmen were free to work their lands as they had done in the past, so long as they regularly paid their tribute. Unlike the Amhara peasantry in the north, however, they did not enjoy the security of hereditary rights of *usufruct* and they were not supposed to carry arms. But if they were fortunate, adroit in registering their claims, diligent in tax payment, and tenacious in litigation, they could hope to wrest title to their own lands from negligent absentee Amhara landlords. This costly process was probably most effectively accomplished where it was accompanied by the adoption of the Amharic language and culture and hence absorption within the dominant ethnic group. Such success stories should not blind us to the terrible exactions which tyrannical governors and landlords forced upon their subjects, turning some into slaves in the process.

More generally, the political history of this ethnically diverse state is the familiar long drawn out battle between centripetal and centrifugal forces. The emperor's title 'King of Kings' (*Negusa Nagast*) with its biblical cadences proudly proclaims the supremacy of the centre within an increasingly tightly ruled union of kingdoms and principalities. Traditionally, the emperor armed with the motto 'Conquering Lion of Judah', is first and foremost a war-leader and, until recent times, his court was a peripatetic military headquarters with his principal ministers and courtiers holding military titles. Francisco Alvarez, chaplain to the first regular Portuguese embassy in the sixteenth century on the eve of the Galla invasions, has left a vivid picture of the emperor's progress as he moved in state round the country, showing the flag and quelling rebellious local leaders. Bare-headed save for his crown, he travelled on the back of a mule enclosed within an elaborate moving tent of red curtains. Further ahead marched twenty pages, and in front of them six saddled mules and six saddled horses, each led by four men. The emperor himself was always accompanied by four lions, and a hundred men each carrying special jars of Tejj mead (the traditional aristocratic drink), and a hundred others carrying baskets of bread. These provisions were placed in the emperor's tent when he camped and were offered to guests. Portable church altars were also included in the procession. Each altar was carried by four priests, with four other priests in attendance, and preceded by two deacons – one with a thurible and cross, the other carrying a bell to warn people off the road to make way for the king. Armed guards rode on the flanks of the royal party, others galloping on ahead to clear the imperial path. So the reigning emperor Lebna Dengel (1508–1540) proceeded in state round his dominions.

As God's Vice-Regent and 'Elect of God', the emperor ruled by divine decree, with a special relationship with the Almighty, enshrined in the claim to descent from Menelik I, the son of Solomon and the Queen of Sheba. This royal charter is proclaimed in *The Glory of Kings* written in the thirteenth century. Although not strictly or literally a divine king, as the Lord's anointed the emperor's person was treated with immense reverence (as the 1974 revolution itself showed). He was traditionally shielded from mundane social intercourse, living in ceremonial seclusion and imperial splendour, replying to those who addressed him directly through an official spokesman. His subjects prostrated themselves in his presence, and even when royal commands were relayed by messenger at a distance they were received with such deference that those to whom they were addressed were expected to strip to the waist. The royal drums were beaten when imperial proclamations were issued even in the provinces.

The emperor did not, however, perform special ritual acts in order to promote the prosperity and well-being of his people. Rather his office was buttressed by the Church, without the loyal support of whose leaders he could not rule effectively. The Patriarch (*abuna*) installed the emperor and administered the vital oath of allegiance binding the emperor and his subjects. In theory claimants to the throne were required to possess the necessary Solomonic ancestry, but this is not so difficult as it sounds given the bilateral kinship system of the Amhara (Haile Selassie, for instance, traced his Solomonic descent through his grandmother).

Since all Amharas, many Tigreans, and members of numerous other ethnic groups are connected by descent or marriage in one way or another, eligibility for the supreme office is wide. It has been successfully claimed by men (and women) of very varied origin, as Theodore's meteoric rise from local warrior brigand to provincial governor and eventually emperor illustrates. Often rival claimants have fought for the crown, victory going to the one whose military ascendancy and popularity were such that the Patriarch judged it prudent to recognize him as the Lord's choice. Once enthroned, the new ruler lost no time in rounding up his most dangerous relatives (if he could find them), and consigning them to gloomy mountain fortresses where they were confined, sometimes in consideration of their royal blood in elegant gold chains. The newly installed emperor was equally prompt to consolidate his control over all the military forces in the realm and to appoint his ministers and court, hearing complaints and judging cases as the final authority in the land – as the aged Haile Selassie did until he was deposed in September 1974 – another example of the supreme authority being necessarily also the supreme source of justice.

Equally, the new ruler had to review all the titles and offices allocated by his predecessors. In principle all titles, honours, and offices were at the disposal of the reigning emperor, although in practice some tended to become hereditary. The most successful emperors exercised the most exquisite statecraft in promoting and demoting followers, stationing them when necessary in regions where they would have little opportunity to build up a local following. Some local chiefs, often non-Amhara, were too important to ignore and might have to be allowed to hold *gult* estates in their own territory. Nevertheless, even within the reign of a single emperor fortunes were liable to wax and wane with alarming rapidity and often in the most unexpected ways. Francisco Alvarez, to whom we owe so much for his excellently observed accounts of life at the Ethiopian court in the sixteenth century, has left us a characteristically poignant description of this practice – known in Amharic as *shum-shir*, which we might translate loosely as 'hire and fire'. Referring again to Lebna Dengel, 'The Prester John,' he records, 'deposes them and appoints them whenever he pleases, with or without cause; and on this account there is no ill humour here and if there is any it is secret, because in this period that we remained in the country I saw great lords turned out of their lordships and others put into them, and I saw them together, and they appeared to be good friends. (God knows their hearts.)'

Each title-holder, especially if he were entrusted with admini- strative authority (as most *gult*-holders were), maintained a satel- lite court modelled on that of his liege, the emperor, exacting tribute from his subjects, part of which he passed on to the imperial treasury, raising a levée when required, and in the mean- time administering justice, and distributing largesse and hospit- ality in the image of his master.

Thus the Amhara peasantry and other less privileged peasant communities 'carried on their backs' (as the local expression has it) a smaller leisured élite (*mekwanint*). And just as the peasantry were divided into two categories, the laity and those in holy orders, so their better-off kinsmen held either religious offices, or administrative or military positions. The spectacular somersaults characteristic of the careers of the élite combined with shared kinship connections to blur the distinction between the common people and their masters. Local big-men could on occasion seize the imperial throne and poor peasants could realistically hope to rise to the rank of their distant aristocratic relatives. Today it is unusual to trace a powerful 'noble' line going back more than three generations, and it is thus difficult to speak of a clearly defined and persisting aristocracy or nobility. Hence comparisons with feudal Europe or Tokugawa Japan throw into relief the unusually open and fluid nature of Ethiopian stratification. In its own curious way, appearances notwithstanding, Ethiopia was a country of *nouveaux riches*.

Nevertheless, locally entrenched power combined with weakness at the centre has from time to time permitted the empire to dis- solve into a loose aggregrate of rival kings and princes. This was the situation in the eighteenth century 'Era of the Judges' from which, a hundred years later, Menelik II (1889–1913) trium- phantly rescued his country. Menelik, the Louis XIV of Ethiopia, was probably the last of the old-style redistributive rulers whose way of life differed in degree rather than kind from that of his subjects, and who depended for his survival and success on their loyalty rather than on external support. Most of his wealth seems to have remained where it was obtained – in his own land.

Requests   **Decisions**

Chart of the Ethiopian Government, *c.* 1967
(from C. Clapham, *Haile-Selassie's Government*, Longman, 1969, p. 191)

To sum up, Ethiopian history displays an erratic movement towards increasing centralization, associated with technological developments (especially in military organization and weapons), and more recently bureaucratization. All this has been achieved, at considerable cost, in an expanding empire where until the last few decades communications were extremely slow and difficult. In this tradition, the despotic ruler seeks to break, disperse and neutralize all alternative seats of power and to banish all threats to his absolute authority. He adroitly emphasizes his uniqueness and undermines rival power-holders by playing them off against each other, governing in the provinces with a realistically loose rein partly by indirect rule; in the true tradition of the Sun King all successes redound to his credit, while his failures are blamed on unworthy and irresponsible members of his government (who are then sacked) or upon external foes.

These are the time-worn methods of successful imperial autocracy as realized so magnificently by Menelik II in the nineteenth century and by Haile Selassie in this. Both men needed no lessons in the art of statecraft and, as a feat of endurance and survival in a period of such radical social change, Haile Ṣelassie's achievement is by any political standards truly exceptional. His amazing dexterity in holding the balance between the forces of innovation and tradition for so long is a tribute to the political genius which made him, for all his faults, one of the world's leading statesmen. While introducing a parliament with elected members, but no political parties, and a palace government responsible ultimately to him, Haile Selassie used (and no doubt abused) every political device to buttress his own personal authority (see diagram). He and his ministers applied with consummate skill the old rules of point and counterpoint in every major department of government and the armed forces. Thus while some of the 'patriots' who so bravely fought the Italians in 1935 were awarded the highest honours others were ignored or passed over in favour of quislings and collaborators. The deputy of a powerful minister or general was often deliberately chosen from a hostile ethnic group or from among his superior's known personal enemies. The military as a whole were likewise divided into many different rival groups led by commanding officers with opposed interests and as little *esprit de corps* as possible. Thus was fostered the byzantine atmosphere of conspiracy and intrigue which appeared to paralyse so many attempts to change the Ethiopian political system.

These modern developments have been accompanied by a much sharper division between the successful political élite and the peasantry, the rich getting richer and the poor poorer; in the appalling famine in 1973 and 1974 destitute pastoralists, tenant farmers, and agricultural as well as urban labourers starved to death when there was no national shortage of food. New military hardware, particularly American rocket-firing jet fighters were regularly used to cow recalcitrant peasants in the provinces with little discrimination between those who were Amhara and those who were not; this again greatly strengthened the power of the centre. It took the unexpected intervention of devastating and persistent drought against which all the modern protective devices were of little avail, to create a situation where the entire traditional order was threatened.

This is not the place to assess the ensuing revolution sparked off by students and staff at the Haile Selassie I University – which, while genuinely populist in origins, was soon 'hijacked' by the military. Two points, however, are particularly relevant. Haile Selassie and his ministers owe their downfall directly to their failure to redistribute a reasonable proportion of the vast fortunes which they had built up by their exploitation of the country and its people. Above all, they are bitterly condemned for their shameless and callous indifference to the plight of their starving subjects and for the obscene contrast between their luxurious life and that of the starving peasantry. The proclamation which announced the assumption of power by the Armed Forces Co-ordinating Committee on 12 September 1974 after Haile Selassie had been deposed, begins as follows: 'Although the people of Ethiopia have looked, in good faith, upon the Crown as a symbol of their unity, Haile Selassie I, who has ruled the country for more than fifty years ever since he assumed power as a Crown Prince, has abused the authority, dignity and honour of office for the personal benefit and interest of himself, his immediate family and retainers.' On this basis and under the slogan 'Ethiopia First' the Armed Forces' Co-ordinating Committee waged its campaign against the old, feudal order and prepared the public for the overthrow of the emperor. Despite the uncompromising centralist policies of the new rulers, which have rekindled the bitter separatist struggle in Eritrea and stimulated other local uprisings, Ethiopia still appears to retain a surprising degree of cohesion. This is surely intimately connected with the extraordinarily intricate web of cross-cutting commitments and interests which, in the style of his predecessors, Haile Selassie fostered. In this way and through the creation of a highly westernized military and civilian élite, the former emperor seems to have done much to prepare his own nemesis.

ALL THE KING'S MEN: BAGANDA BUREAUCRACY

Our final vignette is that of the much smaller conquest kingdom of Buganda.[10] Unlike the surrounding 'Interlacustrine Kingdoms',[11] with their caste-like divisions between Hamitic pastoral aristocrats and indigenous commoner cultivators (as for instance Rwanda), the Baganda state is basically ethnically and culturally homogeneous. In these propitious conditions, we find the same centralizing processes at work – but pushed further along the road to effective autocracy before British intervention arrested them and attempted to democratize the traditional pattern of Baganda rule.

In 1890, when Lugard concluded his treaty with them, the bellicose Baganda boasted nearly a million people and claimed almost as many tribute-paying subjects in the neighbouring territories (including part of the country ruled by their traditional foes the Banyoro).[12] Both in the surrounding Bantu kingdoms and amongst the uncentralized Nilotic and Nilo-Hamitic peoples to the north, their military supremacy was undisputed, and seems largely to have been based upon the sheer size, ruthless efficiency and professionalism of their armies. The domestic economy was mainly in the hands of their womenfolk and was based on that unusually prolific, undemanding and hardy staple, the banana.

10. For an excellent comprehensive analysis, see L. A. Fallers (ed.), *The King's Men: Leadership and Status in Buganda on the Eve of Independence*, Oxford University Press, 1964.
11. That is, the Bantu kingdoms between and round the east African Great Lakes.
12. See J. Beattie, *The Banyoro State*, Oxford University Press, 1973.

Fire-arms do not seem to have been important until quite late in the nineteenth century, when muskets bought from Arab traders were issued by the king to an élite corps of fusiliers, a sort of praetorian guard, recruited from the palace pages who were destined to become leading administrative officials.[13] The journalist and explorer Stanley has left a detailed account of the very considerable forces mustered by Mutesa I (1856–84) in his 1875 campaign against the Buvuma Islanders. The various units then totalled some 125,000 Baganda warriors (excluding non-Baganda levies), with a naval flotilla of 230 war canoes, the largest seventy-two feet long. With such resources no less than sixty-six major campaigns were undertaken in Mutesa's twenty-eight year reign. No wonder Ganda today say 'In the old days the work of men was war.' Indeed it was. Buganda was a war-machine. The armies were sent out regularly each dry season to bring in the harvest of much-needed plunder – cattle, slaves, and wives – whose capture helped feed the war-machine and spurred it to further rapacious exploits.

It is a curious though easily understandable irony of British colonial history that Buganda was the very territory where the policy of indirect rule was conceived and applied so enthusiastically by Lugard and his successors; yet what this amounted to was largely *direct* domination by the Baganda, who convinced the British that they were the natural rulers of most of this part of Africa and possessed a unique genius for government. Thus the Baganda obtained British warrant for extravagant territorial claims (in for instance Bunyoro) and, as the new protectorate government extended its rule to the north and east, Ganda 'agents' were employed to bring 'enlightenment' and their administration to the more 'backward' surrounding tribes. So Uganda began its career with the Ganda firmly established as a privileged power élite; the consolidation and extension of their unique position by later generations of Western-trained Ganda who dominated the country's civil service and business has generated strong feelings of resentment from less-favoured ethnic groups.[14] As the late king,

13. Some indication of the crucial political significance of this élite militia can be gained from the fact that in 1888 (foreshadowing later developments) they led a successful *coup* against the reigning king.

14. See D. A. Low and R. C. Pratt, *Buganda and British Overrule, 1900–55: Two Studies*, Oxford University Press, 1960.

Sir Edward Mutesa II has put it,[15] the Anglo-Bagandan agreement of 1900 which governed relations between the two parties for almost sixty years, was so effective 'it gave the most powerful group in the country a vested interest in retaining the *status quo*'.

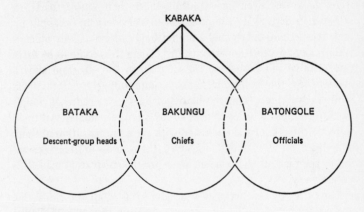

The Baganda Political System
(from L. A. Fallers (ed.), *The King's Men*, Oxford University Press, 1964)

In their Baganda mandarins the British had acquired a cheap local supply of officials, and all that was now missing was a militia to enforce this dual Baganda-British mandate on recalcitrant subjects. The basis for this was the various residual elements (some deserters, others simply redundant) from the forces of the former Turko-Egyptian régime in the Sudan. These consisted of a Muslim diaspora of mainly Nilotic origin (including representatives of the Shilluk, Dinka, Bari, and Kakwa tribes as well as some Lugbara and Acholi and even people from the Nuba Hills). From a synthesis of these and other uprooted tribesmen, brought together under the banner of Islam, there developed a new tribal entity known as Nubis. After absorbing many further elements from the 'savage' uncentralized northern tribes, the Nubis became a distinctive military caste, a kind of east African janizaries, which despite or perhaps because of its marginal and partly alien identity formed the core of the Ugandan army and ultimately thrust one of its typical representatives, General Amin, to supreme power. This

15. Sir E. Mutesa II, *Desecration of my Kingdom*, Constable, 1967, p. 62.

new and largely colonial creation thus played as significant a role in Uganda's history as the archetypal Baganda.

The traditional Baganda kingdom was divided into patrilineal clans with their own chiefs and estates. Successive kings (*Kabakas*) were, however, even more adroit than their counterparts in Ethiopia in destroying the power of local leaders, in breaking up their estates, and in creating a professional cadre of chiefly officials whom they appointed and controlled. There thus came to be three categories of official whose jurisdiction, as our diagram shows, overlapped: the traditional *bataka* clan-heads, the *bakungu* administrative chiefs, and the *batongole*, a special cadre of 'king's men' loyal only to him and used to spy on other officials. All these were allocated land and entrusted with the administration of those who lived on it. Commoners owed their lords military service rather than labour in the fields, since banana cultivation made this unnecessary.

Thus the *Kabaka* became 'King and head of all the clans'. He was, as Fallers says:[16] 'the unique despotic pinnacle of Ganda society', the 'first in the nation', the 'fire', the 'lion' and more esoterically, the 'queen termite' which Baganda says devours its subjects. As in Menelik's Ethiopia, by the middle of the nineteenth century, this kingdom – about a quarter of the size of England in extent – was 'governed by a corps of chiefs who owed their positions largely to the personal grace of the Kabaka who might appoint, dismiss and transfer them at will. A chief might one day stand at the pinnacle of wealth and influence, the ruler of a large district and the recipient of lavish tribute from the people and estates from his King; next day having incurred the monarch's disfavour he might be stripped of property and office, lying in stocks, the object of scorn and physical tortures of a most imaginative kind.' Tax collection, by specialized collectors independent of the administrative chiefs, was more highly centralized than in Ethiopia at the same period; in contrast to the latitudinarian Amhara system of royal succession, in Buganda only those whose fathers or paternal grandfathers had actually held the office had a legitimate title to the throne. The crucial choice amongst this

16. L. A. Fallers (ed.), *The King's Men: Leadership and Status in Buganda on the Eve of Independence*, Oxford University Press, 1964, p. 68.

narrowly circumscribed category of royal heirs (the so-called 'Princes of the Drum') was made, in consultation with senior chiefs, by the *Katikkiro* or Prime Minister, a commoner appointed by the late king. Although the king's nominated councillors led by the *Katikkiro* could exercise restraint on royal policies, the most effective sanction against regal despotism probably lay in the rebellious potential of ambitious princes and heirs to the throne. Wars of succession bulk very large in Ganda history.

With so firm a grasp of secular power a rich adornment of ritual (such as in Lubemba, or even Ethiopia) would seem superfluous. Thus although the kabakaship provided an enduring national symbol, especially potent in times of crisis, it was not deified. The most significant symbols of kingship were probably the sacred fire and the royal drums. When the *Kabaka* was deported in 1953 by the British governor, the fire was extinguished and the drums fell silent; and when he came back in triumph two years later, the fire was re-kindled and the drums exuberantly celebrated his return. Most authorities stress the manipulative, instrumental attitude of successive *Kabakas* towards religion, suggesting that by the nineteenth century the king was not so much a god or equal of the gods but rather their superior. His honours' list extended to the skies, where some spirits owed their fortunate position to loyal service during their earthly lives to the monarch. At the same time, he was not above listening to the spirit-inspired dreams of diviners – a practice apparently continued by General Amin.

Under British rule, Buganda was thus a state within a state, and only prepared to surrender its unique quasi-independence in return for control over the whole of Uganda. The nearer Uganda came to independence the more clearly defined and bitter became the struggle between Baganda interests and those of other tribal groups. In the ensuing conflict, especially acute in the last decade of British rule, the alignments of other ethnic interests partly reflected the long-standing division between Buganda's 'natural' (if sometimes ambiguous) allies in the other Bantu kingdoms (Bunyoro, Toro, and Ankole) and the acephalous northern Nilotes and Nilo-Hamites who were prominently represented in the army. In a fruitless effort to secure Bagandan cooperation in the developing central legislature, the *Kabaka* was sent into exile in 1953. When he returned as a martyr and conquering hero two years later, Buganda had secured a new treaty which augmented rather than diminished her special status. Encouraged by this success, for the next five years Buganda campaigned for further autonomy, and if necessary separate independence, largely ignoring national party politics. In 1959, in a gesture prefiguring General Amin's recent expulsion of the Ugandan Asian community, Indian traders were forced to close their businesses in Buganda, and there were other powerful manifestations of local xenophobia and Ganda chauvinism.

Having failed to secure self-government separately from the rest of Uganda, this policy of non-participation was reversed at the eleventh hour in time to bring Uganda to independence under the strange partnership of Milton Obote's Uganda People's Congress and the recently formed and ultra-traditional *Kabaka Yekka* ('Kabaka Only') party. Since Obote was prime minister it was natural that the *Kabaka* should become president. This ill-starred alliance, inadequately reinforced by Obote's marriage to a Ganda girl of good family, soon fell apart. The fate of the Banyoro 'lost counties' assigned to Buganda by the British, and a political scandal alleging that Obote and Amin were involved in gold-smuggling and clandestine political intrigue in Zaire provoked a struggle which reached its climax in the spring of 1966. When the Baganda lost the first issue and pressed the second, Obote arrested several of his ministers, suspended the constitution, and abolished the office of president. The *Kabaka* replied, rather pathetically, by requesting the central government to quit his kingdom – thus in effect declaring independence unilaterally – and Obote sent in the army led by Colonel Amin. On 24 May 1966, the *Kabaka's* palace was stormed after heavy fighting, but the *Kabaka* and some of his senior ministers escaped to Britain leaving Amin's forces to rampage round the kingdom pursuing old scores.

The new Uganda constitution of 1967 made Obote executive president, setting the seal on Buganda's defeat, and ushered in a completely new political order; at a stroke all the Bantu kingships were abolished, inaugurating the era of the Common Man, as Obote called his new policy. Buganda was ignominiously split into four administrative districts under the direct control of the central government. The wheel had indeed turned full circle: indirect rule which had come in with the *Kabaka* had gone out with him. Obote created special security units directly responsible to himself, and purged his party of dissident non-Lango tribesmen, only the army remaining to be cauterized. Apparently in direct response to an attempt by Obote to do this General Amin seized power in January 1971. The Nubis chance had come and they took it.[17] For the time being anyway the final *coup de grace* to the Baganda was administered by a motley assemblage of marginal ethnic elements united by professional and confessional loyalties and in firm control of the means of destruction. The Common Man – as Ali Mazrui discerns him in the shape of the Ugandan soldiery – had taken over.

The reversion of Uganda to ruthless military despotism reminiscent of the old *Kabakas* is less remarkable than the triumphant emergence of such a parvenu ethnic group as the Nubis – a reminder that culturally distinct communities form and dissolve more often than we usually suppose. Apparently permanent major ethnic blocs such as the Baganda, with their splendid chauvinism and impressive substantiality, encourage us to overlook more shadowy but equally significant cultural phenomena. It is not often that we can see so clearly the actual genesis of ethnic groups. But we must postpone further discussion of this until our next chapter and return to our present brief: the comparative anatomy of centralized power.

STATECRAFT AND DESPOTISM

Power is never truly absolute, for the simple reason that the central authority cannot rule alone; ruling necessarily entails subsidiary agents. As we should expect and as our examples confirm, the larger, more heterogeneous and complex the state is, the more elaborate the ancillary machinery of government. Likewise, the more the central authorities seek to control their subjects and the more difficult communications are, the greater the energy

17. For a fascinating analysis of these developments, see Aidan Southall 'Amin's Military Coup in Uganda: Great Man or Historical Inevitability?', *Third International Congress of Africanists*, Addis Ababa, 1973.

and resources required. Shortage of personnel encourages an indirect, feudalistic approach but may be compensated for by a régime of arbitrary terror, such as the classical oriental despotisms and modern tyrannies where the sheer capriciousness and unpredictability of repression generates a wary and fearful compliance. If it is sufficiently brutal, fitful coercion can be very effective. Nevertheless, the most capricious dictators need assistants. Some devolution of authority is essential in even compact and homogeneous tribal states such as Lubemba and Buganda.

As soon as central power is thus conceded, subordinates may become insubordinate and establish their own power bases from which to challenge and ultimately menace their master. There is thus an inherent frailty in authority – however solid and eternal it may seem. Absolute despotism on the scale achieved in traditional China, where hundreds of millions were ruled by governments which survived in relative peace and tranquillity for several centuries is a truly astonishing feat.

As our African examples demonstrate, most traditional states share with their modern counterparts the battle between central and provincial pressures. To some extent both forces may benefit when the state expands its frontiers by conquest. Defeat, however, with its frustrated hopes of plunder damages the prestige of the centre and stimulates restlessness and potential discontent amongst those who have lost most. The exigencies of patriotic defence against an external enemy may temporarily silence internal disaffection, but not for ever.

In general authority must secure as wide a measure of popular support as it can, even if loyalty and 'patriotism' have to be dinned into the heads of truculent and recalcitrant subjects. Adjustments have to be made on both sides. Hence, as Balandier points out,[18] 'power tends to develop as a relation of domination, but the consent that legitimizes it tends to reduce its control'. It is this mixture of stick-and-carrot, combined with the frequent contradiction between self-interest and communal interest, which lies behind the characteristic ambivalence of power. Acton's famous lines on the corrupting influence of power specify more than a psychological failing of venal politicians; they point

18. G. Balandier, *Political Anthropology*, Allen Lane, 1970, p. 40.

up the inevitable ambiguity of power among uncentralized peoples like the Lugbara and Nyakyusa (p. 95) as well as in centralized states. The ultimate test of a ruler's authority is therefore whether he possesses the power of life and death over his subjects.

The critical dynamics of power (and power-sharing) focus on three crucial and closely related factors: the structure and maintenance of the governing class, the organization of state taxation, and the function of the military. The three 'R's of government, then, are ruling, revenue and repression. The more decisively the ruler can control the selection, placement, promotion and dismissal of his senior officials, the stronger his position. In traditional kingdoms the king is obliged to share power with other hereditary dignitaries, often – as in Ashanti and among the southern Bantu generally – the leaders of kinship groups or other powerful groups within the state. As in feudal Europe and Japan such fragmentation, amounting to a kind of indirect rule within the state, inevitably reduced the strength of the centre. To use the organic analogy, the head could not function effectively without the consent and cooperation of the limbs and other parts of the body. Our Amhara and Baganda examples and on a much vaster scale that of traditional China, show how hard the central authorities struggled to overcome these devolutionary forces. The key lies in a special cadre of officials uniquely responsible in all important respects to the sovereign, the neutralization and confusion of other independent sources of authority, and a realistic tolerance of local-level autonomy. Of course the bureaucracy must not be allowed to get out of hand, to become itself the centre of power as it has in some western democracies.

The ruler's position is also affected by other qualified claimants. A large aristocracy (such as the Bemba crocodile clan) provides a natural mafia and may encourage wide participation among those directly attached to the rulers as clients and dependants. As Machiavelli pertinently observed of sixteenth-century France, although an abundance of nobility provides no necessary safeguard against foreign conquest, a successful conqueror will not find it easy to keep the prize. On the other hand, frustrated nobles and princes are an internal hazard, since each will be tempted to seek his own kingdom – either by displacing the existing ruler, or by hiving off his own personal following. These ambitions may be partially satisfied by enlarging the existing state through conquest and allocating each prince a larger domain, but this seldom provides a complete or lasting remedy. Most states of this type grow to a critical mass which is largely determined by the economic resources available, and the effective range of authority. They are then apt to fragment into a series of derivative kingdoms which reproduce the cycle of expansion and fission. As the Chinese historical novel, *The Romance of Three Kingdoms*, observes with lofty fatalism, 'The conditions under heaven are such that, after a long disunity, there will be unity; after a long unity, there will be disunity.' [19]

A large cohort of eligible leaders intensifies the traumas of succession. Even under the most favourable circumstances, the transition from one reign to another creates widespread uncertainty and anxiety, threatening the very foundations of the state. It is as if the whole state was being reborn [20] – and the national birth-pangs find expression in the elaborate rituals which install the new king. The potential for upheaval is great and will be increased by an unwelcome profusion of candidates. Hence the more clearly defined and exclusive the criteria of eligibility, the less turmoil there is likely to be in the interregnum following the death of one ruler and the appointment of his successor. The simplest procedure is the designation by the incumbent of his own successor. This has the additional advantage of ensuring continuity, following George Orwell's axiom that 'a ruling group is a ruling group as long as it can nominate its successors'. But the impatient heir apparent may be tempted to accelerate the natural course of events. (In the business world, pre-selection of this kind may turn one firm into a recruiting agency for its competitors.)

Other less stringent succession rules which, while still leaving some room for manoeuvre, seek to reduce wasteful rivalry and strife, incorporate restrictive clauses such as those of the Bemba rule limiting eligibility to the sons or grandsons of rulers, or the Nupe stipulation that only actual sons born to reigning monarchs

19. Quoted from F. L. K. Hsu, *Under the Ancestor's Shadow: Kinship, Personality and Social Mobility in China*, Stanford University Press, 1971, p.5.

20. G. Balandier, *Political Anthropology*, Allen Lane, 1970, p. 113.

can claim the throne. But even cast-iron principles cannot eliminate the possibility of violent power struggles especially where, as in traditional Buganda, the state is so tightly organized that violence may be the only means by which the masses can exert any influence over their political destiny.

Having developed and implemented the successful formula for central autocracy – a personally dedicated, American-style bureaucracy – the ruler must ensure that his rewards and promotions do not lead to an uneven concentration of power outside his control which could recoil against him. Effective despotism demands the same unflinching vigilance as more egalitarian forms of government. If some hereditary offices and titles have to be conceded, it is crucial to maintain a firm grip on the placement and promotion of subordinate officials.

The rulers of feudal Japan, which in the Tokugawa period was less centralized than Menelik's Ethiopia, were able to exert some control over the aristocracy by holding aristocratic hostages at the shogunal court. In pre-revolutionary China, where there was virtually no effective local feudal aristocracy, the mandarin bureaucracy ruled over a system of lineage units and attached estates which was at the local level self-regulating to a considerable degree. Not only was the lineage system convenient for predatory expansion and land-holding but also it 'relieved the state of a great part of the burden of social control'.[21] As in Ethiopia, Buganda, and modern bureaucratic states, Chinese officials were frequently moved from province to province to prevent local attachments which might compromise their loyalty to the centre. Magistrates were never allowed to serve in their own districts, and ambitious young bureaucrats were appointed as censors and spies to watch the provincial administration, paying particular attention to local tax registers. In the fifteenth century, eunuchs began to play a key role at the imperial palace and rose to high positions in the state bureaucracy, the security service and the military. We have already noted in Ethiopia and Buganda an equally shrewd appreciation of the advantages of dependent officials whose origins render them political if not actual eunuchs, and there are many other examples, the best-known, probably, the Turkish Ottoman

21. M. Freedman, *Chinese Lineage and Society*, Athlone Press, 1967, p. 29.

empire. Although slavery theoretically no longer exists, modern totalitarian states show an equally acute understanding in employing for their most delicate security tasks faceless men whose backgrounds make them insecure and extremely vulnerable and whose lack of local involvement prevents their developing local loyalties.

Yet even with careful recruitment, difficulties can occur and further precautionary measures will probably be required. Over-successful personalities who are seen as potential threats to the central authorities, may be dispatched on particularly dangerous missions – from which they may never return – or be sent into the political wilderness of some insignificant province, or of an embassy abroad where their opportunities for plotting are negligible.

REVENUE AND REPRESSION

It is in the interest of the central government to exercise a complete monopoly over the collection and disbursement of revenue. Where taxation rests in the hands of a general fief-holding élite, as in feudal Europe and until very recently in Ethiopia, the sovereign cannot exert the control possible where a separate cadre of functionaries are employed solely for this purpose, as in Buganda. The separation of powers – between administrative and fiscal officials – is clearly to the ruler's advantage. The possibilities for dislocating and abrogating the tributary-redistributive nexus are then greatly increased. Subjects who bear tribute directly to their lord, especially when he also depends on their labour and military support, have more leverage than they do when the strands which humanize and give moral weight to patronage are coldly re-arranged in totally separate extractive relationships to the detriment of the client.

Hence specialization of bureaucratic function and personnel is an important facilitating factor in despotism, as all our examples confirm. In pre-colonial Africa, this demand for a rootless, dependent and dependable cadre of functionaries, agents, and soldiery played a significant if inadvertent role in the spread of Islam. Immigrant Muslims, some literate in Arabic, like the Christian janizaries in the Ottoman empire, provided the heads of traditional African states with reliable mercenaries whose precarious local position made them completely dependent and completely loyal. This pioneering use of alien Muslim immigrants was followed by the European colonial authorities who thus inadvertently further encouraged the diffusion of Islam in Africa.[22]

Nowhere is the need for such aliens more significant than in the armed forces which maintain order, defend the state, and extend its frontiers. Armies whose members have feudalistic or quasi-feudalistic attachment to intermediary chiefs cannot develop the unswerving *esprit de corps* and unlimited commitment to the central authorities which effective despotism demands. There is consequently an intimate and vital connection between military leadership, rights over land and other resources on which to support troops, and the power and autonomy of local leaders. Whether of slave, captive or other alien origin, rootless mercenaries are the ideal instruments of absolute rule. No despotic régime has any hope of survival unless it can gain direct and total control of the means of destruction (to borrow Jack Goody's apt phrase); or failing that, so arrange the command and composition of rival forces (as in Ethiopia) that their capacity to act concertedly against the centre is minimized.

Yet even a personal security force contains within itself the seeds of mutiny and the potentiality for seizing political control. The Nubis illustrate a process which the post-independence military coups of the Third World have rendered commonplace and which has even re-appeared in contemporary Europe. Such trends remind us that in *realpolitik* might is always right. However, there is one saving grace which mollifies even the most brutal military tyrannies: the more the military become involved in the day-to-day business of governing, the more they are exposed to the same pressures and political constraints as their civilian predecessors. The masterly assurance of the military when they assume power often soon evaporates as they become more and more politicized.

For these and other reasons, although superiority in fire-power and military manpower remain decisive, ultimately few tyrannies

22. See I. M. Lewis (ed.), *Islam in Tropical Africa*, Oxford University Press, 1966, pp. 30ff.

achieve complete and absolute security. The oppressed take courage in contemplating and exploring the frailties of authority. Here our examples and other evidence suggest that where secular power is weak, overstretched or under especial stress, it turns to ritual as an ancillary source of legitimacy and of symbolic strength. In our brief catalogue of cases the Bemba best exemplify the sanctification of power in an idiom familiar to us which, as was noted in chapter 5, was most flagrantly displayed in Mr Nixon's extraordinary career as president of the United States. The deification of high office, widely realized in the shape of the sun-king – who is often also a rain-king – must be understood in its political context. Amongst the Bemba deification empowers an office which has little else to sustain it, and the same holds true in even less centralized societies where leaders reign rather than rule. At the other end of the political spectrum, in the vast, un-wieldy empires of south-east Asia and pre-Conquest America, absolute despotism also depended heavily upon mystical support. To some extent the modern personality cult of national leaders in new states seems designed to achieve the same effect. As George Orwell put the matter in 1984, 'if one is to rule and continue to rule one must dislocate the sense of reality'. This is what myths of divinely instituted regal omnipotence attempt and sometimes realize. 'Power', as Balandier says, 'is never completely emptied of its religious content.'[23]

23. G. Balandier, *Political Anthropology*, Allen Lane, 1970, p. 100.

Chapter Ten

The Law of the Jungle

We now look at the opposite end of the political spectrum and ask how people govern themselves in the initially appealing conditions of the 'non-state'. Usually it is not that the state has withered away, but rather that it has never blossomed. To what extent, then, is community life feasible without the state government we take for granted? Can the spirit of the hippy commune sustain substantial viable groups? How large are the biggest communities that can be held together by 'minimal government', and what are their characteristics? What does politics mean in such circumstances? How much social discipline is required, and how is it applied? What limits the unfettered pursuit of self-interest and constrains violence?

As usual the best basis for studying these issues is the ethnographic specifics. We begin therefore with Evans-Pritchard's classic analysis [1] of the Nuer of the southern Sudan as he found them in the 1930s, living in what he calls 'ordered anarchy'. Following their expansion at the expense of the neighbouring Dinka (many of whom they had incorporated), the Nuer number about a quarter of a million. They form a distinctive linguistic and cultural entity, but for all their ethnic arrogance they are not traditionally a political unit. In this respect they recall Metternich's description of Italy as a 'geographical expression'. They are a tiny nation, but not a state. If then the Nuer do not constitute a single political unit, what are their significant political groups and how is politics organized?

We cannot locate chiefs and other obvious positions of political leadership, for there are none. So we must look at small-scale social activity and cooperation and this takes us directly to the Nuer economy which, as the reader will recall, combines pastoral-

1. E. E. Evans-Pritchard, *The Nuer*, Oxford University Press, 1940.

ism with cultivation. Although the Nuer see themselves primarily as cattle-herders, they have a transhumant régime, concentrating in villages in the wet season, and dispersing in cattle-camps in the dry. The villages with their fields provide the primary reference groups and the basic political units in Nuer society. Adjoining villages form distinctive neighbourhoods, which cluster together in ever-widening circles until the largest territorial aggregates are reached. These units, which we can arbitrarily call 'tribes', have populations ranging between 5,000 and 45,000 and are the largest named sub-divisions within the Nuer nation.

Tribal solidarity reflects shared interests in common arable land, pastures, water supplies, and fishing preserves, and may be mobilized in defence of these or in their enlargement. Each tribe, through its elders and leading big-men, can act as a sovereign political body *vis-à-vis* other tribes. And as it acts concertedly externally, so its members have both an obligation (in practice often very attenuated) and also the means to settle internal disputes peacefully; the tribe is the largest 'peace-group'. In practice, however, tribal cohesion is an emergent property and only effectively realized in inter-tribal conflict. Paradoxically we can most effectively demonstrate the strength (or weakness) of tribal loyalty by reference to the rules governing conflict. A kind of Geneva Convention regulates appropriate degrees of violent behaviour. Men of the same village or camp should fight only with wooden clubs and not with spears. Men of distant villages and camps, even if they are members of the same tribe, may uninhibitedly spear each other to death. The same nice discriminations of closeness and remoteness are reflected in the rates of compensation for injuries or death sustained in fighting. Within the same village and between neighbouring villages there is strong pressure to restore peace, and swingeing damages are not demanded. In such circumstances twenty head of cattle are the appropriate compensation for homicide. Between distant villages, however, where sentiments of mutual unity are weak, the tariff is higher – ranging between forty and fifty head of cattle for a man's life. Finally, at the level of the tribe, the cut-off point is reached: there is no provision for compensation in inter-tribal conflict. Disputes within tribes can be regulated and brought to a peaceful conclusion, but those between tribes cannot. Intra-tribal hostilities partake of the character of feud; those between tribes are more in the nature of all-out war.

The component villages of Nuer tribes are thus arrayed in feuding sections, but when threatened by an external foe they can combine to defend their wider joint-interests. When the external danger disappears, internal differences reassert themselves and the tribe collapses into its constituent villages. Between the village, the minimum unit, and the tribe, the maximum, political loyalty is almost infinitely elastic. Unity is achieved through the fusion of component sections, disunity by their fission into smaller segments. Tribes and their divisions form a Chinese-box structure of interlocking parts; each Nuer tribesman is a born situationalist whose political identity changes chameleon-like with circumstances.

The political gradations within tribes are of degree rather than kind; Nuer constantly ally with people whom in other contexts they fight. This is not remarkable in itself, for political expediency and opportunism are hardly unusual. The special flavour of the Nuer system is the systematic arrangement of political units in a constant and pervasive pattern of complementary opposition. Political allegiance is actualized in the same way, at the same levels, and according to the same segmentary principles in every Nuer tribe. Tribes may be evanescent: but Nuer politics have a sublime symmetry.

THE SEGMENTARY LINEAGE SYSTEM

These various layers or levels of identity and commitment, each mutually exclusive, reflect geographically localized economic interests and are further buttressed by the Nuer age-set system, which is arranged on a tribal basis, each tribe having its own independent (though corresponding) sets of initiated men. In the absence of chiefs or some more formal apparatus of government, it is doubtful if such fluid political groupings could operate effectively without additional support. This additional support is provided by a separate but complementary organization of clans and lineages. The Nuer are divided into a large number of patrilineal clans and lineages which are paired with corresponding tribal units.

In practice each tribe is identified with a corresponding clan, and every tribal division with a linked lineage segment. Thus territorially founded political groups are transformed into kinship units, and politics become a matter of kinship connections. Genealogies become political charters expressing political allegiance in the language of kinship. The closer people are through shared ancestry, the stronger their political adherence. As the Arab proverb proclaims: 'Myself against my brother; my brother and I against my cousin; my cousin and I against the outsider.' This is the guiding motto of the Nuer and other segmentary lineage systems, where collateral segments or 'branches' stemming from one common ancestor unite in opposition to those descended from another. The unit represented by any particular ancestor subsumes those of his descendants and is in turn subsumed within all wider, higher-order segments based on more remote ancestors. The further back descent is traced, the larger, more comprehensive, and also the weaker the units become.

However, the relationship between these two principles of kinship and physical proximity is complicated. A tribe is not literally a clan, nor a tribal division a lineage segment. Clans and their component segments are scattered widely in Nuerland, with little or no regard for geographical boundaries. Hence every tribe is actually heterogeneous in clan composition, and only *one* of those represented in its territory is identified with it politically in the way we have described. This *dominant* clan is usually the one considered to have first settled in the area and thus to 'own' the tribal territory. Although it is not necessarily the most numerous, its members constitute a local élite, receiving more respect and consideration than those of other clans, and exerting greater influence in the general assemblies of elders who regulate the business of the group. They tend to have more land and cattle, and these and other distinctions are reflected in the high blood-price demanded if one is killed. As might be expected of aristocracy however weakly developed, particularly where it is intimately associated with politics, the genealogies of dominant clansmen are

usually longer and more impressive than those of ordinary tribesmen.

For all their fierce egalitarianism, there is thus a significant
element of stratification in Nuer society. This is largely based on
the ascribed status of the dominant clans (*dil*), whose members the
Nuer honour in their pastoral idiom with the title 'bull' (*tut*).
'Wherever there is a *dil* in a village, the village clusters around him
as a herd of cattle clusters around its bull.'[2] However status is not
exclusively a hereditary endowment: it can also be achieved by
outstanding mastery of all those virile pursuits which the warrior
Nuer hold in high esteem.

The complementary role in this strife-ridden society is the professional peace-maker, the Nuer 'leopard-skin priest'. Leopard-skin
priests act as vital go-betweens and mediators in intra-tribal feuds
and, as befits their neutral role, do not normally belong to
dominant clans or their segments. They are mystically connected
with the earth, in which they may dig symbolic frontiers between
hostile parties in an effort to create peace and a climate for negoti-
ation. Their persons are sacred, so that murderers can safely seek
sanctuary in their company until tempers have cooled, and their
appeals for peace are issued in the knowledge that they can curse
recalcitrant adversaries who ignore their conciliatory efforts.

Nuer priests are committed to the peace of the tribes within
which they live and disengaged from their fractricidal feuds. In a
wider confrontation between the Nuer as a whole and the
northern Sudanese Arabs, or the British, they can assume the
larger role of prophets. Here we see an incipient political nationalism in a society whose members, although they speak the same
language, share the same culture, and belong by birth to clans
transcending tribal divisions, nevertheless are enclosed within
small, mutually hostile local groups and usually only fight other
Nuer.

THE SOMALI SOCIAL CONTRACT

The pastoral northern Somali, whose nomadic life we examined in
chapter 6, throw further light on the politics of segmentary line-

2. E. E. Evans-Pritchard, *The Nuer*, Oxford University Press, 1940, p. 215.

age organization. They are a people who, despite a vigorous sense of communal identity, reinforced by centuries of devotion to Islam, did not traditionally form a single political unit. It is only within the last hundred years, and more particularly since the Second World War, that the cultural nationalism of this nation of some three million people has begun to seek and achieve political fulfilment.

The Nuer, we have seen, employ kinship to help essentially territorial units to limp along. In the predominantly nomadic economy of the northern Somali, local attachments to wells, trading centres, and vaguely defined grazing areas constitute little more than a loose sheet anchor, and lineage rather than territory is the prime mover in social structure. Political allegiance is a direct function of agnatic pedigree so the paternal genealogies that are dinned into infants map out the political world in which they will live as adults. As Somalis themselves put it, converting politics into snobbery, what a person's address is in England his genealogy is in Somalia. When one meets a stranger the first question one asks is not, 'Where do you come from?' but 'Whom do you come from, who are your ancestors, what is your genealogy?' Social and political distance are measured in the 'number of ancestors' the parties 'count apart'. The nomad will press a stranger to recite his genealogy until a familiar name and reference point is reached and then adjust his behaviour accordingly.

Here, more pervasively and directly than amongst the Nuer, politics follows the blood, and political relations are determined by patrilineal ancestry. By the age of six or seven, children can reel off impressive genealogies including thirty or more named ancestors, each – potentially at least – a significant point both of unity and division. This method of 'placing' people in the modern political world of nationalism after independence in 1960 posed serious problems for the sophisticated. In the nationalistic euphoria of the early 1960s, when 'tribalism' was a dirty word, it was insulting to ask people their lineage identity. With characteristic ingenuity the political élite spoke of their 'ex-tribe', as though lineage loyalties had lost their compulsion and no longer mattered. When it was never more alive, by a clever trick of language (in-

cluding the incorporation of the English prefix 'ex' into Somali),
tribalism was officially abandoned, and one could, with perfect
propriety and due deference discover who was who by asking
who used to be who ! When the military seized power in Somalia
in October 1969, and launched a vigorous campaign against
'tribalism', even the term 'ex' was banned.

A Somali's genealogy is a bill of rights and a political manifesto,
proclaiming allegiances which he can adopt for his own interests
and which he may be obliged to assume in support of kinsmen.
The political groups which the various names in the genealogy
represent are mobilized according to the principle of segmentary
opposition, units of equivalent genealogical position being activated in Chinese-box fashion. There is, however, one important
qualification. Lineages descended from collateral ancestors, for
example brothers, may be formally equivalent but actually unequal in manpower and fighting strength; then they are likely
to ally with more distantly related groups, disregarding the
segmentary lineage principle. It follows from this, and is partly a
testimony to the absence of any other basic principle of social
grouping, that genealogies are not automatically adjusted (as they
tend to be among the Nuer) to correspond with actual alignments
at any moment.

In this faction-ridden society viable political units may sometimes deviate from a strict adherence to the principle of the
brotherhood of the closest, but can at least defend their members'
lives and property. And since all such groupings are relative
and impermanent (and likely to be re-convened on subsequent
occasions), the genealogies remain relatively uninfluenced by
current political exigencies and provide permanent membership of
a rich diversity of lineages. Ultimately, and this has implications
to which we shall return later, the whole Somali nation (including
the southern cultivators referred to on pages 165–6) possesses a
single pedigree, so that in principle every individual can trace his
origins back to the founding eponym from whom the Somalis take
their name.

The schizoid shifts of loyalty and allegiance in this political
vortex take place through an expedient and discriminating use of
an egalitarian social contract. Contract (*heer*), defines and mobilizes

The social contract as the basis of Somali society (after a contemporary Somali illustration in M. H. Galaal, *Anthology of Somali Oral Literature*).

effective agnatic unity (*tol*), at a specific genealogical level, and temporarily abridges and abrogates loyalty at all other levels. This is most clearly seen in the most permanent and frequently employed political unit the '*diya*-paying group', which takes its name from the Arabic term for blood-money.

Most people most of the time are effective members of such groups, which consist typically of a few, small, closely related lineages from four to eight generations in depth and with a population of up to two or three thousand men. These are true peace-groups, in that their common contractual agreements (which are recorded in writing) stipulate that they exist for the mutual benefit and security of their members. Each individual contracts to pay and receive damages (for death or injury) incurred by or due to a fellow member according to an agreed tariff. This refers essentially to external relations, members of the group being bound to support each other in all significant transactions with the outside world. At the same time, internal violence is regarded as a particularly serious offence. Different groups recognize this in two conflicting fashions. Some set a higher price on bloodshed within the group than outside it, demanding higher internal blood-compensation payments. Others, like the Nuer, reduce the damages for internal homicide. Both practices emphasize that this primary unit of allegiance is a fortress within whose sheltering walls each member can feel secure. If he or his property is attacked his colleagues will rally to his defence, and if he is killed by an enemy group they will exact vengeance and see that his dependants do not go hungry.

Something of the character of these tiny republics in this turbulent society can be gleaned by looking at an actual *diya*-paying treaty. A typical example is that of the Hassan Ugaas lineage (some 1,500 in male population), delivered to their local District Commissioner and dated 8 March 1950.[3] This reads:

1. When a man of the Hassan Ugaas is murdered by an external group, twenty camels of his blood wealth [one hundred camels] will be taken by his 'next of kin' [his sons, brothers, father, and possibly uncles], and the remaining eighty camels shared amongst all the Hassan Ugaas.
2. If a man of the Hassan Ugaas is wounded by an outsider and his

3. I. M. Lewis, *A Pastoral Democracy*, Oxford University Press, 1961, p. 177.

injuries are valued at thirty-three-and-a-third camels [a standard rate for non-fatal but quite serious injuries], ten camels will be given to him and the remainder to his lineage [the Hassan Ugaas comprise four component lineages].

3. Homicide between members of the Hassan Ugaas is subject to compensation at the rate of thirty-three-and-a-third camels, payable only to the deceased's next of kin. If the culprit is unable to pay all or part, he will be assisted by his lineage.

4. In cases of assault within the Hassan Ugaas for which compensation up to the value of thirty-three-and-a-third camels is payable, only two thirds will be paid.

5. Insult compensation (*haal*) of 150 East African shillings is payable to the person attacked when a man of the Hassan Ugaas joins another to fight with a third.

6. If one man of the Hassan Ugaas insults another at a Hassan Ugaas council meeting, he will pay 150 shillings to the offended party.

7. If a man of the Hassan Ugaas marries a girl already betrothed to another man of the group, or a widow whom it is the customary right of another to marry, he shall pay *haal* of five camels to the aggrieved party.

8. If the Hassan Ugaas kill a man of another group they will pay his blood-wealth in equal shares [amongst the four lineages] by 'penis-counting' [i.e. according to their relative strength in male members].

9. Compensation for serious wounds valued at thirty-three-and-a-third camels or more, owing to a person of another group, will be paid collectively by all the Hassan Ugaas by penis-counting.

10. This contractual agreement (*heer*) cancels all previous agreements of the Hassan Ugaas.

Contracts of this sort, binding closely connected kin, are made by the heads of families meeting together as an *ad hoc* assembly; every adult man has the right to air his views, and issues of group policy are debated and decided in the same open fashion. For all their corporateness and solidarity, however, these are not fixed local groups. The nomadic economy precludes this; and the members of a group are usually only found camped side by side for mutual safety and defence in time of war and feud. At other times, individual members are widely scattered.

In the arid environment of these nomads conflict regularly

erupts as pressure on the available water and pasture resources builds up. Disputes between the members of two *diya*-paying groups readily escalate to involve wider collateral kin on both sides. An outburst of temper over the highly symbolic as well as practical issue of precedence at a watering-point, may quickly develop into generalized enmity between ever-expanding circles of kin, as larger lineages are mobilized and old scores revived. Group identities are systematically enlarged until lineage patriotism is stretched to its widest limits in forces which may contain over 100,000 warriors.

With cohesion on this scale, precarious and ephemeral as it is, the existing *diya*-paying treaties of component lineages must be set aside and replaced, for the time being at least, by wider and more comprehensive treaties of alliance. These new defence pacts are simply more grandiose versions of the contractual agreements between smaller lineages, and the latter are resuscitated as soon as peace is restored and lineage loyalty reverts to lower levels in the system.

The effort of sustaining such wide-ranging lineage solidarity for any length of time is immense: fratricidally rivalrous lineages are eager to recover their freedom of action and manoeuvre and to withdraw from commitments which they honour with extreme reluctance. As the situation changes, groups form, coalesce, fall apart and reform, and different ancestors at different points in the genealogies are picked out as the significant foci of unity or disunity in the kaleidoscopic configurations of Somali politics. And a form of social contract which, in such anarchic conditions, comes astonishingly close to realizing the myths of the seventeenth-century contractarian political philosophers, gives specific definition to the diffuse and latent loyalties of lineage. It enables men to act overwhelmingly in one lineage capacity while reserving their right to act in another (mutually incompatible) capacity on a future occasion. Thus the Somali pastoralists keep as many options open as possible.

Leadership in this intensely egalitarian society is largely informal and, where every issue is endlessly debated, skill in public oratory and poetry is an enormous asset which, combined with energy, courage, political acumen and wealth, can win a man respect and influence amongst his peers. At some levels of lineage grouping (those we might identify as clans) there are honorific titles sometimes referred to as sultans. But these are mere figureheads: such notables, where they occur, do not enjoy the majesty or power which this Arabic title suggests. Yet, if the Somali nomads have thus even less of the incipient ascribed social differentiation which we found in Nuer tribes, this is not to say that their attitudes towards power are entirely straightforward. As in so many highly egalitarian cultures, traditional attitudes towards power and authority are distinctly ambivalent. Like the Americans, the Somalis are fascinated by royalty and noble titles, and display that persistent snobbery of which only the most ruthlessly republican peoples seem capable.

For all their hardy individualism and egalitarianism, the figure of the tyrant and despot holds a curious fascination for the pastoral nomad, and possibly because of the enormous obstacles which would have to be overcome to wield effective power in such unpropitious conditions. From this perspective it seems it is a truly prodigious feat for a man to exercise unquestioned authority over thousands or millions of subjects. And, since such power is usually also associated with an uncompromising command of ruthless force, it inevitably strikes a chord in the heart of the Somali warrior and wins his grudging if not entirely unqualified admiration.

As a nation of warriors the Somalis, like the Nuer, could scarcely survive without professional peace-makers. The most fundamental occupational distinction is in fact between men of god (singular *wadaad*) and warriors (singular *waranleh*, literally 'spear-bearer'). The men of god constitute a kind of loose 'hagiarchy' (to borrow Ernest Gellner's term for their Berber equivalent), seeking to reconcile the strife-torn laity through their commitment to peace and harmony within the Islamic community. As ideally ascetic pacifists, who should be selflessly dedicated to the wellbeing of their fellow men, these Muslim priests and saints share the aura of compensatory sanctity which generally attaches to the poor and secularly weak. Possessing, either by birth, achievement, or both, something of the charismatic divine energy known in Arabic and Somali as *baraka*, they provide convenient go-betweens in lineage conflict and represent the widest, transcendental values of Somali culture. When, in the scramble for Africa at the close of the nineteenth century, their country was partitioned amongst the Ethiopians, British, French and Italians, religious figures in this tradition, the most famous being Sayyid Muhammad 'Abdille Hassan (1864–1920),[4] led the call to arms against the usurping 'infidels' and are honoured today as heroes in the nationalist struggle.

The national identity which these pioneers sought to mobilize had stronger roots than its Nuer counterpart. Unlike the latter (but like the Tiv) the Somalis, as we have seen, traditionally formed a single lineage with the potential for unity. They were also ultimately a peace-group; for the same tariff of indemnities for homicide and other injuries applied throughout the nation, component units of which could compose their differences at any level. (We shall examine how this actually worked in practice and consider its implications later in this chapter.)

Having been arbitrarily divided amongst foreign colonial rulers, the Somalis characteristically sought to achieve independence as a single ethnic state. With few parallels in the tribally hetero-geneous states of modern Africa, in 1960 the former British and Italian Somalilands united to form the Somali Republic (known since the Revolution of 1969 as the Somali Democratic Republic). This state, however, left under alien rule three parts of the nation: the neighbouring Somali communities in the former French territory of the Afars [5] and Issas (since independence in 1977, the Republic of Djibouti) the eastern Ogaden region (named after a Somali clan) of Ethiopia, and a large part of the former Northern Frontier District of Kenya. Somali nationalist aspira-tions towards further unification wax and wane as the political climate changes in these regions.

4. For a brief account of Shaikh Muhammad's heroic and extraordinarily successful holy war against the 'infidel' British, Italians, and Ethiopians which dominated the colonial history of the region from 1900–1920, see I. M. Lewis, *A Modern History of Somalia: Nation and State in the Horn of Africa*, Longmans, 1979, chapter 4.

5. The Issa are the largest Somali lineage in this region, and their traditional rivals, the Afar, who are now politically dominant locally, are a related Cushitic-speaking people with a similar, primarily pastoral way of life.

THE TONGA TOURNIQUET

Segmentary systems (whose component parts need not always be lineages) dramatically display the interplay between the fundamental political principles of confrontation and coalition. They offer unity at one level at the price of disunity at the next, of friendship at the cost of enmity, and entail a continuous and exhausting oscillation in attitudes and behaviour towards the same people, whose positions are regularly re-defined in true 1984 style. War and peace alternate in a seemingly everlasting series of trade cycles. As Leach says with reference to the Kachin,[6] in such circles 'cooperation and hostility are not very different'. These systems thrive on acute and endemic crisis, which they also foster, perpetuating strife and guaranteeing that once one party has taken up a position on an issue whatever its actual merits, its structurally defined adversaries automatically assume the opposite stance. The results are wasteful and disruptive, and greatly reduce the efficiency of government in a modern political context, such as that of the Somali Republic.

Nevertheless, as we have seen, in a fashion that recalls Durkheim's notion of mechanical solidarity such organizations do provide an ordered political framework – in some respects analogous to that of the contemporary international political arena – and a systematic, if schizoid schema of identities, rights and obligations. That they do not break down entirely may indeed be partly ascribed not only to the external pressures bearing upon them, but also to this constant juxtaposition of loyalties, whereby allies of yesterday become enemies today and friends again tomorrow. This constant interaction between its component parts contributes to the segmentary system's internal momentum.

All the units involved here are of the same kind and vary in the same way, the smallest being microcosms of the largest. Social attachments are over-specialized and under-differentiated. Diversification introduces new possibilities. Where people are attached to each other not simply in one all-pervasive way, and where their various relationships are mutually conflicting rather than mutually reinforcing, new patterns of social integration arise. Incom-

6. E. R. Leach, *Political Systems of Highland Burma*, Athlone Press, 1954, p. 153.

patible loyalties which, from the perspective of the individual 'tear him apart' (as we say), can have a positive social impact. The Nuer have chosen, somewhat improvidently, to allow territorial and kinship ties to run in parallel, thus compounding existing cleavages in their society. What would have been the outcome if these two allegiances had been set against each other, as kith versus kin?

The Plateau Tonga of southern Zambia provide an instructive and suggestive answer. Here we encounter another egalitarian people who, at first sight, seem to possess even less formal political organization than either the Nuer or Somali. In a setting characterized by such stately chiefdoms as those of the Bemba, Lozi and Ngoni their fierce individualism made a memorable impression on the expatriate officials who had the almost impossible task of administering them. It is equally in character that the Tonga, who today number some 100,000, should have become one of the most go-ahead and entrepreneurially successful groups in the country.

The Tonga have a mixed economy, growing maize and rearing cattle, and this division between fixed and movable resources provides the economic foundation of their political structure. Cattle are inherited matrilineally, and the Tonga as a whole are divided into a number of dispersed, exogamous matrilineal clans which, they say, God provided so that they could 'marry properly'. Villages, which thus consist of members drawn from different clans, form round a man of strong personality, and are in turn loosely grouped in wider clusters based upon a local rain-shrine, whose custodian commands respect and influence. Such big-men usually claim a connection with the first settlers of the area, and may themselves become the foci of rain cults when they die. Peace and rain figure prominently in the blessings expected from such leaders and their spirits. There are thus areas of ritual cooperation and harmony transcending the village, although the latter remains the primary locus of territorial allegiance.

Villages are not systematically arranged in a segmentary hierarchy as amongst the Nuer, nor are they associated with particular 'dominant lineages'. On the contrary the ties of kith and kin, though both respected, are kept separate and Tonga loyalties pull in different directions. Local farming interests tie them to their neighbours who belong to different clans. Wider, inter-village and inter-rain-shrine interests connect the dispersed clan members who share rights in cattle and owe each other various duties and obligations. They may not marry each other, but they help each other in marshalling marriage payments and inherit each other's widows. In much the same style as the Somali *diya*-paying group, though scattered in different village settlements, the members of a matrilineage form a corporate group legally responsible for the interests and actions of its members. In cases of homicide, like its Somali counterpart, this matrilineage acts as a vengeance group seeking reparation. An individual is also a member of his father's matrilineage and thus has dual matrilineal identity.

Kinship (traced both maternally and paternally) and locality here work at cross purposes, weaving an intricate web of overlapping and clashing, rather than coincident cleavages. Tension and conflict on one front are thus automatically checked by overriding common interests which quickly mobilize their forces on another. The paralysing impact of these built-in safety mechanisms is vividly seen in the following little drama taken directly from Elizabeth Colson's lucid analysis.[7]

At a beer party, a man of the Eland clan in his cups killed a man of the Lion clan who lived in a neighbouring village. The murderer was arrested by the police and sentenced to a year's imprisonment for manslaughter. Lions, however, were far from satisfied with this outcome, and broke off relations with all members of the Eland clan living in the vicinity. Eland men in Lion villages and Lion men in predominantly Eland villages told Elizabeth Colson that, prior to the advent of British administration they would have fled to friendly territory in such circumstances. This was now impossible, so the Lions effectively ostracized their Eland fellow villagers. Eland wives living with Lion husbands were similarly taunted and threatened which inevitably disturbed their husbands, so the dispute began to sour marital relations. The situation became intolerable as more and more relationships became infected by the feud. Under these pressures, through the good offices of common in-laws, the Elands proffered compensation, and agreement was reached on the cattle to be paid. Peace returned

7. E. Colson, 'Social Control and Vengeance in Plateau Tonga Society', *Africa*, vol. 23, 1953, pp. 199–211.

to the troubled villages and people resumed their normal patterns of social intercourse.

But, as so often happens, the Elands were slow in paying the compensation they had promised. The next development was tragic. The son of an Eland woman married to a Lion man fell sick and died. Divination disclosed that the child had been struck dead by the avenging spirit of the murdered Lion man, outraged that the compensation for his life had not been handed over. Again the women began to press their husbands and kinsmen to settle the dispute. Since the matrilineal vengeance groups of the two sides were dispersed and many of their women married to men of other clans, it was extremely difficult for either party to maintain a consolidated front against the forces favouring a prompt and effective settlement. So the inquest on the child's death was followed by a meeting at which mutual relatives of the two enemies acted as mediators, and this time the cattle requested were paid and the feud resolved, at least for the time being.

To appreciate the full integrative force of such social cross-currents the reader has only to consider what the position in contemporary Northern Ireland would be if the Catholics and Protestants intermarried and were as intimately entwined as the Elands and Lions. A few simple principles of social attachment combined with a very flexible pattern of informal leadership, based largely on achievement, can sustain the diffuse social integration individualists like the Tonga require. Many will envy them.

The pressures for peace we have just examined include both secular and sacred episodes. Taboos on commensality during hostilities have an equally devastating impact on normal social intercourse and maintain order and harmony in much the same way. The Tsembaga swidden cultivators of the Bismarck mountains in New Guinea provide a ready example, from that paradise of little big-men where, with the possible exception of hunting bands and hippy communes, we find the most uncentralized, acephalous political systems of all. This 'society' which, like so many others in New Guinea, is minute (just over two hundred people) is divided into exogamous 'clans' and 'sub-clans', dispersed in various local settlements grouped round big-men. On the widespread principle of hospitality that those who eat together are friends, Tsembaga taboos make it impossible for enemies to eat food grown in the same garden or cooked over the same fire. This interdiction has paralysing implications when conflict flares up between the members of different clans living, like the Tonga, cheek-by-jowl in the same local community. Such disputes, known appropriately as 'brother fights', have so many ramifying repercussions for almost every member of the community, including wives and neutral parties, that communal life quickly grinds to a halt. The only possible alternative to a peaceful solution may be for the whole settlement to disintegrate and disperse.[8]

This atmosphere is typical of a region where those who aspire to dominate their fellows strain and struggle unremittingly in a Hobbesian free-for-all. Culture-units in New Guinea[9] on average number only 1,500 people, and in such small communities the political careers of posturing big-men inevitably dominate. Life seems based on the simple but all-pervasive imperative: transact. The ensuing tit-for-tat exchange of honours and blows which, as we saw in chapter 7, big-men organize and direct, is the main instrument of politics. Indeed it is the core of politics. Ties to locality, clan, sometimes to a group of clans, but above all to those who collaborate together in ceremonial exchange and ritual, provide the basic loyalties with which would-be big-men conjure as they joust for power. If the Nuer and Somali can be said to be systematic situationalists. New Guinea leaders are natural existentialists. Their politics is directed by a hedonistic pursuit of short-term glory, in a Keynesian frenzy of entrepreneurial activity and speculation. Successful men pull themselves up by their boot-strings only to collapse again under the strain of retaining prominence in a world where all men are in principle equal and everyone is on the make.

In the luxuriant ecology pigs breed like rabbits and, unlike cattle, compete directly with man for food and only contribute to his diet when they are slaughtered, so there is little heritable patrimony to pass on and no organized ascribed status even on the minimal scale of the Nuer. By the same token, while ties based

8. R. A. Rappaport, *Pigs for the Ancestors*, Yale University Press, 1967, p. 111.
9. New Guinea's total population of 1,500,000 is estimated to contain over 1,000 distinct cultural groups.

on descent, flexibly interpreted, have some significance, there is
no enduring, comprehensive structure of segmentary units. Alliance and aggression ebb and flow under the management of
ambitious big-men, true impressarios who manipulate the various
principles of social attachment within the rules of the political
game to suit their interest.

As Anthony Forge puts it: [10] 'All the segments that actually
exist are compared solely in terms of their land holdings, numbers
and ferocity of their members and so on, as they actually are at
the moment, matters which can easily be changed, not with any
sort of reference to their past.' He invokes de Tocqueville to
remind us that in such circumstances '. . . not only does democracy
make every man forget his ancestors, but it hides his descendants,
and separates his contemporaries from him; it throws him back for
ever upon himself alone, and threatens in the end to confine him
entirely within the solitude of his own heart'.[11] We catch an
authentic glimpse of the isolation and loneliness of those who
seek power even in the cramped circumstances of New Guinea
politics in Forge's moving account [12] of a failed Abelam big-man.
Brinkmanship is essential to the histrionic displays by which
leaders test and affirm their rival claims, and cross-cutting commitments of the Tsembaga type have an important role in the
general maintenance of harmony and order. Where order teeters
dangerously on the edge of anarchy, every straw must be desperately clutched at.

REPARATION AND RETRIBUTION

As our discussion of politics has moved to the uncentralized end
of the political spectrum we have spoken increasingly of 'social
control' rather than 'politics' in the narrow sense. It is now time
to examine more explicitly some characteristic features of social
control and their relation to different types of political system.
Although extreme forms of violence, including homicide, may be

10. A. Forge, 'The Golden Fleece', *Man* (N.S.), vol. 7, 1972, p. 533.

11. A. de Tocqueville, *Democracy in America*, vol. 2,. Harper & Row, New York, 1965,
p. 92, (first published 1871).

12. A. Forge, 'Tswamung: A Failed Big-Man', in S. Kimball and J. Watson (eds.),
Crossing Cultural Boundaries, Chandler, San Francisco, 1973.

accepted daily occurrences amongst people who consider themselves a community, contrary to what our conventional notions of law and order might lead us to expect, this is not because there are no mechanisms for peace-making and settling disputes. Indeed rather the contrary. For, as we have seen amongst the Nuer and Somali where feud is a widespread and recurrent social phenomenon, specialized means of restoring amicable relations are well developed. Those who live to fight must possess some equivalent of the International Red Cross as referees and boundary-men to keep the score and to act, when necessary, as go-betweens and mediators. Passive neutrality can be activated into mediation and small, in some sense marginal groups can make a prosperous living as professional 'honest Johns' between the big battalions.

Those who do well in the service of peace and understanding can operate in many unexpected circumstances. In his fictional account of the mafia, Mario Puzo describes the crucial pacificatory role in mafia feuds of the Bocchicchio clan, a group possessing a unique reputation for 'honour' (a primary asset in all negotiators) matched only by their ruthless ferocity in exacting vengeance. This unusually tightly knit kinship group was formerly in the garbage trade; having prudently decided to diversify, it is now, we learn, 'an instrument for peace in America'. When representatives of one hostile mafia clan wish to meet the leaders of their adversaries, the 'saintly' Bocchicchios provide hostages who, on account of the clan's special reputation, are regarded as 'gilt-edged insurance'.

Even the most contentious and violent of communities must, if its members are to survive, have some form of neutral mediatory agency, and the next question that arises is how disputes are actually settled. The prior question as to what offences or wrongs are recognized can be quickly disposed of. In principle all societies recognize that human life and property, whatever price is placed upon them, have to be protected, and that their violation constitutes a wrong or offence which has to be rectified or punished. Beyond this the elaboration of substantive law is largely a matter of material technology and cultural sophistication and need not detain us further. What must concern us, however, is how the social context or milieu of a dispute affects its treatment and outcome. The penalty can only be fitted to the crime by reference to the social distance of the parties involved.

Take homicide. What matters is not the act of killing, but who you kill. In peacetime homicide is a crime, and the more heinous the closer the relationship between the killer and his victim. (This is why contemporary intra-familial murders are such a source of morbid concern not only to sociologists but also to the public.) In time of war, however, killing the enemy is a glorious act of heroism, earning praise, and in particularly dangerous circumstances medals and promotion. At the same time there may be, even between the most implacable and unsentimental of foes, some residual compunction and a grudging recognition that the taking of life is in some ultimate sense wrong. For who knows, peace may come. Even those who reject the idea of the brotherhood of man, out of hand, may fear the pollution which murder is so widely held to engender. In this context it becomes possible to charge American soldiers with misconduct for butchering innocent civilians even when the latter are only 'Oriental human beings' – a marginal sub-category whose members are supposed to 'breed like flies', to 'value life lightly', and to provide the regulation fodder for Oriental despotism.

As we have seen, the contours of the widest Nuer 'peace-group', the tribe, can be precisely determined by the treatment of homicide as a compoundable wrong, or as a praiseworthy achievement. Here, in an egalitarian society, social distance is traced horizontally and only a few significant differences are based on relative status. In more stratified, class or caste-based societies it is measured vertically, as formerly in England, and in India where the penalties for murder related directly to the caste of the victim. According to the traditional Indian calculus, the murder of a Brahmin required twelve years' penance, that of a Kshatriya nine years', of a Vaishya three and of a Shudra merely one: untouchables are not even mentioned (for the meaning of these occupational terms, see p. 191). In such societies the significance (or insignificance) of a person's life can be accurately computed.

On the whole, whatever the social distance of the parties, attacks on property and persons in uncentralized societies tend to be treated as wrongs, demanding reparation (if necessary in kind), rather than as crimes demanding punishment. The amount of damages sought varies with the social distance of the parties, as indeed does the probability of obtaining a ready and satisfactory settlement. In all communities the pressure to compose differences harmoniously is strongest in the smallest constituent groups, where prolonged conflict makes life intolerable. We have already seen the Nuer sliding scale of degrees of acceptable violence and the corresponding index of indemnities. The uncentralized segmentary Tiv of Nigeria have very similar arrangements, and we have noticed how the amount of blood-wealth claimed in cases of internal homicide within the Somali *diya*-paying group reflects the closeness of the parties.

But how in such segmentary societies where the ultimate sanction is self-help, the taking of the law into one's own hands, is payment of indemnities actually enforced? The ethnographic literature is often disappointingly vague on this point. Among the Somali nomads, the recalcitrant member of a *diya*-paying group who refuses to pay an internal fine or to contribute his share of an outgoing due is liable to be seized summarily by his peers and tied, none too gently, to a tree while several of his most coveted livestock are slaughtered under his eyes to feast the elders of the lineage. This sanction is also applied amongst the Gurage and in certain neighbouring Galla communities in Ethiopia.

Fürer-Haimendorf[13] reports a similar practice among the uncentralized Konyak Nagas, where the village councillors collect a fine from one who has abused a fellow villager and use it to provide a meal for themselves. More serious offences call for more drastic remedies. Thus, the Konyak execute persistent offenders who repeatedly cause serious damage to their neighbours' lives and property, and, since the shedding of blood within the community even in righteous indignation is morally wrong, carry out their sentence by tying up the culprit with a minimum of violence and consigning his body, duly weighted, to the waters of the nearest river. Although they may not resort to drowning, the Galla similarly execute persistent recidivists with the same scrupulous care to avoid spilling any of the culprit's blood. Somali, likewise, do not tolerate habitual trouble-makers within the *diya*-paying group

13. C. von Fürer-Haimendorf, *Morals and Merit*, Weidenfeld & Nicolson, 1967, p. 91.

and will ultimately get rid of them in one way or another. The commonest remedy is to exile such useless drones: but I have also heard of cases where miscreants of this kind were killed in such a way that their death could be attributed to a third party against whom claims for damages were promptly lodged! Insurance fraud is a far from modern invention.

Except where external pressures are acute, or Tonga-type cross-cutting ties interpose their pacificatory pull, disputes outside these basic 'peace-groups' are far less readily settled and self-help in the form of direct counter-attack is the usual sanction to obtain redress. Significant differences between the procedures invoked by the Nuer and Somali illustrate the principles which govern how violations of rights and possessions are evaluated and dealt with. In both societies saintly non-combatants are summoned to mediate between hostile warrior groups. Where the disputants themselves are in a conciliatory frame of mind, these men of god can bring the two sides together, acting as emissaries between them, but they can do little more. There is no question of their undertaking any judicial role; they may act judiciously but they are not a judiciary. No one asks them to pronounce on the merits of each party's case, and they would soon be out of business if they attempted to do so.

But for the Somali this is only part of the story. These pastoral nomads also possess well-recognized arbitrating procedures in the form of *ad hoc* courts specifically appointed to judge between the contending parties. Their members, usually not more than half a dozen in number, are laymen, not priests, selected for their wisdom, knowledge of custom, and impartiality. These wise elders, meeting informally in the shade of a tree, listen first to the case as it is presented by the aggrieved party, either directly or by a spokesman chosen for his skills as a persuasive orator. Important points made in the course of the hearing are repeated loudly by a 'recorder' so that nothing of substance escapes the attentive audience of the proceedings. The plaintiff's submission is followed by that of the defendant, who presents his case in much the same way, attempting to deny or rebut his opponent's accusations. Neither side is cross-questioned by the judges. But once both have finished their submissions and the judges are satisfied that they have fully seized the crux of the issue, they prudently send the recorder to collect their fee before proceeding. The litigants are now invited to present witnesses, and either principal may be requested to support his case by pronouncing a 'triple oath' which, if found to be perjurious, automatically annuls his marriage.

With these devices the judges finally arrive at a decision which they urge both parties to accept with good grace since it is based on previous precedents and issued in the name of Somali custom to which they all steadfastly adhere. Whether or not this verdict is accepted depends largely on the eagerness of the contestants to compromise, on their respective assessments of the reasonableness of the judgment, and upon the collateral pressure of public opinion. Even if the loser fails to comply with the decision, his position will be weakened by losing his case.

These Somali courts are thus not simply 'moots' (such as those described for the Tiv), or general talk-ins (or outs) in which all concerned cathartically ventilate their grievances without seeking an external opinion. On the contrary they offer judgments that in their setting have much in common with those of the International Court at the Hague. Like the latter, the Somali elders have no formal power to enforce their decision. All the *diya*-paying groups, miniature republics though they are, do however subscribe to a common body of customary law which is like a co-ordinated and mutually accepted body of international law. Unlike the Nuer, all the Somalis recognize the same code of wrongs and accept that every category of delict can be compounded by the payment of the appropriate damages. In this respect, the entire Somali nation despite its size, behaves like a Nuer tribe, and so displays a denser and more comprehensive sense of common national identity.

The pronounced emphasis on reparation and restitution which is typical of dispute settlement in such uncentralized societies (and of informal jural activity elsewhere) is closely associated with the evaluation of injuries and violations of rights as *wrongs* rather than as *crimes*, the former, as the Kachin so vigorously assert, characteristically entailing debts. Yet something of the same commendable concern to repair strained relations rather than to honour abstract notions of justice informs the judicial process of many more centralized traditional societies. But, in total refutation

of the erroneous speculations of Durkheim and Maine, as centralization develops so does the range of wrongs that are redefined
as crimes against the state, for which punitive rather than
restitutive measures are required.

The transition from an egalitarian segmentary order involving
wrongs, debts, and damages, ultimately backed by self-help, to
the other extreme is very clear in Edmund Leach's classic analysis
of politics in Highland Burma. As he says, in the traditional
democratic Kachin system 'disputes are settled by arbitration
rather than arbitrary judgment. A law-suit involves a debt (*hka*)
and the settlement of the debt is a matter for the agents (*kasa*) of
the disputing parties.' Arbitration is supplied by a council of elders
in much the same fashion as amongst the Konyak Nagas or
Somalis. However in the transitional would-be hierarchically
organized structure called *gumsa* which the Kachins aspire to
create in the image of the Shan states, chiefs enter the picture,
since outbreaks of violence are felt to infringe their dignity and
power. Such acts amount to a kind of lese-majesty since, by definition, only land-owning chiefs possess 'the right to commit violence'. Hence, if one party assaults another who does not belong
to the chief's lineage, the latter is nevertheless outraged, even
desecrated, since this is a hostile act directed against the chief's
local tutelary spirit (*nat*). So even though a chief is not always
called upon to judge offences, he is implicated in them and has a
vested interest in seeing that disputes are contained and satisfactorily determined.

Precisely because political power and judicial authority are so
intimately bound together we speak of an area over which a
sovereign or central government effectively exerts power as lying
within its 'jurisdiction'. And in the same way, we speak of a
ruler's 'writ' as extending over a determined group or territory.
Increasing assertion of centralized power, such as in Ethiopia and
Buganda, always means that the central authorities claim the
right to determine all disputes between their subjects, even if
they do not exercise this right in all cases. As Schapera says,[14]
speaking of the southern Bantu kingdoms, the administration of
justice is a major duty of all rulers. Under the British system of

14. I. Schapera, *Government and Politics in Tribal Societies*, Watts, 1956; p. 78.

indirect rule, therefore, officially-recognized chiefs were regularly ranged in order of precedence according to the judicial powers allocated to their courts.

The general pattern is clear and unambiguous. For all their much vaunted oriental despotism, successive pre-revolutionary Chinese governments were frequently content to allow many local issues to be settled by self-help, as long as the outcome did not jeopardize wider state interests. Maurice Freedman[15] in a characteristically judicious assessment of the evidence concludes: 'Government existed, but its political and legal abstentions promoted self-help. Lineages depended on one another, especially for women, and they might make common cause in the face of a common danger ... The lineages at arms were part of a system in which the pre-existing ties between them, the interests of neutral neighbouring lineages, and, in the last resort, the concern of the state prevented controlled fighting breaking down into ruthless warfare.'

In this generous spirit even the most resolutely centralist governments will often tolerate a certain level of local turbulence provided the masses pay their taxes and do not molest the property or threaten the interests of the mighty. If the locals keep the peace themselves so much the better. Thus under the British in India and in Africa and the Dutch in Indonesia, as under their successors today, at village level local 'custom' (a convenient and flexible catch-all) may be followed so long as due homage is paid to the ultimate supremacy of the laws of the state – concessions which may promote a more or less officially recognized jural dualism. Yet as we move from uncentralized to centralized polities, in the official law of the land wrongs increasingly become crimes (though some may remain in a restricted 'civil' sector), restitution cedes ground to punishment, judgment becomes more impersonal and abstract (and theoretically more 'perfect'), and courts with teeth replace their well-intentioned pacificatory predecessors. The law of the jungle with all its weaknesses and strengths bows, at least formally, before the majesty of centralized state justice.

THE SWING OF THE PENDULUM

Our previous examination of the logistics of centralized rule took much for granted. As we contemplated formally appointed rulers vigorously pulling the levers of power we did not ask how their centralized machinery came into being. Having examined the non-state, we can ask the wider, more fundamental question: why do states exist, how do they arise? What forces transform acephalous segments into the hierarchical centralized state?

Our brief forays into the political cultures of resolutely uncentralized peoples show clearly that political inequalities are no novelty to them. Their acute sensitivity to the slightest and subtlest differences in power drives their members to struggle so hard to maintain equality. What militates against the entrenchment of political cleavages and the development of permanent and pervasive stratification is not ignorance or lack of interest in power but that everyone in principle wants it and is prepared to fight for it. In this Hobbesian maelstrom everyone is his own Leviathan, and the populist diffusion of power defuses its intrinsic potential for stratification and inequality – at least it almost does, but not completely. Everywhere individuals differ in ambition and fortune. There are always potential big-men ready to get bigger – if only they have the opportunity. That chance, as we have seen in our discussion of New Guinea exchange systems and entrepreneurs (p. 232), occurs frequently during radical socio-economic change. Then pipe-dreams and castles-in-the-air may become realities as opportunists rise to the challenges facing them.

Control of access to new economic opportunities offers substantial dividends and enables an astute local big-man to become bigger, with a following recruited partly through kinship and partly through economic incentives. Thus, by managing the supply of local products (including labour) to outside markets – or *vice versa* – the successful entrepreneur enhances his political status which, subject to customary and other environmental constraints, he will try to consolidate. Social upheaval, cultural confusion, and general social turbulence provide the spur to speculation in circumstances where if the risks are greater it is easier to take them. For when values are in a state of flux it is easier to renege on traditional obligations and to find convincing excuses. Men on the make constantly use new justifications and ideologies to protect them from the claims and envy of the less successful. In such circumstances the protestant ethic, or something remarkably like it, is in the air and new religions may find ready converts amongst social climbers. Nothing succeeds like success, and all that remains to be done is to institutionalize the new inegalitarian dispensation – to convert the self-made man into a hereditary office.

We have outlined a very common scenario for the rise of social stratification and the foundation of dynasties. All we need now are a few examples. We can start with the tendency for wider-based leadership to develop amongst the Nuer and nomadic Somali at times of national crisis. This short-lived incipient stratification is taken a stage further as we have seen amongst the southern cultivating Somali, where the development of chieftaincy is clearly associated with the transition from nomadism to a sedentary economy. These germs of statehood achieved their most impressive realization in the Geledi sultanate which, from its strategic hold on the lower Shebelle River, controlled the vital trade-routes between the coast and hinterland in the nineteenth century, and so dominated southern Somalia. As the richest and most powerful political unit outside the ancient cities of the coast it was also the most stratified: its fields were tended by slaves, and its livestock by client herdsmen.[16]

Although the ultimate origins of this small Somali state are now too remote to probe in detail, we are better informed about parallel political developments further to the west amongst the Galla. In the troubled conditions of the eighteenth century prior to Menelik's final imposition of the *pax Amharica*, the Galla who had moved north from the traditional Boran pastures and settled as cultivators began to produce a new pattern of social stratification. Local war-leaders became increasingly important figures and started pressing individual claims to land. There arose a new landed military élite with tenant and client followers. The rich resources of western Ethiopia – slaves, gold, ivory, animal skins, coffee, and civet – were carried along trade routes through the

16. Cf. V. Luling, *A Somali Sultanate*, in press.

territory dominated by these bellicose leaders who were naturally anxious to participate in this lucrative traffic. They were able to impose market and transit taxes, using the proceeds to buy firearms or further land. Land, trade and war formed a trinity of high-yield assets in these local brigands' investment portfolios. With increasing pressure on land, more land meant more followers; more followers made it possible to win more land by conquest, and the possession of both allowed a leader to control markets and trade routes. The circle was complete.

This stratification spiral reached its climax in the formation of a series of Muslim states along the Gibe River, where the Galla were intruding into territory formerly dominated by the centralized Kaffa and related tribes.[17] In some cases, significantly, the founders of dynasties were non-Galla foreigners, and hence ideally placed to innovate. It is also no accident that they embraced Islam, the religion of dissidence and defiance in Christian Ethiopia; in other areas more acquiescent Galla became Christian. Nevertheless it would be wrong to underestimate what the burgeoning jargon of development studies calls the 'demonstration effect' of the neighbouring Amhara and other kingdoms, especially since some of the state terminology appears to come from these sources. Even these impressive examples would not have inspired ambitious Galla to construct states without the precipitating impact of the economic and military factors we have outlined. Here, consequently, we have to stand the old colonial slogan on its head and say that 'the flag follows trade'.

In Edmund Leach's subtle analysis[18] of the dialectic between segmentary and state government among the Burmese Kachin we find remarkably similar forces at work. Using the economic surplus of trade, mineral resources, and rice cultivation, Kachin big-men strive to convert themselves into Shan princes by exploiting the potential for differentiation and inequality that already exists in their segmentary order. With the élitist model of Shan Buddhist culture as their inspiration, such Kachin knights attempt to trans-

17. Cf. H. S. Lewis, *A Galla Monarchy: Jimma Abba Jifar, Ethiopia, 1830–1932*, University of Wisconsin Press, Madison, 1965.

18. E. R. Leach, *Political Systems of Highland Burma*, Athlone Press, 1954; and for a stimulating recent critique, see J. Friedman, 'Tribes, States and Transformations', in M. Bloch (ed.), *Marxist Analyses in Social Anthropology*, Malaby, 1975, pp. 161–202.

form common lineage ties and affinal connections into hierarchical landlord–tenant relationships. And sometimes they succeed, although egalitarian pressures soon build up, causing a revolutionary explosion and an attempted restoration of the old democratic order. The Kachins, in the picture Leach paints, live in a perpetual identity crisis, and are constantly torn between two diametrically opposed cultures and self-images – the one as democratic as the other is hierarchical. How the overall situation is assessed must depend upon the time-scale within which it is viewed. In the short-term, and under certain ecological and demographic conditions, movement in one direction may appear. But on a longer-term view the troughs and peaks may assume a more regular pattern, suggesting a series of cycles rather than a shift to entirely novel formations. Or reality may be a mixture of both, since the dialectic between localist democracy and autocratic centralism is not necessarily entirely closed.

Leach draws his paradigm for the oscillating politics of the Kachin from the sociologist Pareto's concept of 'moving equilibrium' and the alternating dominance of the 'lions' and the 'foxes'. This is extremely close to the theory of state-formation advanced by the famous fourteenth-century Berber historian and sociologist, Ibn Khaldun. According to this philosopher, wild anarchic nomads, the true wolves of the desert, possess the vitality and *esprit de corps* which enables them to carve out empires amongst their more submissive sedentary neighbours. But no sooner have they settled down to enjoy victory than they grow soft and indolent, and are easily defeated by a fresh nomadic intrusion. The tamed wolves, enfeebled by their association with the sheep, are no match for their feral cousins in the desert. Nothing lasts unless it is renewed and rejuvenated by fresh blood from its original source. The momentum and dynamism which empowers segmentary nomads to create states contains within itself the seeds of its own decay, and necessitates a return to the tribal womb, the source of new life. This circulation of élites in the lives of states and dynasties revolves, Ibn Khaldun argues, on a three generational cycle.

Since Ibn Khaldun was a north African reflecting on the history of his homeland, it is not perhaps remarkable that this cyclical model aptly describes the pre-colonial history of the Muslim states of the region, in particular the dialectical relation between the ruling coastal dynasties and the marauding desert nomads of the interior who rejected their authority but also replenished it.[19] The same paradoxical antithesis between the unruly founders of dynasties and their destroyers occurs along the other margins of the Sahara – in the Hausa-speaking Muslim states of the western Sudan created by the nomadic Fulani.

It would be absurd to argue that, by some curious law of opposites, states were invariably founded by leaders from 'non-states'. But the knowledge that this can and does happen helps to correct the crude evolutionary view that, because states and non-states are structurally poles apart, they are necessarily separated by a long chain of intermediary stages. Even if the political history of mankind can in some sense be viewed as a long winding staircase of evolutionary stages, we must concede that sometimes the steps can be taken at a run – even at the risk of falling downstairs !

This meeting of extremes has a wider context in the classical 'conquest theory' of state formation, according to which states arise when one group or culture successfully imposes its will over another. It is indisputable that many traditional states have been formed in such circumstances. It is the common strand in the political history of such otherwise disparate and unconnected cases as those of Rwanda, the interlacustrine kingdoms, the Barotse, Ethiopia, those of the Incas and Aztecs, and the classical despotic empires of south-eastern Asia; in most of these examples and many others the conquering élite is culturally distinct from its subjects to whom it is linked by a hierarchical system of patronage. In others (such as Lubemba, Buganda, the Zulu and other southern Bantu) there are few if any marked cultural differences between rulers and ruled. Hence as the nineteenth-century political philosopher John Stuart Mill argues,[20] cultural homogeneity may promote democracy, but it evidently does not guarantee it nor preclude the development of centralist autocracy. Moreover, if in some cases conquest and state formation seem to be favoured by the cultural differences of the parties, in other cases

19. Cf. E. Gellner, *Saints of the Atlas*, Weidenfeld & Nicolson, 1969.
20. J. S. Mill, *Considerations on Representative Government*, Blackwell, 1861, pp. 291–2.

(such as the Nuer and Dinka), conquest does not spawn states, perhaps because the cultural gap is smaller and more easily bridged.

Hence conquest is by no means a sufficient condition for the rise of states. Nor does it appear to be a necessary condition. Segmentary societies can assume the characteristic features of statehood as a result of what perhaps might be best described as 'peaceful penetration'. This theoretical situation has strong analogies with the feud-ridden world of the Nuer and Somali. An unruly people at odds with each other seek the help of external mediators to compose their differences. The visiting peace-makers prove successful and popular, and stay. Eventually they become indispensable and their pacificatory role acquires a political edge. This is essentially the genesis of the 'hagiarchal' state realized by communities of saints in Muslim societies, of which the Sanusi of Cyrenaica [21] provide the outstanding example. What wisdom and conciliatory words have achieved may later require consolidation and defence by force as those who came to make peace make war.

So we are brought back to the vital factor of military technology in the rise and fall of states. The tactical advantages conferred by mastery in fire-power are immediately apparent. We are, however, apt to forget – despite Jack Goody's [22] strenuous efforts to remind us – that in the pre-industrial technologies of Africa 'horse-power' often played an equivalent role, especially in the Savanna states, with equestrian aristocracies cavalierly ruling pedestrian peasants.

Techno-environmental factors cannot therefore be brushed aside, even if we cannot concede the full formative force with which the more simplistic evolutionary cultural ecologists would endow them. Here, perhaps, the important conclusions are straightforward. Large permanent political communities need strong organization to hold them together, although there may be 'economies of scale'. Small fleetingly mobilized groups, such as Nuer tribes or Somali lineages, are more easily and simply organized. The bigger and more specialized the apparatus of government, the greater the economic surplus needed to maintain it and hence the more extractive and intensive the economy. But even

21. E. E. Evans-Pritchard, *The Sanusi of Cyrenaica*, Oxford University Press, 1949.

22. J. Goody, *Technology, Tradition and the State in Africa*, Oxford University Press, 1971.

these modest conclusions, which are scarcely more than truisms, do not entitle us to conclude that centralized states necessarily represent a high-energy form of civil life which is more efficient and satisfactory. Just as states can thrive in areas of low population density, so such highly intensive forms of economy as wet-rice cultivation permitting very high concentrations of population, do not necessarily beget high degrees of centralization. Wittfogel's famous theory linking irrigation cultivation with oriental despotism is much less deterministic and more subtle than many of those who work in his shadow suppose. 'It is only above the level of an extractive subsistence economy', the master cautiously specifies, 'beyond the influence of strong centres of rainfall agriculture, and below the level of a property-based industrial civilization that man, reacting specifically to the water-deficient landscape moves towards a specific hydraulic order of life.'[23] With so many elaborate qualifications, who needs counter-arguments or negative instances?

NEW NATIONS

On the face of it the nationalist struggles of nineteenth-century Europe and twentieth-century Africa and Asia seem very different. In Europe the independence battle-cry was not 'one man, one vote', but rather 'one nation, one state'. In Europe, nationalism was a grievance which could only achieve redress by the grant of sovereign statehood. Asian and African politicians also fought for freedom from colonial rule in the name of nationalism. But the entities they represented were certainly *not* nations. With rare exceptions (in sub-Saharan Africa, Somalia, Swaziland and Basutoland), the units for which self-government was claimed were patchworks of tribes and language-groups thrown together by the fortuitous vagaries of European colonization. They were mostly composite, culturally plural countries with no natural traditional common denominator save that imposed by European conquest and rule. Despite their own very different nationalist tradition, their European founders had evidently shared Edmund Leach's view that 'there is no intrinsic reason why the significant frontiers of social systems should always coincide with cultural frontiers'.[24]

23. K. A. Wittfogel, *Oriental Despotism*, Yale University Press, 1957, p. 12.
24. E. R. Leach, *Political Systems of Highland Burma*, Athlone Press, 1954, p. 17.

And, as we have seen, culturally heterogeneous 'plural' states were not a European invention.

Third World nationalism thus reverses its European counter-part, and the post-independence period is dominated by 'nation-building' as newly sovereign states, having achieved the political kingdom, seek the more elusive goal of cultural integrity. Shortly before his death, Tom Mboya diagnosed the position with can-dour: '. . . we have still to achieve complete nationhood. Such nationhood requires commitment, a sense of identification and the submerging of tribal as well as racial loyalties to national loyalty.' [25] As Ken Minogue succinctly puts it in his valuable recent survey: 'In modern nationalism, politics comes first and national culture is constructed later.' [26]

But what of the traditional communities of the Third World, are they not nations? I consider that they are, and have thus deliberately spoken of Nuer nationalism, Somali nationalism etc. But is this view really defensible? Here we need to review the strange career of the term 'tribe'. Originally the Latin term *tribus* meant the early political divisions or patrician orders (that is 'estates') of the Roman state, and was completely devoid of con-descending atavistic connotations. Despite its noble origins, in the eighteenth and nineteenth centuries colonizing Europeans applied the term indiscriminately to the 'uncivilized' archaic communities of Asia and Africa before the imperial partition. The term thus referred to distinctive cultural entities, whose members spoke the same language or dialect and generally lived in a common terri-tory; they might or might not acknowledge the authority of a single chief and so form a political as well as a cultural unit. Tribal natives everywhere were in principle rustic children of nature living in their primordial condition, and tribes consequently rep-resented the antithesis of civilized societies.

This is seen with particular clarity in the case of that halfway house to western civilization – the continent of India. There the majority of people, while not enjoying the ultimate privilege of being European, nevertheless lived in castes which represented a

25. T. Mboya, 'The Impact of Modern Institutions on the East African', in P. H. Gulliver (ed.), *Tradition and Transition in East Africa*, Routledge & Kegan Paul, 1969, p. 93.
26. K. Minogue, *Nationalism*, Batsford, 1967, p. 154.

distinct step forward on the evolutionary scale. Outside the caste system, beyond the pale on the very margins of the Indian states, roamed the unruly 'tribesmen', true creatures of nature (and sometimes for the more romantically inclined English also 'nature's gentlemen'). Unlike the dark continent of Africa, India was not all unrelieved gloom, for it was a country of 'castes *and* tribes'.

Both in Africa and Asia the word 'tribe' thus embraced a truly catholic collection of different communities: tiny traditional kingdoms; stateless societies large and small; vast linguistic congeries such as the Ibo, Yoruba, and Hausa-speaking peoples in West Africa, or the Galla in north-east Africa; and cultures whose technologies and economies ranged from the simplest hunters and gatherers to the most complex wet-rice producers. Despite these enormous variations, most of these 'tribes', even if they were not actual political units, were indeed communities with some sense of common cultural identity and exclusiveness – particularly in contexts of competition or conflict with other comparable populations. 'We the Tikopia' – the phrase Raymond Firth found often on the lips of the inhabitants of the tiny Pacific island of Tikopia – is a statement, a declaration of identity, which all tribes will echo. Even those who traditionally devote so much energy to killing each other still acknowledge a common bond that is unique and totally distinctive.

Colonization encouraged new and wider intercourse between peoples who had previously had little in common, often not even enmity, and also facilitated the emergence of entirely new tribal communities. The most effective common political denominator was the subjection of the various tribes within a colony to a single, alien administration. In Africa these political circumstances underlie the rise of the utopian doctrine of Pan-African solidarity and its associated francophone creed *négritude*. Both asserted the rights of the colonized to freedom and self-determination on the basis of a nationalism which was general rather than specific to any particular colony, and which sought to transcend and subsume petty tribal divisions. If this assumed the form of an inverted racialism (the precursor of the more directly aggressive Black Power) that is scarcely surprising. Nor is it difficult to appreciate how the same circumstances naturally cast 'tribalism' in the dark role of a negative, destructive divisiveness to be extirpated. The ideal of an independent nationhood inevitably relegated tribalism to the status of a dangerous subversive factionalism, and a convenient stick to beat one's political opponents.

But old ghosts are not so easily laid. As a basis for sentiments of identity, common economic interests, and political commitments, tribalism has become perhaps the most pervasive single force in the modern urban politics of new states, most of whose governments acknowledge tacitly if not explicitly that balanced tribal representation is a pre-requisite for stable government. There are other important bases of association and loyalties connected with occupation, schooling, class, and religious adherence which infiltrate behind and across tribal lines, yet modernization everywhere has paradoxically been accompanied by an immense politicization and expansion of traditional tribal loyalties. New groups like the Nubis come into being; people who in their daily rural lives hardly gave a thought to the fact that ultimately they were Bemba rather than Ngoni, or Ibo rather than Hausa or Yoruba, have, through the pressure of urban interaction, become much more aware of their political identities. Hume's view that nations are groups of individuals who, by constant intercourse, acquire common characteristics, must be set in a wider context of social interaction.

There is in fact a two-fold process in play. Traditional particularistic loyalties are revived or extended and invested with new and sometimes entirely novel political force, especially by the intelligentsia and politicians on the make. When they are needed, new tribal identities may be conjured up out of thin air. Ultimately, in the competitive conditions of modern urban life one's identity is defined in terms of the existing big tribal blocs. Thus, in Nigeria, people who are not Ibo by birth but belong to neighbouring tribes pass themselves off as Ibo vis-à-vis Hausa and Yoruba, just as associates of the Bemba do vis-à-vis Ngoni or Lozi in Zambia. This extension of tribal loyalties is sometimes called 'super-tribalism'.

This intense, politicized tribalism brings the wheel full circle, whether we describe them in terms of 'ethnicity' (a popular bland catch-all), or more laboriously and misleadingly as 'primordial loyalties.' They all thrive in modern urban conditions that are the precise opposite of the rustic world which the word 'tribe' was first invoked to describe. The modern situation and the contemporary rhetoric of Third World politicians (and that of those who study their affairs) returns 'tribe' once more to something much closer to the original Latin usage, but the stigma lingers on.

So today Asia and Africa suffer not from a deficiency but from a surfeit of nations. Not only have those communities traditionally designated tribes all the characteristics by which political scientists and philosophers habitually define 'nations', but their modern political activities are in all essential respects identical to those generally attributed to nationalism elsewhere. In perhaps the most trenchant and certainly the wittiest brief survey of the subject, John Argyle [27] shows how modern African tribal associations engage in all the activities of their nineteenth-century European counterparts. In addition to obvious economic and political services, they foster the study of folklore, history and philology, the establishment of an authentic vernacular literature, the foundation of schools and other educational facilities – in short they promote all those cultural activities which have such tremendous symbolic significance in the rise of nations. If, as Elie Kedourie eloquently asserts,[28] nationalism is not a universal phenomenon, it is certainly not (as he suggests it is) peculiarly European : since, even if it goes by the alias tribalism, it flourishes so profusely in Africa and Asia. Ken Minogue,[29] who appears to take a broader view, finds the elusive essence of nationalism in those 'who speak the same language'. This definition, which is reminiscent of Samuel Johnson's famous remark that 'languages are the pedigree of nations', certainly raises no problems for our argument. Indeed it happens to be the way in which Somalis (and I suspect many other peoples) define friends as those 'who understand each others' speech' – a definition which is reproduced in a recent primer for adult education written in the new national (and nationalistic) Somali script.

But enough of generalities. Let us take a specific example, and

27., W. J. Argyle, 'European Nationalism and African Tribalism', in P. H. Gulliver (ed.) *Tradition and Transition in East Africa*, Routledge & Kegan Paul, 1969.

28. E. Kedourie, *Nationalism*, Hutchinson, 1966, p. 74.

29. K. Minogue, *Nationalism*, Batsford, 1967, p. 131.

one of which I have practical as well as theoretical knowledge. The campaign for the unification of the Somali territories and the formation of an enlarged Somalia to include the Somali-occupied regions of the French Territory of the Afars and Issas, Ethiopia, and Kenya, is by any definition a nationalist movement. Yet, perfectly understandably, the same struggle for what is in effect Somali-determination appears to the French, Ethiopians, and Kenyans as divisive 'tribalism'. But if unity at the level of a population of several million which has already partial status as a nation-state earns the title 'nationalism', how are we to describe the situation at lower lineage levels *within* this group? Are these smaller segments significantly different? My answer is that they are not: that they are simply smaller units of the same kind which, in the modern world, cannot realistically hope to exist (however much they might like to) as separate, viable, independent political communities.

Some impression of the intense chauvinistic pride of these major segments in the Somali nation, as impressive and compelling as anything called nationalism anywhere else, can be gained from the following personal experience. In 1962 I had the honour to deliver a public lecture at the embryonic national university of the Somali Republic. The cumbersome title 'The Historical and Sociological Background to the Migration of Peoples in the Somali Peninsula' scarcely seemed calculated to inspire nationalistic fervour, or for that matter enthusiasm of any kind. However it drew a capacity audience which became increasingly animated and, eventually, seething with emotion as I laboriously and dryly recounted my reconstruction of the order in which the major Somali lineages had assumed their present geographical positions. Historical precedence raised a whole penumbra of political issues and brought my attentive listeners to a frenzy of excited debate and controversy. In an atmosphere of turmoil familiar to anyone who has participated in large, rancorous political assemblies, the courteous chairman rose to declare, with masterly understatement, that since there were no further questions he would close the meeting, and we both beat a hasty retreat. There was more than a whiff of the authentic smell of nationalism there.

The political divisions which we have referred to before (pp. 325–33) are the very stuff of Somali politics and, indeed, are the price of the Somalis' otherwise enviable possession of a ready-made nationhood. The divisions are unusual in being between segments of a single comprehensive cultural unit, whereas tribalism usually operates in a pluralistic, culturally heterogeneous setting. This segmentary order of divisions which is fundamental to politics and which makes nonsense of the spurious distinction between nations and tribes, can be formulated more generally and more familiarly as follows. A committed internationalist condemns parochial nationalism (little Englanderism) just as unequivocally as a nationalist condemns tribalism, a tribalist clannishness, and a clansman familism. The range of reprobation is as elastic, relative and arbitrary as the terms themselves. None refer to units which differ significantly in kind rather than degree. When all is said and done they are all simply *groups*. It is perhaps as well that we should fully understand this. Whether we disparage them with the label tribalism or dignify them with the title nationalism, local level loyalties of this kind are everywhere rampant today. Amongst the Basques, in Ulster, Wales, the Middle East, and the Black ghettoes of the United States, we confront the same phenomenon – a desperate quest for political autonomy and cultural dignity.

This renaissance of the 'little tradition' reflects many conflicting forces. Paramount seem to be increased interaction and competition between groups fostered by modern communications, and the search for a comfortable and comforting sense of togetherness and identity in a world dominated by bewilderingly massive and impersonal political blocs whose policies the ordinary citizen can do little to influence. These monstrous modern conglomerates, political juggernauts rather than Leviathans, whose formation is both encouraged by and promotes the ever-increasing range and deadliness of modern weapons, stretch the bounds of viable patriotism beyond breaking point. If law and order break down that is scarcely surprising : how could it be otherwise where the sense of community is so atomized and fitful? After all even in the highly 'personalized' (from our modern perspective) parish-pump world of segmentary societies, the most effective and enduring loyalties derive from cross-cutting entanglements. Those who seek relief from the afflictions of the modern world in a romantic return to the tribal womb may perhaps find their best hope here – at the costs we have indicated.

Chapter Eleven

Anthropology and the Contemporary World

The evolutionary paradigm may be out of fashion in social science epistemology, but the growth of knowledge in academic disciplines is still generally considered to follow an evolutionary pattern, in which each successive stage represents a distinct advance on more primitive earlier phases. Such scientific progress is, moreover, increasingly seen nowadays as consisting not so much of regular linear lines of progress, but rather of erratic Kuhnian 'break-throughs', in which new paradigms render obsolete earlier theories. Such an absolutist and discontinuous view of change necessarily emphasises differences and incompatibilities between competing ideas and theories. The charting of such irregular paradigm shifts in the progress of knowledge is one of the main tasks of historiographers and philosophers of science. This is naturally best developed in subjects with a long and closely-studied history.

Social anthropology, as we have seen, only really began to assume its distinctive character following the First World War (1914–18).[1] It is thus not surprising that, although important initiatives are now being made (especially by George Stocking and his collaborators)[2] the history of social anthropology remains largely unwritten and its historiography very underdeveloped.[3] It is thus appropriate to be somewhat more cautious in mapping and assessing new movements and trends, than their partisan protagonists themselves can be expected to be. Such a circumspect approach may also find certain methodological virtues where others see only vices and, in reviewing successive

1. Above, pp. 52–60.

2. G. Stocking (ed.), *Observers Observed, History of Anthropology*, Vol. I, Madison, University of Wisconsin, 1983; *Functionalism Historicized, History of Anthropology*, Vol. II, Madison, University of Wisconsin, 1984.

3. See, however, I. Langham, *The Building of British Social Anthropology*, Dordrecht, Holland, D. Keidel Publishing Company, 1981.

approaches and theories, emphasise compatible positive features rather than antagonistic incompatibilities. In this vein, in earlier chapters we have adopted an eclectic methodology which, loosely grounded in structural functionalism, included insights from Lévi-Straussian structuralism and, in a general sense, classical Marxism and history. Although not everyone will agree, I would argue that cumulatively these and other theoretical developments have contributed to the subtlety and sophistication which social anthropology now deploys in the comparative study of societies and cultures. They have also opened our subject's frontier to other disciplines – provoking recurrent identity crises within the anthropological community itself. The survey of trends and developments with which we conclude this book thus inevitably raises the question of the enduring nature of social anthropology in this wider, contemporary context.

MARXIST CURRENTS

It is convenient to begin this review by considering the impact on Anglo-Saxon anthropology of modern Marxist currents, often linked with Structuralism (and hence sometimes referred to as structural Marxism).[4] Whether through the works of Godelier,[5] Terray[6] or other French anthropologists, what Peter Worsley dubs the 'functionalist Maxism of Althusser' enjoyed considerable vogue in the 1970s. In Britain especially, the importers of this interpretative ideology met, or confronted, an older more empiricist Marxist strain, prominent, as we have seen, in the works of Gluckman and the Manchester School, Goody, and others, which had strong links with the political economy orientation of such prominent British Marxist historians as Hill, Hobsbawm and E. P. Thompson. Specialising in the production of 'abstract theoretical analyses' (a number of which have been quite influential), this French-inspired 'structural Marxism'

4. See e.g., M. Bloch, *Marxism and Anthropology*, Oxford, Clarendon Press, 1983; J. S. Kahn and J. R. Llobera, *The Anthropology of Pre-capitalist Societies*, London, Macmillan, 1981.

5. M. Godelier, *Perspectives in Marxist Anthropology*, Cambridge University Press, 1977.

6. E. Terray, *Marxism and 'Primitive Society'*, London, 1972.

seemed largely to have abandoned Marx's vital sense of history. It is here particularly that it parted company with the work of serious British and American scholars. As Ortner observes;[7] 'structural Marxism was largely non-historical, a factor which, again, tied it to earlier forms of anthropology'. And, she shrewdly suggests, 'that it was in part this comfortable mix of old categories and assumptions wrapped up in a new critical rhetoric that made structural Marxism so appealing in its day'.

It may be remarked, en passant, that few if any of those working in this imported French Marxist tradition seem to have turned their attention to contemporary Marxist societies. It was left to others, outside this genre, to contribute the few social anthropological studies made in this period of power and politics in actual Marxist regimes.[8] Nevertheless, in addition to contributing a number of useful individual studies (according to some opinions, despite rather than because of Marxist inspiration) [9] this renewed interest in Marxist sociological analysis in Anglophone anthropology prompted, or reinforced, the growth of a generally more critically informed and systematic exploration of ideology, power and inequality.

GENDER STUDIES

Marxist anthropology thus claims to share some of the credit for the renewed interest in women and gender roles kindled in anthropology by wider feminist currents in Western society at large. There is, of course, a long, distinguished tradition of research on the domestic role of women by a number of senior generation women social anthropologists (such as Catherine

7. S. Ortner, 'Theory in Anthropology since the Sixties', *Comparative Study of Society and History*, 1984, 26, (1), p. 141.

8. See e.g., I. M. Lewis, 'Kim Il-Sung in Somalia', in P. Cohen and W. Shack (eds.), *The Politics of Office*, Oxford, 1979; C. Humphrey, *Karl Marx Collective*, Cambridge University Press, 1983; T. Dragadze (ed.), *Kinship and Marriage in the Soviet Union*, London, Routledge and Kegan Paul, 1984.

9. For a valuable sceptical critique of Africanist workers in this style, see D. Brown, 'Warfare, oracles and iron: a case study of production among the pre-colonial Klowe, in the light of some recent Marxist analyses', *Africa*, 54, 2, 1984.

Berndt,[10] Elizabeth Colson,[11] Phyllis Kaberry,[12] Hilda Kuper,[13] Audrey Richards,[14] and Monica Wilson [15]) which compliments the immensely influential work of Margaret Mead and other contemporaries [16] in American cultural anthropology. These pioneering women anthropologists did not concentrate exclusively on the role of women, but also sought to produce comprehensive studies of the communities they worked in. To a varying degree, this often led them to be treated by male informants as men or as bisexual, this being the price of access (facilitated in a colonial context) to the men't world.

The corresponding limitations on access to the world of women which male anthropologists encounter is, naturally, a further justification for the more rigorous and systematic focus on women by women anthropologists which gathered momentum in the 1970s.[17] Few social anthropologists today would be likely to dispute Annette Weiner's judgement that 'any study that does not include the role of women – as seen by women – as part of the way the society is structured remains only a partial study of that society'.[18] How, indeed, could it be otherwise when the demographic importance of women is considered? But it is not just that ignoring women excludes the female dimension in a society. As we have seen in a number of contexts in earlier chapters, male roles and male-dominated institutions, practices and beliefs themselves are not fully understandable without reference to women. So, for instance, the varying status

10. 'Women's Changing Ceremonies in Northern Australia', *L'Homme*, 1950, 1, pp. 1–87.

11. *Marriage and the Family among the Plateau Tonga*, Manchester University Press, 1958.

12. *Aboriginal Woman: Sacred and Profane*, Routledge, 1939.

13. *An African Aristocracy*, Oxford University Press, 1947.

14. *Land, Labour and Diet in Northern Rhodesia*, Oxford University Press, 1939.

15. *Reaction to Conquest*, Oxford University Press, 1936.

16. *Sex and Temperament in Three Primitive Societies*, New York, New American Library, 1935.

17. See e.g., R. Reiter (ed.), *Toward an Anthropology of Women*, New York, Monthly Review Press, 1975; S. Ardener (ed.), *Perceiving Women*, New York, Wilely, 1975; M. Z. Rosaldo and L. Lamphere (eds.), *Women, Culture and Society*, Stanford University Press, 1974; C. MacCormack and M. Strathern (eds.), *Nature, Culture and Gender*, Cambridge University Press, 1981.

18. A. Weiner, *Women of Value, Men of Renown*, Austin: University of Texas Press, 196, p. 228.

of women in patrilineal groups affects and reflects the very nature of patriliny,[19] and the prominence of women in spirit-possession cults illuminates the character of male authority.[20]

More radically, feminist anthropologists reasonably ask : to what extent is the male dominance enshrined in the ethnographic record itself a product of male dominance, and corresponding reporting bias, in the anthropological profession itself? Are the cultures anthropologists study really so chauvinistic, or has anthropological male-bias misconstrued gender roles by listening only to official male ideology and discourse? [21] Finally, in this context, what biological factors underlie (and constrain) the cultural and social construction of gender?

In such a rapidly expanding field it would be premature to proffer answers to all these questions. What we can perhaps safely say is: in some societies, careful studies by feminist anthropologists have established that male-dominance is not an artefact of male-biased reporting, but an authentic native cultural product; [22] in these and other cases the extent to which a self-conscious parallel women's culture, or counter-culture, exists (as in many, if not all Islamic communities) [23] varies considerably. Equally, granted the unique part played by women in biological reproduction, female gender is not universally construed as necessarily more 'natural' than masculinity. There is a constant danger here of ethnocentrically projecting Western folk assumptions and hence forgetting that 'nature' and 'culture' are themselves cultural artefacts.[24]

CONSTRUING ETHNOGRAPHY

This more explicit focus on gender, coinciding with feminist

19. See above, p. 258.

20. Cf. above, pp. 85–9, and I. M. Lewis, *Ecstatic Religion*, Penguin Books, 1971. It is thus perhaps not inappropriate that this book should have been used in some women's groups in consciousness-raising sessions.

21. Cf. K. Milton, 'Male Bias in Anthropology', *Man* 14, 1, 1979, pp. 40–54.

22. e.g., P. Jefferey, *Frogs in a Well*, London, Zed Press, 1979.

23. See e.g., M. Strobel, *Muslim Women in Mombasa, 1890–1975*, New Haven, Yale University Press, 1979; P. Holden (ed.), *Women's Religious Experience*, London, 1983.

24. See e.g., M. Strathern, 'No Nature, No Culture: the Hagen Case', in C. MacCormack and M. Strathern (eds.), *Nature, Culture and Gender*, 1980, pp. 174–222.

currents in their own societies as well as in those they study, is one of the many elements contributing towards the formation of a more self-conscious, reflective, and reflexive anthropology, in which the descriptive writing of ethnography itself comes under increasingly sharp scrutiny. Attention here concentrates on the paradoxical contrast between the deeply subjective character of the fieldwork experience and the uniquely privileged status accorded to the resulting ethnographic text. Unlike theory which is by nature ephemeral, ethnographic texts possess enduring value and authenticity. Yet as James Clifford [25] reminds us, ethnographic data are not 'discovered like a note in a bottle'. Malinowski, the founder of the genre of 'ethnographic realism', was himself well aware of the anthropologically constructed character of ethnography. 'In Ethnography', he wrote [26] perceptively, 'the writer is his own chronicler and the historian at the same time, while his sources are no doubt easily accessible but also supremely elusive and complex; they are not embodied in fixed material documents, but in the behaviour and in the memory of living men. In Ethnography, the distance is often enormous between the brute material of information – as it is presented to the student in his own observations, in native statement, in the kaleidoscope of tribal life – and the final authoritative presentation of the results.'

Ethnography, thus, is inevitably selective and heavily edited, reflecting the anthropologist's own pre-occupations and, according to influential professional opinion, his own personality. 'The social anthropologist', Evans-Pritchard wrote,[27] 'discovers in a native society what no native can explain to him and what no layman, however conversant with the culture, can perceive – its basic structure ... a set of abstractions ... fundamentally an imaginative construct of the anthropologist himself'. Similarly, while celebrating the ethnographer's art of 'thick description', Clifford Geertz also advised that once you know what view an

25. Fieldwork, Reciprocity, and the Making of Ethnographic Texts: the Example of Maurice Leenhardt', *Man*, 1980, 15, 3.

26. *Argonauts of the Western Pacific*, London: Routledge & Kegan Paul, 1922, pp. 3–4.

27. 'Social Anthropology: Past and Present', the Marett Lecture 1950, reprinted in *Essays in Social Anthropology*, London, Faber, 1962.

anthropologist holds of himself, you can predict what he will say about the people he studies, all ethnography being 'part philosophy and a good deal of the rest confession'.[28] Edmund Leach is more forthright 'every anthropological observer ... will see something that no other such observer can recognise, namely a kind of harmonic projection of the observer's own personality'.[29] Here Margaret Mead's [30] and Derek Freeman's [31] diametrically opposed accounts of Samoa might be cited as illustrations: Mead's carefree, sexually permissive Samoan adoleccents were, according to Freeman, on the contrary just as strait-laced and guilt-ridden as their American contemporaries of the 1920s.

In this line of reflective commentary, what began as the biography of culture is reconstrued as anthropological autobiography. If biography is always, inevitably, tinged with autobiography, there is a danger here that, taken to extremes, this view of ethnography might help to license a perennially popular style of analysis which, under a vague, general epistemological canopy, and ignoring relevant comparative ethnography, reinvents anthropology in the same of each culture the anthropologist studies. Here, totalising general theory is liable to become part of the anthropological persona and specific cultural and social phenomena may be interpreted particularistically without reference to significant ethnographic parallels. The door is then effectively closed to any systematic empirically grounded comparative sociology of culture.

An excessive preoccupation with the observer's subjectivity is apt also to ignore the extent to which anthropologists become 'impressarios' (Malinowski's term) for the peoples they study and, frequently, unconscious promoters of the ideas and concepts they have absorbed in the course of fieldwork. Such 'secondary

28. C. Geertz, 'The Cerebral Savage', *Encounter*, 28, 1967, pp. 25–32.

29. 'Glimpses of the Unmentionable in the History of British Social Anthropology', 13, 1984, p. 22.

30. *Coming of Age in Samoa*, New York, 1928.

31. *Margaret Mead and Samoa: the Making and Unmaking of an Anthropological Myth*, Cambridge, Harvard University Press, 1983; see also A. B. Weiner, 'Ethnographic Determinism: Samoa and the Margaret Mead controversy', *American Anthropologist*, 85(4), 1983, pp. 909–19.

ethnocentricity' (as Herskovits called it) is undoubtedly a marked feature of many theoretical debates where cultures, as it were, argue through their unwitting anthropological protagonists.[32] The tension between biography and autobiography in ethnographic accounts assumes a further twist when, as increasingly today in Europe,[33] Japan [34] and India [35] (as well as elsewhere in the Third World), native social anthropologists study their own (or closely related) cultures. Such auto-anthropology (of which Jomo Kenyatta was an illustrious African pioneer) [36] reverses the traditional inter-cultural distancing between observer and observed, as the native anthropologist moves from his own particular culture to the cosmopolitan cultural pluralism of anthropological theory. Subjectivity may be most obvious here but for many, as in Black Studies, this becomes a virtue since it is held to permit unique cultural insights inaccessible to the alien anthropologist with an inevitably much poorer command of the local language. There are thus many possible permutations in the complex dialogue between anthropological observer and observed which, despite these variably compounded subjective factors, aspires to achieve ethnographic reporting with an accuracy and authenticity transcending the idiosyncratic personality of the chronicler. This is not, I think, an entirely illusory aspiration as indeed can

32. Cf. I. M. Lewis, *Religion in Context*, Cambridge University Press, 1986, Chapter 1.

33. For an interesting account of the Italian situation, see G. R. Saunders, 'Contemporary Italian Cultural Anthropology', *Annual Review of Anthropology* 13, 1984, pp. 44–66; and on the Mediterranean, D. G. Gilmore, 'Anthropology of the Mediterranean Area', *Annual Review of Anthropology*, 11, 1982, pp. 175–205. For an excellent Portuguese example of this genre, see J. Cutileiro, *A Portuguese Rural Society*, Oxford, Clarendon Press, 1971.

34. See C. Nakane, *Japanese Society*, Berkeley, University of California Press, 1970; E. Ohnuki-Tierney, *Illness and Culture in Contemporary Japan: an Anthropological View*, Cambridge University Press, 1984.

35. See L. P. Vidyarthi, 'The rise of social anthropology in India (1774–1972)', in *The New Wind: Changing Identities in South Asia*, ed. Kenneth David, Mouton, The Hague and Paris, pp. 61–83; A. Beteille and J. N. Madon (eds.), *Encounter and Experience: Personal Accounts of Fieldwork*, Delhi, 1975; M. N. Srinivas, A. M. Shah, E. A. Ramaswamy (eds.), *The Fieldworker and the Field*, Delhi, Oxford University Press, 1979.

36. J. Kenyatta, *Facing Mount Kenya*, London, Secker and Warburg, 1938. For a vigorous West African view of modern social anthropology in general, see M. A. Onwuejeogwu, *The Social Anthropology of Africa*, London, Heinemann, 1975. More generally on Third World auto-anthropology, see H. Fahim (ed.), *Indigenous Anthropology in Non-Western Countries*, Durham, North Carolina Academic Press, 1982.

be illustrated by reference to the Trobriand Islanders themselves, where successive ethnographic studies, exploring aspects of Trobriand society neglected or under-reported by Malinowski confirm the general accuracy of his pioneering accounts. [37] Without wishing to discount the subjective factor, perhaps the most impressive endorsement of the fidelity of the foreign fieldworker's reportage is that provided (if it is) by native, 'auto-anthropologists' whose negative assessments, likewise, must surely be especially devastating. If I may strike a personal note here, I am certainly particularly sensitive to criticism from professional Somali historians and anthropologists and am gratified when their work confirms my own studies of their culture and society. [38]

A new genre of 'experimental ethnographies' seeks to confront these problems directly. These works 'integrate within their interpretations, an explicit epistemological concern for how they have constructed such interpretations and how they are representing them textually as objective discourse about subjects among whom research was conducted.' [39] Surely this is a welcome development. However, even here there are catches. There is a danger that the writer of the ethnographic text may become so self-indulgently intrusive that the culture, which he seeks to depict in all its rich authenticity, recedes into the background and becomes merely a pale outline or setting for the anthropologist's exercises in introspection. [40] Ethnography then becomes anthropological travellers' tales. Then not only women

37. See e.g., H. A. Powell, 'Competitive Leadership in Trobriand Political Organization', *Journal Royal Anthropological Institute*, vol. 90, 1960; A. Weiner, *Women of Value, Men of Renown: new perspectives in Trobriand exchange*, Austin, Texas University Press, 1976; J. W. Leach and E. Leach (eds.), *The Kula: new perspectives on Massim exchange*, Cambridge, 1983.

38. Cf. I. M. Lewis, *A Pastoral Democracy*, Oxford University Press, 1961 (new edition, Africana, 1982), and S. S. Samatar, *Oral Poetry and Somali Nationalism*, Cambridge, 1982. In this vein most anthropologists, I am sure, must envy the warm memorial tribute paid to the late Meyer Fortes by the Tallensi anthropologist, Dr. Moses Anafu, 'Meyer Fortes: a personal memoir', *Cambridge Anthropology*, special edition, vol. 8, 1983, pp. 9–13.

39. G. E. Marcus and D. Cushman, 'Ethnographies as Texts', *Annual Review of Anthropology*, 11, 1982, p. 25.

40. Unfortunate examples it seems to me are J. Favret-Saada, *Deadly Words: Witchcraft in the Bocage*, Cambridge University Press, 1980; P. Riesman, *Freedom in Fulani Social Life (an introspective ethnography)* Chicago University Press, 1977.

but, in extreme cases, an entire culture is liable to be silenced, the anthropologist (of all people) perpetrating a kind of inadvertent ethnocide. Perhaps with this danger in mind, some of the newer discussions of subjective fieldwork experience are published separately from the corresponding technical ethnographic accounts. [41]

SEMANTIC ANTHROPOLOGY

This more explicit attention to the relationship between presentational style and content in the fieldwork mode of ethnographic production (and reproduction) has, as already implied, strong literary affinities. Evans-Pritchard, while apt to dismiss Malinowski's functionalism as a 'mere literary device', regularly presented social anthropology as the 'translation of culture'. Sharing Malinowski's fascination with literally transcribed native texts (hard data comparable to historical documents) and stressing his discipline's links with literature (as well as with history), when he succeeded Radcliffe-Brown as head of the Institute of Social Anthropology at Oxford in 1946, Evans-Pritchard welcomed research workers trained in English literary criticism by the legendary F. R. Leavis at Cambridge. This modest 'borrowing' from English Literature (reflected in such enterprises as the Oxford Library of African Literature [42]) has since been repaid handsomely, if indirectly, in the massive diffusion from anthropology (and linguistics) to literature of structuralist and poststructuralist (including structural Marxist) ideas and techniques. The flowering of these heady stylistic movements in the con-

41. See e.g., J. Middleton, *The Study of the Lugbara: Expectation and Paradox in Anthropological Research*, New York, Holt, Rinehart and Winston, 1970; P. Rabinow, *Symbolic Dominance: Cultural Form and Historical Change in Morocco*, Chicago University Press, 1975, and the same author's *Reflections on Fieldwork in Morocco*, University of California Press, 1977. Cf. N. Barley, *The Innocent Anthropologist*, London, 1983, and the same author's *Symbolic Structures*; see also, P. Loizos *The Heart Grown Bitter: a chronicle of Cypriot-War Refugees*, Cambridge University Press, 1982; and A. F. Robertson, *Community of Strangers. A Journal of Discovery in Uganda*, London, Scolar Press, 1978.

42. Edited by Evans-Pritchard, Godfrey Lienhardt (who had read anthropology and English literature at Cambridge) and the linguist, W. H. Whiteley.

temporary literary world under the general title of semiotics
has in turn reinforced similar, parallel currents in anthropology
itself. The ensuing semiotic writing is not always best known
for its clarity of expression. Nevertheless, the general aim of the
semiotic literary project, as such contemporary critics as Terry
Eagleton see it, [43] is through 'discourse theory' to arrive at a
more 'complete and satisfactory understanding' of the text.

It is thus not surprising that today there should be a much
stronger concurrence between social (and cultural) anthropology
and literary studies, than at the time of Evans-Pritchard's
tentative overtures in the early 1950s. Even for those whose
enthusiasm for the more abstruse aspects of semiology is limited,
it is salutary to be reminded periodically that 'Semantic Anthropology is not a subfield but merely . . . what anthropology is
centrally concerned with'. [44] So the popularity in recent years
of the term 'meaning' in the title of publications signals less a
new direction than a renewed (or re-invigorated) commitment to
the abiding core preoccupation of social (and, as I see it, cultural)
anthropology. After all, as with Malinowski's treatment of the
Kula, or Radcliffe-Brown's of Andaman myths, even classical
functionalist accounts sought in one way or another to elucidate
meaning.

MEDICAL ANTHROPOLOGY

The pervasive search for meaning in cultural symbols brings us
naturally, in one of its most concrete contexts, to the important
contemporary growth area of medical anthropology. Within the
wider framework of cosmology and symbolism, medical anthropology examines the culturally specific elements in the perception, diagnosis and treatment of sickness. It thus includes ethno-

---

43. *Literary Theory*, Oxford, Blackwell, 1983.
44. See M. R. Crick, 'Anthropology of Knowledge', *Annual Review of Anthropology*,
1982, 11, pp. 287–313 and *Explorations in Language and Meaning: Towards a Semantic
Anthropology*, London, 1976, Malaby. Cf. Also D. Parkin (ed.), *Semantic Anthropology*,
London, Academic Press, 1983.

biology (or ethno-physiology and ethno-anatomy) as well as ethno-medicine (and ethno-psychiatry). [45]

Particularly in the United States, interest in this cross-cultural approach to diagnosing and treating illness is evidently partly a product of the practice of Western, biologically oriented medicine in culturally plural contexts. In the less well-endowed circumstances of Third World countries, where 'cosmopolitan' medical provision reaches only a fraction of the population, the question of how to assess and accommodate traditional therapeutic practices is an issue of immediate practical significance. [46] At the same time, in Western industrial countries, increasing public interest in 'alternative medicine' also encourages this developing trend. This trend is at the same time reinforced by growing Western interest in 'alternative medicine'. [47]

One important consequence has been to highlight the cultural status of Western medical assumptions themselves, a point long ago made by the great Russian pioneer of ethno-medicine and specialist on shamanism, S. M. Shirokogoroff. [48] The perception of Western medicine as a cultural artefact has in turn prompted examination of the *practice* of Western doctors, focussing attention on the culture of medical care and on the language of medical discourse. [49] At least in Britain, with the work of J. Loudon, [50] V. Skultans [51] and C. G. Helman, [52] it has become clear that general medical practitioners (physicians) constitute an exotic group, often reinforcing local ethnomedical folk beliefs rather than practising the biomedicine taught in medical school.

45. For a convenient survey see, A. Young, 'The Anthropologies of Illness and Sickness', *Annual Review of Anthropology*, 1982, 11, pp. 257–85. See also J. M. Janzen, *The Quest for Therapy in Lower Zaire*, Berkeley, University of California Press, 1978. For an excellent auto-anthropological monograph, bridging medical and semantic anthropology, see H. Ngubane, *Mind and Body in Zulu Medicine*, London, Academic Press, 1977.

46. For Africa see e.g., M. Last and G. Chavunduka (eds.), *The Professionalisation of African Medicine*, Manchester University Press, 1986.

47. P. Worsley, 'Non-Western Medical Systems', *Annual Survey of Anthropology*, 1982, 11, pp. 315–48.

48. *The Psychomental Complex of the Tungus*, London, 1935.

49. See e.g., L. Romanncci-Ross, D. E. Moerman and L. R Tancredi (eds.), *The Anthropology of Medicine; from Culture to Method*, Massachusetts, 1983.

50. J. Loudon (ed.), *Social Anthropology and Medicine*, London, Academic Press, 1976.

51. V. Skultans, *Ritual and Intimacy*, London, Routledge, 1974.

52. C. G. Helman, *Culture, Health and Illness*, Bristol, J. Wright, 1984.

As might be anticipated, the cultural construction of illness and health seems most marked in mental illness where those who work in the field of 'transcultural psychiatry' have discovered a series of 'culture-bound' (i.e. culture-specific) reactive syndromes.[53] Psychiatric disorders, in fact, raise in an acute form the issues of distinguishing between human universals and cultural specifics in interpreting behaviour and expression. As elsewhere, the symptoms which are often diagnosed as florrid 'schizophrenia' or 'acute psychosis' in immigrant Black patients in the United Kingdom usually prove more amenable to short-term treatment than ostensibly identical symptoms in members of the local native populations.[54]

On the other hand, intriguing parallels sometimes occur in diagnosis and treatment. So, for example, the modern Western psychodynamic ('transactional') understanding of neurosis as a product of interpersonal tensions is closely in line with the Zande theory of witchcraft (discussed above).[55] Indeed, the degree of coincidence is so close here that, apparently without appreciating the irony of the situation, a leading American trans-cultural psychiatrist [56] solemnly warns of the dangers of prematurely introducing this psycho-dynamic approach in cultures where people traditionally believe in witches!

More generally, the interface between social (and cultural) anthropology and psychology, sometimes under the banner 'psychological anthropology' continues to be a focal point in the disentanglement of cross-cultural (biological) universals, and culture specifics involved in cognition and perception,[57] as for example, in the perception and identification of colour. Here the decisive anthropological studies of Berlin and Kay, demonstrating the existence of a cross-cultural stock of basic colour

53. P. M. Yap, 'The Culture-Bound Reactive Syndromes', in W. Caudill and T. Y. Lin (eds.), Mental Health Research in Asia and the Pacific, Honolulu, East–West Center Press, 1969.
54. R. Littlewood and M. Lipsedge, Aliens and Alienists, Harmondsworth, Penguin, 1982.
55. Above, pp. 69–84.
56. A. Kiev, Transcultural Psychiatry, New York, Free Press, 1972, pp. 171–2.
57. See B. Lloyd and J. Gay (eds.), Universals of Human Thought. Some African Evidence, Cambridge University Press, 1981; M. Cole, J. Gay, J. A. Glick and D. Sharp, The Cultural Context of Learning and Thinking, New York, Basic Books, 1971.

terms (white, black, red, green, blue, yellow, brown, pink, orange and grey) utilised, partially or fully, in a predictable order in different languages is confirmed by physiological research demonstrating that the same colour distinctions are made by pre-verbal infants and by macaque monkeys.[58] More generally, further interdisciplinary progress is apt to be hampered by the very different ways in which psychologists and anthropologists are prone to use the term 'cognition'. Psychologists normally restrict this term to refer to the actual (ultimately physiological or biochemical) processes of thinking (as in Piaget's evolutionary model of the cognitive development of children from 'preoperational', to 'concrete operational', to 'formal operational') at the *individual* level. Anthropologists, on the other hand, employ 'cognition' to refer essentially to *what* people think – their collective cultural representations – rather than to *how* they think. But our anthropological appropriation of the term 'cognition' (and glib references to getting inside people's heads) implies – which is by no means established [59] – that *what* people (collectively think, and *how* individuals think, is one and the same thing! [60] As earlier chapters have shown, people in different cultures seem to think similarly (if not identically) with *different* cultural constructs and cosmologies.

On a wider canvas, wider than we can possibly explore here, biologically based trans-cultural psychological phenomena lead us towards the broader inter-disciplinary subject frame of socio-biology [61] (or biosocial anthropology),[62] whose existence as an

58. See B. Berlin and P. Kay, *Basic Color Terms, their Universality and Evolution*, Berkeley, University of California Press, 1969; for an eloquent attempt to reassert the primacy of culture in colour discrimination see M. Sahlins, 'Colours and Cultures', *Semiotica*, 16, 1976, pp. 1–22.

59. G. Jahoda, *Psychology and Anthropology*, New York Academic Press, 1982; R. M. Farr and S. Moscovici, *Social Representations*, Cambridge University Press, 1984.

60. These issues are, unfortunately, confused in C. R. Hallpike's otherwise notable effort to apply Piagetian concepts in anthropology, *The Foundations of Primitive Thought*, Oxford, Clarendon Press, 1979.

61. See e.g., E. O. Wilson, *Sociobiology*, Cambridge (Mass.), Belknap, 1975; and *On Human Nature*, London, Harvard University Press, 1978; and R. Dawkins, *The Selfish Gene*, London, Oxford University Press, 1976.

62. R. Fox (ed.), *Biosocial Anthropology*, London, Malaby Press, 1975. For powerful critiques of these revivals of projective, sociocentric biology ('born-again Darwinism'), see M. Sahlins, *The Use and Abuse of Biology: an Anthropological Critique of Sociobiology*, Ann Arbor, University of Michigan Press, 1976, and H. Callan, 'The Imagery of Choice in Sociobiology', *Man*, 19, 3, 1984, pp. 404–20.

exciting, if highly controversial area within (sometimes co-terminous with) ethology we can do no more than register here. Without presuming to suggest that this applies to the whole subject area, it seems to me that attempts to extend sociobiology to religion [63] are of less interest to social anthropologists, than recent neuro-chemical discoveries on the endogenous endorphin (and possibly other parallel) systems, associated with euphoria and absence of pain, since these indicate a natural, universal base, much more material than Marx can ever have imagined, for religious experience as, literally, the 'opium of the people'.[64]

URBANISM AND ETHNICITY

If ethnic demography has played a not insignificant role in the emergence of medical anthropology, urban anthropology (and the study of urban ethnicity) follows in the wake of the mushrooming cosmopolitan cities in and outside the Third World [65] whose growth is so closely linked with ethnic migration, particularly from rural origins. In Europe the American pattern of devolopment here tends to be repeated. In Britain, after the first flutter of interest in 'Race Relations' aroused by the early wave of West Indian immigration in the 1950s, the expansion of research on ethnic relations in the 1960s and 1970s reflected increased public consciousness of cultural pluralism 'at home' in the metropolis.[66] This encouraged a growing focus on ethnicity as a theoretical issue, both in European urban contexts and in the Third World,[67] necessitating (somewhat belatedly) comparisons with the urban situation in the United States which, historically, had been mainly analysed by ethnographically oriented sociologists and ecologists under the intel-

63. e.g., V. Reynolds and R. Tanner, *The Biology of Religion*, London, Longman, 1983.

64. R. Prince (ed.), *Shamans and Endorphins*, Ethos, 1982, 10, 4.

65. See e.g., J. Abu-Lughod and R. Hay (eds.), *Third World Urbanization*, London, Methuen, 1979; P. Lloyd, *Slums of Hope?*, Manchester University Press, 1979; M. Kenny and D. E. Kertzer (eds.), *Urban Life in Mediterranean Europe: anthropological perspectives*, Urbana, University of Illinois Press, 1983.

66. See M. Banton, *Race Relations*, London, Tavistock, 1967; J. L. Watson (ed.), *Between Two Cultures*, Oxford, Blackwell, 1977.

67. A. Cohen (ed.), *Urban Ethnicity*, London, Tavistock, 1974.

lectual leadership of the famous 'Chicago Empirical School' associated with such illustrious names as Robert E. Park,[68] Louis Wirth,[69] Cayton and St Clair Drake.[70] The 'melting-pot' ideology naturally emphasised acculturation, treating 'minority' cultures in urban contexts as conservative, maladaptive residues, 'survivals' resisting cultural change to the dominant white mode.

Within this tradition, Oscar Lewis[71] developed his controversial concept the 'culture of poverty', a distinctive self-perpetuating sub-culture of deprivation, rather than a product of exploitation and oppression – which is how more recent urban anthropologists in America tend to see urban ghetto behaviour. This latter perspective which emphasises the influence of external forces, treats urban ethnicity as a reactive construct, viewing culture more generally as a political phenomenon or even, as with the transactionalists, as a survival 'strategy' for an interest-group.[72] While this approach has helped to elucidate the behaviour and ideology of a wide range of occupational[73] and other groups in industrial towns, it risks underestimating the subjective aspect of ethnicity – the compelling psychological 'roots' element which underlies cultural identity.[74] Also, although notable efforts have been made (as for instance by the Swedish anthropologist, Ulf Hannerz, working in an American black ghetto) to delineate a theoretically distinctive urban anthropology,[75] apart from its obvious practical significance, most of the results so far obtained seem to fit into the general framework of comparative social (and cultural) anthropology. The most pervasive connecting thread here is, perhaps, the (self-) definition of

68. See R. Turner (ed.), *On Social Control and Collective Behaviour*, Chicago, Chicago University Press, 1967.

69. *The Ghetto*, Chicago, Chicago University Press, 1928.

70. *The Black Metropolis*, London, Jonathan Cape, 1945.

71. O. Lewis, *La Vida: A Puerto Rican Family in the Culture of Poverty*, New York, Random House, 1966.

72. N. Glazer and D. P. Moynihan (eds.), *Ethnicity, Theory and Experience*, Cambridge, Harvard University Press, 1975; A. Cohen (ed.), *Urban Ethnicity*, London, Tavistock, 1974 and, for the most abstract expression of the 'transactionalist approach', F. Barth (ed.), *Ethnic Groups and Boundaries*, London, Allen and Unwin, 1969.

73. See e.g., S. Wallman (ed.), *The Social Anthropology of Work*, London, Academic Press, 1979.

74. Cf. A. L. Epstein, *Ethos and Identity*, London, Tavistock, 1978.

75. U. Hannerz, *Exploring the City*, New York, Columbia University Press, 1980.

network and group boundaries, and the contextual mobilisation
and expression of identity – surely the most abiding and fundamental theoretical concern in anthropology.[76] Certainly this is a
prominent theme in recent work on Latin American cities, which
are now a major focus of attention in urban anthropology.[77]

APPLIED ANTHROPOLOGY

Unemployment and poverty in ethnic urban ghettoes have
brought the Third World and its problems home to the indus-
trialised West just as the latter has exported underdevelopment
in its exploitation of Third World labour and markets.[78] To the
extent that our subject seeks to understand this complex world,
it must constantly adjust its focus and thrust as the world
changes. Medical anthropology, as we have seen, is both a natural
outgrowth of 'semantic anthropology' (or 'symbolic anthropology') and, like urban anthropology, directly related to world
demographic trends and on-going historical change in the industrial and post-industrial era.

If these developments seem almost inevitable enlargements of
the scope of academic social anthropology, the use of anthropology in development has a more practical, a-theoretical ring,
disturbing to professional purists. The latter tend to regard
'applied anthropology' with suspicion and embarrassment, the
sort of activity likely to appeal to the least academically able. In
fact, however, those who are attracted to applied work are often
academically highly qualified, radical activists who are not prepared to sit tight and ignore pressing social and political problems in their own and other countries and who find the aims of
anthropological advocacy and 'action anthropology' inspiring. In
any event, the fact of the matter is that the majority of profes-
sionally qualified social anhropologists who seek to practise their

76. Cf. A. Cohen, *Two-dimensional Man*, London, Routledge, 1974.

77. See e.g., L. A. Lommitz, *Networks and marginality: Life in a Mexican Shanty Town*, New York, Academic Press, 1977.

78. For West Africa see, K. Hart, *The Political Economy of West African Agriculture*, Cambridge University Press, 1983; and more generally P. Worsley, *The Three Worlds: Culture and World Development*, London, Wiedenfeld, 1984.

discipline are nowadays likely to do so in some applied field at home or overseas. Those who enjoy the privilege of teaching and research in academic institutions should, I believe, recognise this and view applied anthropology as a challenge, offering the opportunity, complex though it is, of using anthropological skills positively. This may often involve counselling against a particular development project whose effects appear, in the light of anthropological insights, likely to prove inequitable or generally harmful. As Raymond Firth observes,[79] 'an important part of the anthropologist's job', here, 'is to expose the difficulties, the contradictions, the conflicts of interest in a situation in order that false hopes of easy solutions should not mislead'. In similar vein, Allan Hoben, an academic anthropologist with a considerable experience of development work, sees our most general contribution as being 'to challenge and clarify, and hence to help revise, explicit and implicit assumptions made by those responsible for planning and implementing development policies about problems to be solved and about the institutional linkages between proposed policy interventions and their impact on income, asset distribution, employment, health, and nutrition'.[80] This is quite a wide field and it needs to be stressed again here that the anthropologist's expertise is based on his existing ethnographic experience of particular forms of social and cultural organisations and, more widely, on the application of his sensitive qualitative techniques of data collection to other appropriate cultural contexts.[81]

There are limits to the range of feasible anthropological technology-transfer, and nothing is gained by making exaggerated claims in the name of professional competence. Above

79. R. Firth, 'Engagement and Detachment: Reflections on Applying Social Anthropology to Social Affairs', *Human Organization*, Vol. 40,m No. 3, 1981, pp. 193–201.

80. A. Hoben, 'Anthropologists and Development', *Annual Review of Anthropology*, Vol. 11, 1982, p. 370.

81. As well as material in such specialized journals as *Human Organization*, and *Practical Anthropology*, for recent discussions see, N. Long, *An Introduction to the Sociology of Rural Development*, London, Tavistock, 1977; G. Cochrane, *The Cultural Appraisal of development Projects*, New York, Praeger, 1979; A. F. Robertson, *People and the State: an Anthropology of Planned Development*, Cambridge University Press, 1984. W. L. Partridge (ed.), *Training Manual in Development Anthropology*, Washington, American Anthropological Association No. 17, 1984.

all, we should guard against becoming involved in the professional legitimation of projects (with or without 'hidden agendas') which seem more for the benefit of the developers than for the 'underdeveloped' clients. Here there are indeed serious and complicated ethical issues of which we need to be constantly reminded. There is a real danger that 'Social Soundness Analyses' for USAID or other development agencies, governmental or voluntary, may become routine certificates of fitness,[82] issued perfunctorily by anthropologists who are more concerned about their consultancy fees, *per diems* and future contracts than about their own professional standards. When this happens anthropologists will have indeed joined the ranks of the 'Development Set' delineated by Ross Coggins : [83]

> The Development Set is bright and noble,
> Our thought are deep and our vision global;
> Although we move with the better classes,
> Our thoughts are always with the masses.
>
> Development Set houses are extremely chic,
> Full of carvings, curios, and draped with batik.
> Eye-level photographs subtly assure
> That your host is at home with the great and the poor.

This uncomfortably accurate portrait of 'jet-setting international 'experts' is a terrible warning to those anthropologists who in good faith venture into this ethical minefield. On the other hand, those academic anthropologists who understandably feel that their worst forbodings have been appallingly realised by such prostitution of their subject, risk further compounding professional odium by giving a dog a bad name, and may, ultimately, be accused of neglecting their professional responsibilities. For, like it or not, social anthropology is being applied in the name of development and this field must be expected to

---

82. Cf. P. Benedict, 'The Bureacratization of Anthropology in AID', *Practical Anthropology*, 3(2), 1981; D. W. Brokensha, 'The Anthropologist and Project Consultancies', *Practical Anthropology*, 3(2), 1981.

83. R. Coggins, 'The Development Set', *Adult Education and Development*, September, 1976; see also E. C. Green, 'Have Degree will Travel: a consulting job for AID in Africa', *Human Organization*, Vol. 40, no. 1, 1981; and, for a powerful analysis of all these issues, R. Chambers, *Rural Development: Putting the Last First*, London, Longman, 1983.

expand as more and more development agencies (non-govern-mental as well as governmental) seek the advice of anthropolo-gists as, in effect, 'human factor' experts. This, ironically, far outstrips anything that ever happened during the colonial period in which anthropology allegedly existed to serve the exploitative interests of colonial regimes! In fairness, it also has to be said that in many colonial territories expatriate officials, involved in development, were better informed in their knowledge of local languages and customs, and morally more committed to the well-being of those they administered, than their contemporary development agency counterparts. It is partly an implicit recog-nition of this disparity in knowledge which informs the growing demand for the recruitment of anthropological development experts.

This market will attract (and already is attracting) an increas-ing number of 'social soundness' arbitrators. In America, academic anthropologists have realised that if they are not prepared to help to ensure, through their professional and other organisations, that properly qualified people are employed for appropriate applied tasks, they risk endangering the credibility of their discipline.[84] On more theoretical if less humanistic or ethical grounds, it can also be argued that the development context often provides a unique opportunity for testing anthro-pological analyses which, if they are accurate, must have some bearing on how social change occurs. Purist theorists who ignore development anthropology may have fewer ethical problems (though some are intrinsic to the discipline), but they thus miss the special insights into the nature of social and cultural processes (including those of development agencies) which such quasi-experimental situations permit.

WHERE THE ACTION IS

Evidently as social anthropologists (of whatever nationality)

84. Similar professional concerns are increasingly evident in the affairs of the British Association of Social Anthropologists and of its derivative Group for Anthropology in Policy and Practice (formed in 1981).

become increasingly engaged today in research (pure and applied) in and outside urban centres in the West, as well as in the Third World, they rub shoulders with an ever-widening circle of colleagues from other social science disciplines, ranging from economics, through social history to psychology. The issue of academic subject boundaries is thus apt to arise frequently and sometimes acutely. Social anthropology, according to one witty (functionalist) definition, is what social anthropologists do. So if they do everything, everything is social anthropology. This risks stretching holism and tautology too far. We need at least to recall and restate our characteristic research technique. This is ethnography, a sensitive qualitative approach in which the anthropological observer's questions are posed for him as he immerses himself in the life of the people he studies and which he thus experiences and registers subjectively as well as objectively. The 'field' may now be such familiar home ground as a street corner, a neighbourhood, a factory or other workplace, a voluntary fire service, a phychiatric centre, a charismatic church or any other area of contemporary urban (as well as rural) activity where people interact intensively in a particular cultural style characterised by shared values and understandings.

This biographic approach to the interactions binding people together, treats their shared frame of reference and activity as in some sense culturally specific; a generative product – but also a symbolic property. Here as A. L. Kroeber [85] foresaw over a quarter of a century ago, anthropology is no longer 'concerned above all else with primitives, nor [does] it see in them the primary claim to its own intellectual autonomy'. At the same time, the rigid boundaries drawn by their rival proponents between 'social anthropology' which privileges reified 'society' and 'cultural anthropology' which privileges reified 'culture' appear increasingly arbitrary and mutually permeable or, perhaps more accurately, alternative sides of the same coin. This is why I have deliberately tended to juxtapose these terms in this final chapter, since one treats culture as a medium for social relations (or, sometimes, as their content) while the other treats

85. A. L. Kroeber, *Anthropology*, New York, Harcourt, Brace & Co., 1948, p. 847.

society as a display of culture.[86] I, at any rate, see a significant convergence here.

More generally, if geographers or psychologists (and, indeed, sociologists) should come to appreciate the special virtues of this style of ethnographic 'thick description' and even seek to adopt our research methodology that, of course, is flattering.[87] Beyond this methodology, we retain our cross-cultural comparative perspective which acts as a constant, in-built corrective to the ethnocentric proclivities of other disciplines to which we are nevertheless drawn by converging subject matter and aims. Here, the current emphasis in social anthropology on spatial dynamics (regional analysis, rural–urban relationships, the role of the state) and on temporal co-ordinates gives new substance to our traditional links with both geography and history.

History has long been an obvious neighbour and sparring-partner here under the recurrent rubrics of social change, process, or 'practice'.[88] And as soon as we thus focus on how people act over time (and their presumed motivations) we inevitably reach also the straddling common interests of psychology (and even of psychoanalysis). This is not, I think, accidental. We have many common aspirations as well as deficiencies. Anthropologists and historians can provide convincing accounts of the cultural context of ideology and behaviour. What they do not succeed in doing completely is in predicting how individuals will act and think (or think and act) in a given situation. Real people are not enculturated robots. Except when the stress (in history or psychology) is on the *individual* role-player, culture-bearer and culture-representative, the idiosyncratic actor is missing from the picture. From commonsense, everyday experience, we all know that individual personalities matter and that, in the final analysis, our lives depend on how they manipulate sacrosanct structures. With the aid of collateral disciplines, the ultimate challenge for social and cultural anthropology is somehow to achieve this understanding of individual idiosyncrasy and in-determinacy within the socio-cultural contexts we translate.

86. Cf. G. Watson, 'The Social Construction of Boundaries between Social and Cultural Anthropology in Britain and North America', *Journal of Anthropological Research*, Vol. 40, no. 3, 1984, pp. 351–66.

87. See M. Hammersley and P. Atkinson, *Ethnography: Principles in Practice*, London, Tavistock, 1983.

88. Cf. P. Bourdieu, *Outline of a theory of Practice*, Cambridge University Press, 1978.

Bibliography

Agitator, London, 1971.

W. ALLAN: *The African Husbandman*, Oliver & Boyd, 1965.

S. ANDRESKI: *Social Science as Sorcery*, Penguin, 1974.

B. W. ANDRZEJEWSKI and I. M. LEWIS (eds). *Somali Poetry*, Oxford University Press, 1964.

E. ARDENER: 'The New Anthropology and its Critics', *Man* (N. S.), vol. 6, 1971, pp. 449–67.

W. J. ARGYLE: *Oedipus in Central Africa*, University of Natal, 1971. 'European Nationalism and African Tribalism', in P. H. Gulliver (ed.), *Tradition and Transition in East Africa*, Routledge & Kegan Paul, 1969.

T. ASAD (ed.): *Anthropology and the Colonial Encounter*, Ithaca Press, 1973.

C. R. BADCOCK: *Lévi-Strauss: Structuralism and Sociological Theory*, Hutchinson, 1975.

G. BALANDIER: *Political Anthropology*, Allen Lane, 1970.

J. A. BARNES: 'Durkheim's Division of Labour in Society', *Man* (N. S.), vol. 1, 1966, pp. 158–75.

F. BARTH: 'Economic Spheres in Darfur', in R. Firth (ed.), *Themes in Economic Anthropology*, Tavistock, 1967.

P. T. W. BAXTER: 'Distance makes the heart grow fonder', in M. Gluckman (ed.), *The Allocation of Responsibility*, Manchester University Press, 1972.

J. BEATTIE: *The Banyoro State*, Oxford University Press, 1973.

S. BELLOW: *The Victim*, Penguin, 1966.

P. BERGER: *Invitation to Sociology*, Penguin, 1970.

P. L. VAN DEN BERGHE: *Caneville*, Wesleyan University Press, Middletown, Connecticut, 1964.

G. BERREMAN: *Hindus of the Himalayas: Ethnography and Change*, University of California Press, 1972.

K. BIRKET-SMITH: *The Eskimos*, Methuen, 1959.

M. BLOCH: *Placing the Dead*, Academic Press, 1971.

P. BOHANNAN: *Tiv Farm and Settlement*, H.M.S.O., 1954.

P. BOHANNAN and L. BOHANNAN, *Tiv Economy*, Longman, 1969.

T. B. BOTTOMORE and M. RUBEL (eds): *Karl Marx: Selected Writings in Sociology and Social Philosophy*, Penguin, 1970.

E. S. BOWEN (Laura Bohannan): *Return to Laughter*, Gollancz, 1954.

P. BROWN: 'Sorcery, Demons, and the Rise of Christianity from late Antiquity into the Middle Ages', in Mary Douglas (ed.), *Witchcraft Confessions and Accusations*, Tavistock, 1970.

J. W. BURROW: *Evolution and Society*, Cambridge University Press, 1966.

A. BUTT: 'Training to be a Shaman', in S. Wavell, A. Butt and N. Epton, *Trances*, Allen & Unwin, 1966.

J. CAMPBELL: *Honour, Family and Patronage*, Oxford University Press, 1964.

C. CASTANEDA: *The Teachings of Don Juan: A Yaqui Way of Knowledge*, Penguin, 1970.
Journey to Ixtlan, Penguin, 1974.

R. CHALMERS: *A History of Currency in the British Colonies*, London, 1893.

C. CLAPHAM: *Haile-Selassie's Government*, Longman, 1969.

H. CODERE: *Fighting with Property*, Augustine, New York, 1950.

A. COHEN: *Two-Dimensional Man*, Routledge & Kegan Paul, 1974.

E. COLSON: 'Social Control and Vengeance in Plateau Tonga Society', *Africa*, vol. 23, 1953, pp. 199–211.

G. CONDOMINAS: *Nous Avons Mangé La Forêt*, Mercure de France, Paris, 1957.

H. C. CONKLIN: *Hanunóo Agriculture: A Report on the Integral System of Shifting Agriculture*, F.A.O. Forestry Development no. 12, New York, 1957.

H. COX: *Feast of Fools*, Harvard University Press, 1970.

D. DAMAS: 'The Diversity of Eskimo Societies', in R. Lee and I. DeVore (eds.), *Man the Hunter*, Aldine, Chicago, 1968.

K. DAVID: 'Until Marriage Do Us Part: A Cultural Account of Jaffna Tamil Categories for Kinsmen', *Man* (N. S.), vol. 8, 1973, pp. 521–35.

J. DAVIS: 'Gifts and the U.K. Economy', *Man* (N. S.), vol. 7, 1972, pp. 408–29.

M. DOUGLAS: 'The Lele of the Kasai', in D. Forde (ed.), *African Worlds*, Oxford University Press, 1954.
The Lele of Kasai, Oxford University Press, 1963.
'Raffia Cloth Distribution in the Lele Economy', *Africa*, vol. 28, 1958, pp. 109–22.
(ed.) *Witchcraft Confessions and Accusations*, Tavistock, 1970.

M. DOUGLAS and P. KABERRY (eds.): *Man in Africa*, London, 1969.

P. DRUCKER and R. HEIZER: *To Make my Name Good: Re-examination of the Southern Kwakiutl Potlatch*, University of California Press, 1967.

L. DUMONT: *Homo Hierarchicus*, Paladin, 1972.

É. DURKHEIM: *The Division of Labour in Society*, Free Press, New York, 1947. (First published in 1893 as *De la Division du travail social: étude sur l'organisation des societés supérieures*.)
The Elementary Forms of the Religious Life, Allen & Unwin, 1915. (First published in 1912 as *Les Formes élémentaires de la vie religieuse*.)
The Rules of Sociological Method, Free Press, New York, 1965. (First published in 1895 as *Les Règles de la méthode sociologique*.)

P. EINZIG: *Primitive Money in its Ethnological, Historical and Economic Aspects*, Pergamon, 1966.

S. EPSTEIN: 'Productive Efficiency and Customary Systems of Rewards in Rural South India', in R. Firth (ed.), *Themes in Economic Anthropology*, Tavistock, 1967.
South India: Yesterday, Today and Tomorrow – Mysore Village Revisited, Macmillan, London, 1973.

E. E. EVANS-PRITCHARD: *Witchcraft, Oracles and Magic among the Azande*, Oxford University Press, 1937.
The Nuer, Oxford University Press, 1940.
Nuer Religion, Oxford University Press, 1956.
The Sanusi of Cyrenaica, Oxford University Press, 1949.
The Azande: History and Political Institutions, Oxford University Press, 1971.

L. A. FALLERS (ed.): *The King's Men: Leadership and Status in Buganda on the Eve of Independence*, Oxford University Press, 1964.

S. FELDMAN: *Cognitive Consistency*, Academic Press, 1967.

R. FIRTH: *We, the Tikopia*, Allen & Unwin, 1936.
Primitive Polynesian Economy, Routledge & Kegan Paul, 1939.
Social Change in Tikopia, Allen & Unwin, 1960.
Symbols, Public and Private, Allen & Unwin, 1973.
(ed.), *Man and Culture: An Evaluation of the Work of Bronislaw Malinowski*, Routledge, 1957.

R FIRTH and B. YAMEY (eds.): *Capital, Savings and Credit in Peasant Societies*, Allen & Unwin, 1964.

FOOD AND AGRICULTURE ORGANIZATION: *Expert Consultation on the Settlement of Nomads in Africa and the Near East*, F.A.O., R.P. 20, Rome, 1972.

D. FORDE: (ed.), *African Worlds*, Oxford University Press, 1954.
'Double Descent among the Yakö', in A. R. Radcliffe-Brown and D. Forde (eds.), *African Systems of Kinship and Marriage*, Oxford University Press, 1950.

D. FORDE and P. M. KABERRY (eds.): *West African Kingdoms in the Nineteenth Century*, Oxford University Press, 1967.

A. FORGE: 'The Golden Fleece', in *Man* (N.S.), vol. 7, 1972, pp. 527–40. 'Tswamung: A Failed Big-Man', in S. Kimball and J. Watson (eds), *Crossing Cultural Boundaries*, Chandler, San Francisco, 1973.

M. FORTES: *Kinship and the Social Order*, Aldine, Chicago, 1969.

R. FORTUNE: *Manus Religion*, American Philosophical Society, Philadelphia, 1935.

G. FOSTER: 'Peasant Society and the Image of Limited Good', *American Anthropologist*, vol. 67, 1965, pp. 293–315.

R. FOX: *Kinship and Marriage*, Penguin, 1967.

J. G. FRAZER: *The Golden Bough*, Macmillan, London. (First published 1890.)

M. FREEDMAN: *Chinese Lineage and Society*, Athlone Press, 1966. *Lineage Organization in South-Eastern China*, Athlone Press, 1958. *Rites and Duties, or Chinese Marriage*, London School of Economics, 1967.

D. FREEMAN: *Report on the Iban*, Athlone Press, 1970.

J. FRIEDMAN: 'Tribes, States and Transformations', in M. Bloch (ed.), *Marxist Analyses and Social Anthropology*, Malaby, 1975, pp. 161–202.

C. VON FÜRER-HAIMENDORF: *Morals and Merit*, Weidenfeld & Nicolson, 1967.

M. H. GALAAL: *Anthology of Somali Oral Literature*, Ministry of Higher Education, Mogadishu, 1972.

C. GEERTZ: *Agricultural involution: The Process of Ecological Change in Indonesia*, University of California Press, 1970.

E. GELLNER: *Saints of the Atlas*, Weidenfeld & Nicolson, 1969. *Words and Things*, Penguin, 1968.

A. VAN GENNEP: *The Rites of Passage*, Routledge & Kegan Paul, 1960. (First published in French in 1908.)

A. GIDDENS: *Capitalism and Modern Social Theory*, Cambridge University Press, 1971.

M. GLUCKMAN: 'Kinship and Marriage among the Lozi of Northern Rhodesia and the Zulu of Natal', in A. R. Radcliffe-Brown and D. Forde (eds), *African Systems of Kinship and Marriage*, Oxford University Press, 1950.

Order and Rebellion in Tribal Africa: Collected Essays, Routledge & Kegan Paul, 1963.

J. GOODY: 'A Comparative Approach to Incest and Adultery', *British Journal of Sociology*, vol. 7, 1956, pp. 286–305.

'The Mother's Brother and the Sister's Son in West Africa', *Journal of the Royal Anthropological Institute*, vol. 89, 1959, pp. 61–86.

Technology, Tradition and the State in Africa, Oxford University Press, 1971.

The Domestication of the Savage Mind, Cambridge University Press, 1976.

K. GOUGH: 'Changing kinship usages in the Setting of Political and Economic Change among the Nayars', *Journal of the Royal Anthropological Institute*, vol. 82, 1952, pp. 71–88.

'Nayar: Central Kerala', in D. Schneider and K. Gough (eds.), *Matrilineal Kinship*, Cambridge University Press, 1962.

M. GRIAULE: *Conversations with Ogotemmêli*, Oxford University Press, 1965.

S. GUDEMAN: 'The Compadrazgo as a reflection of the natural and spiritual person', *Proceedings of the Royal Anthropological Institute*, 1971, pp. 45–72.

P. GULLIVER (ed.): *Tradition and Transition in East Africa*, Routledge & Kegan Paul, 1969.

J. A. HADFIELD: *Dreams and Nightmares*, Penguin, 1954.

LORD M. HAILEY: *African Survey*, Oxford University Press, 1957.

S. HALL: 'The Hippies: An American Movement', in J. Nagel (ed.), *Student Power*, Merlin Press, 1969.

C. R. HALLPIKE: 'Social Hair', *Man* (N.S.), vol. 4, 1969, pp. 256–64.

M. HARRIS: 'The Cultural Ecology of India's Sacred Cattle', *Current Anthropology*, vol. 7, 1966, pp. 51–66.

J. HARRISON: *Prolegomena to the Study of Greek Religion*, Cambridge University Press, 1903.

M. HERSKOVITS: 'The Cattle Complex in East Africa', *American Anthropologist*, vol. 28, 1926, pp. 229–72; 361–88; 633–64.

R. HERTZ: *Death and the Right Hand*, Routledge & Kegan Paul, 1960.

T. HEYERDAHL: *The Kon-Tiki Expedition*, Penguin, 1963.

The Ra Expeditions, Penguin, 1973.

P. HILL: *Migrant Cocoa Farmers of Southern Ghana*, Cambridge University Press, 1963.

A. HOBEN: *Land Tenure Among the Amhara of Ethiopia: The Dynamics of Cognatic Descent*, University of Chicago Press, Chicago, 1973.

F. L. K. HSU: *Under the Ancestor's Shadow: Kinship, Personality and Social Mobility in China*, Stanford University Press, 1971.

H. S. HUGHES: 'History, the Humanities, and Anthropological Change', *Current Anthropology*, vol. 4, 1963, pp. 140–45.

D. HYMES (ed.): *Reinventing Anthropology*, Vintage Books, New York, 1974.

F. A. J. IANNI: *A Family Business: Kinship and Social Control in Organized Crime*, Routledge & Kegan Paul, 1972.

A. H. M. JONES and E. MONROE: *A History of Abyssinia*, Oxford University Press, 1935.

S. JONES: 'The Waigal Horn Chair', *Man* (N.S.), vol. 5, 1970, pp. 253–7.

H. A. JUNOD: *The Life of a South African Tribe*, Neuchâtel, 1913.

E. KEDOURIE: *Nationalism*, Hutchinson, 1966.

K. E. KNUTSSON: *Authority and Change: A Study of the Kallu Institution among the Macha Galla of Ethiopia*, Etnografiska Museet, Gothenburg, 1967.

T. S. KUHN: *The Structure of Scientific Revolutions*, University of Chicago Press, 1970.

A. KUPER: *Anthropologists and Anthropology: The British School, 1922–1972*, Allen Lane, 1973; Penguin, 1975.

J. LA FONTAINE: 'Gisu Marriage and Affinal Relations', In M. Fortes (ed.), *Marriage in Tribal Societies*, Cambridge University Press, 1962.

I. LAKATOS and A. MUSGRAVE (eds.): *Criticism and the Growth of Knowledge*, Cambridge University Press, 1970.

P. LAWRENCE and M. J. MEGGITT (eds.): *Gods, Ghosts, and Men in Melanesia*, Oxford University Press, 1965.

R. LAYTON: 'Myth as Language in Aboriginal Arnhem Land', *Man* (N.S.), vol. 5, 1970, pp. 483–97.

E. R. LEACH (ed.): *Aspects of Caste in South India, Ceylon and North-west Pakistan*, Cambridge University Press, 1960.

Genesis as Myth and Other Essays, Cape, 1969.

Lévi-Strauss, Fontana, 1970.

Political Systems of Highland Burma, Athlone Press, 1954.

A. LEGESSE: *Gada: Three Approaches to the Study of African Society*, Free Press, New York, 1973.

D. N. LEVINE: *Wax and Gold: Tradition and Innovation in Ethiopian Culture*, University of Chicago Press, 1965.

C. LÉVI-STRAUSS: *The Raw and the Cooked*, Cape, 1970.

The Savage Mind, Weidenfeld & Nicolson, 1966.

'Structural Analysis in Linguistics and in Anthropology', in C.

Lévi-Strauss, *Structural Anthropology*, Penguin, 1972.

'The Structural Study of Myth', in C. Lévi-Strauss, *Structural Anthropology*, Penguin, 1972.

H. S. LEWIS: *A Galla Monarchy: Jimma Abba Jifar, Ethiopia, 1830–1932*, University of Wisconsin Press, Madison, 1965.

I. M. LEWIS: *The Anthropologist's Muse: An Inaugural Lecture*, London School of Economics, 1973.

Ecstatic Religion, Penguin, 1971.

'From Nomadism to Cultivation: the Expansion of Political Solidarity in Southern Somalia', in M. Douglas and P. Kaberry (eds.), *Man in Africa*, Tavistock, 1969.

(ed.), *Islam in Tropical Africa*, Oxford University Press, 1966.

Marriage and the Family in Northern Somaliland, East African Studies, no. 15, East African Institute of Social Research, Kampala, Uganda, 1962.

A Modern History of Somalia: Nation and State in the Horn of Africa, Longmans, 1979.

A Pastoral Democracy, Oxford University Press, 1961.

K. LITTLE: *West African Urbanization: A Study of Voluntary Associations in Social Change*, Cambridge University Press, 1965.

P. LLOYD: *Africa in Social Change*, Penguin, 1971.

J. LOCKE: *The Second Treatise on Government*, Blackwell, 1966. (First published 1690.)

P. LOIZOS: 'Changes in Property Transfer among Greek Cypriot Villagers', *Man* (N.S.), vol. 10, 1975, pp. 503–23.

D. A. LOW and R. C. PRATT: *Buganda and British Overrule 1900–55: Two Studies*, Oxford University Press, 1960.

F. D. LUGARD: *The Dual Mandate in British Tropical Africa*, Blackwood, 1922.

S. LUKES: *Émile Durkheim: His Life and Work*, Allen Lane, 1973.

V. LULING: *A Somali Sultanate*, in press.

A. MACFARLANE: *Witchcraft in Tudor and Stuart England*, Routledge & Kegan Paul, 1970.

W. MACGAFFEY: *Custom and Government in the Lower Congo*, University of California Press, 1971.

W. J. M. MACKENZIE: *Politics and Social Science*, Penguin, 1969.

D. MCKNIGHT: 'Sexual Symbolism of Food among the Wik-Mungkan', *Man* (N.S.), vol. 8, 1973, pp. 144–209.

J. F. MCLENNAN: *Primitive Marriage*, University of Chicago Press. (First published 1865.)

H. MAINE: *Ancient Law*, Dent. (First published 1861.)

L. MAIR: *Marriage*, Penguin, 1971.

B. MALINOWSKI: *Argonauts of the Western Pacific*, Routledge & Kegan Paul, 1922.

A Diary in the Strict Sense of the Term, Routledge & Kegan Paul, 1967.

Myth in Primitive Psychology, Kegan Paul, 1926.

R. A. MANNERS and D. KAPLAN (eds.): *Theory in Anthropology*, Routledge & Kegan Paul, 1968.

J. MAQUET: *The Premise of Inequality in Ruanda: A Study of Political Relations in a Central African Kingdom*, Oxford University Press, 1961.

J. MARKAKIS: *Ethiopia: Anatomy of a Traditional Polity*, Oxford University Press, 1975.

L. MARSHALL: 'Sharing, Talking and Giving: Relief of Social Tensions among !Kung Bushmen', *Africa*, vol. 31, 1966, pp. 231–49.

M. MAUSS: *The Gift*, Routledge & Kegan Paul, 1969. (First published in French in 1925.)

M. MAUSS and H. BEUCHAT: 'Essai sur les variations saisonières des sociétés Eskimos', first published in *Année Sociologique 1904–1905*, reprinted in M. Mauss, *Sociologie et Anthropologie*, 3rd edn, Presses Universitaires de France, Paris, 1966.

A. C. MAYER: *Caste and Kinship in Central India*, Routledge & Kegan Paul, 1960.

T. MBOYA: 'The Impact of Modern Institutions on the East African', in P. H. Gulliver (ed.), *Tradition and Transition in East Africa*, Routledge & Kegan Paul, 1969.

M. J. MEGGITT: *The Lineage System of the Mae-Enga of New Guinea*, Oliver & Boyd, 1965.

J. MIDDLETON: *The Lugbara of Uganda*, Holt, Rinehart & Winston, 1965.

Lugbara Religion, Oxford University Press, 1960.

J. S. MILL: *Considerations on Representative Government*, Blackwell, 1861.

K. MILLET: *Sexual Politics*, Hart-Davis, 1971.

K. MINOGUE: *Nationalism*, Batsford, 1967.

T. MONOD (ed.): *Pastoralism in Tropical Africa*, Oxford University Press, 1975.

L. H. MORGAN: *League of the Troquois*, Corinth, New York. (First published 1857.)

H. S. MORRIS: 'Some Aspects of the Concept Plural Society', *Man* (N.S.), vol. 2, 1967, pp. 169–84.

D. MORRIS: *The Naked Ape*, Corgi, 1969.

G. P. MURDOCK: *Social Structure*, Macmillan, New York, 1949.

M. MURRAY: *The Witch-cult in Western Europe*, Oxford University Press, 1963.

E. MUTESA II: *Desecration of my Kingdom*, Constable, 1967.

S. NADEL: *A Black Byzantium*, Oxford University Press, 1942.

R. NEEDHAM: *Structure and Sentiment*, University of Chicago Press, 1962.

S. ORTIZ: *Uncertainties in Peasant Farming: A Colombian Case*, Athlone Press, 1973.

G. ORWELL: *1984*, Penguin, 1954.

M. PAMMENT: 'The Succession of Solomon', *Man* (N.S.), vol. 7, 1972, pp. 635–43.

E. PARTRIDGE: *Shakespeare's Bawdy*, Routledge & Kegan Paul, 1969.

S. PIDDOCKE: 'The Potlatch System of the Southern Kwakiutl: A New Perspective', in E. LeClair and H. K. Schneider (eds.), *Economic Anthropology*, Holt, Rinehart & Winston, New York, 1968.

J. PITT-RIVERS: 'The Kith and the Kin', in J. Goody (ed.), *The Character of Kinship*, Cambridge University Press, 1974.
'On the word "Caste" ', in T. O. Beidelman (ed.), *The Translation of Culture*, Tavistock, 1971.

H. A. POWELL: 'Competitive Leadership in Trobriand Political Organization', *Journal of the Royal Anthropological Institute*, vol. 90, 1960, pp. 118–45.

M. PUZO: *The Godfather*, Pan, 1971.

A. H. QUIGGIN: *The Story of Money*, Methuen, 1956.

A. R. RADCLIFFE-BROWN: *The Andaman Islanders*, Cambridge University Press, 1922.
Structure and Function in Primitive Society, Cohen, 1952.

A. R. RADCLIFFE-BROWN and D. FORDE (eds.): *African Systems of Kinship and Marriage*, Oxford University Press, 1950.

R. RAPPAPORT: *Pigs for the Ancestors*, Yale University Press, 1968.

K. J. V. RASMUSSEN: *Intellectual Culture of the Hudson Bay Eskimos*, Gyldendalske Boghandel, Nordisk Forlag, Copenhagen, 1930.

R. REDFIELD: *The Little Community*, University of Chicago Press, Chicago, 1955.

G. REICHEL-DOLMATOFF: 'The Cultural Context of an Aboriginal Hallucinogen: *Banisteriopsis caapi*', in P. T. Furst (ed.), *Flesh of the Gods*, Allen & Unwin, 1972, pp. 84–113.

A. RETEL-LAURENTIN: *Oracles et Ordalies chez les Nzakara*, La Haye, Mouton, Paris, 1969.

A. RICHARDS: 'Keeping the King Divine', *Proceedings of the Royal Anthropological Institute*, 1968, pp. 23–36.

D. RICHES: 'Cash, Credit and Gambling in a Modern Eskimo

Economy', *Man* (N.S.), vol. 10, 1975, pp. 21–33.

B. RUSSELL: *History of Western Philosophy*, Allen & Unwin, 1946.

R. SALISBURY: *From Stone to Steel*, Cambridge University Press, 1963.

I. SCHAPERA: *Government and Politics in Tribal Societies*, Watts, 1956.
'Kinship and Marriage among the Tswana', in A. R. Radcliffe-Brown and D. Forde (eds.), *African Systems of Kinship and Marriage*, Oxford University Press, 1950.

E. SCHILLEBEECKY: 'Some Thoughts on the Interpretation of Eschatology', *Concilium*, vol. 1, 1969, pp. 22–29.

D. SCHNEIDER: 'Double Descent on Yap', *Journal of the Polynesian Society*, vol. 71, 1962, pp. 1–24.

D. SCHNEIDER and K. GOUGH (eds.), *Matrilineal Kinship*, Cambridge University Press, 1962.

H. K. SCHNEIDER: 'Economics in East African Aboriginal Societies', in E. LeClair and H. K. Schneider (eds.), *Economic Anthropology*, Holt, Rinehart & Winston, New York, 1968.

W. A. SHACK: *The Gurage: People of the Ensete Culture*, Oxford University Press, 1966.

U. SHARMA: 'Theodicy and the Doctrine of Karma', *Man* (N.S.), vol. 8, 1973, pp. 347–64.

J. SINGH UBEROI: *The Politics of the Kula Ring*, Manchester University Press, 1962.

E. SMITH: *The Migrations of Early Culture*, Manchester, 1915.

A. SOUTHALL: 'Amin's Military Coup in Uganda: Great Man or Historical Inevitability?', in *Third International Congress of Africanists*, Addis Ababa, 1973.

H. SPENCER: *Principles of Sociology*, London, 1882.

B. SPOONER: 'Towards a Generative Model of Nomadism', *Anthropological Quarterly*, vol. 44, 1971, pp. 198–211.

H. N. C. STEVENSON: 'Status Evaluation in the Hindu Caste System', *Journal of the Royal Anthropological Institute*, vol. 84, 1954, pp. 45–65.

G. W. STOCKING: 'What's in a Name? The Origins of the Royal Anthropological Institute (1837–71)', *Man* (N.S.), vol. 6, 1971, pp. 369–90.

M. N. SRINIVAS: *Religion and Society among the Coorgs in South India*, Oxford University Press, 1952.

A. STRATHERN: *The Rope of Moka: Big-Men and Ceremonial Exchange in Mount Hagen, New Guinea*, Cambridge University Press, 1971.

R. H. TAWNEY: *Religion and the Rise of Capitalism*, Penguin, 1969.

S. TAX: *Penny Capitalism*, U.S. Government Printing Office, Washington D.C., 1953.

K. THOMAS: 'The Relevance of Social Anthropology to the Historical Study of English Witchcraft', in Mary Douglas (ed.), *Witchcraft Confessions and Accusations*, Tavistock, 1970.
Religion and the Decline of Magic, Penguin, 1973.

A. DE TOCQUEVILLE: *Democracy in America*, vol. 2, Harper & Row, New York, 1965. (First published 1871.)

C. TURNBULL: *The Mountain People*. Cape, 1973.

V. TURNER: *The Drums of Affliction*, Oxford University Press, 1968.
The Forest of Symbols, Cornell University Press, 1970.

S. A. TYLER (ed.): *Cognitive Anthropology*, Holt, Rinehart & Winston, 1969.

E. TYLOR: 'On a Method of Investigating the Development of Institutions: Applied to Laws of Marriage and Descent', *Journal of the Anthropological Institute*, 1889, pp. 245–73.

E. ULLENDORFF: *The Ethiopians: An Introduction to Country and People*, Oxford University Press, 1965.

A. VAYDA (ed.): *Environment and Cultural Behavior*, Doubleday, New York, 1969.

A. DE WAAL MALEFIJT: *Religion and Culture*, Macmillan, New York, 1968.

L. WARNER: *A Black Civilisation*, Harper, 1937.

A. D. WEISMAN: 'Reality Sense and Reality-Testing', *Behavioural Science*, vol. 3, 1958, pp. 228–61.

E. M. WEYER: *The Eskimos*, New Haven, 1932.

M. WILSON: *Good Company: A Study of Nyakyusa Age-Villages*, Oxford University Press, 1951.

K. A. WITTFOGEL: *Oriental Despotism*, Yale University Press, New Haven, 1957.

J. WOODBURN: 'Stability and Flexibility in Hadza Residential Groupings', in R. Lee and I. DeVore (eds.), *Man the Hunter*, Aldine, Chicago, 1968.

E. WOLF: *Peasants*, Prentice-Hall, 1966.

A. B. WYLDE: *Modern Abyssinia*, Methuen, 1901.

N. YALMAN: *Under the Bo Tree: Studies in Caste, Kinship and Marriage in the Interior of Ceylon*, University of California Press, 1967.

M. YOUNG: *Fighting with Food: Leadership, Values and Social Control in a Massim Society*, Cambridge University Press, 1972.

Index